T0358202

Contemporary Economists in the West

Historical Materialism
Book Series

VOLUME 325

The titles published in this series are listed at *brill.com/hm*

Contemporary Economists in the West

Critical Essays on Oppenheimer, Stolzmann, Amonn, Petry, and Liefmann

By

Isaak Il'ich Rubin

Translated with Introduction and Commentary

Richard B. Day

BRILL

LEIDEN | BOSTON

The Library of Congress Cataloging-in-Publication Data is available online at https://catalog.loc.gov
LC record available at https://lccn.loc.gov/2024029971

Typeface for the Latin, Greek, and Cyrillic scripts: "Brill". See and download: brill.com/brill-typeface.

ISSN 1570-1522
ISBN 978-90-04-70565-4 (hardback)
ISBN 978-90-04-70566-1 (e-book)

Dedicated to Philip, Amelia, Monica, Mason, Elizabeth

∴

Contents

Foreword   XI
Preface   XV

PART 1
The Economic Theory of Franz Oppenheimer

Introduction by the Editor   3

1 Oppenheimer's Two Formulae of Value   9

2 A Critique of Oppenheimer's First Formula of Value
   Value and Income   19

3 A Critique of Oppenheimer's Second Formula of Value
   The Value of Products and the Value of Labour   28

4 Skilled Labour   34

5 The Theory of Monopoly   41

6 Surplus Value as Monopoly Income   48

7 The Contradiction between Oppenheimer's Theory of Value And His
   Theory of Surplus Value   55

8 Oppenheimer as Critic of Marx   65

PART 2
Rudolf Stolzmann and the Social Method in Political Economy

Introduction by the Editor   81

1 The Social-Organic Method   88

2 Stolzmann and the Theory of Labour Value   105

3 Stolzmann's Theory of Value and Distribution   116

4 Stolzmann as Critic of Marx   129

PART 3
Alfred Amonn and the Social Method in Political Economy

Introduction by the Editor   151

1 Amonn's Doctrine on the Subject Matter of Theoretical Economics   156

2 Critique of Amonn's Doctrine   167

PART 4
Franz Petry and His Attempt at a Social Interpretation of Marx's Theory of Value

Introduction by the Editor   191

1 Isaak Rubin on Franz Petry   194

PART 5
The Economic Theory of Robert Liefmann

Introduction by the Editor   213

1 The Psychological Conception of Economy   217

2 Money Economy   229

3 Capitalist Economy   239

4 The Theory of Prices   260

Appendix 1: The Austrian School   291
Appendix 2: Isaak Il'ich Rubin on Supply, Demand, and Price
    Determination   305
References   311
Index of Names   316

Foreword

Isaak Il'ich Rubin understood the study of political economy to include the economic, political, social and historical contradictions of capitalist society. In an essay on Marx's method, published three years before *Contemporary Economists in the West*, Rubin wrote of the need to combine two points of view, one dealing with *objective changes in the means of production*, the other with *social relations* between people in the process of production.

> In conceptual terms, Marx's economic theory is closely related to his sociological theory …. We can study the labour activity of people, joined together in a society, from two different perspectives: either as the aggregate of means of production and technical devices, with whose assistance man overcomes nature and produces the products he requires, or as the sum total of social relations that connect people in the process of production. Hence the difference between the technical and the economic – between the material-technical process of production and its social form, between the productive forces and the social relations of production among people. Both the theory of historical materialism and Marx's economic theory revolve around one and the same basic question of the relationship between the productive forces and the production relations among people. The subject of investigation is the same in both cases: *the change of production relations among people in accordance with development of the productive forces.*[1]

The essays translated in this volume are particularly concerned with the sociological dimension of Marx's political economy. For centuries prior to capitalism, philosophers and theologians typically conceived human life in terms of community. Man, as Aristotle said, is a social being. In pre-capitalist Europe, the life of most people was limited to domestic requirements and toil in the fields. Everyone had a practical 'place' in work and a spiritual 'place' in the divine hierarchy. There was class oppression, to be sure, but the consciousness of most people was formed in a world of *Gemeinschaft*, or social relations anchored in an unchanging mode of production and stable personal ties with neighbours and family. This world was shattered by the industrial revolution, which replaced *Gemeinschaft* with *Gesellschaft* – a new and rapidly changing

---

1 Rubin 2018a, pp. 543–4.

order in which social production relations were dehumanised by the capitalist market, the commodification of labour, and machine technology.

By the time Rubin wrote his essays on *Contemporary Economists in the West*, the focus of bourgeois economic theory was on rationalising and legitimating the 'natural' order of capitalism. The Austrian school of marginal utility, which dominated German-language debates following the decline of the German Historical School, interpreted economic relations in terms of radical individualism and subjective-psychological calculations of self-interest. Carl Menger, one of the founders of the Austrian school, published his *Grundsätze der Volkswirtschaftslehre* (*Principles of Economics*) in 1871. Menger believed 'the phenomena of economic life, like those of nature, are ordered strictly in accordance with definite laws' that are 'entirely independent of the human will'.[2] Menger's emphasis upon individual judgements of marginal utility had the effect of conceptually dismantling community into a simple sum of individual choices. Menger wrote that economic actors are driven exclusively by '*individual* economic aims' and '*individual* interests'.[3] He considered the analytical theory of marginal utility to be analogous to the method of the natural sciences. The difference was that instead of *imagining* 'atoms' and 'forces', economists had the advantage of studying the observable behaviour of 'human individuals and their efforts'.[4]

In *Contemporary Economists in the West*, Rubin assumes that readers are familiar with the principal tenets of Austrian theory. With that fact in mind, as editor of this volume I have added to Rubin's original text two appendices: first, an essay on the theory, methodology, and social-political significance of the Austrian school that Rubin wrote in 1926 for *The Great Soviet Encyclopaedia*; second, a brief exposition of Rubin's personal assessment of the role of supply and demand in the determination of market prices and the distribution of social labour. These documents provide important background for Rubin's essays in this book. They are, however, rather technical, so that readers, depending upon their familiarity with the subject matter, will need to decide for themselves the most appropriate time to turn to them.

The authors whose work Rubin analyses in this volume were dissenters from the new marginalist orthodoxy. Like Adam Smith and other classical political economists, they believed that individual behaviour is socially formed by institutions and even normative expectations. Since this discussion occurred between German writers, the influence of philosophical idealism, particularly the work of Kant and Hegel, frequently appears. Kant believed that the innate

---

2   Menger 2007, p. 48, italics added.
3   Menger 1985, p. 194.
4   Menger 1985, p. 142n.

freedom of individuals could only be secured in a law-governed civil society. In terms of moral philosophy, he situated individual judgements within the moral universe of a categorical imperative; that is, a universal law of reason that proscribed treatment of others merely as means to one's own ends (which, of course, is precisely the result of the commodification of labour). Hegel, in the dialectical movement of his *Philosophy of Right*, also imposed normative restraints upon civil society by incorporating it within a community of ethical consciousness that is formed by shared historical experience and rationally articulated in the laws of the modern state.

Viewing culture as dependent upon the mode of production, Marx had little interest in Kantian moral philosophy. Nevertheless, the challenge that he did take from Hegel was to provide a scientific account of civil society and the market in terms of historically formed production relations between people. The whole of Marx's work is a journey, through social contradictions, from the abstraction of the individual commodity producer in the first chapter of *Capital* towards the concrete community of communism. In communism, Marx expected that the abstract individual would be replaced by *social individuals*, whose production relations would no longer be mediated by commodity fetishism and the movement of things but instead by *social property* and by a *socially determined plan* (the analogue of Hegel's ethical laws of the modern state). Social reason would govern the movement of things, and market relations would be replaced by mutual recognition in a social whole that would organise the contributions of each and satisfy the human needs of all.

In *Contemporary Economists in the West*, Rubin critically assesses the efforts by several economists to replace the abstractions of marginalism by restoring social context to political economy. In his essay on Franz Oppenheimer, he examines a reinterpretation of the labour theory of value in the context of class relations imposed by political force and monopolistic economic power. In his commentary on Rudolf Stolzmann, he reviews a sophisticated attempt to reassert the primacy of the whole by drawing upon the traditions of German idealism. Turning to Alfred Amonn, he applauds the importance that Ammon assigned to social context while criticising his failure to explain how social forms are themselves determined by the relations of production. The author whom Rubin found most intriguing in this collection was Franz Petry, who proposed to reinterpret Marx in terms of the value-oriented neo-Kantian philosophy of history associated with Heinrich Rickert. Finally, as if to prove his case against marginalism by invoking a *reductio ad absurdum*, Rubin concludes with an essay on Robert Liefmann, an extreme proponent of the psychological method who undertook to eliminate objective causality entirely from economic theory.

Although Rubin's essays are at times challenging, any undergraduate in the Economics Department of a modern university will readily recognise his principal concerns. Marginal utility theory is the core of today's 'microeconomics', in which people are transformed into indifference curves, budget lines, and individual demand schedules, while firms become isoquants, budget lines, and marginal product curves. The forms of social relations are replaced by equations, and any notion of class interest in determining economic behaviour is excluded by the rules of self-interested individual choice. The remarkable irony is that these tributes to abstraction claim to project a state of social harmony and economic equilibrium in which every consumer is a 'sovereign' – at the same time as the real world is dominated by corporations that often have greater revenues than many 'sovereign' states.

The philosopher Georg Lukács once commented that the bourgeoisie is at home with its pseudo-science of 'false consciousness', for to embrace the methodology of dialectical causality would be to anticipate the 'self-negation of the capitalist class'.[5] For the bourgeoisie, Lukács wrote, 'it is a matter of life and death to understand its own system of production in terms of eternally valid categories: it must think of capitalism as being predestined to eternal survival by the eternal laws of nature and reason'.[6] To acknowledge the social and economic contradictions of capitalism, even in theory, 'would be tantamount to observing society *from a class standpoint other than that of the bourgeoisie.* And no class can do that – unless it is willing to abdicate its power .... Thus the barrier which converts the class consciousness of the bourgeoisie into "false" consciousness is objective; it is the class situation itself'.[7]

Lukács and Rubin were contemporaries. Lukács was one of the foremost dialectical philosophers of the time, just as Rubin was one of the most gifted expositors of the role of dialectical causality in Marx's understanding of political economy.[8] Their shared commitment was to comprehend the contradictory forms of modern society as a whole and thereby to understand and anticipate the movement of history. Both believed that 'partial' and 'formal' bourgeois sciences, conceived as wholly separate domains of social theory, are ideological instruments of the ruling class whose purpose is to occlude historical and economic contradictions and thus to immobilise social consciousness in the immediacy of the existing order.

Richard B. Day

---

5 Lukács 1971, p. 64.
6 Lukács 1971, p. 11.
7 Lukács 1971, p. 54.
8 See, in particular, Rubin 2018b, pp. 728–817.

Preface

The purpose of this book is to familiarise readers with the economic theories of some of the most prominent of today's West-European economists and to give a critical analysis of their doctrines from the viewpoint of Marxism.

The essays included in this book are linked by a community of ideas. The economists whose names appear in the chapter headings of our book interest us not only as colourful scientific individualists, each with his own unique individual attributes – these economists also have something in common, which is the fact that they can all be viewed as striking heralds of the profound crisis being experienced by today's bourgeois theoretical economics. It is with good reason that Stolzmann devoted his latest book, which appeared in 1925, to 'the crisis in modern political economy'. All of the economists whom we analyse express resolute dissatisfaction with the current condition of theoretical economics and make vain attempts, each in his own way, to lead it out of a blind alley. These futile efforts, generated by the crisis of modern economic thought, are in turn glaring symptoms of that same crisis.

The crisis of economic thought to which we refer has much to do with the collapse of hopes that were previously placed on the Austrian school. At the end of the nineteenth century and the beginning of the twentieth century, it might have seemed that Austrian theory was destined to play the role of a centre of gravity that would more or less successfully unify and reconcile the feuding trends of bourgeois economic thought. The starting points of the psychological theory, brilliantly developed by Menger,[1] Wieser,[2] and Böhm-Bawerk,[3] became symbols of faith for the majority of bourgeois economists. Supporters of this approach captured one university chair after another and, intoxicated with their victories, confidently promised in the near future to reconstruct the whole edifice of economic science upon the basis of new principles. Events, however, did not follow these promises. The Austrian school turned out to be powerless to rebuild the entire structure of economic science and did not get beyond its original psychological premises. These psychological ideas propelled the thinking of economists in a misleading direction and into

---

1 [Carl Menger (1840–1921), founder of the Austrian school and a proponent of marginalism and the 'subjective' theory of value.]

2 [Friedrich von Wieser (1851–1926), Professor of Political Economy at the University of Vienna.]

3 [Eugen Böhm Ritter von Bawerk (1851–1914), major contributor to the Austrian school and frequent critic of Karl Marx.]

a dead end, from which there was no exit that led to an understanding and explanation of the real phenomena of capitalist economy. The period of tumultuous successes for the Austrian school was quickly followed by a period of impotently marking time and sceptically reflecting upon the reasons for their failure.[4]

Today, with more or less certainty, we can say that the Austrian theory's period of virtually limitless dominance in official bourgeois science has ended or is now ending. The poverty of the Austrian school's scientific accomplishments is evident, and a negative or at least sceptical attitude towards the individualistic-psychological method of studying economic phenomena is spreading rapidly. On the one hand, we see in scientific circles a growing interest in classical theory, which the Austrian economists, in their day, declared to be finally jettisoned. On the other hand, economists of the so-called 'social' direction are showing an indistinct but strong attraction towards a convergence of political economy with sociology. Finally, even scholars who retain the individualistic point of view are putting the purely psychological method of research in the background compared to the mathematical method (e.g. Schumpeter)[5] or are searching for a new foundation for the psychological method (e.g. Liefmann).[6] Among representatives of the first, neo-classical trend, we can certainly include Oppenheimer, who is building his economic system on a joint basis of classical theory and warped Marxism. The psychological direction is represented in our book by Liefmann, but we pay most attention to the social direction in the persons of its representatives Stolzmann, Amonn, and Petry.

Among the trends in contemporary economic thinking that we have mentioned, the most interesting and promising is the social direction. Its supporters are looking for new paths for economic science and justifiably reject both the traditional path of naturalistic objectivism, which found expression in the system of the classics and ended with the absurdity of their vulgar successors, and

---

4 [Many mainstream economists today would say that in the 1930s John Maynard Keynes helped to resolve the crisis to which Rubin refers by developing a new *macroeconomics* in *The General Theory of Employment, Interest and Money* (Keynes 2007), which was subsequently reconciled with microeconomic theory in the 'neo-classical synthesis'.]

5 [Joseph A. Schumpeter (1883–1950), one of the most famous of twentieth-century economists, author of several books on the theory of economic development, history of economic thought, business cycles, and the socio-economic prospect of capitalism being replaced by socialism.]

6 [Robert Liefmann (1874–1941), Professor of Economics at the University of Freiburg, was best known for his work on cartels and trusts and on the relation between economics and psychology.]

also the path of naturalistic subjectivism represented by the Austrian school. In opposition to naturalistic subjectivism, which starts from the psychological experiences and behaviour of separate individuals, supporters of the social method put forth the idea of the *socially conditioned behaviour of the individual*. In contrast to naturalistic objectivism, whose attention is fixed upon material-technical elements of the economic process, they uphold the need for a study of the *social form of the economy* as social relations between people. Both of these ideas create a certain theoretical affinity between representatives of the social method and the supporters of Marxist theory.

However, the existence of such a theoretical affinity must not conceal from readers the fundamental differences of principle between the social method of modern economists and the sociological method of Marx. In the hands of today's economists, the social method is taking a form that is fraught with serious dangers for scientific research: it appears in close connection with philosophical idealism. Representatives of the social method, in agreement with Marx's ideas, insist upon the need to study the social form of the economy. But what this social form of the economy is, and what place it occupies in the process of social development – in their answers to these questions they sharply differ from Marxism. According to Marx's teaching, a given social form of economy (or a system of production relations between people) grows up on the basis of a determinate condition of society's material productive forces, and it changes depending upon changes in the latter. Development of the social form of an economy is intimately dependent upon development of society's material productive forces.

Representatives of the social method decisively repudiate such a 'materialistic' understanding of the social form of an economy. In Stolzmann's opinion, the social form of an economy cannot be regarded as a necessary, causally conditioned result of a determinate condition of the productive forces. This would mean reducing human personality to the role of a materialistic marionette. Stolzmann recognises man as the free creator of his own destiny and asserts that the sphere of social regulation of the economy (i.e. interpersonal relations) is the sphere of operation for free human will, which endeavours to realise certain ethical ideals and purposes. The material process of production is subordinate to the law of causal necessity, but the law of moral freedom operates in the sphere of social regulation of the economy. The economist must approach an explanation of the social form of an economy – this sphere of freely realised moral purposes – with a *teleological* (purposeful) method of investigation, not a *causal* one.

In Stolzmann's view, therefore, the social form of an economy is separated from the process of material production by the same deep gulf as the otherworld of ethical teleology is from the empirical world of causal necessity. *Detachment of the social form of the economy from the material process of production* is the characteristic feature of today's supporters of the social method. While in Stolzmann's case this detachment appears in the acute form of ethical teleology, which has grown up on the basis of Kantian idealistic ethics, with Petry it takes the more subtle form of a gnoseological[7] teleology that bears the imprint of the neo-Kantian doctrine of Rickert and Windelband.[8] Even in Amonn, who avoided any intrusion into the sphere of philosophy and remained on the ground of strictly scientific causal research, we find deliberately severed all the threads that connect the social form of the economy with the material process of production.

In our essays devoted to Stolzmann, Amonn, and Petry, we endeavour as much as possible to illuminate both the right and the left among modern supporters of the social method in political economy. We note with appreciation the fruitful critical work that these economists have accomplished in their struggle against vulgar economics and the Austrian school. We cannot help but sympathise with the endeavour to direct economic science along the path of investigating the social form of the economy. But we also consider it necessary to explain in detail the profound difference between Marx's teaching – in light of which the social form of an economy turns out to be inseparably connected with the process of development of society's material productive forces – and the doctrine of contemporary economists who dig an impassable abyss between these two sides of a single social process. We hope that our analysis of the theories of Stolzmann, Amonn, and Petry will help the reader to relate critically to the constructions of supporters of the social method, which at first sight appear to have an important similarity with the constructions of Marx.

I.I. Rubin

---

7 [In common English-language usage today, the term 'gnoseology' has been replaced by 'epistemology'. For the difference between these terms, see Curado and Gouveia 2017, pp. 336–7. Here 'epistemology' is said to ask what knowledge is, while 'gnoseology' asks how knowledge is possible. But the distinction can be said to be only abstract and conceptual, for 'every theory of knowledge shows a mixture of epistemological and gnoseological accounts'. In this volume, Rubin will make reference to gnoseology in his analysis of Franz Petry.]

8 [The reference is to Heinrich John Rickert (1863–1936) and Wilhelm Windelband (1848–1915), who together led the Baden school of neo-Kantians Baden school of neo-Kantians.]

PART 1

The Economic Theory of Franz Oppenheimer

∵

Introduction by the Editor

Franz Oppenheimer graduated from Kiel University in 1908 after completing a thesis on David Ricardo. The following year, with the support of Adolph Wagner and Gustav von Schmoller,[1] he became a *privatdozent*[2] at the University of Berlin. In 1919 he acquired a full professorship in political economy and sociology at the University of Frankfurt, where he remained until his retirement in 1929. He spent the next four years in a rural cooperative that he had helped to organise near Berlin before the war, and from 1934–35 he taught in Palestine. He gave guest lectures in Paris and America, and in 1936 he became an honorary member of the American Sociological Association. In 1938 he fled Germany and eventually settled in Los Angeles, where in 1941 he helped to establish *The American Journal of Economics and Sociology*.

Oppenheimer was the author of approximately 40 books and 400 academic articles.[3] His most important work was the four-volume *System der Soziologie* (*System of Sociology*, 1922–29), of which the second volume was an enlarged edition of *Der Staat* (*The State*, first published in 1908), while the third volume was a revised edition of *Theorie der reinen und politischen Oekonomie* (*The Theory of Pure and Political Economy*), which first appeared in 1910.[4] The *System* was 4,500 pages in length, devoted to social psychology, political and economic theory, and economic and social history. Oppenheimer regarded himself as a liberal socialist and even a 'true disciple of Marx' – although, as Rubin mentions

---

1 Both of the Historical School.
2 An unsalaried lecturer, surviving on fees from students.
3 See 'A Bibliography of Franz Oppenheimer, 1864–1943' (Fuss 1946).
4 *Der Staat* (Oppenheimer 1908), first translated into English by John M. Gitterman as *The State: Its History and Development Viewed Sociologically* (Oppenheimer 1926) and republished many times since. A recent French translation also includes a thoughtful introduction to both *The State* and *The Theory of the Pure and the Political Economy*: see Oppenheimer 2013. Other informative works on Oppenheimer include Lowe 1965; Heinmann 1944; Honigsheim 1948. There is also a polemical article by N.I. Bukharin in the book *Ataka: Sbornik teoreticheskikh stat'ei* (Bukharin 1924, pp. 51–77). Another Marxist response to Oppenheimer can be found in chapter 2 of Grossmann 1992, online at http://www.franz-oppenheimer.de/f043a.htm, accessed 17 July 2019.

    The American Journal of Economics and Sociology, Vol. 3, No. 3 (April 1944) has a collection of essays in memory of Franz Oppenheimer and provides a partial bibliography of his works from 1895–1929 on pp. 519–21. For Oppenheimer's final judgement of the state of economic theory, and particularly the theory of Alfred Marshall, see his 'Critique of Political Economy: A Post Mortem on Cambridge Economics' (Oppenheimer 1942–44).

in the following essay, he also had a reputation among socialists as 'an ambitious *litterateur* who wants to create a name for himself as a Marx-destroyer'.

In *The State*, Oppenheimer saw two ways to ensure human sustenance: either by labour (the 'economic means') or by robbery (the 'political means'). Since robbery involved less effort, 'Wherever opportunity offers, and man possesses the power, he prefers political to economic means for the preservation of his life'.[5] The result was a 'conquest' theory of the state, beginning with 'robbery and killing' in border fights.[6] But once herdsmen conquered sedentary peasants, they soon discovered that a murdered peasant could no longer be a ploughman: it was better to abandon robbery and instead to institutionalise a more sustainable appropriation of the peasant's surplus by controlling the access to land. 'The herdsman in the first stage is like the bear, who for the purpose of robbing the beehive destroys it. In the second stage he is like the bee-keeper, who leaves the bees enough honey to carry them through the winter'.[7]

Erosion of the centralised feudal state comes with money economy and mobile property, which creates the industrial city. Initially the city offers the peasant exchange of 'equivalent values' and 'the honour of free labour',[8] but technical changes in agriculture also enable landlords to rid themselves of redundant peasants, leading to creation of a dispossessed proletariat. 'For the first time there appears, in the terminology of Karl Marx, the "free labourer" ... competing with his own class in the labour markets of the cities'.[9]

Speaking of Germany in his own day, Oppenheimer referred to a 'robber state' in which the ruling class consisted of 'the great landed magnates who at the same time are the principal shareholders in the larger industrial undertakings and mining companies', along with 'the captains of industry' and bankers who had also become important landowners.[10] As in feudal times, 'the great

---

5   Oppenheimer 1926, p. 53.
6   Augustin Thierry had already provided a 'conquest' theory of the state in the 1840s. See Plekhanov 1956, ch. 2, 'French Historians of the Restoration', pp. 26–44.
7   Oppenheimer 1926, p. 65. The economist Mancur Olson later appropriated Oppenheimer's idea in his distinction between 'roving' and 'stationary' bandits. See Olson 1993, pp. 567–76.
8   Oppenheimer 1926, p. 241. The central authority grants charter rights to the cities and weakens turbulent nobles by creating its own 'officialdom' to expedite tax collection and administration. With the possible exception of Ancient Egypt, says Oppenheimer, 'This revolution of the political mechanism was everywhere put into motion by development of the money economy' (Oppenheimer 1926, p. 249).
9   Oppenheimer 1926, p. 253.
10   Oppenheimer 1926, p. 259.

mass of men' lived in bitter poverty, condemned to 'hard, crushing, stupefying forced labour' in exchange for subsistence wages, resulting in a class struggle 'carried on by strikes, cooperative societies and trades unions'.[11]

Oppenheimer explains capitalist exploitation in terms of monopolistic power that originates in the control of land. One-half of the acreage in pre-war Germany was owned by 200,000 large estates, leaving the other half divided among five million small farmers.[12] It was this class monopoly of land that continuously created the oversupply of 'free labourers': 'The cause of the permanent reproduction of the reserve army and thus of capitalism is to be found in the countryside'.[13] Since capitalism presupposes a reserve army of labour that it cannot create for itself, it followed that capitalism must end when rural areas become depopulated or are reorganised on the basis of small farms and cooperatives.

> The guilty party, the sole author responsible for all the vices of the social economy, is ... large-scale land holdings. Capitalist property is only a 'secondary' and *derivative* usurpation; it cannot be an agent of exploitation, it cannot engender 'surplus value' unless it economically exists alongside large-scale landed property; then and only then can the 'social relation of monopoly' be preserved because a continuous stream of 'free' workers, more than capital can employ, arrive in the urban labour market ....[14]

Oppenheimer believed the solution to class inequality and exploitation was to replace class monopoly with market competition. Between 1893 and 1920,

---

11 Oppenheimer 1926, p. 266.
12 In his essay on Oppenheimer's work in sociology, Paul Honigsheim describes the class structure of German society before the First World War as follows:

    In pre-war Germany the Junker class of eastern Germany had a virtual monopoly on the leading positions in the administration and in the army. They were the owners of baronial estates, dependent on the labor of very poorly paid agricultural workers, partly seasonal workers of Polish origin. They treated the relatively few middle-class farmers living near their estates as dependent clients. As a result, the younger sons of these middle-class farmers and, to an even greater degree, the agricultural workers themselves migrated to the cities, where they swelled the numbers of industrial workers until the supply exceeded the demand to such an extent that there was no alternative for them but to accept the wages and working hours imposed by the ascendant class of industrialists. There they lived in rookeries owned by middle-class citizens with moderate liberal views. They also organized themselves into moderate socialist or Catholic labor unions.

    See Honigsheim 1948, p. 332.
13 Oppenheimer 2013, p. 310.
14 Oppenheimer 2013, p. 319.

he tried four times to establish self-managing agricultural settlements, three of them in Germany and the fourth in Palestine.[15] A cooperative society would enable workers and farmers to organise and employ themselves. Instead of workers competing for jobs, jobs would compete for workers. Social classes and the political state would then gradually disappear.[16]

> There will be no 'surplus value' for the capitalist class, because the labourer himself can form capital and himself become an employer. Thus the last remaining vestige of the political means will have been destroyed, and economic means alone will exercise sway. The *content* of such a society is the 'pure economics' of the equivalent exchange of commodities against commodities, or of labour power against commodities, and the political *form* of this society will be the 'freemen's citizenship'.[17]

In the essay that follows, Isaak Rubin assesses Oppenheimer's study of value theory in *Wert und Kapitalprofit* (*Value and Capital Profit*, 1916). At a time when marginalism prevailed almost everywhere among non-Marxist economists, and when Marxists – headed by Hilferding, Lenin, and Luxemburg – were already analysing the new phenomena of capitalist imperialism, Oppenheimer naïvely hoped to show how a community of 'liberal socialism' could eliminate injustice by restoring a 'pure economy' of free and competitive markets.

Isaak Rubin on the Economic Theory of Franz Oppenheimer

Franz Oppenheimer is one of today's most prominent economic theorists. The diversity of his scientific interests, his fondness for broad theoretical generalisations, his brilliant literary gift and sharp polemical talent, give Oppenheimer's scientific work a strikingly distinctive character.

Oppenheimer is the creator of an entire 'theoretical system' that attempts to embrace and explain all the basic phenomena of capitalist society. Even Robert Liefmann, who is by no means inclined to exaggerate the contributions of others and is a particularly committed critic of Oppenheimer, acknowledges that,

---

15   Lowe 1965, pp. 137–49.
16   Oppenheimer 1926, p. 276.
17   Oppenheimer 1926, p. 284.

among all the economic works that have appeared in recent decades, Oppenheimer's teaching can most justifiably claim to be 'systematic theory'.[18]

But Oppenheimer is not just an academic scholar. The combative temperament of a social reformer takes him beyond the four walls of his academic office and into the noisy arena of journalism. Oppenheimer wants to use his economic theory to establish a definite system of practical policy and social reforms that he calls 'liberal socialism'. With characteristic passion he wages a struggle on two fronts: against direct apologists for the capitalist system on the one hand, and against Marxism on the other. Oppenheimer opposes proletarian socialism with his system of liberal socialism, and his economic theory is directed against the economic teaching of Marx. He writes books against socialism, comes out with one 'refutation' after another of Marx, and, as he himself acknowledges, has earned a reputation in socialist circles as 'an ambitious writer who wants to create a name for himself as a Marx-destroyer'.[19]

Of course, Oppenheimer thinks such a reputation is completely undeserved. At times he is almost ready to claim that he is a 'true disciple of Marx',[20] who out of respect for that great thinker has the courage to criticise his theory and correct its imperfections. Since Oppenheimer speaks of himself in such terms, it is even less surprising that some of his opponents from the bourgeois camp – who are prepared to consider any economist who mentions surplus value and exploitation of workers to be a Marxist – regard Oppenheimer's teaching as 'an attempt to create a new justification for Marxism and the objective theory of value'.[21]

Oppenheimer's intermediate position between bourgeois and Marxist political economy, and his attempt to oppose Marx's theory with his own, requires Marxists to pay close attention to his doctrine. Marxist literature must submit his teaching to the detailed critical analysis that it deserves in terms of its wide theoretical breadth and also the importance of the practical-political conclusions drawn from it.[22]

It is not our task in this article to provide a critical analysis of all the elements of Oppenheimer's theoretical and practical system. In the first place, we leave completely aside his practical programme of liberal socialism. Secondly,

---

18 Liefmann 1919, p. 793. Needless to say, Liefmann thinks only his own theory fully deserves this honourable title.
19 Oppenheimer 1919a, p. x.
20 Oppenheimer 1919a, pp. ix and x.
21 Liefmann 1919, p. 793.
22 In the Russian Marxist literature, N.I. Bukharin examined Oppenheimer's views in an article included in the collection 'Ataka'; see also B. Bordilina (in the collection *Problemy teoreticheskoi ekonomii*, ed. Sh. Dvolaitsky and S. Chlenov).

from Oppenheimer's extensive theoretical system, we take as the subject of our inquiry only his most basic and initial theoretical doctrines: the theory of value and the theory of surplus value (which is inseparably connected with the doctrine of monopoly). These are the teachings of most interest to us; they serve Oppenheimer as the foundation for erecting his entire theoretical structure, and in the author's mind they are intended to replace the theory of value and surplus value created by Marx, which is the basis of the entire Marxist economic system.

CHAPTER 1

Oppenheimer's Two Formulae Of Value

Oppenheimer takes on the task of providing 'a new foundation for the object-ive theory of value'. He regards himself as continuing the work of the classical writers and Marx. The classical writers, Ricardo in particular, claimed that the value of products is determined by the *'quantity of labour'* expended in their production. In Oppenheimer's opinion, Marx provided an essential correction to the teaching of the classical writers: he taught that the value of products is determined by the quantity of *'labour time'* required for their production. But Marx's theory, too, is not free from errors and contradictions. The objective the-ory of value requires a new foundation, and Oppenheimer proposes his own theory as such a new foundation, according to which the value of products is determined by *'the value of the labour'* they contain. If the theory of the classics can be termed *Arbeitsmengentheorie*, and Marx's theory can be termed *Arbeit-szeittheorie*, Oppenheimer calls his own doctrine *Arbeitswerttheorie*.[1] Oppen-heimer does not stint in praising his 'new' theory: he sees in it the successful completion of more than two centuries of evolution of the labour theory of value and hopes, with its help, to provide 'the first successful resolution'[2] of the most difficult problem in political economy.

The theory of value, formulated by the classics, suffered from the following *three* most important shortcomings:

1) In their theory of the costs of production the classics revolved in *a vicious circle*: they derived the value of one commodity (the product) from the value of other commodities (means of production).

2) They were unable to solve the problem of *skilled* labour, i.e. to explain the exchange of the product of less labour by a skilled worker for the product of more labour by an unskilled worker.

3) Finally, they explained only the laws of price formation of freely repro-duced products, but they did not investigate the exchange of *monopoly* products.

Marx, to some extent, eliminated the first two shortcomings. Defining the value of a product by the quantity of socially necessary labour time, or labour, he 'very

---

1 Oppenheimer 1922, p. 74. [The terms refer respectively to a 'quantity of labour' theory, a 'labour time' theory, and a 'value of labour' theory.]

2 Oppenheimer 1922, p. 53.

© RICHARD B. DAY, 2024 | DOI:10.1163/9789004705661_003

skilfully escaped the vicious circle'[3] noted in point 1). He also succeeded, for the most part, in reducing a smaller amount of skilled labour to a greater amount of simple labour. But Marx did not overcome the third of the above-listed short-comings. The Marxist formula of labour value only applies to the exchange of freely reproduced commodities and does not at all extend to cases of mono-polistic exchange. Marx could not provide a 'comprehensive' formula of value: 'he investigated only part of the problem of value, mistakenly thinking that he was solving the entire problem'.[4]

In proposing his 'new foundation for the objective theory of value', Oppen-heimer hopes that it will completely eliminate all three of the above–mentioned shortcomings. In his theory of value Oppenheimer undertakes the following tasks:

1) to escape the *vicious circle* from which the classical theory of value suf-fered, and
2) to provide a *'comprehensive'* formula of value, covering all cases of exchange without exception, namely: a) the exchange of freely repro-duced products, made by labour of the *same* skill; b) the exchange of freely reproduced products, made by labour of *different* skills, and c) the exchange of *monopoly* products.

Oppenheimer attempts to solve the first of these tasks with his *first* formula of value, which considers the value of the product as part of the *income* of the pro-ducer. He wants to solve the second task in his *second* formula of value, accord-ing to which the value of the product is determined by *the value of the labour* it contains. We must now turn to an examination of these two formulae of value.

In order to disclose the law of the 'static price' of commodities (by which Oppenheimer means their value), it is necessary to investigate the *law of stat-ics or the equilibrium of a market economy*. Although he has no right to do so, Oppenheimer claims for himself the honour of discovering this law, which he formulates as follows: 'The process of a market economy, competition, has a tendency to equalise all revenues'.[5] With *equality of incomes* on the part of individual producers comes the condition of market equilibrium; the market prices of commodities correspond to their 'static prices' (value). 'Such a relation between all prices, in which competition ceases to operate because all reven-ues are wherever possible equalised, we call a *static relation of prices*, and each of these prices – the *static price* of the product'.[6]

---

3 Oppenheimer 1922, p. 11.
4 Oppenheimer 1922, p. 173.
5 Oppenheimer 1922, p. 32.
6 Oppenheimer 1922, p. 36.

In a real capitalist economy, the incomes of different producers are in fact far from equal. They differ according to 1) the personal *skill* of the individual producer and 2), whether he has one or another '*monopoly position*' (monopolies). Consequently, the equilibrium of a market economy occurs not when the incomes of all producers are mathematically equal, but on condition of a 'correspondence of these incomes to the personal skill of the producers, and to their relation to monopoly positions (as active or passive agents)',[7] i.e. as the possessors of a monopoly or as persons suffering from the possession of a monopoly by other producers. 'Skill' and 'monopolies' – these are the two causes that disrupt the equality of incomes between producers. 'Let us call the income of a producer of average skill, without any monopoly, E; the increment (or reduction) for a higher or lower degree of skill we shall call $\pm$ q, and the increment (or reduction) for monopoly $\pm$ m'.[8] In that case, the income of any producer can be expressed by the formula: $E \pm q \pm m$, in which E represents a 'constant sum'. The income of each individual producer consists of this 'constant sum' E, plus (or minus) a certain sum for personal skill (q), plus (or minus) a certain sum (m), depending upon the relation of a particular producer to monopoly positions. As will be apparent from this formula, which includes three unknowns, our investigation must be divided into three levels or stages. First, it is necessary to study the income of the producer and the value of products in 'a society of equals', after which we must turn to the theory of *skill*, and finally to the theory of *monopoly*.

Let us imagine a 'society of equals' in which there is no difference whatever in the 'skill' or 'monopoly position' of individual members. Oppenheimer understands both 'skill' and 'a monopoly position' in a very broad sense that differs from customary usage. The absence of monopoly means to him not only freedom of competition but also the equal provision of means of production to all the producers. Equality of personal skill means that 'there are no *personal* differences of strength and intellectual development, of education, will power and so forth' on the part of individual producers.[9] In other words, there is an assumption of *absolute natural equality between the individual members of society*. In those conditions, 'it is obvious that all producers work for the identical period of time – for they are all assumed to be equally diligent – and *in the static condition all incomes are exactly equal*'.[10] Each member of society receives the identical annual income, which is represented by the letter E.

---

7   Ibid.
8   Oppenheimer 1922, pp. 45–6.
9   Oppenheimer 1922, p. 51.
10   Ibid.

'*Income*' is understood here not as a specific sum of money or exchange values, but rather as a determinate *sum of consumer goods*. Equality of incomes on the part of individual producers means equality in their supply of means of consumption (in the broad meaning of the term). *Equality of incomes* inevitably accompanies any 'society of equals', regardless of whether a natural economy prevails or developed monetary exchange.

Take first a *natural* economy in which there is no exchange at all. Although products here have no exchange value, and the incomes of different producers are not expressed in a common unit (money), nevertheless 'incomes here are completely equal. This means that all of the families that constitute a given society consume the same goods each year: their diet, clothing, housing, adornment, etc. are equivalent (*wertgleich*)'.[11] This 'equivalence' of goods does not mean the equivalence of their *exchange value* or their equalisation through exchange, since the latter does not occur. Nor does it mean any '*substantial equality*' of goods, i.e. complete identity of the consumer ration that accrues as income to individual producers. Oppenheimer assumes that the latter are employed in different crafts – some in hunting, others in agriculture, etc. – and that all producers are free to move from one occupation to another. In the absence of exchange, the various producers acquire as income (and consume) different consumer goods (bread for one, meat for another, fish for a third and so on). 'Nevertheless, the real sums of goods, acquired by the individual private undertakings, are equal and equivalent (*wertgleich*), although they are not identical in substance. They represent *equal amounts of use values, or subjective values*. Given the assumption of equality of skills, anyone who valued someone else's income higher than his own could easily acquire the same income by changing the character of his production'.[12] For example, if a member of society who is engaged in hunting were to conclude that the bread produced by a farmer, in his estimation, is more valuable that the meat he acquires for himself (with an equal expenditure of labour), he would leave hunting in favour of farming.

Hence, Oppenheimer draws the following conclusion, which we shall critically examine below: 'All incomes are equivalent in two respects: first, in terms of costs of production, for they represent equal expenditures of labour power with the same skill, and secondly, in terms of subjective value, for any income can be directly replaced by another. It is true that each individual subjectively evaluates the mass of goods, which constitutes his income, more highly than

---

11   Oppenheimer 1922, p. 52.
12   Ibid.

the incomes of others, but this is possible only in the event that all incomes are equivalent when considered from an "intersubjective" point of view'.[13] In other words, if a hunter subjectively evaluates the meat that he obtains more highly than the bread acquired by the farmer, and the latter subjectively evaluates his bread higher than meat, then from an 'intersubjective point of view' the given quantities of bread and meat (i.e. the incomes of the farmer and the hunter) must be *equivalent*.

As we see, in a 'society of equals', with a natural economy, individuals receive *equal income* – not in the sense of equal exchange value but instead as 'an equal and equivalent' (although not identical) quantity of use values.

This same situation also prevails for a 'society of equals' with a developed *money* economy. In a money economy, 'the sums of use values, comprising the incomes of different individuals, are also equivalent – *objectively* as the embodiment of equal labour expenditures over the same period of time, and *subjectively* as equal subjective or intersubjective values. But here this dual equality is expressed more clearly than before since all incomes also have equal *monetary value*'.[14] Previously, in the natural economy, this equality of incomes was tenuously based on rough indicators of an approximately equal material prosperity in different undertakings. A money economy has 'a finer and more precise scale of the equality of incomes, namely, an exact equality of money income' on the part of individual producers.[15] But it would be a mistake to take this monetary expression of income (or money) as the income itself: the latter consists not of money but of 'a real mass of use values'.[16] Oppenheimer strongly emphasises this idea, which, as we shall see below, has a central place in his scheme.

Consequently, Oppenheimer's first conclusion says: in 'a *society of equals' all producers receive the same income E*, understanding the latter to mean not an equal sum of exchange values but *an equivalent mass of use values* (expressed in a money economy as an equal sum of money).

On the basis of this exposition of the producers' 'income', Oppenheimer turns to a study of the 'static price' or the *value of products*. Once every producer receives the identical income, it is easy to calculate the value[17] of the individual products they make. Let us designate the number of units made by a given producer during the year (for example, poods of bread, meat and so forth), with the

---

13   Oppenheimer 1922, pp. 52–3.

14   Oppenheimer 1922, p. 53.

15   Oppenheimer 1922, pp. 53–4.

16   Oppenheimer 1922, p. 54.

17   Here and in what follows, we use the term '*стоимост*' [value] in place of Oppenheimer's reference to 'static price'.

letter n. In order to acquire income E in the course of a year, the producer must receive from the sale of each unit of his product an income equal to $\frac{E}{n}$. If the 'cost price' for the producer (or cost of production)[18] of one unit of the product is s, then the cost price of each unit of the product is $s + \frac{E}{n}$, i.e. *the costs of production plus the quotient resulting from dividing the producer's annual income by the number of products he makes during the year*.[19] For the sake of simplification, let us assume that the costs of production (s) are zero, i.e. that only the living labour of the producer is expended in making the product. In that case, the value of the product is equal to $\frac{E}{n}$. Let us suppose that, in the given society, E (i.e. the annual income, which is identical for all producers) consists of 3,000 marks. In that case, if the farmer acquires 1,500 poods of grain in a year, and the hunter 300 poods of meat, then the value of a pood of grain equals $\frac{3,000}{1,500} = 2$ marks, and the value of a pood of meat is $\frac{3,000}{300} = 10$ marks. The value of a pood of grain is $\frac{1}{1,500}$ of the annual income E, and the value of a pood of meat is $\frac{1}{300}$ of the same annual income E. *The value of each product is expressed as a determinate share of the producer's annual income.* That is Oppenheimer's second and central conclusion: *the value of the product* (v) *is derived from the income of the producer:* $v = s + \frac{E}{n}$ or, in simplified terms, $v = \frac{E}{n}$.

That is his *'formula of value'*, to which Oppenheimer attaches great significance. In his words, this is 'the formula of the absolute value of each commodity in itself. Its value is expressed not in terms of the value of other commodities, but as *a part of the income, which is equal for all* and consists not of commodities, i.e. exchange values, but instead of use values'.[20] That is precisely why this formula is free from the vicious circle that distinguished the theory of the classics. If the income E consisted of exchange values, then reducing the value of the product to a part of the income would be the equivalent of reducing one value to another value: we would continue to revolve within the same vicious circle that characterised previous formulations of the theory of value. It is precisely in order to avoid that vicious circle that Oppenheimer frequently and insistently repeats that 'income is not exchange value but use value. Any correct theory understands "income" as a real sum of goods and services intended for use (consumption). And something that exists for use is not a commodity or exchange value but simply a use value, or utility'.[21] 'Income, *for the purpose of*

---

18 Since the producer expends his own labour in making the product, by costs of production we here understand only expenditures on material, means of production and other material factors of production.

19 Oppenheimer 1922, p. 55.

20 Ibid.

21 Oppenheimer 1922, p. 46.

comparison, may be expressed in terms of money, i.e. as a sum of exchange values – but, considered in itself, it represents only a sum of use values'.[22] Whereas the classical theory reduced the exchange value of a commodity to the costs of production (i.e. to the exchange value of other commodities) and thereby fell into the vicious circle, that does not apply to Oppenheimer's formula: it begins with income as a real mass of *use values* and examines the '*static price*' (the value) of the commodity as a particular component of that income.[23]

After establishing the formula of the producers' *income* and the *value* of products in the 'society of equals', Oppenheimer attempts to connect that formula with the *labour theory of value*. Until now, we have been considering the income of the producer, or the economic plus (*Lust*) that he derives; now we must examine the minuses or burdens (*Last*) of the producer, consisting of his *labour expenditures* required in order to receive the given income E. We know that in a 'society of equals' all producers expend an equal amount of equally skilled labour, say 3,000 hours of labour per year. Consequently, the income E (3,000 marks) is obtained with the assistance of a determinate labour expenditure (3,000 hours of labour). This means that the real mass of use values, which constitutes the income E, costs the producer 3,000 hours of labour; and conversely, the given some of labour has provided the producer with income E. It follows that *the given sum of labour has the value* (*ist wert*) E, and each hour of labour expended has the value of (*ist wert*) one mark, since an hour of labour yields precisely that income to each producer 'in the form of use values, and with sale of the product, in the form of exchange values'.[24] Therefore, not just the product of labour but also the *labour itself has value*, and the value of the product and the value of the labour spent in its production are equal. *The value of labour* (*or labour time*) *is determined by the value of its product*.

This formula of the '*value of labour*' refers first of all to the labour of an independent producer. But in a 'society of equals', all of whose members are equally supplied with means of production, the same formula also applies to the value of labour (i.e. to the wage) of non-independent workers who are selling their services to others. Once an hour of labour brings an income of 1 mark and thus has a value of (*ist wert*) 1 mark, the non-independent worker (who also has the opportunity to engage in independent production) will not agree to sell his hour of labour for any lower wage. In a 'society of equals' *the wage* of the worker includes the *full product* (or the full value of the product) *of his labour*.[25]

---

22   Oppenheimer 1922, p. 47.
23   Oppenheimer 1922, p. 54.
24   Oppenheimer 1922, pp. 57–8.
25   Oppenheimer 1922, p. 58.

We can see that Oppenheimer proposes the following formulae for a 'society of equals':

1) The formula of '*income*': all producers receive the same income, understanding the latter in the sense of an aggregate of use values.

2) The formula of the '*value of the product*': the value of the product consists of a determinate part of the producer's annual income.

3) The formula of the '*value of labour*': labour has a value that is determined by the value of the product made with its assistance.

4) The formula of the '*wage*'; the worker's wage is equal to the value of his labour.

All of these formulae are closely connected, for each follows from its predecessor. Leaving aside for now the problem of wages and considering only the value of the product, we see that what is most unique in Oppenheimer's new 'formula of value' is that the value of the product is regarded as *part of the producer's annual income*. The concept of 'income', in the sense of a certain mass of use values, is the starting point for all of Oppenheimer's reasoning. With the help of his theory of the value of the product, as part of the producer's income, Oppenheimer hopes to rescue the theory of value from the vicious circle that it suffered with the classics.

However, along with the 'formula of value' that we have described, which reduces the value of the product to the *income* of the producer, we encounter even more frequently in Oppenheimer's writings a second 'formula of value', which says that the value of the product is determined by the '*value of labour*' expended in its production. Because this formula is so central to Oppenheimer's reasoning, he has called his theory of value '*Arbeitswerttheorie*'. Oppenheimer proposes to replace the Marxist '*Arbeitszeittheorie*' with his '*Arbeitswerttheorie*', which says the value of products is determined not by the *quantity of labour* but rather by *the value of labour* expended in their production.[26] By means of this formula, it is easy to explain the fact that the product of two hours of labour by a skilled worker exchanges for the product of four hours of labour by an unskilled worker: these two products embody unequal amounts of labour but the same value of labour (since the value of one hour of labour by the first worker is twice that of one hour of labour by the second worker).

In Oppenheimer's earlier works, his entire theory of value consisted of the *second* formula, which reduces the value of products to the *value of labour*. In

---

26   [See note 23 above.]

his later and main theoretical study, *Wert und Kapitalprofit,*[27] Oppenheimer, as shown above, placed at the forefront of his whole system the first formula of value as part of *income*. He portrayed the second formula of value as deriving from and dependent upon the first formula.

In fact, on the basis of the doctrine of income presented above, it is easy to come to the second formula of value. We have seen that, in the 'society of equals', labour itself acquires value; *'the value of labour'* (or labour time) = *the value of the product* made with the help of that labour. But this equation can be reversed and read from right to left. In that case we get the second formula of value: *the value of the product = the value of the labour* expended in its production. 'All products have a static price (i.e. value, *I.R.*) of the total labour time (or labour) expended upon them'.[28] In the 'society of equals', we previously took 1 hour of labour to have a value of 1 mark. If the producer spent 10 hours of labour making a particular product, the value of this product (not including the value of the raw materials, machinery, etc.) will be equal to the value of the labour expended, i.e. 10 marks. The producer *cannot* get any higher price for his product, for in that case his income would turn out to be higher than the income of other producers. Nor is he *compelled* to accept any lower price for it, for in that event his income would fall below the level of income common to all the producers. To the value of the materials used, the machinery, etc., the producer adds exactly the 'static price of the labour time he has expended',[29] i.e. 10 marks.

Thus, the second formula of value says: *the value of products is proportional to the value of the labour* expended on their production. But, in the 'society of equals', the 'value of labour' of all the producers, given their equal skill and the absence of monopolies, is identical: 1 hour of labour by any producer has the value of 1 mark. If making one product requires an expenditure of 4 hours of labour, while another requires 2 hours – given the equal skill of both producers – then the first product will have twice the value of the second product. If the production of a hundredweight of wheat requires two days of labour, and the production of a pound of copper one day, then one pound of copper exchanges for half a hundredweight of wheat, i.e. one day of labour time by one producer exchanges for one day of labour time by the other producer. In the 'society of equals', therefore, the *law of labour value* developed by Ricardo and Marx prevails. Here the static prices (values) of products are actually proportional to the

---

27   The first edition appeared in 1916.
28   Oppenheimer 1922, p. 58.
29   Ibid.

quantity of labour (or the labour time) expended on their production.[30] But Marx mistakenly took this formula of labour value to be a fundamental economic law: the formula of *Arbeitszeittheorie* is no more than a special case of applying the formula of *Arbeitswerttheorie* (which says the value of products is determined by the value of labour) in the 'society of equals', where the value of all producers' labour is identical.

The Ricardo-Marx law of labour value turns out to be inapplicable where various producers differ from one another according to their personal skill or their relation to monopoly positions. With different 'skills' or 'monopolies', *the values of the products of labour* are proportional not to the *quantities of labour* expended in their production, but instead to *the value of that labour*.

We have now acquainted the reader with both of Oppenheimer's 'formulae of value', which are closely connected. Now we must turn to a critical analysis of them. In the following chapter we shall provide a critical analysis of Oppenheimer's first formula of value, and in the third chapter, an analysis of his second formula of value.

---

30   Ibid.

CHAPTER 2

A Critique Of Oppenheimer's First Formula of Value

Value and Income

Oppenheimer's *first formula of value*, the foundation of his entire theory of value, leads to the following propositions.

In the 'society of equals' all producers expend an equal quantity of identically qualified labour and receive the *equal income* (E), in the sense of an equivalent *mass of consumer goods*. Each individual product has the value of this *mass of consumer goods* (E) divided by the number of products (n) made by the producer in the course of the year. We then get the formula of value: $v = \frac{E}{n}$.[1] The concept of the 'value' of the product is derived from the concept of the producer's 'income' (E) in the 'society of equals'. A critical analysis of this formula of value must for that reason begin with an analysis of the '*income*' (E), which Oppenheimer takes for the basis of all his constructions.

First of all, let us begin with a closer look at Oppenheimer's '*society of equals*'. At first sight it may seem that Oppenheimer is resorting here to the same abstract method of investigation as Marx used in constructing his '*society of simple commodity producers*'. In reality, however, Oppenheimer's 'society of equals' has nothing in common with Marx's 'society of simple commodity producers'.

Marx takes capitalist society as the subject of his study and scrutinises separately the various *types of production relations between people* that prevail within it. Abstracting from any social-class difference between the various producers (i.e. from the production relations between capitalists and workers), in his theory of value Marx investigates the production relations between equal commodity producers who are formally independent of each other. Marx assumes the social-class equality of these 'simple commodity producers', but in no way does he assume absolute equality in terms of their personal and material factors of production. In Marx's society of simple commodity producers, who are making the same product, there can be differences in terms of physical strength, in the intensity and dexterity of their labour, and also in the

---

1 For purposes of simplification, we assume that s = 0, i.e. that there are no expenditures on the purchase of materials, machinery, etc. The complete formula of the value of a product is the following: $v = E/n + s$.

© RICHARD B. DAY, 2024 | DOI:10.1163/9789004705661_004

character of the means of production they use[2] (hence the contrast between individual and socially necessary labour). Furthermore, the producers in different branches of labour may have trained for different lengths of time (creating the distinction between simple and skilled labour).

Whereas Marx has in mind the 'social equality' of commodity producers, Oppenheimer's structure rests upon the fantastic idea of the absolute *natural equality* of individual producers in terms of their physical, intellectual and moral qualities (insofar as they are reflected in their labour activity). There is an assumption of complete equality of their physical strength and intellect, their will and dedication, and the duration and intensity of their labour. There are also no differences whatever in terms of the agility of individual workers within the same trade, how advanced their instruments of production are, or the skills involved in different trades.[3]

Marx's critics, including Oppenheimer, frequently attack him, in their words, for his artificial construct of a society of 'equal' commodity producers. As we see, Oppenheimer himself, having set out to analyse the phenomena of value, constructed a far more artificial and fantastic hypothesis of absolute natural equality between individual producers. Marx's hypothesis is incomparably closer to reality than Oppenheimer's, which is burdened with numerous fantastic and theoretically 'superfluous' assumptions.

However, the main problem with Oppenheimer's theory is not the inclusion of theoretically 'superfluous' assumptions, but rather the absence of those 'necessary' assumptions without which no theory of value can be provided. The latter presupposes an exchange society consisting of '*commodity producers*', i.e. producers who make products for the market and commit their labour to one or another branch of production depending upon the opportunities it provides (with an equal expenditure of labour) for a greater quantity of *exchange value* (expressed in terms of money). Production for the market and the prevalence of exchange value, in the role of regulator of social production (i.e. as regulator of the distribution of social labour between various branches) – these are the necessary prerequisites for a theory of value.

To our astonishment, these prerequisites are missing from Oppenheimer's construction. His 'society of equals' is based upon a natural economy: its individual members, in their production activity, are led by the endeavour to

---

2 Provided that the quantitative difference in the character of the means of production belonging to equal commodity producers does not become a social-qualitative difference between proletarians, who are deprived of all means of production, and capitalists, whose means of production are set in motion by the labour power of others.

3 Oppenheimer 1922, p. 51.

acquire the greatest possible mass of *use values* (goods). It is true that Oppenheimer also envisages the possibility of a money economy in the 'society of equals'. With him, however, this money economy is merely a modified form of natural economy, and money (exchange value) serves only as a more precise measure for a mass of use values. Oppenheimer draws his principal conclusions from analysis of the natural economy that prevails in the 'society of equals'.

We can only be amazed at how Oppenheimer failed to see the fundamental inconsistency and theoretical bankruptcy of his entire construction. He wants to find the laws of a 'market economy' (*Marktwirtschaft*) by analysing a *natural* economy in which neither exchange nor a market exists. He studies the laws of formation of a '*static price*' (exchange value) for products using the example of an economy in which products *do not have* any exchange value or price whatever. True, in the natural economy that he is portraying, Oppenheimer does introduce one important feature adopted from an exchange economy, namely, the possibility for individual producers to transfer from less gainful occupations to ones that are more advantageous.[4] We shall not pause here to prove that, in reality, indifference towards concrete types of labour and mass transfers of individual producers (not entire communities) from less advantageous occupations to more advantageous ones are characteristic features of an exchange economy, not of a natural one. Let us agree with Oppenheimer for the moment and assume, along with him, the possible existence of a natural economy of absolutely equal producers who freely change their occupations depending upon their advantages. Will the '*equality of incomes*' that Oppenheimer talks about be established in such an economy?

Suppose that our 'society of equals' consists of three producers, one of whom is engaged in agriculture, another in hunting, and the third in fishing. There is no exchange, and each producer consumes the entire product that he acquires. Oppenheimer claims that all three producers receive an equal income (E). Does this mean that they all have the same, *identical* items of consumption? No, the incomes of the producers are 'substantially' different: the first acquires and consumes only grain, the second only meat, and the third only fish. Does equality of incomes mean that the farmer can acquire from a neighbouring tribe, in exchange for all of his grain, the same quantity of metal, shall we say, as the hunter might get in exchange for all of his meat? No, that would involve regarding the producer's income as a certain sum of *exchange* values, which contradicts Oppenheimer's construction and its insistence that income be understood in the sense of a mass of use values.[5]

---

4 Oppenheimer 1922, p. 52.
5 Oppenheimer insists upon this because otherwise (i.e. if income were understood as a mass

However, if we are to regard the income of the farmer as a certain quantity of grain, that of the hunter as a certain quantity of meat, and so forth, where is the 'equality and equivalence' of these incomes? In Oppenheimer's opinion, there is in this case an equality of '*subjective values*', which is shown by the fact that not a single producer subjectively appraises the income of another more highly than his own. If the farmer subjectively valued the sum of meat, annually obtained by the hunter, more highly than the sum of grain that he annually obtains for himself (with the same expenditure of labour), he would abandon his work in agriculture in favour of hunting. The same applies to the hunter, the fisherman, etc. But does this mean that each producer subjectively considers his income to be *equal* in value to the income of any other producer? No, Oppenheimer himself recognises that the farmer is engaged in agriculture precisely because he subjectively values the sum of grain, which constitutes his annual income, *more highly* than the sum of meat that constitutes the annual income of the hunter. Conversely, the hunter subjectively values his own income more highly, etc. But if that is the case, then it is obvious that there can be no talk of any equality of 'subjective values', and the whole assertion of the '*equality and equivalence*' of different producers' incomes loses any meaning. Oppenheimer hopes to rescue his position with the following turbid sentence: 'It is true that each individual subjectively values the mass of goods that constitutes his own income more highly than the incomes of other people, but this is possible only in the case where all incomes, from an "intersubjective" point of view, are equivalent (*wertgleich*)'.[6] We shall not accuse Oppenheimer of a contradiction here: previously he was speaking of an equality of 'subjective values', whereas now he is arguing that, despite the inequality of subjective evaluations, there exists an 'intersubjective' equivalence of incomes. But can we accept, as a proven fact, the assertion that it is only possible for every producer to evaluate his own income more highly than the incomes of others if all of these incomes are 'inter-subjectively' (objectively) equivalent? That assertion has certainly not been proven. It is entirely possible that the incomes of our three producers are objectively *non-equivalent*, while at the same time each of them subjectively appraises his own income *more highly* than the incomes of all others. Even Oppenheimer himself often repeats that from the heights of subjective appraisals no conclusions can be drawn concerning the magnitude of objective value.

---

of exchange values) his attempt to derive the product's exchange value from the income of the producer would collapse: it would suffer from the same vicious circle that, according to Oppenheimer, characterised classical theory.

6   Oppenheimer 1922, p. 53.

The failure of Oppenheimer's entire construction inevitably results from the inconsistency of the theoretical task that he poses for himself: to build a theory of exchange economy on the basis of an analysis of natural economy, and to represent the exchange value of a product as a component of the aggregate of use values (that constitute the income E). In order to solve this contradictory task and erect a bridge from natural economy to exchange economy, Oppenheimer included in his view of natural economy the concept of an 'equivalence' of incomes, grown from the soil of *exchange* economy and presupposing an objective, day-to-day *equalisation in exchange* of the various products (use values) as exchange values (expressed in terms of money). But the concept of 'equivalence' of incomes, which is alien to a natural economy, remained deeply contradictory in Oppenheimer's work. He not only failed to demonstrate the fact of equivalence of incomes in the natural economy of the 'society of equals', but he also did not even explain what this objective ('intersubjective') equivalence of incomes might consist of once incomes are regarded not as a certain sum of exchange values but instead as a mass of real use values. In this case we have an interesting example of how closely a particular economic concept (the equivalence of incomes) is tied to a determinate social context (a commodity-exchange economy) or a determinate type of production relations between people: to operate with a given economic concept, outside of the social environment from whose phenomena it is abstracted, can do nothing but damage to science.

Once the assertion of '*equivalence of incomes*' in the natural economy of the 'society of equals' is dropped, the bankruptcy is also revealed of the *formula of value* of the product as a component of income ($v = \frac{E}{n}$). If income is understood as a real quantity of goods intended for consumption (1,500 poods of grain or 300 poods of meat, etc.), then it is not possible to speak of the 'equivalence' of various incomes and the equality of each of them to one and the same magnitude E. Consequently, it is impossible to express the exchange value of a product as a magnitude E, divided by the number of products made (n). If we divide the income of the farmer, regarded as a real quantity of goods (1,500 poods of grain), by the number of poods provided, i.e. by 1,500, what we get is *a unit of the product*, i.e. 1 pood of grain, but by no means do we get the *value* of a pood of grain as Oppenheimer proposes. From the formula $v = \frac{E}{n}$ it is clear that v is a fractional part of E and consequently part of the same genus. If E is an aggregate of consumer goods, then v is also a consumer good – but not at all its 'static price' (exchange value). To regard v as the exchange value of a unit of the product would only be possible if E expressed the *exchange value* of the whole annual output of the producer, i.e. if income is understood to mean a sum of exchange values, not use values. But if the income E is the sum of exchange values of all the products made in a year, then it is obvious that to explain the exchange value of a unit of the product (v) by reference to E is not possible: such an explanation only spins in a vicious circle inasmuch as it derives *exchange value* from *exchange value*. If the income E is a sum of exchange values (and that is the only way it can be regarded), then the formula of the dependence between income and the exchange value of the product ($v = \frac{E}{n}$) turns out to be nothing more than a formula of the dependence between two exchange values, namely, between the exchange value of a unit of the product and the exchange value of the entire annual production. To explain this exchange value (as a unit of the product and as the entire annual production), the investigator has no alternative but to establish a certain relation between the value of a product and the quantity of labour expended by the producer.

As we have seen, Oppenheimer prefers to take as the starting point of his investigation not the relation between exchange value and *labour*, but instead the relation between exchange value and *income* (an aggregate of use values). However, he cannot entirely avoid the problem of labour value. He turns to this problem in his subsequent arguments, where he evidently shares the theory of labour value and recognises, in agreement with Ricardo and Marx, that in the 'society of equals' the value of products is proportional to the *quantities of labour* or labour time expended in their production. We must not, however, be confused by the apparent similarity between some of Oppenheimer's views and the theory of labour value. In fact, Oppenheimer's doctrine is not a correction to but rather a denial of the basic ideas of the theory of labour value.

Oppenheimer's reasoning actually leads, as we have already noted at the end of the previous chapter, to the following. In the 'society of equals' all producers receive an equal annual income E, understood as an aggregate of use values. This income E, divided by the number of products made by the producer in the course of the year, determines the value of one unit of the product. The value of the product, in turn, determines the value of the labour (or labour time) expended in its production. But if the value of labour (or labour time) is determined by the value of the product, then, conversely, all products also have the value of the labour (or labour time) expended upon them.[7] If 4 hours of labour are spent in making product A and only 2 hours in making product B, then

$$\frac{\text{the value of product A}}{\text{the value of product B}} = \frac{\text{the value of 4 hours of labour}}{\text{the value of 2 hours of labour}}$$

7 Oppenheimer 1922, p. 58.

But, given our assumption of equal skill for both types of labour, the value of the two labour expenditures is proportional to their duration. 'Here all labour expenditures are recognised as involving equal skill, i.e. as having the same value. But, on that assumption, the value of labour time is a constant magnitude, and the calculation can be directly based on units of time'.[8] In other words

$$\frac{\text{the value of 4 hours of labour}}{\text{the value of 2 hours of labour}} = \frac{\text{4 hours of labour}}{\text{2 hours of labour}}$$

From these two formulae comes a third:

$$\frac{\text{the value of product A}}{\text{the value of product B}} = \frac{\text{4 hours of labour}}{\text{2 hours of labour}}$$

This third formula, asserting the proportionality of the value of products to the quantity of labour or labour time expended in their production, is also the formula of labour value of Ricardo and Marx. But, with Oppenheimer, this formula of *Arbeitszeittheorie* serves only as an abbreviated and camouflaged expression of the formula of *Arbeitswerttheorie*, which asserts that the *value of products* is determined by the *value of labour*. Here, lurking beneath the formula of Ricardo-Marx, hides the confused and mistaken formula of Adam Smith, which was developed further by vulgar economists and provoked a brutal criticism from Ricardo. However, the formula of *Arbeitswerttheorie* is also not the starting point of Oppenheimer's reasoning. With Oppenheimer, the claim that the *value of the product* is determined by the *value of labour* is simply a conclusion from the reverse assertion, according to which the *value of labour* is determined by the *value of its product*. To escape this vicious circle, Oppenheimer searches for a firm foothold for determining a product's value, and he finds it, as we have seen, in *income* as an aggregate of *use values*, i.e. in use value. Thus, Oppenheimer's entire reasoning leads to the following three propositions: 1) *use value* (in the form of income) determines the value of the product; 2) the *value of the product* determines the value of labour (or labour time); and 3) the *value of labour* determines the wage. This line of reasoning is obscured and partly concealed from the reader's eyes because Oppenheimer is also inclined to state his second formula in reverse order: he claims that the value of products is determined by the *value of labour* or – taking the skill of

---

8 Oppenheimer 1922, p. 69.

labour and its value to be constant – by the *quantity of labour* expended in production. With this claim, Oppenheimer appears at first sight to move his doctrine towards the theory of labour value. But, as we have already noted, this external similarity must not hide from the reader's view the implacable difference in principle between the two theories. Freed from all the complicating and obscuring extensions, Oppenheimer's first formula of value is nothing but an attempt to derive *exchange value* from *use value* (regarded as income). Such a construction fundamentally contradicts the theory of labour value and instead moves Oppenheimer's first formula closer to the Austrian theory. In fact, it is precisely the Austrian economists who take use value as the starting point for explaining exchange value; they are precisely the people who see labour as a 'good', analogous to products (means of production) and having 'value'; it is precisely they who determine the 'value of labour' by the value of the products it creates.

This comparison of Oppenheimer's views with those of the Austrian economists may appear extremely surprising. After all, Oppenheimer often emphasises his disagreement with supporters of the Austrian school and says his goal is to provide a new grounding for an 'objective' theory of value. How did it happen that ideas akin to the schemes of the Austrian school have penetrated into Oppenheimer's 'objective' theory? Those ideas have penetrated through a secret door that Oppenheimer left open for them. From the very outset his goal was to investigate only the *quantitative* side of the phenomena of value; he is interested only in the 'question of the level and measure of value'.[9] He leaves aside the *qualitative* dimension of value phenomena, or the 'question of the cause and essence of value', which in his opinion is 'completely and correctly solved by the subjective school'.[10] Sharing the views of the Austrian school[11] on the fundamental question concerning the qualitative side of the phenomena of value, Oppenheimer unwittingly draws near to the latter whenever he has to give a 'final' explanation of phenomena. Thus, he looks for the final explanation of the value of products in income, as a mass of use values or subjective values. Consequently, in another place, when determining the value of a product by the 'value of labour', he adds that in the latter expression 'the concept of value

---

9   Oppenheimer 1922, p. 6.
10   Oppenheimer 1922, p. 22.
11   'The cause of value is the undisputed "utility" of the goods for which we strive' (Oppenheimer 1922, p. 60). But it would be futile to look for clarity on this question from Oppenheimer. In another place he says that 'the cause of value is costs' (Oppenheimer 1919b, p. 333).

is understood in the same sense as it is by the subjective school'.[12] The attempt to build an objective theory of the 'magnitude' of value, while accepting that the subjective theory is correct concerning the 'source' of value, naturally had to end in covert capitulation to the subjective theory.

---

12   Oppenheimer 1922, p. 69.

CHAPTER 3

A Critique of Oppenheimer's Second Formula of Value

The Value of Products and the Value of Labour

As we have already seen in the first chapter, Oppenheimer's *second formula of value*, according to which the value of the product is determined by the value of the labour embodied in it, represents nothing more than a conclusion from his first formula of value. As a result, it would appear that we can limit ourselves to the critical analysis of the first formula of value that we have given in the previous chapter. If the first formula is untenable, then the second, insofar as it is based upon the first, must also be mistaken. Nevertheless, Oppenheimer's second formula requires a separate critical examination. It plays too important a role in his system to pass without comment. Although, from a logical point of view, Oppenheimer makes the first formula of value (i.e. the doctrine of income) the cornerstone of his latest work, in his subsequent analysis he rarely invokes it. On the contrary, the second formula of value runs like a red thread throughout Oppenheimer's entire study, which rotates, as if on an axle, around the concept of the '*value of labour*'.

Oppenheimer sees the greatest merit of his second formula of value in the fact, as he sees it, that it is a '*universal*' formula of value that applies not just to the '*society of equals*' but also to a '*society of unequals*', comprising producers with different skills, and even to a '*monopolistic*' society with the presence of monopolies. The products being exchanged always contain equal '*values of labour*' even though they frequently have unequal '*quantities of labour*'. Therefore, Oppenheimer's theory of the 'value of labour' (*Arbeitswerttheorie*) embraces an incomparably greater range of phenomena than Marx's theory of 'labour value' (*Arbeitszeittheorie*) does. The latter theory [according to Oppenheimer] is suitable only for explaining exchange in a 'society of equals', but it does not hold for exchange between producers with different skills or different monopoly positions. In fact, if the value of products in the 'society of equals' is proportional to the *quantity* of labour expended (since the latter is not differentiated in terms of skills), in the 'society of unequals' this proportionality is already disrupted. For example, the product of 2 hours of labour by a skilled producer is equal in value to 4 hours of labour from an unskilled producer. The value of the products and the incomes of producers are determined not by the quantity of labour they expend, but instead by *the product of the quantity of*

© RICHARD B. DAY, 2024 | DOI:10.1163/9789004705661_005

labour multiplied by the value of labour. 'It is not the expenditure of labour in terms of time that is of decisive importance, but rather the time expenditure combined with the value' of labour.[1]

In the example that we have given, the 'value' of skilled labour is twice the value of unskilled labour: the latter is 1, the former is 2. Consequently, 2 hours of labour are expended on the first product, and its value is $2 \times 2 = 4$ units. On the second product, 4 hours of labour are expended and its value is $4 \times 1 = 4$ units. In both cases the *value of the expended labour* is the same (despite the different durations), and thus the value of the products is the same. The formula, according to which *the value of products is determined by the value of labour,* is applicable both to cases when products involving quantities of labour (of the same skill) are being exchanged and also to cases when products involving unequal quantities of labour (with different skills) are being exchanged. In all cases of exchange, products are equated that include the same 'value of labour' (although with a difference in the quantity of labour or its duration). The result is that this formula of value [in Oppenheimer's view] corresponds more closely to real phenomena than does the formula of Marx concerning the correspondence of the value of products to the *quantities* of labour expended or the labour time. Marx's *'Arbeitszeittheorie'* must be replaced with Oppenheimer's *'Arbeitswerttheorie'.* The starting point for explaining the value of products must not be the concept of 'labour' (or labour time), but instead the concept of the 'value of labour' (or of labour time).

Oppenheimer wants to use his formula of the 'value of labour' to explain the problem of *skilled labour* and the problem of *monopoly* (in which he also includes the problem of surplus value). For that reason, our critical analysis of this formula must involve two parts: first, we must demonstrate the logical inconsistency and internal contradictions of the formula under scrutiny; second, we must consider the extent to which this formula of value is necessary and useful for explaining the problem of skilled labour and monopoly. The present chapter is devoted to the first task, the next chapter to the second one.

Oppenheimer's second formula says: 'The static price of products is determined by the *value of labour* embodied in them'.[2] Is this a novel thesis? Not at all. In the economists of the seventeenth and eighteenth centuries, who gropingly took the first steps towards the theory of labour value – from Petty to Adam Smith – we meet with the same confusion of concepts: they determine the value of products by the labour expended in their production and the value

---

1 Ibid.
2 Oppenheimer 1922, p. 68.

of that labour. Ricardo sharply protested against this mixing up of concepts, and Marx ultimately overcame it with his teaching that 'labour' – considered as a part of the aggregate social labour, which is distributed between different branches of production and flows from some branches into others as a result of changes in prices and the value of commodities – does not possess any price and value. Insofar as 'labour' in capitalist society becomes an object of trade in the market, an item to be bought and sold, it appears not as a part of the aggregate social labour but rather as a special commodity, 'labour power', with its own value and price (the wage). 'Labour' is understood as a production-labour relation between independent 'simple' commodity producers, expressed in the 'value' of the products of their labour as commodities. 'Labour power' means 'labour' as a commodity, the value of which expresses the production-labour relation between the capitalist and the wage labourer. One can speak of the value of '*labour power*' but not of the value of labour.

Oppenheimer invites us to abandon Marx's distinction and return to the confusion of concepts that prevailed amongst the old-time economists. However, there is a profound difference between the latter and Oppenheimer; the old economists understood the 'value of labour' essentially as the *wage*, whereas Oppenheimer sees in the value of labour something completely different from the wage paid by the capitalist to the worker. According to his doctrine the capitalist, using his monopoly position as owner of the means of production, pays to the worker, in the form of wages, not the full value of his labour but only a part of it. The wage in a capitalist economy is *less* than the 'value of labour'. Consequently, Oppenheimer understands the 'value of labour' not as the static price of 'labour' or of labour power in the capitalist economy (i.e. as the average wage), but instead as the value that labour would have in the absence of a capitalist economy, namely, in a simple commodity economy. But the point is that labour, in the latter, *does not appear in the form of a commodity* or an item for purchase and sale; it has no 'market price' and therefore also no '*static price*' (or average price corresponding to the condition of market equilibrium). And, since Oppenheimer understands the 'value' of a commodity to be precisely its static price,[3] then – to be consistent with his terminology – he would have to come to the following conclusion. In a simple commodity economy labour is not an object of purchase and sale; it has no static price and consequently no value. It is not possible to speak of the 'value of labour' as anything other than the average wage of the worker in capitalist society (i.e. the value of labour power).

---

3 Oppenheimer 1922, p. 21.

Oppenheimer evades such a conclusion. As we have seen previously, he speaks of the 'value of labour' even with regard to the 'society of equals', where there can actually be no talk of a market or a static price of labour. We must, therefore, take note of Oppenheimer's terminological inconsistency involving the ambivalent use of the term 'value': this term denotes both the static price and also something quite distinct from it.

But let us make a concession to Oppenheimer and assume that in a simple commodity economy one can speak of the 'value of labour', taking it to mean the static price that labour *would have* in that economy if it were an item for purchase and sale. We shall not object to the concept of the 'value of labour' and instead assume, in agreement with Oppenheimer, that the value of products is determined by the value of labour. But, in that case, the question immediately arises as to how to determine this *value of labour*. To our astonishment, we find out from Oppenheimer that the value of labour is determined by the value of the products it makes.[4] Accordingly, the value of the *product* is determined by the value of the *labour*, but the value of the *labour* is determined by the value of the *product*. It is difficult to come up with a more striking example of a *vicious circle* than the one that Oppenheimer falls into while eagerly accusing other economists of a similar sin. In his doctrine of the 'society of equals', Oppenheimer attempted to escape from this vicious circle and find a firm foothold in the concept of the income E, as an aggregate of use values. Analysis of the income E gives the value of an individual product ($v = \frac{E}{n}$), and the value of the product, in turn, determines the value of labour. Oppenheimer subsequently forgets about his much-acclaimed discovery of *income* as the starting point of the investigation, being compelled to save the theory of value from its original sin, the vicious circle. In the second part of his study, in the teaching concerning 'skill', Oppenheimer proposes the concept of the '*value of labour*' as the basis for the theory of value, arguing that this concept is the primary and initial one beyond which our investigation need not go.[5] Whereas previously Oppenheimer derived the value of *labour* from the value of the *product*, which in turn is part of the income E, now he proposes to reduce the value of the *product* and the *income* E itself to the value of *labour*.[6] While Oppenheimer's previous mistake consisted of attempting to derive the objective-social concept of exchange value from a heterogeneous subjective-individualistic concept of use value (namely, the income E as an aggregate of consumer goods), now he falls into another error, deriving the value (of the product) from the value (of

4 Oppenheimer 1922, p. 57.
5 Oppenheimer 1922, pp. 69–70.
6 Oppenheimer 1922, p. 74.

labour). Oppenheimer fails to understand that the task of a scientific theory consists of deriving the phenomenon of exchange value from another phenomenon that is not identical to it but also not heterogeneous – one that belongs instead to the same sphere of social economy as do the phenomena of value. This is precisely the demand that is satisfied by Marx's theory, which derives the objective-social concept of (exchange) *value* from the objective-social concept (of socially-abstract) *labour*.

Oppenheimer himself understands that his theory, which determines the value of the product by the value of labour, cannot fail to provoke the charge of a vicious circle. In order to forestall such an accusation, the best he can do is to come out as a principled defender of the vicious circle in the theory of value, against which he himself hurled thunder and lightning. It turns out that the theory of value consists of nothing more than the reduction of one *value* to another *value*. 'Any theory of commodity value that does not lead to another value – and to what other value besides labour value could it lead? – is meaningless on its own and already formally incorrect'.[7] To prove this assertion is extremely easy and, as Oppenheimer suggests, incontestable:

> The problem of value is a problem of measurement, and any measurement comes down to an equation. But the elementary rule says that an equation can only involve magnitudes of the same measurement. This means that I can express length only in terms of a unit of length, weight by a unit of weight, volume by a unit of volume, temperature by a unit of temperature, and so forth. In exactly the same way I can measure value only by a unit of value.[8]

Just as one cannot say that the road from London to Berlin is equal to 99 degrees Celsius, likewise one cannot say that the value of a particular table is equal to 23 hours of labour; what must be said is that the value of the table is equal to the value of 23 hours (or labour of 23 hours).

First of all, we must note that this argumentation by Oppenheimer is strikingly contradicted by the fundamental tasks that he set for himself at the beginning of his work. He previously saw the main sin of the old formulations of the theory of value in the vicious circle; now he claims that the problem of value, by its very nature, cannot break free of such a circle. Previously he decisively repudiated theories that 'start from exchange value for an explanation of exchange

---

7   Oppenheimer 1922, p. 70.
8   Oppenheimer 1922, p. 71.

value';[9] now he just as decisively rejects 'any formula of commodity value that does not lead to another value'.[10]

But let us leave this contradiction behind and consider, on its own merits, Oppenheimer's reasoning in favour of the vicious circle. His basic mistake lies in the assertion that the problem of value is a *problem of measurement*. In justification of Oppenheimer, it must be said that many of the most prominent economists, from the time of the mercantilists up to our own day, share this mistake with him. Every statement of the problem of value in Adam Smith suffers from a duality: it aims to disclose the laws of *a change in value* on the one hand, and to find a suitable *measure of value* on the other. To the same extent as the first task involves the sphere of theoretical political economy, the second, by its very nature, is foreign to it. If our task were actually reduced to a proper measurement of the value of commodities, then Oppenheimer would be correct: to measure one value (i.e. to determine its magnitude) would be possible with the help of another value as the unit. Thus, in the exchange turnover, the value of commodities 'is measured' with the help of another value, namely money. But the task of a scientific theory consists not of finding an 'external' measure of value such as money, but rather of disclosing the laws of a change in value. We must discover the phenomenon whose alterations cause corresponding changes in the value of commodities. That phenomenon relates to value as cause does to effect, and not as the right side of an equation to the left. If value can only be measured with the help of *value*, then to reveal the laws of changes in value means to place the phenomena of value in a causal connection with phenomena that lie *outside the sphere of value*. Such phenomena, according to Marx's teaching, are changes in labour productivity and in the production-labour relations between people that cause corresponding changes in the value of commodities. Thus, completely aside from the question of whether the value of commodities can be *measured* by the value of labour, economic theory must look to *'labour'*, not the *'value of labour'*, for the final *cause* of changes in the value of commodities.[11]

---

9   Oppenheimer 1922, p. 54.
10   To eliminate this gaping contradiction in Oppenheimer, one might say that in his formula, which determines the value of a product by the value of labour, he understands the latter not in the sense of 'exchange value' but instead in 'the sense used by the subjective school' (see Oppenheimer 1922, p. 69). The formula would take the following form: the exchange value of a product is determined by the subjective worth of labour. But that formula would mean abandonment, first of all of the 'objective' theory of value that Oppenheimer wants to justify; and secondly, of his demand that equalisation must involve only 'magnitudes of the same measurement'.
11   See below the chapter on 'Oppenheimer as Critic of Marx'.

CHAPTER 4

Skilled Labour

In the previous chapter we undertook to disclose the logical contradictions of Oppenheimer's second *formula of value*. It is difficult to believe that this formula, built upon a confused concept of the 'value of labour' and revolving within the vicious circle, could actually serve as a useful and instructive tool for solving the problems of *skilled labour* and *monopoly*. Meanwhile, that is exactly the role that Oppenheimer assigns to it. According to Oppenheimer, it is precisely the 'universal' character of the formula of value that constitutes its principal theoretical advantage compared to the Ricardo-Marx formula of 'labour value'. In order to prove how mistaken this assertion by Oppenheimer is, we must turn to an exposition and analysis of his theory of skilled labour and monopoly. A critical analysis of these teachings, on the one hand, will help us to test the 'universal' character of Oppenheimer's theory of value, while on the other hand it will enable us to introduce further parts of Oppenheimer's economic system and to evaluate critically the solution to the problems of skilled labour and monopoly (more accurately, surplus value as monopoly income) that he proposes.

In his doctrine of the 'society of equals' Oppenheimer assumed absolute equality of personal skill on the part of individual producers. At the second stage of his study he withdraws this simplifying premise and turns to a study of incomes and the value of products in a 'society of unequals', whose individual members differ from each other in terms of their personal skill. He thereby turns to an examination of the problem of *skilled labour*. In Marx's theory the problem of skilled labour is considered in the teaching on labour value or the 'society of simple commodity producers'. In the latter, according to Marx's view, it is quite possible to have the existence of diverse trades, which require from the producers a different period of training or instruction. The difference in the period of instruction between a jeweller and a shoemaker (and consequently the different value of the products of an hour's labour on the part of the jeweller and the shoemaker) does not in the slightest degree violate their social-class equality as 'simple commodity producers'.

The problem of skilled labour occupies a different place in Oppenheimer's theory. In the 'society of equals', as we have seen, an absolute natural equality of individuals is assumed, which leads to an exact equality of their 'incomes'. This absolute equality of incomes can be and actually is violated in a real capitalist economy: 1) either by differences in the *'personal skill'* of individual producers, or 2) by differences in their 'material qualification', i.e. their secure access to the means of production. Consequently, all of Oppenheimer's inquiry naturally divides, as we have already seen, into three stages that gradually move the abstract research in the direction of reality. In the first part he studies the 'society of equals'. In the second part he assumes that there are differences of 'personal skill' between individual producers, yet full equality remains in the area of 'material qualification' (or, in his terminology, there are no monopolies). Here Oppenheimer studies the 'society of unequals', or the *problem of skilled labour*. Finally, in the third part he also assumes inequality in the 'material qualification' of various producers (or, in his terminology, the existence of 'monopolies' on the part of some producers in relation to the others). Here he studies the *problem of monopoly*.

In the previous chapter we have already analysed Oppenheimer's doctrine of the 'society of equals'. In this chapter we must deal with his teaching concerning 'skill' or skilled labour. While for Marx this problem is part of the theory of 'simple commodity producers', with Oppenheimer it moves beyond the confines of the theory of the 'society of equals' as a second, distinct part of his study.

The unique way in which Oppenheimer formulates the problem of 'skilled' labour is also explained by the unreasonably broad context in which he uses this particular term. In the 'society of equals', once it is assumed that there is an absolute natural equality of the personal attributes of individual producers, everything that violates that equality must be attributed to a difference of their personal 'skill'.[1] The jeweller, who trains for his trade over a period of ten years, is more skilled than a common labourer, whose work requires no prior instruction; a masterful spinner, who makes twice as much thread in an hour as his unqualified, clumsy or lazy neighbour, has greater skills than the latter; a Böcklin,[2] whose paintings are worth their weight in gold, owes this fact to his greater skill; a footman with a statuesque figure is a skilled worker compared to one whom nature has not blessed with such qualities, etc.[3] The extra skill of all these people is manifested in the fact that: 1) the products of their labour have a higher *value* when sold, and 2) these people receive a higher *income*.[4]

---

1   Oppenheimer 1919b, pp. 380–1.
2   [The reference is to Arnold Böcklin (1827–1901), a famous Swiss painter, graphic artist and sculptor.]
3   Oppenheimer 1919b, pp. 380–2.
4   On p. 379 of *Theorie* (1919b), Oppenheimer defines skill as the ability of the producer to make commodities of a higher value (стоимость), but in *Wert und Kapitalprofit* (1922, p. 62) he refers to the ability to acquire a higher income. The two definitions are incompatible: a

As we see, Oppenheimer combines a whole series of different phenomena into one, and with this confusion of concepts he blocks his own way to a proper understanding of the problem of skilled labour. We have yet to mention that Oppenheimer does not distinguish the question of the value of the products of skilled labour from the question of the value of skilled labour power. But, even with reference to the first of these problems, we see Oppenheimer mixing up the following questions: 1) the question of the value of the products of labour by workers of *different trades* that are distinguished by different *skills*, e.g. the jeweller and the shoemaker (the problem of skilled labour); 2) the question of the value of the products of labour by various producers in *one and the same trade* who differ in terms of skilfulness or the quality of their labour, e.g. a masterful and an artless spinner (the problem of socially necessary labour), and 3) the question of the price of non-reproducible products made by specific individuals (a Raphael or a Böcklin and so forth).

In his latest work, *Wert und Kapitalprofit*, Oppenheimer justifiably sets aside the third question on the grounds that when a painting by Raphael is sold, the issue is 'market price', not the 'static price' (value) that we are examining here.[5] However, he continues and even increases the confusion concerning the problem of *skilled* and *socially necessary* labour, which is the main flaw in his study of 'skill'.

In his most recent work, *Wert und Kapitalprofit*, Oppenheimer considers two types of skill: skill that is '*acquired*' and skill that is '*innate*'. The first is acquired by the producer as a result of 'more prolonged or costly training' for the profession.[6] The second is possessed by producers who stand out from the average due to their 'innate' natural qualities (physical, intellectual or moral), e.g. physical strength, cleverness, strength of will and so forth. Oppenheimer

---

skilled spinner receives a higher income than one who is unskilled, although the price of their products is identical; conversely, the price of the product of an hour's work by the (average) jeweller is higher than the price of the product of an hour's work by the (average) shoemaker, although the skilled shoemaker receives a higher income than an unskilled jeweller. When comparing various trades with different skills (i.e. when investigating the problem of skilled labour), we notice a difference in the price (*стоимость*) of products that are produced during the identical work time. When comparing various workers of one and the same profession (i.e. when investigating the problem of socially necessary labour), we notice that their incomes differ while the prices of their products are the same. The hopeless confusion of these two problems in Oppenheimer (see below) forced him to move from the more correct definition that he gave in *Theorie* to the erroneous definition of skill on the basis of 'income' (*доходности*) to which he later turned in *Wert und Kapitalprofit*.

5   Oppenheimer 1922, p. 67.
6   Oppenheimer 1922, p. 63.

charges Marx with limiting his study to 'acquired' skill without considering 'innate' skill.[7] To explain the latter was especially 'difficult' for previous formulations of the theory of labour value. Oppenheimer hopes that his own theory will easily cope with this difficulty.[8] Let us see what novelty Oppenheimer promises to provide in solving the problem of skilled labour.

We shall begin with 'acquired' skill. Obviously, the producer who has spent certain resources on preparation for his trade receives an *above-average income*, namely E + q (where E is the same income for all unskilled producers and q is a premium for skill). Since E is a determinate sum, it remains to determine the magnitude of q. In this case, that is easy to do. Suppose that a 15-year-old youngster, instead of working in some craft as an unskilled producer, spends another 10 years preparing for the legal profession. That training has cost him 15,000 marks. Moreover, he has lost the income that he would have received for each of the 10 years as an unskilled producer, namely, 3,000 marks × 10 = 30,000 marks. The sum that he has lost is 45,000 marks. Taking the average human lifespan to be 55 years, we find that our attorney, during the remaining 30 years of his life, must receive an annual income bonus for skill (q) in the sum of $\frac{45,000}{30}$ = 1,500 marks. In that case, his annual income will be: E + q = 3,000 + 1,500 = 4,500 marks.[9]

Once we have precisely determined the *income* of a skilled producer, i.e. E + q, we shall also easily determine the *static price* (the value) of an individual product that he makes. If, as we did previously, we use the letter n to designate the number of products made during the year, then the value of each unit of the product is $\frac{E+q}{n}$. Since the value of a product of labour by an unskilled producer is $\frac{E}{n}$, it is clear that the product of an hour of labour by a skilled producer has a greater value than the product of an hour's labour by the unskilled producer. At the same time, though, the 'value of labour' by a skilled producer is correspondingly higher than the 'value of labour' by an unskilled producer, since each hour of labour provides the former with a higher income than the latter. Consequently, the increased value of the *products of labour* by a skilled producer is explained by the increased 'value of labour' they contain. In the exchange of products, made by producers with different skills, *unequal* quantities of labour are exchanged but the 'values of labour' are *equal*.[10]

---

7   Oppenheimer 1922, p. 64.
8   Oppenheimer 1922, p. 65.
9   Oppenheimer 1922, p. 63.
10   [That is, any exchange involves equivalent sums of value, but the hours expended – the 'quantities of labour' – by skilled and unskilled producers to create the same value will be different.]

Does this reasoning from Oppenheimer give us anything new in principle compared to the solution to the problem of skilled labour that we find in Marx and in subsequent Marxist literature? Oppenheimer himself recognises that his explanation 'approximately' repeats the thinking of Marx.[11] The difference between them is that Oppenheimer calculates the monetary expense of preparing for a given profession, whereas from the viewpoint of Marxist theory these *monetary expenditures* (the costs of instruction) in turn are reduced, in the final analysis, to determinate *labour expenditures* (namely, the labour of the instructors, of the student, and of the people providing the material items required for the training). In his explanation of 'acquired' skill Oppenheimer has said nothing new.

The 'novelty' to which Oppenheimer lays claim in this area consists of his response to the problem of 'innate' skill. He solves this problem in an extremely simple way: it turns out that with an innate skill, as distinct from an acquired one, 'the static price (i.e. the value. *I.R.*) of goods being substituted does not vary as a result of the different skills of the labour involved in their production'.[12] Imagine a shoemaker who has innate skill, e.g. greater physical endurance, acumen, dexterity and so forth. Clearly he will receive an income higher than E (i.e. 3,000 marks), namely E + q, while q (the premium for skill) will be higher, the more this particular person is distinguished from the norm by his innate abilities. But does his skill have any influence on the *value* of his product, the shoes? Not at all. The fact is that 'in all branches where highly skilled workers produce substitutable goods, there are competing workers of average skill competing against them'.[13] In close proximity to our shoemaker, other shoemakers are working, who are distinguished by their average physical endurance, acumen and so on. And since the value of every product is determined by the costs of its production in the least favourable circumstances, the result is that in this case also the value of shoes is determined by the costs of *'average'* shoemakers, i.e. those not having any innate skill; the value of shoes must be just sufficient to furnish 'average' shoemakers with the annual income E, that is, 3,000 marks. If the 'average' shoemaker produces 300 pairs of shoes each year, then he must receive 10 marks for each (in addition to the costs of material, etc.; with total costs of 15 marks per pair, the value of a pair of shoes is 25 marks).

Once the value of a pair of shoes is established on the basis of the expenses of 'average' shoemakers (it is equal to $\frac{E}{n} + s = \frac{3,000}{300} + 15 = 25$), then *that is the price*, obviously, for which the shoes made by our 'outstanding' shoemaker will

---

11   Oppenheimer 1922, p. 64.
12   Oppenheimer 1922, pp. 65–6.
13   Oppenheimer 1922, p. 66.

also be sold. His innate skill has no influence upon the value of his product, which is thus determined by the formula $\frac{E}{n} + s$, and not by the formula $\frac{E+q}{n} + s$. The 'innate' skill of our shoemaker can be manifested only in the fact that he: 1) either makes *more units* of the product with the same expenditure of labour, e.g. 400 pairs of shoes, which gives him an income of 10 marks × 400 = 4,000 marks = E (3,000 marks) + q (1,000 marks); or 2) thanks to his ingenuity and dexterity he saves in terms of *expenses* for material and so on; saving 2 marks on each pair of shoes, for 300 pairs he will receive an additional income for his skill (q) of 600 marks, and a total income of E + q = 3,000 + 600 = 3,600 marks.[14] Thus, the 'innate' skill has an influence only upon the *income* of the producer but not upon the *value of a unit of the product*. The producer who possesses 'innate' skill receives supplementary income (q) while selling his product at the same price as the 'average' producers do. One pair of shoes, made during 7½ hours of labour ($\frac{3,000}{400}$), equates to one pair of shoes made by the 'average' shoemaker during 10 hours of labour ($\frac{3,000}{300}$) because the 'value of labour' by the former exceeds the 'value of labour' by the latter.

The reader can be easily assured that Oppenheimer's claim to provide a new solution to the problem of 'innate' skill is based upon a simple misunderstanding. As a solution to the problem of *skilled* labour, Oppenheimer presents us with an analysis of phenomena that was given long ago by Marx in his teaching concerning *socially necessary* labour. In his arguments about 'innate' skill, Oppenheimer studies the value of products and the incomes of different producers in *one and the same trade*, as in the case of the different quality or skilfulness of the labour (of the 'outstanding' shoemaker and the 'average' shoemaker). It is clear that once these producers are making one and the same product, the price of the latter does not depend upon the individual labour expenditures of a given producer. The value of the product is determined by the socially necessary labour expenditures, not by individual labour expenditures. The most skilful producers, whose individual expenses in making the product are lower than what is socially necessary, receive additional income when selling their product at its 'socially necessary' value. In the present case, Oppenheimer is merely repeating the ideas of Marx that were developed in his doctrine of socially necessary labour.[15] But this entire problem has no relation to the problem of skilled labour, i.e. to an explanation of the different value of products made by producers *in different trades* and distinguished by different levels of skill. What is involved in the latter case is not a difference of

---

14   Oppenheimer 1922, p. 67.
15   With the exception that Oppenheimer, like Ricardo, defines value in terms not of 'average' but of 'marginal' producers, i.e. with the highest costs of production.

the 'individual skill' (ingenuity) of producers in one and the same trade, but rather the 'average skill' of different trades (for example, shoemaking and jewellery). Oppenheimer's claim to offer something 'new' concerning this question is based exclusively upon a crude mixing up of the problems of 'skilled' and 'socially necessary' labour – and examples of this confusion can also be found in his earlier works.[16]

As we see, in his explanation of skilled labour Oppenheimer has said nothing that is new in principle compared to Marx. The Marxist theory of labour value gives a completely satisfactory explanation both of the fact that the product of hourly labour by a skilled producer (a jeweller) has a higher value compared to the product of hourly labour by an unskilled producer (a common labourer), and also of the fact that the value of the product of labour by a skilful producer (the master shoemaker) is determined not by his individual costs but by the average socially necessary costs. In explaining the *problem of skilled labour*, Oppenheimer's formula of the 'value of labour' has *no advantages whatever* compared to Marx's formula of 'labour value'. Oppenheimer himself is obliged to recognise that Marx correctly solved the problem of 'acquired' skill. That Marx ignored 'innate' skill (which, as we have seen, he did not in fact do), as Oppenheimer himself acknowledges, is not a 'serious weakness' and 'has no significance for solving the great problems of the theory of value'.[17] Oppenheimer's attempt to show that his formula of *Arbeitswerttheorie* explains the problem of skilled labour better than Marx's formula of *Arbeitszeittheorie* cannot withstand even mild criticism.

---

16   In *Theorie der reinen und politischen Oekonomie* (1919b, p. 379), Oppenheimer does not
       distinguish the skill of 'entire groups of professional workers' and the skill of 'individuals
       within these groups'.
17   Oppenheimer 1922, pp. 172 and 178.

CHAPTER 5

The Theory Of Monopoly

The teaching on *monopoly* is the third part of Oppenheimer's theoretical research, his 'third approximation' to actual economic reality. In the 'society of equals', an absolute equality between producers prevailed. In the 'society of unequals', they differ from one another according to their 'personal skill'. Finally, in a monopolistic society the producers differ from one another in terms of their 'material qualification': they are not equally provided with the products of labour and the means of production. Seizure of the latter (factually or legally) creates 'monopoly positions' for individuals and for entire classes. Whereas unlimited competition previously prevailed (between equal producers in the 'society of equals' and between producers with different skill in the 'society of unequals'), now the seizure of *monopoly positions* actually limits competition and gives monopolists the opportunity to acquire *'monopoly income'* in excess of the normal[1] level and to sell their products for *'monopoly prices'* that are higher than 'competitive prices'. 'Monopoly is a dominant economic position based on the fact that competition cannot operate with complete freedom'.[2]

Thinking that one of the main defects of former theoretical systems, including the Marxist, was the inability the explain monopoly prices, Oppenheimer provides a thoroughly developed theory of monopoly; he sees the main contribution of his theory in solving precisely this problem.

To begin with, Oppenheimer provides an elaborate classification of monopolies, which we must abbreviate here for the sake of clarity in our subsequent exposition:

Monopolies are divided:

A) in terms of their scope of activity into:

    1) *personal monopolies* (a monopoly position belongs to individuals or groups of people, e.g. to a capitalist who has a patent for producing razors, or a coal trust that controls most of the coal production) and

    2) *class monopolies* (an entire social class has a monopoly position, e.g. the land belongs to the class of agriculturalists, and the other means of production to the class of capitalists);

---

1 'Normal' is understood to refer to the level of income that is established with free competition and corresponds to the skill of the given producer (i.e. income E or E ± q).

2 Oppenheimer 1919a, p. 6. Approximately the same definition is given in *Wert und Kapitalprofit* (1922, pp. 93–4).

B)   in terms of their basis into:
    1)   *natural monopolies* (e.g. monopoly possession of the only vineyard that grows a particular variety of grape) and
    2)   *legal monopolies under public law* (e.g. the patent on razors) and private-law monopolies (e.g. an agreement between all the producers, as members of a syndicate, to restrict production and raise prices);
C)   in terms of the position of the monopolist into:
    1)   *monopolies of sellers* (e.g. a trust) and
    2)   *monopolies of buyers* (e.g. the monopoly position of capitalists, as the buyers of labour power,[3] in relation to those who sell the latter, i.e. the workers;
D)   in terms of their relation to static prices into:
    1)   *exchange monopolies* (a monopolist sells or buys at a 'monopoly' price that *diverges* from the competitive static price, e.g. a trust sells its product at a higher price or a capitalist buys labour power at a price below its value) and
    2)   *production monopolies* (e.g. an individual capitalist, who possesses advanced machines that cheapen production, acquires surplus profit or a supplementary revenue although he sells his product *at the same price* as other producers do who work with less advanced means of production).

As we see, Oppenheimer understands the concept of 'monopoly' (as he does 'skill') in a much wider sense than is usually the case. In his eyes all of the following are equally 'monopoly income': 1) the income of a trust from selling the commodity at prices higher than competitive prices (*monopoly* in the precise sense of the word);[4] 2) the average profit of a capitalist, who does not possess any special monopoly, from the purchase and exploitation of the wage labour of workers (*surplus value*);[5] 3) the surplus profit of a capitalist (or supplementary income of a craftsman) who possesses more advanced means of production and sells his products at normal competitive prices (*differential profit* or differential income resulting from the difference between the individual and socially necessary value of the product).[6]

---

3   In place of the term 'labour power', Oppenheimer uses the term 'labour'.
4   In Oppenheimer's terminology, this means the personal monopoly of a seller (in exchange).
5   In Oppenheimer's terminology, this means a class monopoly on the part of buyers (i.e. capitalists as the buyers of wage labour).
6   In Oppenheimer's terminology, this means a seller's personal monopoly in production.

We can already anticipate that Oppenheimer's theory of monopoly will not likely benefit from combining such dissimilar economic phenomena. The three cases that we have mentioned differ sharply from each other in both *qualitative* and *quantitative* terms. Each of the three types of income expresses a different *type of production relations* between people: 1) the first income expresses the production relations between *monopoly* capitalists and capitalists who *do not have* a monopoly, i.e. a restriction of competition is assumed within the class of capitalists; 2) the second income expresses the production relations between the class of *wage workers* and the class of *capitalists as a whole*, who are monopoly owners of the means of production, while unlimited competition is assumed to prevail within the class of capitalists; 3) the third income expresses the production relations between commodity producers *in one and the same branch of production* (whether craftsmen or capitalists), who possess means of production *of different technical productivity* and find themselves in circumstances of unrestricted mutual competition. The third type of income is inherent in any commodity economy (even a simple one), and for that reason it is studied by Marx in the theory of labour value and the teaching on 'socially necessary labour'. The second type of income occurs in any capitalist economy and is therefore studied by Marx in his theory of 'surplus value'. The first type of income occurs only in a special variant of capitalist economy, namely monopoly capitalism, and therefore has to be examined in a special 'theory of monopoly'. In the single concept of 'monopoly', Oppenheimer confuses and combines the *fundamental* characteristics of *commodity* economy (the differential income of commodity producers who possess more advanced means of production), the *basic* features of *capitalist* economy (surplus value), and the *special* features of *monopolistic* capitalism (monopoly profit).

The social-qualitative heterogeneity of these three types of income is also reflected in their *quantitative* aspect. The magnitude of differential income is determined by the difference between the *individual* and the *socially necessary* value (the competitive price) of the product.[7] The magnitude of surplus value is determined by the difference between the value (competitive price) of *labour power* and the value (competitive price) of *the commodity* that is made by wage labour.[8] The magnitude of monopoly income, in the precise sense, is determ-

---

7   'Competitive price' refers here to the average price that is established with free competition and corresponds to the value of the product; deviations of the average price from value do not concern us here.

8   Provided that there are no expenditures on constant capital (material, machines and so forth).

ined by the difference between the *monopoly price* for a particular product and its *value* (the competitive price). Consequently, it is only in the latter case that we can speak of a 'monopoly price' in the strict sense of the word.

Of these three incomes, let us set aside the differential profit of the producer who sells his commodity at competitive prices. Oppenheimer himself recognises that in this case there is no 'monopoly price',[9] and thus the major part of his study is devoted to the two other types of income. By combining them both in the concept of 'monopoly', as N.I. Bukharin has noted, Oppenheimer confuses two heterogeneous phenomena: 'the class monopoly of the capitalists and monopoly within the class of capitalists'.[10] Oppenheimer himself understands the heterogeneous character of these two phenomena and thus distinguishes between a *'class* monopoly' (i.e. the monopoly of the class of capitalists, expressed in the appropriation of surplus value) and a *personal* monopoly (a monopoly of individual capitalists or a group of them who are receiving monopoly profit). Yet he believes that both of these phenomena are subject to identical laws of monopoly. Accordingly, Oppenheimer first considers the general concept of monopoly in order subsequently to turn to 'class' monopoly, i.e. to the theory of surplus value. Let us briefly trace the development of his reasoning.

Any individual who occupies a monopoly position, actually excluding other members of society from freely competing with him, acquires, in addition to the normal income E, a supplementary *monopoly income* (m). His total income is E + m.[11] Hence, it is also easy to find the formula of 'monopoly price' for a unit of the product. If our monopolist, e.g. a trust, each year produces a volume of products n, then the *'static monopoly price'* of a unit of the product is $\frac{E+m}{n}$.[12] At first glance it may appear that this formula is totally indeterminate because the trust, in the capacity of a monopolist, can raise prices on its products to any arbitrary level. But that assumption would be mistaken. The most powerful trust cannot raise prices beyond a certain point. Otherwise consumers, on the one hand, will curtail consumption of the given product and begin partially to replace it with similar but cheaper products (e.g. alcohol or gas in place of kerosene), while on the other hand the high price for this product will sooner or later encourage other producers, who are not members of the trust,

---

9   Oppenheimer 1922, p. 88.
10   Bukharin 1924, p. 54.
11   Here the average personal skill of a producer is assumed. The income of a more highly skilled producer is E + q + m.
12   This applies to conditions in which costs of production for material, machines and so forth are zero. Taking these costs as s, we get the complete formula: (E + m) / n + s.

to expand production of this product. Thus, the monopoly price for the given product (e.g. kerosene) is limited first by *competition* from producers who are not members of the monopoly organisation, and secondly by *competitive* prices on similar products that might serve as surrogates. 'The magnitude of a monopoly mark-up beyond the static price of products is determined within quite narrow confines by the possibility of competition'.[13]

Between every monopolist and his counterpart (e.g. between a trust and its purchasers), a special social relation is established, a *'monopoly relation'*, characterised by the inequality of the two parties and a preponderance of power to the benefit of the monopolist. What the monopolist gains, his counterpart loses.[14] The former acquires a 'monopoly profit'; the latter is compelled to pay a 'monopoly tax' out of his income. The monopolist sees the source of his monopoly profit in his goods or products (e.g. the trust with its kerosene), but in fact the source is the inequality of social power between the two parties.[15] The monopolist, with the aid of his 'monopoly position', extracts from his counterpart, without any compensation, a part of the latter's income and commandeers it for himself: monopoly income is 'surplus value' taken by the monopolist from his counterpart. This appropriation of surplus value is completed in the process of exchange: the monopolist gives to his counterpart less value in exchange for more. Whereas previously, with free competition, *equivalent* products exchanged one for the other, now, with the rule of monopoly, *nonequivalent* products are being exchanged.[16]

Oppenheimer considers his development of the theory of monopoly to be one of his main contributions, and he sees total neglect of monopoly value as one of the main flaws of the Marxist theory of value. At first sight, it may appear that Oppenheimer has in mind here Marx's lack of a theory of monopoly in the exact sense of the word (cartel prices, etc.). It is true that in his theory of value Marx does study only the laws of the formation of competitive prices, but he does so not because the phenomena of monopoly price formation were unknown to him – in his time, by the way, they did not yet play such a role as from the end of the nineteenth century – nor because he did not consider them worth studying. Marx believed that economic theory must study capitalist economy in its 'pure' form, i.e. first and foremost as an economic system based upon free competition between individual capitalists. Only on the basis

---

13   Oppenheimer 1922, p. 93.
14   Oppenheimer 1922, p. 103.
15   Oppenheimer 1922, pp. 99–101.
16   Oppenheimer 1922, p. 106.

of the *theory of value*, which investigates the laws of the formation of competitive prices, is it possible to proceed to an explanation of *monopoly prices* (cartel
prices and so forth).

Does Oppenheimer have any right to rebuke Marx for such a methodological approach to the problem of price and value? Not at all, for Oppenheimer
is himself obliged to resort to the same method. He initially (in his theory of the
'society of equals' and 'skill') gives us a theory of competitive prices, in order
then to turn to a theory of monopoly prices. He builds the latter on the basis
of the former and comes to the conclusion that lawfulness in the formation
of monopoly prices can only be understood from studying lawfulness in the
formation of competitive prices. Thus, on the question of the relation between
competitive and monopoly prices, Oppenheimer claims to add something new
to the theory of monopoly, but in fact he uses the method that was specified by
the classics and by Marx and that has also been further developed by the most
recent Marxists.[17]

Furthermore, Oppenheimer comes to the conclusion – completely unexpected from him – that an economist studying the law of value is generally correct
to ignore the formula of monopoly prices on the grounds that monopolies in
the narrow sense (patents, cartels, trusts and so forth) are *temporary and transient* entities: they appear for a time but are soon swept away by new waves of the
competitive struggle, 'and therefore they are not relevant to a static economy
in the strict sense of the word'.[18] For that reason, the economist is correct not
to include monopoly prices and incomes in his investigation.[19]

But if that is the case – asks the puzzled reader – on what grounds does
Oppenheimer accuse Marxist theory of ignoring 'monopoly value'? To answer
that question we must keep in mind that by monopoly income Oppenheimer
understands, without any distinction, both 'monopoly profit' in the narrow
sense (the profit of trusts and so on) and also 'surplus value' in the general
sense, which is received by every capitalist. While a researcher who is inclined
towards strict differentiation of concepts has a perfect right to regard only the
first phenomenon as pertaining to monopoly, Oppenheimer, to the contrary,
sees the centre of gravity of his entire theory of monopoly precisely in the study
of '*class*' rather than 'personal' monopolies, i.e. in the theory of *surplus value*.
Oppenheimer does not even see any great error, as we have pointed out, in the
economic theorist ignoring the problem of 'personal' monopolies (trusts, etc.),
i.e. exactly those phenomena that really do pertain to the theory of monopoly.

---

17   For example, the work by Hilferding and Nakhimson (Spektator) on cartel prices.
18   Oppenheimer 1922, p. 95.
19   Oppenheimer 1922, p. 96.

This problem, in Oppenheimer's words, is secondary compared to the problem of 'class' monopoly, i.e. surplus value. 'The primary problem is not the surplus profit of a monopolist but rather the normal profit of the capitalist who does not possess any personal monopoly'.[20]

We arrive, therefore, at an initially unexpected conclusion. Accusing the Marxist theory of value of ignoring the phenomena of monopoly, Oppenheimer essentially has in view not so much Marx's fictional ignoring of monopoly price formation in the narrow sense of the word as *Marx's refusal to build the theory of surplus value on the basis of the theory of monopoly* (or, what amounts to the same thing, to equate surplus value with monopoly profit). The trouble with Marx is not so much that he did not include the problem of monopoly in his research as that he consequently failed to provide a correct theory of surplus value. Marx's basic 'methodological downfall' is that 'he did not pose the question of whether surplus value is a monopoly price'.[21] He did not understand that 'the social relation of capital is itself the most typical special case of a monopoly relation'.[22] On the other hand, Oppenheimer sees the greatest contribution of his own theory of monopoly not in explaining the phenomena of monopoly price formation in the narrow sense, but instead in the fact that it makes possible a correct understanding of *surplus value* as a special form of *monopoly income*. In Oppenheimer's view, the central point of his disagreement with Marx concerns precisely this question. We must, therefore, turn to an analysis of Oppenheimer's theory of surplus value.

---

20   Ibid.
21   Oppenheimer 1922, p. 173.
22   Oppenheimer 1919a, p. 12.

CHAPTER 6

Surplus Value as Monopoly Income

On the basis of the theory of value set out above, Oppenheimer believes it is easy and simple to build a theory of *surplus value*. We have seen that whenever a monopolist enters into exchange with someone who does not have a monopoly position, he appropriates a portion of the latter's income and receives 'surplus value'. Conversely, the '*surplus value*' acquired by the class of capitalists is a result of the monopoly of property held by this class (the latter will be understood hereafter in the broad sense as the aggregate of landowners and capitalists). The consequence of this '*class monopoly*' is a restriction of free competition and free economic rivalry among all the members of society. Economists have customarily regarded capitalist economy as a system of free competition, guided exclusively by the operation of economic forces. This is incorrect. Capitalism arose and is maintained by the operation of not just economic but also '*non-economic*' political forces, and the character of these two forces is directly opposite. Economic rivalry or free competition tends to establish complete equality between the individual producers, which is expressed in 'fair' exchange of the products of their labour in accordance with the 'value of labour' embodied in them. This realm of free competition is a sphere of '*natural*' economic laws, a sphere of 'pure economy'. But the operation of foreign '*social*' laws also breaks into this sphere: one class of society, using the methods of 'political' coercion, seizes the land and the means of production and establishes a 'class monopoly', which in fact limits the possibility for other classes to compete freely with the monopolist class. The 'natural' or normal economic laws (or free competition) can no longer appear in pure form, the equality of the producers gives way to social oppression and inequality, and the 'fair' exchange of equivalents is replaced by the exchange of 'non-equivalents': the class monopolist (the capitalists) purchases the labour of the destitute class (the wage workers), paying them less than its full value and appropriating the difference in the form of monopoly profit (surplus value). In place of the *pure economy* (of free competition) we have a *political economy* (or competition limited by monopolies).[1]

What is it that constitutes the 'monopoly position' of the propertied classes in capitalist economy? Its basis is the *seizure of land* in the form of private prop-

---

1   For this reason, Oppenheimer called one of his principal works *Theorie der reinen und politischen Oekonomie* (*The Theory of Pure and Political Economy*).

© RICHARD B. DAY, 2024 | DOI:10.1163/9789004705661_008

erty and the formation of *large landholdings*. With an equal division of the land between all members of society, each would receive a small parcel sufficient for operating his own homestead. But a small band of 'well-armed' people, by the end of the feudal period, seized all the land as private property,[2] drove the peasants from the land, and transformed them into hired proletarians. Established by methods of feudal coercion, large-scale agriculture was preserved under capitalism and continues to be the basis for the monopoly-class rule of the propertied classes. If the land were declared open to everyone who wished to work it, the worker would prefer to set up his own farm and receive the full product (or the full value) of his labour, rather than toil in a factory for a wage far less than the value of his labour. Furthermore, there would be an end to the flow into the cities of former agricultural workers, masses of whom, receiving a beggarly wage from the big landowners, depart for the cities and drive down the level of wages for urban workers. It is only with large-scale land ownership and mass emigration of the population from rural areas to the cities that employers continuously have available a contingent of workers who are ready to sell their labour for a wage less than the full value of their labour. It is only due to monopoly seizure of the land by large landowners that the capitalists were able to have at their disposal the labour of an entire impoverished population and thus concentrate in their own hands monopoly possession of all the secondary means of production (materials, machines, and so forth).

Today, the capitalist class stands opposed to the class of wage workers as the *monopoly purchaser* of their labour. If they refuse to work for a capitalist, the workers, deprived of land and means of production, are only able to obtain a pauper's income with their own independent labour (gathering wild crops and so forth).[3] Thus, the workers have no alternative but to work for the capitalist for a wage that barely provides them with the *social minimum standard of living*. This is the wage level established in capitalist society for workers with average skill. For the *annual wage*, let us use the symbol L (from the word *Lohn*).[4] This sum L is less than the actual 'value of labour' that Oppenheimer, as we already know,[5] takes to mean the full value of the product of labour. Suppose, as we have already done in the first chapter, that the value of the product of a year's work by a worker of average skill is E. In that case, the natural 'value of the labour' of this worker (or the wage he would receive if totally free competition prevailed, i.e. in the absence of any monopolies, including class monopolies),

---

2 Oppenheimer 1919a, p. 78.
3 Oppenheimer 1922, p. 133.
4 [In German: wage, reward or salary.]
5 See our first and third chapters above.

would also be E. The sum E can be termed the 'competitive static price' of labour. But in capitalist society, relying upon their monopoly position as owners of the means of production, the capitalists pay the workers a smaller sum equal to L. This sum L can be termed the *'monopoly static price'* of labour. The difference between these two sums (E–L = P) accrues to the capitalist in the form of *profit* (P) *or surplus value*. The capitalists acquire surplus value because, using their monopoly position, they pay the worker a wage that is *lower* than the 'competitive static price' of labour, or the natural 'value of labour'. *Surplus value* is a special form of *monopoly income*. Consequently, Marx was mistaken in asserting that the capitalist buys the worker's labour power at its value. Marx erroneously claimed that the origin of surplus value must be sought in the process of *production*, not in the process of *exchange*.[6] It is precisely in the process of exchanging a wage for the worker's labour that the capitalist, armed with a class monopoly, appropriates for himself the difference between the 'monopoly price' of labour that he pays out (the wage payment) and the full 'value of labour'.

This leads Oppenheimer to a number of extremely important social-political conclusions. Contrary to the view of socialists, the basic shortcoming of capitalist economy is not the prevalence of unlimited free competition but rather the opposite, curtailment of the latter by 'class monopolies', beginning with large land ownership. The working class suffers not from *'free competition'* but instead from its *limitation*. Consequently, to eliminate the distress of the working class there is no need to replace the system of free competition with a socialist, organised economy. On the contrary, what is needed is to remove all restrictions on free competition: the *elimination of large land ownership* and the transfer of parcels of land to all who wish to work it will break the 'class monopoly' of the capitalists and guarantee to every toiler the full product of his labour. After class monopolies are eliminated, free competition between independent commodity producers will yield only beneficial consequences: its result will be a 'just' and equivalent exchange of goods, equally securing the interests of all participants in exchange and eliminating the exploitation of one person by another. The future economic organisation can only be called 'socialist' in the sense that no one will acquire surplus value or non-labour income. However, it will also be based on unrestricted free competition and therefore can be called 'liberal'. It will be socialism built upon the prevalence of free competition, or a *'liberal socialism'*.[7]

---

6 Oppenheimer 1919a, p. 118.
7 Oppenheimer 1919a, p. 103.

Turning to a critique of Oppenheimer's theory of surplus value, we shall set aside his social-political conclusions and concentrate on the theoretical side of his teaching. The final part of Oppenheimer's theory, the doctrine of monopoly and surplus value, strikingly reveals the fundamental dualism of his system. Marx's teaching has not been without influence on Oppenheimer: he understands that capitalist economy cannot be studied apart from social relations between the classes that constitute capitalist society. Oppenheimer acknowledges Marx's 'everlasting service' in his teaching that value and capital are expressions of determinate social relations between people.[8] But, instead of following Marx's example and seeing capitalist society as a single social process, the two sides of which (economic and social) are inseparably bound together, Oppenheimer follows Dühring's[9] lead and sees it as the result of a *mechanical summation* of two heterogeneous forces that are foreign by nature and hostile to each other, namely, the *'economic'* and *'non-economic'* (or political) forces. The sphere of operation of 'natural' economic laws, and of the free play of 'economic' forces of unrestricted competition, is invaded by the distorting activity of 'social' relations of force and political 'coercion', which help some social groups seize lucrative 'monopoly positions'. The operation of free competition is curtailed by monopolies (particularly class monopolies), and the 'just' and 'normal' exchange of equivalents gives way to the 'unjust' exchange of non-equivalents, in which the monopolist renders to his counterpart (e.g. the capitalist renders to the wage worker, whose labour is being bought) less value in exchange for more value. We have, therefore, the opposition and struggle between two forces that are foreign to each other by nature: on the one aside, the *'natural'* or 'production' categories, *'economic'* rivalry, free *competition*, the exchange of *equivalents* and the absence of exploitation – on the other side the 'social' or 'distributional' categories, *'non-economic'* (political) coercion, *monopolies*, the exchange of *non-equivalents* and the appropriation of *surplus value* (monopoly income). Oppenheimer characterises operation of the former forces as the *normal*, proper development of the economy, and operation of the latter as a *violation* and *corruption* of this proper course of development.

The result is a complete rupture and an impassable gulf between the 'economic' and the 'social' sides of the economy. Instead of showing how the operation of 'economic' forces creates certain forms of 'political' violence, how the development of free competition inevitably causes class differentiation in

---

8 Oppenheimer 1919a, pp. 12 and 117.
9 [The reference is to Eugen Dühring (1883–1921), a German philosopher-economist and prominent critic of Marxism.]

the society of commodity producers and the emergence of 'class monopolies', Oppenheimer turns the two sides, which have been abstracted from reality, into autonomous and heterogeneous forces, while actual reality is turned into the result of a mechanical summation of these heterogeneous forces. 'Capitalism is the illegitimate son of the unnatural union of two forces that are hostile from the beginning: one founded upon the conquest of ancient rule, which created the feudal state and large land ownership, and the other, freedom'.[10] Marx incorrectly saw 'capitalism as a normal phase of economic development'. In fact, 'capitalism is the result of a non-economic *disruption* of normal economic development, namely, a seizure of the land by force of arms, which created the basis for class monopoly'.[11]

If the capitalist economy (like the feudal) is merely a 'disruption of normal economic development', then surplus value is also nothing more than an 'abnormal' income based upon monopoly. The idea that surplus value is appropriated by the capitalists due to their 'class monopoly' over the means of production was expressed and developed by Marx himself. But it never entered his head to equate this '*class* monopoly', which constitutes the basis of the whole of modern society, with the '*personal* monopolies' of individual capitalists and their groups (patents, trusts, and so forth). The former expresses the production relations between the class of capitalists as a whole and the class of wage workers; the latter affect only the redistribution of the whole mass of surplus value, which is appropriated by the capitalist class, between individual capitalists and groups of capitalists. The former is a *permanent* and fundamental feature of *any* capitalist economy, including '*pure*' capitalism; the latter reaches its greatest development only in the most recent epoch of '*monopolistic*' capitalism. The former is the necessary and inevitable result of the complete *development of free competition* in a society of commodity producers; the latter represents temporary, sporadic *restrictions* of free competition, i.e. monopolies in the precise meaning of the word. To say that surplus value is simply a 'monopoly income' is to explain a *fundamental* phenomenon by a *derivative* one. To say that surplus value only appears in the presence of monopolies, and not with free competition, is to claim that it does not exist in capitalist society – the only economic system in world history in which free competition has developed widely. It means calling the system of free competition, with the inevitable class differentiation of commodity producers that it creates, a monopoly, and calling a non-existent economic system, combining

---

10   Oppenheimer 1919a, p. 73.
11   Oppenheimer 1919a, p. 74.

extensive development of commodity exchange with the absence of class differences between commodity producers – free competition.

Oppenheimer's theory suffers, therefore, from an illegitimate confusion of such heterogeneous phenomena as monopoly in the strict sense of the word (patents, trusts and so forth) and monopoly incomes, on the one hand, and 'class monopoly' and surplus value on the other. The inadmissibility of such conceptual confusion is evident not just in the methodological considerations that we have outlined, but also in the development of Oppenheimer's own reasoning. If surplus value could really be explained on the basis of a theory of monopoly, then all of the fundamental conclusions that Oppenheimer draws in his general theory of monopoly income would likewise have to be applicable to surplus value. In fact, however, Oppenheimer is himself compelled to notice a whole series of fundamental and decisive *differences* between monopoly incomes in general and surplus value. In his general teaching about monopoly, Oppenheimer comes to the following conclusions: 1) in capitalist society, monopolies in the narrow sense of the word ('personal monopolies') appear only *temporarily* and to some extent by chance; 2) the process of competition has a constant tendency to *destroy* the monopolies that appear in individual sectors; and 3) the level of monopoly prices is limited, to some degree or other, by the level of *competitive prices* (for the same products or their surrogates) and tends in equilibrium to be equalised with the latter.

Oppenheimer forgets about all these basic provisions of his general theory of monopoly the moment he turns to an exposition of surplus value. The latter, in his portrayal, has traits that markedly differentiate it from monopoly incomes. The 'class monopoly' of the capitalists and their appropriation of surplus value are *permanent* features of capitalist economy. Unlike monopoly in the narrow sense of the word, they appear not at specific locations in the capitalist economy but instead cover its entire surface, so to speak, with an unbroken web. The web is everywhere, permanent and steadfast: waves of competition are powerless to sweep it away, unlike cases of monopoly incomes in the narrow sense (from patents, cartels and so on). This means that the price of labour power (the wage) is also regulated by *laws that are different* from the 'monopoly price' of products in general. The latter have no precisely determined level and show a tendency towards equalisation with the competitive price. But the wage in capitalist society has a constant,[12] precisely determined level and, in

---

12   Of course, a 'constant' level of wages, as with prices of production, only occurs in the form of fluctuations of the actual wage around a normal level, which remains 'constant' when there is no change in the conditions that determine the value of labour power.

Oppenheimer's view, *does not display* even the slightest tendency to equate with the 'competitive price of labour' (or the 'value of labour', which, according to Oppenheimer's theory, is equal to the full product of labour).

As we can see, Oppenheimer's own portrait reveals sharp features of difference between surplus value and monopoly income in the narrow sense of the word. The former phenomenon displays greater *constancy* and is more clearly governed by laws than the latter. Oppenheimer himself acknowledges that the 'primary problem' for an economist is not the surplus profit of a monopolist but surplus value.[13] It would seem, therefore, that only one conclusion can be drawn: it is necessary to start with an investigation of the 'primary problem' of surplus value in order subsequently, on that basis, to study the process of the distribution of surplus value between monopolists or monopolistic groups. Oppenheimer turns the entire investigation on its head and offends the fundamental rules of methodology by suggesting that we derive one phenomenon, which is distinguished by a more constant and law-governed character, from another that is more sporadic and less law-governed. The combination, within the single concept of 'monopoly', of such heterogeneous economic phenomena as surplus value and monopoly in the narrow sense, impairs Oppenheimer's theory both of monopoly and of surplus value. A concept of monopoly that includes not just monopoly in the narrow sense, but also surplus value and even differential profit, cannot help but suffer from theoretical indeterminacy. A theory of surplus value, regarded as monopoly income, is nothing but an attempt to resurrect the old doctrine of the utopian socialists concerning the right of the worker to the full product of his labour.

---

13   Oppenheimer 1922, p. 96.

CHAPTER 7

The Contradiction between Oppenheimer's Theory of Value And His Theory of Surplus Value

We have concluded that Oppenheimer's theory of monopoly can scarcely do what he promised, namely, reveal 'the secret of surplus value that not even Marx could disclose'.[1] But we cannot stop at this conclusion. We must still, so to speak, confront Oppenheimer's *theory of surplus value* with his *theory of value*, which we have outlined previously. This confrontation must resolve the question that we posed in our initial chapters: is it true that Oppenheimer's formula of *Arbeitswerttheorie* is universal in scope and fully applicable, as he claims, to *monopoly exchange*? We shall see that Oppenheimer's teaching with regard to surplus value as monopoly income – in addition to its internal inconsistency, which we demonstrated in the previous chapter – leads to a whole series of contradictions with his theory of value.

Oppenheimer's theory of monopoly is replete with a *dualism* between the natural, normal laws of free competition and the abnormal laws of monopoly. Meanwhile, Oppenheimer's goal in his theory of value is to provide *a single, universal formula of value* for both freely reproduced and monopoly products.[2] In the theory of monopoly he sees an abyss between a 'pure' economy of free competition[3] and a 'political economy' with monopolies. Nevertheless, he hopes to provide 'a more general formula, embracing both cases'.[4] Oppenheimer does not notice how naïve his promise is, from a theoretical point of view, to give a common formula for the phenomena of a free economy and of a monopoly economy after he has declared the former to be a 'normal' type and the latter its 'violation'.

Not only does Oppenheimer not notice the irreconcilability between his quest for a 'common' formula of value and the dualism of his construction, but it is precisely in the monism of his theory of value that he sees its principal

---

1 Oppenheimer 1922, p. 109.
2 Ibid.
3 We use the word 'free' throughout to refer to an economy founded upon free competition: a 'free' economy includes both the 'society of equals', consisting of producers with the same skill, and a 'society of unequals', whose individual members differ from one another in terms of their personal skill (but do not possess any monopolies).
4 Oppenheimer 1919b, p. 454.

merit. In Oppenheimer's view, Marx's theory of value applies only to a 'society of equals' – in which the products of equal quantities of labour are exchanged – and with certain reservations to a 'society of unequals' (since Marx equates a lesser quantity of skilled labour with a greater quantity of simple labour). At best, Marx's theory applies only to a 'free' economy or to a system of free competition, but not at all to a '*monopoly*' economy (which is what a capitalist economy is): in the latter, products of *unequal quantities of labour* exchange for one another (e.g. the capitalist receives 12 hours of the worker's labour for the product of 6 hours of labour). Marx cannot provide a 'general' formula of value for both a free economy and a monopoly economy, and precisely this point strikingly reveals the superiority of Oppenheimer's theory, which says that the value of the product is determined by the value of the labour it contains. This formula is also fully appropriate for a *monopoly* economy.

Indeed, let us suppose that in the course of a year (with an expenditure of 3,000 hours of labour), a worker earns 1,500 marks. This means that each hour of labour brings him an income, or creates a product with a value of ½ mark *for him*.[5] 'Thus an hour of his labour has a value of ½ mark'. The capitalist (who does not differ from the worker in terms of personal skill) receives an income of 15,000 marks for the same amount of time. Accordingly, for him 'each hour of labour has a value of 5 marks'. In that case, it is not at all surprising that the product of 10 hours of labour by the worker exchanges for the product (or income) of one hour of labour by the capitalist. Nevertheless, in this case 'equal *values of labour* are exchanged, for 10 hours of labour by the worker have the value of 5 marks, and 1 hour of labour by the capitalist also has a value of 5 marks'.[6]

This reasoning applies to any case of monopoly exchange. Let a monopolist exchange the product of one hour of his labour for the product of 3 hours of labour by his counterpart. 'Since we measure the value of labour by the real income it yields, the value of the monopolist's labour is three times greater than the value of the labour by his counterpart'.[7] Consequently, the product of *1 hour of labour* by the monopolist incorporates the same 'value of labour' as the product of *3 hours of labour* by his counterpart. Oppenheimer's formula, according to which the value of the product is determined by the value of the labour, turns out to be true *in every case of exchange without exception*, includ-

---

5 The product that the worker produces for himself is obviously his wage, not the product that he produces for the capitalist.

6 Oppenheimer 1919a, pp. 112–13.

7 Oppenheimer 1922, pp. 104–5.

ing *monopoly* exchange: 'in every case' the exchange of commodities involves exchange of 'equal values of labour'[8] – not of different quantities of labour as Marx claimed.

It may appear at first sight that Oppenheimer has faithfully fulfilled his promise to give us a 'universal', monistic theory of value. He has performed a miracle before our eyes: 'normal', 'free' exchange was only recently separated by an impassable gulf from 'monopoly' exchange, which 'corrupts' normal development of an economy, yet now it turns out that in both cases exchange is completed according to one and the same formula. But if that is so – let us put the question to Oppenheimer – what explains his *sharp contrast* between the 'free' exchange of 'equivalent' products and the 'monopoly' exchange of 'non-equivalent' products? On the one hand, we are told that *'equal values of labour'* exchange in a capitalist economy. On the other hand, we learn that the laws of capitalist exchange and distribution strikingly differ from the 'laws of comparing the value of labour'.[9] On the one hand, Oppenheimer takes pride in his formula of value, which embraces both *free* and *monopoly* exchange. Yet, on the other hand, he emphasises that 'where the market is perfectly free, *equivalent* products are balanced, but where monopoly exists *non-equivalent* products are involved'.[10]

What we have learned, therefore, is 1) that in all cases of exchange, including monopoly exchange, *'equal values of labour'* are exchanged, and 2) that with the dominance of monopoly *'non-equivalent* products' are exchanged. Do not these two propositions contradict one another? After all, Oppenheimer sees the 'equivalence', or the value correspondence of products, in an equality of the 'values of labour' that they embody (as distinct from Marx, who sees products as equivalent when they contain equal amounts of labour – referring, of course, to labour that is socially necessary and simple). In that case, it is one or the other: either it is true that monopoly exchange is also subject to a 'universal formula', which says that *'equal values of labour'* always exchange, although in that case we have no grounds for speaking of the *'non-equivalence'* of the products being exchanged; or else, with monopoly, the products being exchanged are truly *'non-equivalent'*, but in that case it would be strange to claim that *'equal values of labour'* are being exchanged. Oppenheimer must abandon either his formula of *value* or his doctrine of *surplus value*. In fact, if equal values of labour are also exchanged in monopoly exchange, what that means is that the capit-

---

8   Oppenheimer 1919a, p. 111.
9   Oppenheimer 1922, p. 176.
10   Oppenheimer 1922, p. 106.

alist pays the full value of the worker's labour. If the capitalist pays less than its value for the worker's labour, it cannot be claimed that in this case equal values of labour are being exchanged.

This glaring contradiction between Oppenheimer's theory of value and his theory of monopoly is an inevitable consequence of the *fundamental dualism* that distinguishes his doctrine. Insofar as he sharply counterposes the 'normal' laws of free competition to the 'abnormal' phenomena of monopoly, he must make a pointed distinction between 'equivalent' and 'non-equivalent' exchange. On the other hand, insofar as he wants to provide a 'universal' formula of value, he is compelled to erase the difference between the two types of exchange. Hence, exchange of the value of the product of 1 hour of labour by the monopolist (the capitalist) for the product of 10 hours of labour by his counterpart (the worker)[11] is regarded by Oppenheimer as an exchange both of equal values of labour and also of unequal values of labour. This dualism is also closely connected with a dualism in the determination of 'labour value', which, as we saw in the third chapter, moves in a vicious circle. Since Oppenheimer takes the 'value of labour' as his starting point for determining the value of the product, in the case that we have been considering he cannot fail to see that the exchange between the two parties involves labour expenditures of unequal value,[12] and consequently 'non-equivalent' products are being exchanged. On the other hand, since he derives the 'value of labour' from the value of its product, he concludes that once the product of 1 hour of labour by the monopolist actually does exchange for the product of 10 hours of labour by his counterpart, then obviously the value of one hour of labour by the former is 10 times greater than the value of 1 hour of labour by the latter; and it follows that in this case the products being exchanged contain both unequal quantities of labour and equal 'values of labour'.

Oppenheimer sees the main superiority of his formula of value over Marx's in the fact that the latter is applicable only to free competition, while the former holds true for all cases of exchange, including monopoly exchange. We have already convinced ourselves of how illusory this superiority is. Apart from the indeterminate and internally contradictory character of his concept of 'the value of labour', in the final analysis it fails to serve even the sole purpose for which it was designed, namely, to work out a 'universal' formula of value for freely reproduced and monopoly goods. It is true that Oppenheimer

---

11   Assuming that they are both equally skilled.

12   Since both parties are equally skilled, the value of their labour expenditures is proportional to the length of time spent by each.

verbally subsumes monopoly exchange under the formula of an '*equality of values of labour*', but only to recognise the next moment that in the given case '*non-equivalent*' products are being exchanged, i.e. containing *unequal* values of labour. But such recognition is tantamount to acknowledging that Oppenheimer's theory of value, which holds that the products being exchanged contain equal 'values of labour', is *inapplicable to monopoly exchange*, i.e. suffers from the same fault for which Oppenheimer reproaches Marx's theory.

We shall not, however, be too severe concerning Oppenheimer's contradictions and shall endeavour, as much as possible, to keep them out of what he goes on to say. Oppenheimer himself does not indicate any way out of the glaring contradiction that we have mentioned. With every good intention to interpret Oppenheimer's presentation to his advantage, we suggest that the contradiction could only be eliminated by assuming that Oppenheimer uses the term 'value of labour' in *two different senses*. First of all, by the '*natural value of labour*' he means the value that the expended labour (taking into account both its quantity and its quality) would have in the complete absence of monopolies: secondly, he understands the '*value of labour*' in general terms to be the value attributed to labour on the basis that its product in the given circumstances (of free competition or monopoly exchange) actually exchanges for a determinate quantity of other products. The product of 1 hour of labour by the monopolist and 10 hours of labour by his counterpart[13] contain unequal 'natural values of labour', for with free competition the value of the first product would be ten times less than the value of the second product; yet they contain equal 'values of labour' insofar as the latter are determined by the factual value (or more accurately, by the average price, which deviates from value) of the products in the given circumstances, i.e. with the prevalence of monopoly. Thus, the exchange between the monopolist and his counterpart will actually represent an exchange of equal 'values of labour' and simultaneously an exchange of unequal 'natural values of labour' (or 'non-equivalent products').

If Oppenheimer were inclined to look for an escape from the contradiction inherent in such a *dualistic* use of the term 'value of labour',[14] he would have

---

13   Assuming they have equal skills.

14   This is apparently Oppenheimer's intention. He notes that with free competition 'equal *natural values* of labour' are exchanged (1919a, p. 6). In his general formula of value, extended to monopoly exchange, he says that exchange of commodities always involves 'equal *values* of labour' (1919a, p. 111). 'With the prevalence of monopoly, unequal 'natural' values are equalised, i.e. have equal value' (1919a, p. 114). This strange-sounding assertion, that 'unequal' values are essentially 'equal' values, only makes sense with the assumption that the beginning of the sentence refers to 'natural' values, while the end of the sentence refers to 'value' in general (more accurately, to average prices).

to abandon the constant juggling with this concept first in one sense and then in the other. He would confront the need to provide an unequivocal answer to the question: *exactly which* of the two concepts of the 'value of labour' is his theory of value based upon, and does he determine the value of products by the '*natural* value of labour' or simply by the '*value* of labour'? In the first case, it is evident that in monopoly exchange, in which unequal 'natural values of labour' are treated as equal, no 'universal' formula of value applies. If Oppenheimer, in order to maintain the operation of his general formula, should say that the value of products is determined not by the 'natural value' but simply by the 'value of labour', that would essentially mean that, to whatever extent the presence of monopolies skews the exchange proportions of products (i.e. the average prices) relative to the 'natural value of labour', we shall take the very fact of exchange of the given commodities as proof of the equality of the 'values of labour' expended in their production. In other words, in response to the question of whether there *exists* any lawfulness whatever in the process of establishing the average prices of commodities, we reply that we shall always *presuppose* such lawfulness. No matter what happens in the formation of a product's average price, we shall say that it corresponds to value ('the value of labour'), for we determine the value of the commodity only of the basis of its actual average prices. However much the value of the product diverges from the value of the labour it contains (e.g. the value of a monopolist's product is ten times higher than the 'natural value of labour'), we shall easily overcome the problem by saying that the value of labour itself has changed (e.g. that the value of a monopolist's labour is ten times greater than the value of his counterpart's labour).

Such an argument, from the methodological point of view, amounts to complete *abandonment of the theory of value*:[15] the economist is restricted to ascertaining the average prices of products, declaring that any state of *average prices* of commodities corresponds to their *values*. For Oppenheimer, such an argument is all the more inadmissible, since he not only promises that his theory of value will explain the objective lawfulness of the movement of prices, but he also builds his theory on the concept of the 'value of labour'. The result is a completely incongruous position: on the basis that the year's income of the capitalist (e.g. the owner of shares) is 100 times more than the income of the worker, Oppenheimer declares that the 'labour' of the former has 100 times more value than the labour of the latter. What 'labour' can be involved in explaining an

---

15   In addition, as we have noted above, it fundamentally contradicts Oppenheimer's teaching that the capitalist (as monopolist), pay the worker less than the value of his labour.

economic system whose distinctive feature is receipt of 'non-labour' income by whole classes of the population (capitalists and landowners)? The explanation of such a system must be found in the appropriation by one social class of the *labour* of another, not in any different *'value of labour'* on the part of the two classes.

Although the *logical* contradiction of the whole course of his arguments eluded Oppenheimer, he could not fail to notice the *sociological* absurdity of the conclusions to which they led him. In his latest work, *Wert und Kapitalprofit*, where Oppenheimer attempts to systematise and theoretically ground his views, he directly acknowledges the failure of his attempts to explain the income of capitalists by the high value of their 'labour'. Citing the explanation that he gave in an earlier work, *Theorie der reinen und politischen Oekonomie*, Oppenheimer continues: 'I do not deny that this solution is somewhat *unsatisfactory*'. The capitalist receives a profit that is independent of any labour. It seems strange, therefore, to refer to the income of a degenerate descendant of a millionaire as the 'value' of his labour. In such cases the 'term "value of labour" becomes something *exactly the opposite* of its normal meaning'.[16] How does Oppenheimer propose to overcome these difficulties? Very simply: he suggests to the reader, who may be 'too bewildered' by a bold application of his formula of the 'value of labour' to non-labour incomes, that he decline such an application and, on this issue disagree with him (i.e. with Oppenheimer). He reassures the reader that the formula 'value of labour' in fact refers only to the problem of the 'substance of value'.

> As far as the question of the substance of value is concerned, of course it would be very satisfying to arrive at a single formula that would equally cover all cases, even the most extreme. Our formula does this in full measure for a 'pure economy'; it is applicable to a political economy, with relations that are distorted by a class monopoly, only with the help of a method that is perhaps questionable (*bedenkliche Wendung*). If, on this basis, someone refuses to recognise this formula as universal, then so be it. However, this is scarcely of any consequence for our theory as a whole, since the question of the substance of value is a purely academic and aesthetic problem, so to speak.[17]

---

16   Oppenheimer 1922, pp. 146 and 147.
17   Oppenheimer 1922, p. 147.

We do not intend to enter here into a discussion of whether the problem of the 'substance of labour' is academic or not. But we cannot fail to note that the words Oppenheimer uses amount to a total renunciation of the tasks that he took on at the outset of his study. Oppenheimer rejected the Marxist determination of the value of products by the quantity of socially necessary labour they contain, and he did so precisely on the grounds that this formula only applies to a *pure* economy (of free competition), but not to a *political* economy (a monopoly economy). He saw the principal merit of his own formula, according to which the value of the product is determined by the value of the labour, precisely in the fact that it embraces both free competition and *monopoly*. In his theory of monopoly, Oppenheimer assigned the principal importance to class monopolies, which explain the origin of '*surplus value*', i.e. non-labour incomes. But it turns out, in the final analysis, that the formula of *Arbeitswerttheorie* is *inapplicable* precisely to non-labour incomes. But, in that case, there is ultimately no basis for Oppenheimer's paramount argument in favour of replacing the Marxist theory of value with his own formula of *Arbeitswerttheorie*. Oppenheimer's acknowledgement demonstrates that the internal contradictions of his system, though partially hidden by a dualism of terms, is ruptured with such force at the decisive point that even the author himself gives up any attempt to apply them. Oppenheimer's acknowledgement cannot be regarded as anything other than the *collapse of his theory of value*.

It remains for us now to provide some *short summaries*.

In his theory of value Oppenheimer had two main objectives: 1) to escape from the *vicious circle* and 2) to provide a 'universal' formula of value, identically applicable to the exchange of *freely reproduced* and *monopoly* products. Oppenheimer attempted to solve the first task in his initial formula of value ($v = \frac{E}{n}$), according to which the value of a product is defined as part of the *income* of the producer. In order to avoid the vicious circle, Oppenheimer understands (E) not as a sum of exchange values but rather as a real mass of *consumer goods*. But there is no bridge that leads from income, understood as a mass of consumer goods, to the *exchange value* of the product.

Oppenheimer's second formula is built upon the internally contradictory concept of the '*value of labour*', which he understands as the value that labour would have in the absence of a capitalist economy, i.e. in a society where labour is not generally an item for purchase and sale and therefore has no price and no value. The second formula of value clearly spins in a *vicious circle*: if the value of the product is determined by the value of labour embodied in it, then the value of the labour, in turn, is determined by the value of the product produced through its use. This vicious circle is so obvious that Oppenheimer could do nothing but unexpectedly proclaim himself to be a principled defender of the vicious circle in the theory of value.

Oppenheimer saw the principal advantage of his *Arbeitswerttheorie*, compared to Marx's *Arbeitszeittheorie*, in the fact that it is directly applicable not only to the exchange of freely reproduced products but also to the exchange of *monopoly* products. This advantage turns out to be illusory. There is an insurmountable contradiction between Oppenheimer's *Arbeitswerttheorie* and his theory of monopoly and surplus value. Either it is true that, in all cases of monopoly exchange, equal 'values of labour' are exchanged, in which case Oppenheimer's claim that the capitalist does not pay the full value of the worker's labour is incorrect. Or else the capitalist really does pay for the worker's labour a price that is lower than the value of labour, in which case unequal values of labour are exchanged and therefore the formula of *Arbeitswerttheorie* is *not applicable* to cases of monopoly exchange. In his most recent work, Oppenheimer is compelled to acknowledge this fact directly. With this acknowledgement, the main – one might even say the sole – argument that Oppenheimer gives in support of his *Arbeitswerttheorie* collapses.

Furthermore, it is precisely at this point that the *superiority* of Marx's theory is revealed when compared to Oppenheimer's theory. If we omit 'personal monopolies' from our study and focus our attention on 'class monopolies', which, as Oppenheimer himself recognises, play an incomparably more important role in capitalist economy, then we come to the following unexpected conclusion. The formula of *Arbeitswerttheorie* is *inapplicable* to cases of exchange between a capitalist and a worker, as Oppenheimer was ultimately forced to acknowledge. Meanwhile Marx, who taught that the capitalist buys from the worker not his labour but his labour power, paying for it according to its value, was also able to demonstrate that this exchange, with all of its specific features, which cannot be underestimated, still occurs *on the basis of and within the limits of* a general law of value. The result, therefore, is a paradox. *Arbeitswerttheorie* was summoned up by Oppenheimer exclusively in order to cover cases of monopoly exchange that Marx supposedly ignored. Meanwhile, if we take the most important group of monopolies, namely class monopolies and the exchange between capitalist and worker that is based upon them, we see that this exchange occurs according to Marx's formula of *Arbeitszeittheorie*; Oppenheimer is forced to acknowledge that his own formula of *Arbeitswerttheorie* does not extend to this exchange. Now we could, if we were of a mind to do so, turn Oppenheimer's own arguments against him. For Oppenheimer, the decisive criterion for assessing the correctness of various formulae of value is the possibility of extending one or another formula of value to monopoly exchange. We can now see that Oppenheimer's formula of *Arbeitswerttheorie* does not apply to monopoly exchange, and Marx's formula of *Arbeitszeittheorie* does cover cases of monopoly exchange (insofar as class monopolies are the issue). Consequently, the latter formula – from the point of view of the criterion set out by Oppenheimer himself – deserves unconditional preference. Even on this point, which Oppenheimer took to be the Achilles heel of Marxist theory, the undoubted superiority of the latter is evident.

CHAPTER 8

Oppenheimer as Critic of Marx

In nearly all of his works Oppenheimer pays considerable attention to Marx. On the one hand, he considers himself to be 'a true student of Marx'.[1] On the other hand, Oppenheimer's 'corrections' reduce Marx's theory to nothing, and his critique has earned him the reputation of 'an ambitious *litterateur* who wants to create a name for himself as a Marx-destroyer'.[2]

In our previous chapters we have tried to demonstrate that Oppenheimer's economic theory can make no claim to being a 'perfect' edifice.[3]

But even though he was unable to resolve the disputed questions of our science with his own economic theory, perhaps Oppenheimer did manage with his critical arguments to show the failure of Marxist theory. That is the question we shall address in this chapter. It would take us too far astray here if we were to examine all of Oppenheimer's critical comments and correct the numerous misunderstandings and mistakes that are easily found in his exposition and criticism of Marx. We shall deal only with the central and most fundamental points of his criticism.

With the help of his theory, as we have seen, Oppenheimer hopes to correct the fundamental deficiencies of classical theory, which: 1) revolved in a vicious circle; 2) could not resolve the problem of skilled labour; and 3) ignored the phenomenon of monopoly. Oppenheimer attributes only the third of these inadequacies to Marxist theory, which is 'free of the main objection that has justifiably been raised against all the objective theories of value. It does not revolve in a vicious circle'.[4] As for the problem of skills, it is true that Marx could not explain 'innate skill', but this 'aesthetic shortcoming' does not involve any 'serious weakness' and 'is not important for resolving the great problems of the theory of value'.[5] Thus, Marxist theory is free of the first two shortcomings that afflicted classical theory.

---

1 Oppenheimer 1919a, pp. ix, x.
2 Oppenheimer 1919a, p. x.
3 Oppenheimer 1922, p. 74n.
4 Oppenheimer 1922, p. 177.
5 Oppenheimer 1922, pp. 172 and 178. We have shown above, in our chapter on skilled labour, that the phenomena Oppenheimer considers under the heading 'innate skill' are explained by Marx in his teaching on socially necessary labour. Not understanding this, Oppenheimer enormously extended the concept of 'skill' and mistakenly narrowed the Marxist concept

© RICHARD B. DAY, 2024 | DOI:10.1163/9789004705661_010

Likewise, Oppenheimer attaches no significance to arguments from Marx's critics concerning a 'contradiction between the first and third volumes of *Capital*', between the theory of value and the theory of prices of production. He not only has no objection to Marx's position – which has evoked fierce attacks from his critics – regarding the correspondence between the sum of prices of production for the total mass of commodities and the total sum of their labour values, but he even adopts that position in his own theory.[6]

Rejecting all of these arguments from Marx's critics, Oppenheimer concludes that they are incapable of refuting Marxist theory. But Oppenheimer hopes to confront Marx's theory with 'stronger arguments'.[7] These arguments amount to the accusation, already familiar to us, that Marx 'studied only a part of the problem of value, mistakenly claiming to resolve the entire problem'.[8] Marx ignored the *problem of monopoly* and thus foreclosed the possibility for a correct understanding of *surplus value*. To ignore monopoly amounts to ignoring the 'non-economic' (social-political) forces that, through their intervention, disrupt the activity of purely economic forces. Marx's merit is that he saw in capital a social relation between the class of capitalists and the class of wage workers. But he mistakenly described this relation as a purely economic 'production' relation, whereas in reality capitalism is a 'social relation of distribution'[9] that is founded upon the non-economic factors of compulsion and subordination that capitalism adopts from feudal society. Ignoring these non-economic factors of capitalism was the cause of Marx's 'methodological

---

of 'socially necessary labour': he understood the latter to mean merely a correspondence of labour expenditures with the extent of social need. See Oppenheimer 1922, p. 178 and 1919a, p. 116.

6 Oppenheimer 1922, pp. 144–5 and 172. Interpreting ideas developed by Marx in his theory of prices of production (without giving the source), Oppenheimer simultaneously attributes to Marx ideas that contradict what Marx actually said. Marx supposedly claimed that 'the profit of every individual capitalist entrepreneur is extracted from workers employed in the given enterprise' (Oppenheimer 1922, pp. 139, 143). Such a notion would make it difficult for Marx to understand the process of equalisation of the rate of profit on capital. To explain the latter process, Oppenheimer partly borrows from Marx himself: he says that the entire income extracted from the labour of the entire working class becomes the property of the entire class of capitalists and is divided between individual capitalists in proportion to the magnitude of their capital (p. 140). Every capitalist receives 'a dividend on his shares in the class monopoly' (p. 143). Oppenheimer then has the audacity to say that 'Here lies the secret of the equalisation of profits on all capitals, over which Marx racked his brains' (p. 140).

7 Oppenheimer 1922, pp. 172 and 173.

8 Oppenheimer 1922, p. 173.

9 'Marx saw in capitalism a social production relation. He was mistaken: it is a relation of social distribution' (Oppenheimer 1919b, p. 572).

original sin': his failure to understand *the monopoly character of surplus value.*[10] Marx portrays surplus value purely as a result of the economic laws of 'free competition': the capitalist acquires surplus value through buying the 'labour power' of the worker (manifested, let us say, in 12 hours of labour) at its full value, which is equal to the labour value of the products needed for its reproduction (requiring, say, only 6 hours of labour to produce). In Oppenheimer's opinion, the capitalist buys not 'labour power' but 'labour time', or the 'labour' of the worker, while paying him – as a result of [the capitalists'] class monopoly position – a sum below its 'natural value', which is equal to the value of the 'full product' of the worker's labour.

For the sake of clarity, we can present the basic disagreement between Marx and Oppenheimer on this point in the following manner:

In Marx's opinion:

1)   the value of the product made by the worker is 12 hours of labour;

2)   the value of the worker's labour power is 6 hours of labour;

3)   the average wage is equal to the value of the product of 6 hours of labour.

In Oppenheimer's opinion:

1)   the value of the product created by the worker is 12 hours of labour;

2)   the value of the worker's 'labour' is 12 hours of labour;

3)   the average wage is equal to the value of the product of 6 hours of labour.

We see that Marx and Oppenheimer agree on the first and third points: they both begin with the fact that the average wage is less than the value of the product of the worker's labour. But they decisively disagree on the second point. In Marx's opinion, the value of the worker's labour power is *less* than the value of the product of his labour and (tends to be) *equal* to the average wage. In Oppenheimer's opinion, the value of the worker's 'labour' is *equal* to the value of the product of his labour and *greater* than the average wage. The wage is a 'monopoly' price, but not the 'natural' price of the worker's 'labour'.

---

10   Oppenheimer 1922, pp. 173 and 176. This is also the origin of the second essential mistake in Marx's economic theory, his erroneous theory of 'the accumulation of capital', according to which the capitalist relation reproduces itself by virtue of purely economic laws that are inherent in capitalism (the rising organic composition of capital, the relative decline of the number of employed workers, the reserve army and the 'impoverishment' of the workers). Oppenheimer believes that the capitalist relation is constantly reproduced only in the presence of large-scale land ownership, which is founded on the 'non-economic' fact of seizing the land. Oppenheimer gives a more detailed criticism of Marxist theory from this point of view in his earlier work *Das Grundgesetz der Marxschen Gesellschaftslehre* (1903). We do not include an analysis of this specialised question in our article, the more so since in his subsequent and basic theoretical work *Wert und Kapitalprofit* Oppenheimer focuses his criticism on the Marxist theory of surplus value.

Oppenheimer's objections to Marx's teaching on the value of labour power can be reduced to *three* sorts of arguments:

First, Oppenheimer asserts that if Marx were to draw all the conclusions from his own theory of labour value, he would have to recognise that the value of 'labour power' is equal to the full value of the product of labour. In order to arrive at such a conclusion, it would have been enough for Marx to make a *simple transposition* in the 'equation of value'.

Second, as Oppenheimer shows with the aid of mathematical calculations, Marx's claim that the value of labour power is less than the value of labour's product leads to internally contradictory and *absurd conclusions*.

Third, and finally, Oppenheimer objects essentially to Marx's well-known conclusion that the worker sells his *labour power* to the capitalist and not his *labour*.

Let us consider the first two of Oppenheimer's arguments and then turn later to the third one.

Oppenheimer attempts to show, first of all, that his formula of the full product of labour (i.e. the formula that says the 'value of labour' equals the full value of labour's product) is no more than *a necessary conclusion resulting from the theory of labour value* that Marx himself defends.

> Marx's theory of labour value can be presented in the form of the following equation: the value of the product equals the labour time embodied in it. But this formula can also be read in reverse. With the help of a simple transposition we get the following formula: the value of the labour time equals the product of the [labour]. Thus the wage of the worker would have to consist of the full product of the [labour] (after the deduction of costs, i.e. the labour of other workers). We would then get the formula of the full product of labour.[11]

However, everyone knows that the worker in fact receives only a part of the value of the product produced by his labour. Our formula of the 'full product of labour' is at odds with actual capitalist reality. This fact of the deviation of the actual wage from its 'natural' level is explained by the existence of monopoly. Having ignored monopoly, Marx found this way out of the contradiction to be foreclosed. Thus Marx was forced to reject any 'transposition of the equation' and to resort to an artificial construction, according to which the worker sells not his '*labour*' but rather his '*labour power*', the value of which is less than the

---

11   Oppenheimer 1922, pp. 178–9.

value of the product of the worker's labour. But this construction by Marx inevitably leads to internal contradictions that Oppenheimer reveals with the help of mathematical formulae:

> In purely formal terms it (Marx's construction) already leads to impossible conclusions. Suppose that v, the daily product of the average worker, has the value of twelve hours of average and necessary labour. In that case we get the formula: $v = 12 \, t$, and through transposing we get the formula: $12 \, t = v$. Now, assume that the capitalist purchases 'a', the 'labour power' of the worker, for 6 t. Accordingly, $a = 6 \, t$. But this labour power delivers twelve hours of labour, or 12 t. The employer receives 12 t for 6 t. Consequently, $12 \, t = \frac{v}{2}$. But the previous formula said that $12 \, t = v$. It follows that $v = \frac{v}{2}$, i.e. we get an impossible conclusion.[12]

This whole argument by Oppenheimer is founded upon a deeply mistaken approach. The equation $[v = 12 \, t]$ says that the *value* of the product = the labour embodied in it (or the labour time). By transposing, Oppenheimer gets the equation: the *value* of the labour (or labour time) = its product $[12 \, t = v]$. We have noted elsewhere the formal error of such a transposition:

> The transposition of an equation means a complete transfer of the left part of the equation to the right and vice versa. A correct transposition would give the following formula: the labour time embodied in the product equals the *value* of the product. In quantitative terms, this formula in no way contradicts the Marxist theory. Oppenheimer reaches his formula of the full product of labour with the help of a transposition that is clearly incorrect: he leaves the word 'value' on the left side of the equation, but 'product' is carried over to the right. This would be the same as if a mathematician transposed the expression $\log 100 = 2$ as $\log 2 = 100$.[13]

Now that we are familiar with Oppenheimer's doctrine concerning the 'value of labour', it will be an easy matter for us to disclose the basic source of his mistaken and overly daring treatment of the equations. Oppenheimer takes the view that the *value* of the product is determined by the *value* of the labour. From his viewpoint, the formula $v = 12 \, t$ means that the value of the product v is equal to the *value* of 12 hours of labour. The formula equates one value with

---

12   Oppenheimer 1922, p. 180.
13   See Rubin 1924, p. 113.

another value and therefore has the same kind of magnitudes on both sides and can be transposed into the reverse formula, saying that the value of the labour equals the value of its product. But to interpret the Marxist formula of value that way means attributing Oppenheimer's ideas to Marx in advance.

Let us analyse the formula v = 12 t from the viewpoint of Marxist theory. It is absurd to think that the *product* v equals 12 *hours of labour*, just as it is silly to think that the *value* of the product v equals the *value* of 12 hours of labour. From Marx's viewpoint, the formula can only take the following form: the *value* of the product v equals 12 *hours of labour*, or V (v) = 12 t.[14] On the left side is the *value* of the product; and on the right, a certain quantity of *social labour* (but not the *value* of the labour). In value, an attribute that appears to be inherent in the thing itself, Marx saw the expression of the production-labour relation between people as commodity producers. The formula, according to which the value of the product is determined by social labour, expresses the connection between the social-production relations of people and their embodied expression in the value of the product. In Oppenheimer's eyes, the formula of value is an equation, the two sides of which are isomorphic (the value of the product and the value of the labour). For Marx, the formula of value expresses the causal link between a social phenomenon (the development of the productivity of social labour) and its embodied expression (the value of the products). The concepts of 'social labour' and 'value' are homogeneous only in one sense – namely, that they belong to the realm of the social economy – but they are not qualitatively of the same type. Hence, in the strict sense of the word, Marx's formula of value must not be expressed in the form of an equation that equates value to labour, but rather in the form of a proportion that equates the relation of the values of two products to a relation of the quantities of social labour required for their production. Strictly speaking, Marx does not claim that the *value* of a pood of wheat equals 12 hours of *labour*, and that the value of a pood of rye is 6 hours; he says that the *value* of a pood of wheat is to the *value* of a pood of rye as 12 hours of *labour* is to 6 hours of *labour*. Marx's formula is expressed most accurately in the form of a ratio: $\frac{V(v)}{V(a)} = \frac{12t}{6t}$ – not in the equations V (v) = 12 t and V (a) = 6 t.[15]

---

14   Here and in what follows the capital letter V stands for 'value' and the letter in brackets refers to the commodity (which can be either a thing or labour power).

15   It is characteristic that in the first chapters of *Capital* and *Critique of Political Economy*, where Marx often uses equations, he always equates the value of one product with the value of another, but not value with labour. He writes that 20 yards of linen = 1 coat and so forth, but he avoids saying that the value of 1 coat = × days of labour, preferring in this context to say that 1 coat 'represents' or 'expresses' (*darstellen*) × days of labour (*Kapital*, Vol. I, 1914, p. 13 [See Marx 1976, p. 136 *et passim*]). Such use of words by Marx is not an

This explains how incorrect it is to apply to the Marxist theory of value the method of 'transposing equations', to which Oppenheimer so readily and frequently has recourse. Oppenheimer's formula of value amounts to *an equation* in which the value of a product is equated to the value of labour – an equation that, with equal success, can be read from left to right or from right to left. 'If the value of the commodity is equal to the value of the labour embodied in it, then the value of the labour is also equal to the value of the product in which it is embodied'.[16] This device of rearranging the two sides of an equation, which Oppenheimer frequently repeats,[17] serves as a striking illustration of the vicious circle in which his theory of value revolves: the value of the product is determined by the value of the labour; and the latter, in turn, by the value of the product. The question of the causal connection between the two phenomena is not even raised; thus each of them, with the same success, can take the place of either cause or effect.

The formula of Marx's theory of value is distinguished by a completely *different methodological character*. The basic feature of Marx's method consists of the fact that the social form of the products derives from the social form of labour, and that changes in the value of commodities are explained by changes in the productivity of social labour. But it would be completely absurd, of course, to reverse Marx's formula of value and say that Marx derives the development of the productivity of labour from changes in the value of commodities. Marx's theory of value does not give us an 'equation' of labour with value: it reveals the causal connection between phenomena and gives us a formula in which one series of phenomena (the development of labour productivity) plays the role of cause, and the other (changes in the value of products) plays the role of effect. Whereas Oppenheimer's 'equation of value' is distinguished by the complete 'reversibility' of its elements (i.e. the possibility of inter-changing them), Marx's *causal formula* does not have this characteristic: it is 'irreversible'.

---

accident and strictly follows from his views on the relation between social labour and the value of products: 'If we say that, as values, commodities are simply congealed quantities of human labour, our analysis reduces them, it is true, to the level of abstract value, but does not give them a form of value distinct from their natural forms. It is otherwise in the value relation of one commodity to another. The first commodity's value character emerges here through its own relation to the second commodity' (Marx 1976, pp. 141–2). In the strict sense of the word, an 'equation' is simply a formula equating the value of one commodity to the value of another, not a formula determining the value of the commodity by the quantity of social labour required for its production.

16   Oppenheimer 1919a, p. 127.
17   See Oppenheimer 1919b, p. 459; 1922, pp. 178–9 et seq.

We come to the conclusion that it is fundamentally incorrect to see an 'equa-tion' in Marx's formula. Marx's goal is not to demonstrate an equation of *value with labour*: what he studies is an *'equation' of different types of social labour*, established by means of an *'equation' of their products as values* in the process of market exchange. Nevertheless, for the sake of clarity, let us agree to express Marx's formula in terms of the equation V (v) = 12 t – without, however, for-getting for a moment that the left side of the formula refers to the 'value' of the commodity, the right to 'social labour', and that these are qualitatively dif-ferent magnitudes. Through transposition, as we have seen, Oppenheimer gets something different from this formula: the 'value of 12 hours of labour' equals the value of the product V (v). We now know that such a transposition is based upon a profound error – conversion of a definite quantity of *social labour into the 'value of labour'*. With a proper transposition of this formula, we would get the following formula: 12 t = V (v).[18] This formula means that a certain quantity of *social labour* (i.e. labour viewed as a social function) *is expressed* in the value of the product v. But in no way does it mean – as Oppenheimer thinks – that the *value* of the given labour as a commodity (i.e. labour as something bought and sold) is *equal* to the value of the product v. From our transposition – if only it is done correctly – we do not get any formula of the full product of labour. Oppenheimer's first argument is based, therefore, on a crude substitution of the *value of labour* in place of a *quantity of labour*.

Oppenheimer's *second* argument, his attempt to lead the Marxist doctrine concerning the value of labour power to absurd conclusions, relies upon the same mistake. Oppenheimer tries to discredit Marx's theory with the help of mathematical proofs. The capitalist buys labour power (a) (expressed in a 12-hour working day) for a wage that is equal to the product of 6 hours of labour. Therefore, V (a) = 6 t, or V (a) = V $\left(\frac{v}{2}\right)$.[19] Now, in place of the labour power (a) Oppenheimer puts the 12 hours of labour in which it is expressed. We then get: V (12 t) = V $\left(\frac{v}{2}\right)$. But earlier, through transposition, we got the formula: 12 t = V (v).[20] Assuming that the left sides of both equations are equal, Oppenheimer concludes that the same applies to the right sides; that is, V (v) = V $\left(\frac{v}{2}\right)$ or v = $\frac{v}{2}$. This clearly absurd conclusion proves, in Oppenheimer's opinion, how incor-rect is Marx's theory of value.

---

18   If the formula V (v) = 12 t means that the value of the product v *expresses* 12 hours of social labour, then the formula 12 t = V (v) means that 12 hours of social labour *are expressed* in the value of the product v.

19   Since v is the product of 12 hours of labour, V (v) = 12 t. Hence V $\left(\frac{v}{2}\right)$ = 6 t. Thus, in place of the expression 6t, we can use the expression V $\left(\frac{v}{2}\right)$.

20   By transposing the formula, Oppenheimer wants to get V (12 t) = V (v). But we have already shown that the correct transposition leads to a different formula, namely, 12 t = V (v).

This argument from Oppenheimer rests on the unstated assumption that the left sides of both equations are equal, i.e. that V (12 t) = 12 t.[21] But it is precisely that assumption that is incorrect. What is meant by the expression V (12 t)? It signifies that the labour itself has become a commodity that is bought and sold in the market and has a definite value. But this labour-commodity[22] has a value that is less than the value of the product that it produces. And this is precisely the foundation of the capitalist economy. Assuming that V (12 t) = 12 t, Oppenheimer incorrectly attributes to Marx his own idea that *the value of the labour equals the value of its product*. Meanwhile, Marx decisively rejects this idea and proves that as soon as economic conditions appear in which 'labour' acquires 'value' (i.e. becomes a special sort of commodity, labour power), this value of 'labour' is *less* than the value of the product it creates. By comparing two formulae: 1) V (12 t) = V $\left(\frac{v}{2}\right)$ and 2) 12 t = V (v), we can come to only one conclusion, namely that V (12 t) <12 t, or that the value of 'labour' as a commodity (the average wage) is less than the value of the product created by that labour. But it is by no means true that these two formulae yield the 'impossible' conclusion that v = $\frac{v}{2}$.

It is very interesting that Oppenheimer's 'new' argument, which is finally to prove the error of Marxist theory, was properly appraised long before Oppenheimer's works ever appeared. Consider the following quotation:

> If a labourer works for 12 hours and receives the product of 6 hours labour as wages, then the product of the 6 hours constitutes the *value* of 12 hours labour (because the wages [represent] the exchangeable commodity for [12 hours of labour]). It does not follow from this that 6 hours of labour are equal to 12 hours,[23] or that the commodities in which 6 hours of labour are embodied [are] equal to the commodities in which 12 hours of labour are embodied.[24] It does not follow that the value of wages is equal to the value of the product in which the labour is embodied.[25] It follows only that the value of labour (because it is measured by the value of labour power, not by the labour carried out), the value of a given quantity of

---

21   Oppenheimer makes this suggestion covertly since in his 'equations' he writes simply v in place of V (v) and 12 t in place of V (12 t). But while it is true that 12 t = 12 t, we can see that it is completely incorrect to say that V (12 t) = 12 t.

22   Since Oppenheimer denies that the worker sells his labour power, we are provisionally using the expression 'labour-commodity' (in the sense of labour power).

23   [i.e. that 6 t = 12 t]

24   [i.e. that v = $\frac{v}{2}$]

25   [i.e. that V (12 t) = 12 t]

labour contains less labour than it buys;[26] that, consequently, the *value of the commodities* in which this purchased labour is embodied, is very different from the value of the commodities with which this given quantity of labour was purchased, or by which it was commanded. Mr. Malthus draws the opposite conclusion. Since the *value* of a given quantity of labour is equal to its value,[27] it follows, according to him, that the value in which this quantity of labour is embodied is equal to the value of the wages.[28]

One might think that this excerpt was aimed directly at Oppenheimer's argument outlined above. Meanwhile, it was written by Marx half a century before Oppenheimer's works appeared, and it was aimed at Malthus, who wrote a century ago.[29]

Oppenheimer's attempt to reduce the Marxist formula of value to absurdity has not succeeded. The absurd conclusion (namely, that $v = \frac{v}{2}$) is only reached, given Oppenheimer's assumption that V (12 t) = 12 t; that is, that the worker sells not his labour power but rather his labour, the value of which equals the value of the product he creates. But Marx, as we know, denies that proposition and contends that the 'labour' sold by the worker to the capitalist, in return for the wage, itself takes on the character of a special commodity, 'labour power', whose value is less than the value of the product created by the worker's labour; in other words, V (12 t) <12 t. For that reason, Oppenheimer is obliged to turn from formal-mathematical arguments to substantive objections to Marx's position. Oppenheimer – and here we come to his third argument – objects to Marx's position that the worker sells his labour power and not his labour; he suggests that the worker sells precisely his *labour* and by no means his *labour power*. In support of his opinion, Oppenheimer offers the following considerations.

If the worker sold his labour power to the capitalist, his ability to work after the labour process 'would be exhausted to the extreme, for he would not be left with the slightest strength for any of his own purposes. Evidently Marx used this word in precisely that sense'.[30] But the fact is that the worker, in most cases, does not sell his labour to the point of completely exhausting his labour power; upon leaving the factory he still finds within himself the strength to dig in his

---

26   [i.e. that V (12 t) <12 t]
27   [i.e. that V (12 t) = V (12 t)]
28   [i.e. that 12 t = V (12 t)]
29   Marx 1972, pp. 25–6.
30   Oppenheimer 1922, p. 182.

garden or play soccer. Obviously, he does not sell all of his labour power but only a definite quantity of his labour.

It would be redundant to dwell on the theme of how mistaken it would be to attribute to Marx the view that sale of 'labour power' can only mean sale of labour power to the point of the worker's complete physical exhaustion. Marx readily acknowledged the possibility of an improvement in the worker's conditions of labour (shortening the working day and so forth) – an improvement, however, that can 'in no way alter the fundamental character of capitalist production'.[31] If we understand work in the economic rather than the physical sense, as a person's constant and regularly resumed participation in the production process, then, of course, there is no doubt that the worker sells to the capitalist his entire labour power or his entire capacity for labour. It would only be possible to deny this in the event that the worker spent only a part of his working day in the capitalist's factory and, for the rest of the time, regularly worked for himself in his own shop. Even Oppenheimer would hardly want to claim that such circumstances are typical for a capitalist economy.

Sensing the weakness of his argument, Oppenheimer hurries to reinforce his claims with new arguments, namely, through 'investigation of the term "labour power" in its strictly scientific meaning'. In Oppenheimer's opinion, it is necessary to make a 'strict distinction' between three different concepts: 1) 'labour' (*Arbeit*) is a *physical* concept; 2) 'labour power' or 'labour capacity' (*Arbeitsvermögen*) is a *physiological* concept; and 3) labour or 'labour expenditure' (*Arbeitsleistung*) is an *economic* concept.[32] Leaving aside the first concept, let us consider the latter two. Just what is 'labour power' (labour capacity)? Oppenheimer defines it by using Marx's words: 'We mean by labour-power, or labour-capacity, the aggregate of those mental and physical capabilities existing in the physical form, the living personality, of a human being, capabilities which he sets in motion whenever he produces a use-value of any kind'.[33]

Can the worker sell his labour power or his labour capacity? Not at all, answers Oppenheimer. Indeed, labour power is an inseparable attribute of the organism of the worker and could only be sold along with the latter. Only in a slave economy is 'labour power' sold together with the person of the slave, who was a commodity and had exchange value. In a capitalist society labour power is not an 'economic object' or a commodity. The 'free worker' does not sell his person and thereby his labour power; he only sells his labour or 'labour expenditure', which is specified in terms of skill and duration. Labour power

31   Marx 1976, p. 763.
32   Oppenheimer 1922, p. 183; Oppenheimer 1919a, p. 122.
33   Marx 1976, p. 270.

is the 'material condition' for labour, but the two must not be confused – just as the steam engine must not be confused with the energy it develops. Imagine that the owner of a steam engine hires it out for a time while reserving his property right in it. What is he selling? Obviously, not the engine itself but only the energy it develops during a certain period of time. Likewise the worker, hiring out his labour power, sells only the energy that it produces, or his labour. In the contract between the capitalist and the worker, the item being bought and sold is only labour, not 'labour power'.[34]

Is Oppenheimer correct in claiming that 'labour power' is a physiological concept and labour an economic one? Not at all. Labour power and labour can both be regarded in physiological as well as economic terms. A physiologist can study both the worker's capacity for labour in general and also his concrete labour expenditure. Accordingly labour, just like labour power, can serve as a physiological concept. On the other hand, 'labour power' and labour can each take on particular social-economic features and serve as an 'economic' concept. Marx is not interested in a physiological distinction between potential and actual labour, but rather in distinguishing the social-economic relations that are established between people, depending on whether the person involved is a commodity owner, who owns the product in which his labour is embodied – or a wage worker who is compelled to create, by means of his work, products owned by the employer. Labour and 'labour power' are essentially two social-economic concepts that reflect the difference between two economic structures (a simple commodity economy and a capitalist economy) and two social types of production (of an independent craftsman and a wage worker). At the basis of this distinction lies a different relation of the immediate producers to the material means of production. Where the producers combine in their own hands both the personal and material factors of production, they exchange with each other the products of their labour and thereby their labour. Where the direct producers are separated from the material factors of production, they are deprived of any possibility to exchange their 'labour' with other members of society because the necessary conditions of exchange do not exist; nothing remains to the worker but to alienate the personal factor of production (labour power), which is separate from the material factor and counterposed to it (with the result that this material factor of production acquires the character of 'capital'). The distinction between 'labour power' and 'labour' reflects the difference between a personal factor of production that is separated from the material factor in class-specific terms – and a personal factor that is joined together with

---

34   Oppenheimer 1922, pp. 184–6.

the material factor in the hands of one and the same class. Obviously, the difference between them has not just a physiological but also an economic character. With his famous teaching that the worker sells not his 'labour' but his 'labour power', what Marx has in mind is to mark the fundamental social-economic difference between the independent commodity producer and wage labourers.

The fact that this was precisely Marx's goal in his teaching on labour power is evident throughout his entire exposition. He points out that the transformation of labour power into a special commodity is possible only when the following two basic conditions prevail. First, 'labour-power can appear on the market as a commodity only if, and in so far as, its possessor, the individual whose labour-power it is, offers it for sale or sells it as a commodity. In order that its possessor may sell it as a commodity, he must have it at his disposal, he must be the free proprietor of his own labour-capacity, hence of his person'.[35] This feature distinguishes the capitalist economy from a slave economy or any other type that is founded on the absence of freedom for the direct producer. 'The second essential condition which allows the owner of money to find labour-power in the market as a commodity is this, that the possessor of labour-power, instead of being able to sell commodities in which his labour has been objectified, must rather be compelled to offer for sale as a commodity that very labour-power which exists only in his living body'.[36] This feature distinguishes a capitalist economy from one of simple commodity production; in other words, the production relation between the capitalist and the wage labourer (expressed in the opposition of 'capital' to 'labour power' or 'wage labour') is distinguished from the production relation between independent commodity producers (who exchange the products of their labour and, through them, their 'labour' itself).

Of course, Oppenheimer is perfectly correct in pointing out that sale by the worker of his labour power (labour, in his terminology), is clearly different from sale of the worker's person in a slave economy. But Marx himself, as we have seen, emphatically underlines this difference. However, if the sale of labour power is clearly different from sale of the worker's person, there are still no grounds for confusing the sale of 'labour power' with alienation of 'labour' in the form of the finished products of labour, which characterises exchange between independent commodity producers. But Oppenheimer's doctrine leads to exactly that confusion by asserting that the worker alienates his 'labour'. Oppenheimer ignores the most important feature of capitalist eco-

---

35   Marx 1976, p. 271.
36   Marx 1976, p. 272.

nomy, which lies in the fact that the entire process of production – including the process of applying the personal labour of the direct producers (the workers) – is directed and controlled not by the will and discretion of the latter but instead by the will and discretion of the employer. The latter, therefore, even prior to commencement of the labour process, legally possesses and economically disposes of the workers' capacity for labour, or his labour power. With his captious and sometimes scholastic criticism of the Marxist doctrine on labour power, Oppenheimer displays a total misunderstanding of the sociological character of Marx's teaching on the subject.[37]

---

37   Even economists who have no sympathy for Marxism are compelled on this question to defend Marx against Oppenheimer's attacks and to recognise that 'one of Marx's greatest scientific services' lies in the distinction he made between labour and labour power. See Budge 1920, p. 85. But Budge commits the opposite error to Oppenheimer's: he recognises 'labour power' (i.e. wage labour) as an economic category, yet he mistakenly denies that character to 'labour', which he regards as a purely technical category (p. 87). On this point Budge shares the widespread confusion that we encounter below in the articles on Stolzmann and Ammon.

PART 2

Rudolf Stolzmann and the Social Method in Political Economy

∵

Introduction by the Editor[1]

By the mid-nineteenth century, theoretical political economy reached a critical juncture. John Stuart Mill's *Principles of Political Economy* (1848) had become a standard textbook after Mill refined Ricardo's doctrine in response to some of the more perceptive critics. Marx, of course, was at the early stages of his own critical reinterpretation of Smith and Ricardo, but among non-Marxist economists the most important new developments after Mill came in the 1870s with the marginalist revolution. Marx's work, in today's terminology, began with the 'supply side', that is, with value and income distribution, which Marx saw being objectively determined by conditions in production. The theory of marginal utility, which originated almost simultaneously in the work of Carl Menger (in Austria), William Stanley Jevons (in Britain), and Léon Walras (in France), took the opposite approach of explaining demand in terms of consumers' subjective appraisals of utilities resulting from incremental purchases of alternative goods. Marginalism created the illusion of 'consumer sovereignty' while occluding issues of property ownership, production relations, and income distribution between social classes.

During the same period, significant changes were also occurring in ethical philosophy. Hegelianism had run its course in Germany, and in England the utilitarianism of Jeremy Bentham and John Stuart Mill proffered a normative ethics that excluded metaphysics and any notion of the *a priori*. A good action depended upon its consequences, and the criterion for judging a good action was its effect in maximising happiness for the greatest number. Bentham's utilitarianism and the doctrine of legal positivism shared a commitment to science as the only source of genuine knowledge.[2] By the 1870s, however, just as margin-

---

1 There is very little English-language literature on Stolzmann. For some background to the present article, readers may look at Lechner 2017, pp. 145–52; see also Lechner 2017b. For Stolzmann's disagreements with Austrian theory, see Esser 1971. Several commentaries on Stolzmann's *Die soziale Kategorie in der Volkswirtschaftslehre* appeared at the time of publication. These include reviews by C.H. d'Eppington in *The Economic Review*, 7 (1897), pp. 130–1; E. Castelot in *Journal des Economistes: Revue mensuelle de la Science Economique et de la Statistique*, 5e Serie, Tome XXVII (Juillet à Septembre 1896), pp. 282–4; M. François Simiand in *L'Année Sociologique*, ed. Émile Durkheim, Vol. 1 (1898), pp. 472–5.

2 James E. Crimmins (2020) comments that Bentham 'carried over into moral science the basic principle that people can only know, in any certain or scientific sense of that term, that which can be observed and verified … . He rejected all forms of idealism in philosophy and insisted that in principle all matter is quantifiable in mathematical terms, and this extends to the pains and pleasures that we experience – the ultimate phenomena to which all human activity (and social concepts, such as rights, obligation, and duty) could be reduced and explained'.

© RICHARD B. DAY, 2024 | DOI:10.1163/9789004705661_011

alist theory claimed to be a new, objective science of economics, neo-Kantian philosophers in Germany were arguing that even the scientific method presupposes *a priori* concepts and principles.

For Kant, the *a priori* categories of Understanding form and give meaning to sense impressions; in these terms, the world, *as we know it*, is one of natural causality defined by the activity of our own consciousness. With regard to moral philosophy, Kant's 'categorical impetrative' projected a timeless and universal 'kingdom of ends' that would include all 'rational beings as ends in themselves, and also the special ends which each may propose to himself.'[3] Kant recognised that this *noumenal kingdom* can never exist, but he argued that in the *phenomenal* world our own reason still commands us to strive for an *ethical commonwealth* that may be progressively realised in human history. The supreme moral law – never to treat others merely as means to our own ends – led to the dilemma of how the ideal of an ethical commonwealth might be reconciled with the self-interest of a market economy. As Kant said, poverty was always a 'great temptation to vice'.[4]

Rudolf Stolzmann, as Rubin explains in the following essay, brought to political economy a 'social-organic-ethical' method that was heavily indebted to Kantian traditions and to the neo-Kantian philosophy of Heinrich Rickert.[5] An exponent of the social law position in economics, Stolzmann rejected the notion of pure economic theory or immutable economic laws. He believed that social 'facts' are constituted by legal and ethical 'forms' that make social regulation possible. Political economy was 'a science of the means for achieving ethical ends'.[6] 'The social element must be present from the very beginning (*a priori*) as a *constitutive* category that internally penetrates all economic concepts and relations'.[7]

The purpose of capitalism, for Stolzmann, was to satisfy needs in the most efficient manner compatible with social justice. Taking needs as given, he related wages to the socially necessary compensation for the 'last' (or marginal) worker, and profits to the needs of the 'last' capitalist, with rent as the residual. These 'teleologically given and purposively fixed sums' were the starting point for any economic investigation. Wages and profits were categories of distribution, not of social production. Every member of society must be guaranteed

---

3   Kant 1923, p. 51.
4   Kant 1991, p. 193.
5   In 1925 Stolzmann dedicated *Wesen und Ziele der Wirtschaftsphilosophie* (*The Nature and Goals of Economic Philosophy*) to Heinrich Rickert. For a brief account of Rickert's philosophy, see the introduction to Rubin's essay on Franz Petry in this volume.
6   Stolzmann 1909, pp. 111–12.
7   Stolzmann 1909, p. 114.

economic security, and interactions between individuals must serve the collective purpose of sustaining community:

> The task of social economics consists of historically and systematically regarding the national economy as an ethical purposive formation, as a spiritual creation of the social ideal but one that is realised and embodied in the existing regulated matter of social life and expressed in distinct national economic institutions and phenomena.[8]

Isaak Rubin was unimpressed by the teleological structure of Stolzmann's neo-Kantianism, yet he still regarded him as a 'first-class' economist and a 'major and original thinker' who provided 'a devastatingly critical analysis of the doctrine of the Austrian economists. This is Stolzmann's great and indisputable service'. Rubin included Stolzmann in this book because he also found some affinity between Stolzmann and Marx. In the first chapter of *Capital* Marx explained that commodities only come into the world insofar as 'they possess a double form, i.e. natural form and value form'.[9] Indeed, this was the theme of Rubin's best-known book, *Essays on Marx's Theory of Value*:

> *The value-form of the product of labor is not only the most abstract, but is also the most universal form, taken by the product in bourgeois production, and stamps that production as a particular species of social production, and thereby gives it its special historical character ....the 'value form' is the most general form of the commodity economy*; it is characteristic of the social form which is acquired by the process of production at a determined level of historical development. Since political economy analyzes a historically transient social form of production, commodity capitalist production, the 'form of value' is one of the foundation stones of Marx's theory of value.[10]

In the essay that follows, Rubin takes care to explain that while Marx saw 'value' as the objective measure of abstract labour and the social form for mediating exchange relations, he understood the latter in terms of dialectical causality, not teleological purpose. The principal flaw that Rubin found in Stolzmann's work was his failure to reconcile obvious natural causality (law-governed nature and the material-technical conditions of production) with teleological purpose. For Stolzmann, 'The ethical "idea" stands opposed to

---

8   Stolzmann 1909, p. 137.
9   See Marx 1976, p. 138.
10   Rubin 1973, p. 114 *et passim*.

empirical "reality", which it must transform and spiritualise'. The ethical factor, being created by an act of free human will, '*escapes* from the world of causally conditioned phenomena', and the result – instead of the unity of a social economy – is an insurmountable dualism. The ideal of social regulation turns out, in Rubin's words, to be simply 'a two-faced Janus looking in different directions'.

Stolzmann envisioned a law-governed social whole that only Marx could realistically anticipate through critical investigation of the regulating role of the law of value in commodity exchange. Marx's method involved analytical deconstruction of society into its fundamental elements – 'a small number of determinate, abstract, general relations such as division of labour, money, value, etc.'[11] – followed by dialectical reconstruction of those elements in order to comprehend a whole that is internally contradictory and formed not by the pull of teleology but instead by the force of economic crises and class contradictions. This, Marx said, was the 'scientifically correct method' of demonstrating that 'The concrete is concrete because it is the concentration of many determinations'.[12] In *Capital*, it is the singular law of value, moving from abstract to increasingly concrete expression, that explains exchange value, income distribution, and the allocation of productive forces. It is also the law of value that points beyond capitalism to social ownership of the means of production, creating the first real, not imagined, prospect of a totality of conscious social self-regulation in the form of economic planning.

Isaak Rubin on Rudolf Stolzmann

Rudolf Stolzmann is the foremost representative, perhaps even the author, of the *social method* in the form that we often encounter among contemporary European economists. Stolzmann counts Rodbertus and Adolph Wagner among his predecessors, while Marx also had a strong influence upon him. It is no exaggeration to say that the starting point for Stolzmann's critical position, which has led him to attempt a complete reconstruction of economic theory, corresponded precisely with the position that Marx took in his brilliant and profound criticism of the 'three-sided formula' of vulgar economics.

Vulgar economists attributed the origin of different forms of income (wages, profits, and rents) to the operation of material-technical factors of production (labour, means of production, and land). Following Marx, Stolzmann decisively

---

11   Marx 1993, p. 100.
12   Marx 1993, p. 101.

rejects such a 'naturalistic' explanation of social phenomena. Like Marx and Rodbertus, he draws a sharp distinction between technical factors of production (labour, means of production, and land) and their specific social forms that inhere in capitalist production (wage labour, capital, and landed property). Generalising this antithesis between factors of production and their social form, Stolzmann comes to a broader antithesis between the 'matter' of the economy, which is subordinate to the rule of *natural* categories, and social 'regulation' of the economy, which is the sphere of operation for *social* categories. For Stolzmann, neglect of the social form of the economy is the most significant flaw both of naturalistic objectivism, represented in the teachings of the classics and their followers, and also of naturalistic subjectivism, which finds its proponents among the Austrian economists. One of Stolzmann's foremost services is his brilliant critique of both variants of economic naturalism.

In Marx and Rodbertus we find a principal source for the ideas that have inspired Stolzmann's thinking. We can locate a second ideological source, no less influential for him, in Kantian idealistic philosophy. Finally, it seems likely that a third set of influences on Stolzmann's system originated with the ethical tendency of economic thought that prevailed in Germany during the second half of the nineteenth century. In the spirit of Kantian philosophy, Stolzmann strictly separates the world of empirical reality, which is subject to the law of causal necessity, from the world of ethical ideals and purposes, which demands realisation by virtue of its inherent value. For Stolzmann, this Kantian antithesis, between the world of *causal necessity* and the world of *moral freedom*, approximates the previously mentioned antithesis between the *matter* and *form* of the economy; more precisely, in his thinking the latter antithesis is nothing but the form in which the first antithesis manifests itself in the economic sphere. The social form of the economy (or in Stolzmann's terminology, social regulation of the economy) can be regarded as a totality of social norms and institutions created by the free will of man for the purpose of realising certain ethical ideals. For this reason, the social form of the economy must be investigated from a *teleological*, not a *causal*, point of view; in place of Marx's sociological method, Stolzmann follows his own *'social-organic-ethical'* method.

The joining of the *social* method with *idealistic* philosophy, as proclaimed by Stolzmann, is an inevitable consequence of the collapse of the naturalistic tendency in economic thought on the one hand, and of the prevalence of idealistic philosophy in bourgeois scholarly circles on the other. One need not be surprised, therefore, by the fact that Stammler, almost simultaneously with Stolzmann, came out with his teaching regarding the matter and form of the economy in his well-known book *Economy and the Law*,[13] which corresponds in many ways to Stolzmann's ideas. It is true that Stolzmann regards the social form of the economy primarily in terms of the ethical purposes it realises, whereas Stammler looks at the juridical forms in which the former is implemented. But, despite this difference, the very idea of counterpoising the matter to the form of the economy, on the basis of a Kantian contrast between the world of causality and the world of teleology, is common to Stammler and Stolzmann, both of whom can be regarded as fathers of the new union of the social method with idealistic philosophy.

Thanks to its wide philosophical-sociological sweep and brilliant literary quality, Stammler's book made an incomparably greater impression on broad circles of the reading public and even among scholars than did Stolzmann's *Die soziale Kategorie in der Volkswirtschaftslehre* (*The Social Category in Economic Science*), published in 1896. On the other hand, being a jurist by profession, Stammler avoided going deeply into purely economic problems. Stolzmann, in his persistent scientific-literary work over the span of three decades, has proved to be a first-class economist and has taken on a task that never occurred to Stammler – that of completely reconstructing economic science on the basis of the social method.[14]

Stolzmann's first work, *Die soziale Kategorie in der Volkswirtschaftslehre* (1896), was devoted almost exclusively to the investigation of purely economic problems and avoided crossing over into the area of philosophy. In that work, which has primarily a critical character, Stolzmann outlined his own system only in general terms while giving prominence, as the book's title makes clear, to the antithesis between natural and social categories in the economy. In his next voluminous work, *Der Zweck in der Volkswirtschaft* (*Purpose in the National Economy*, 1909),[15] Stolzmann developed his own theory in detail and, as this title also suggests, forcefully promoted the importance of the teleological method of research. But, in this work too, discussion of philosophical questions, while given a place of honour, are still supplementary to the economic investigation. Finally, in his most recent works, *Grundzüge einer Philosophie der Volkswirtschaft* (*Principles of a Philosophy of Economics*, 1920)[16] and

---

13   [Rudolf Stammler (1856–1938), German legal philosopher. The reference is to Stammler 1896.]
14   Stolzmann is not an academic scholar but holds a high position in the judicial establishment. He has not followed the typical academic career – a rare exception in Germany – and it was only after several decades of scientific work that he received the title of Doctor *honoris causa*.
15   Stolzmann 1909.
16   Stolzmann 1925a.

Die Krisis in der heutigen Nationalökonomie (*The Crisis in Today's National Economy*, 1925),[17] Stolzmann took the opposite route of descending from general philosophical positions to economic problems. Attempting in these writings to provide a general philosophical foundation for his theory – even though, as a Kantian, he sees philosophy's centre of gravity in the theory of knowledge, not in ontology and metaphysics – Stolzmann did not refrain from entering into the realm of metaphysics. Here we learn that the antithesis between natural and social categories in the economy is merely an expression of the fundamental philosophical antithesis between empirical reality and the ethical idea, between the world and the 'I', between the empirical 'I' and the transcendental 'I'.

The first two of the aforementioned works by Stolzmann are voluminous and ponderously written, intended for the specialised reader and hardly accessible to the wider reading public. For the latter, Stolzmann intended the newer works mentioned above, in which he provides a more or less concise and accessible outline of his philosophical views and his economic system. Stolzmann's attempt to make his ideas accessible to a broader public is probably due in part to the revival of interest in the social method that has been evident in recent years on the part of broad circles of scholars and the reading public. This fact probably also explains the revival of Stolzmann's literary activity; over the past decade, in addition to the two works already mentioned, he has written a number of interesting articles that have been published in the journals.[18]

---

17   Stolzmann 1925b.

18   For the interested reader we include a list of these articles: 'Die Kritik des Subjektivismus an der Hand der sozialorganischen Methode' (Stolzmann 1914); 'Die Kritik des Objektivismus und seine Verschmelzung mit dem Subjektivismus zur sozialorganischen Einheit' (Stolzmann 1915); 'Die soziale Theorie der Verteilung und des Wertes' (Stolzmann 1918); 'Das Reinoekonomische im System der Volkswirtschaft' (Stolzmann 1919); 'Liefmanns rein psychisches System der Volkswirtschaft' (Stolzmann 1922). The reader will find Stolzmann's best short presentation of his own economic theory in the above-mentioned article (Stolzmann 1915). A complete presentation of Stolzmann's system can be found only in his lengthy work *Der Zweck in der Volkswirtschaft* (1909).

CHAPTER 1

The Social-Organic Method

Stolzmann is sharply critical of economists who devote their attention entirely to the investigation of natural-technical economic categories. In his opinion, a national economy can be understood only as a unity of continuously interacting natural and social categories.

Stolzmann understands *natural* categories to include 'all causal connections that are based upon the mechanism of nature – which is independent of human will – and that are once and for all *given in the causality* of natural laws'. 'Natural categories include both the basic natural-technical and the (individual) psychological conditions that are also called *constant* and "eternal", since they form the unchanging material, the *matter* of all economic forms'.[1] In his economic activity man is compelled to take into account both the laws of external nature and the psycho-physiological properties of his own nature. This accounts for the presence of natural-technical and individual-psychological principles in his activity.[2] Thus, insofar as the economic activity of people is directed to satisfying human needs, it is conditioned by laws of nature – of both external nature and the nature of man himself – that are necessary and independent of human will.[3] This includes the '*matter*' (*Stoff*) of the economy, which is subordinated to the operation of '*natural categories*'.

However, if we leave aside the fantasy of Robinson Crusoe, the economic activity of people always occurs within a society, within a certain social context. From the very outset it has not only a natural-technical but also a social-ethical character. A man not only confronts nature but is also connected with other people, and 'insofar as a man is connected with other people, he is guided by the *social principle*, or by "practical reason" and the ethics it necessarily entails'.[4] Every individual is woven into a system of social institutions and norms that determine his behaviour and his economic activity. The economy is a sphere governed not only by natural categories but also by '*social categories*'.[5] The 'matter' of economic life does not exist in isolation, apart from a certain social form

---

1 Stolzmann 1909, p. ii. Unless otherwise indicated, all italics are from Stolzmann.
2 Stolzmann 1909, p. 105.
3 Stolzmann 1925b, pp. 91–3.
4 Stolzmann 1909, p. 105.
5 Hence the title of the well-known work by Stolzmann: *Die soziale Kategorie in der Volkswirtschaftslehre* (1896).

© RICHARD B. DAY, 2024 | DOI:10.1163/9789004705661_012

or a certain 'social regulation'.[6] The 'forces of nature and the instincts of man represent the "matter" that awaits human "regulation" – not technical regulation but regulation with the aid of *law* and *morals*'.[7] Social regulation of the economy finds expression in a totality of norms and institutions that regulate the mutual relations between members of a society.

We can regard social regulation, on the one hand, as the basis (or *cause*) of economic phenomena and, on the other hand, as the *purpose* that is realised by way of the latter. 'In the first sense, this is *objectively implemented* regulation, which corresponds to the economic system and follows from the existing legal and moral order. From this regulation comes the social part of the causal connections'[8] that operate in economic life. But apart from this, social regulation may be seen 'as an idea, as something desirable or as the representation of purpose'.[9] In other words, social regulation can be seen both from the *causal* and from the *teleological* (goal-oriented) point of view. From the former point of view, the economic system appears as a system of causally conditioned phenomena in which social regulation plays a role as one of the factually acting causes (together with nature). From the latter point of view, the economy appears as a system of purposes that are being realised – specifically, those ethical ideals and norms that find their expression in the given type of social regulation (i.e. interpersonal relations). For now, let us deal with regulation in the *first* sense, i.e. regulation that factually operates as one of two basic causal series that condition economic phenomena (the second causal series originates in nature).

Social regulation, as 'an *embodied* idea and *realised* purpose, acts in a way similar to any other cause' and does not differ in this respect from natural categories.[10] 'Wherever people associate socially, we see regulation and the subordination of all economic desires and activities to morals and law'.[11] From a *causal* point of view, the activities of economic subjects are factually conditioned by *two* causal series: by the natural-technical conditions of production and by the regulating social norms that correspond to the given state of laws and rights.

---

6   Stolzmann uses the following terms in just about one and the same sense: social category, social regulation, regulation, and the structure of the economy.
7   Stolzmann 1909, p. iii.
8   Ibid.
9   Ibid.
10   Stolzmann 1909, p. iv.
11   Stolzmann 1909, p. 35.

In view of what has been said, the economy can be understood only as *a unity of matter and regulation*, or of natural and social categories. Only the economy of an isolated Robinson Crusoe can be understood with the aid of natural categories alone and be viewed as a relation between man and nature. 'In the context of a *social* economy *all* phenomena are the inseparably *unified* result of *both* categories'.[12] 'The matter of natural categories, thanks to the regulation that forms it, turns into the unity of a social economy'.[13]

Two conclusions follow from the unity of natural and social categories in the economy: 1) the economist has no right to ignore the natural-technical *'matter'* of the economy; and 2) even less can he study matter that is not formed by a certain *social regulation*.

'Regulation does not occur as a naked idea somewhere in the vacuum of space but can be embodied only in the matter of things'.[14] If 'an investigation of social matter apart from concrete regulation leads to no end', the reverse also holds: 'regulation, without the matter that is being regulated, is completely impossible'.[15] 'Natural factors only act within the limits of social regulation, but the opposite is also true; the latter, without the former, is no more than a formalistic and dead thing'.[16] To ignore the natural aspect of the economy is inadmissible.[17]

The majority of economists, however, have sinned in the opposite direction. They have either devoted their attention exclusively to the natural side of the economy, ignoring its social regulation, or else they have proposed first to study the 'purely economic', i.e. natural categories, in order then to take an additional look at the role of social moments. Stolzmann fundamentally repudiates such a method of investigation. From the very outset the 'matter' of the economy only exists in a socially formed manner, and the economist can only investigate it on that basis. On their own, 'natural categories create only the *possibility* for the emergence of economic phenomena. The appearance of the latter depends upon a *socially implemented* mode of production. Economic phenomena are not self-subsistent and independent of social regulation'.[18] 'Natural and social categories act *simultaneously and jointly* in the economic phenomena of all social life, from the very origins of the latter and onward into any conceivable

---

12   Stolzmann 1909, p. 131.
13   Stolzmann 1909, p. 55.
14   Stolzmann 1909, p. 48.
15   Stolzmann 1909, pp. 48–9.
16   Stolzmann 1909, pp. 51–2.
17   Stolzmann 1909, pp. 43–4.
18   Stolzmann 1909, p. 131.

future'.[19] Thus, any study of economic life has, as its presupposition, the presence of a determinate social regulation of the economy.

The relation between the technical and social causes that act upon the
economy is best regarded in the form of an interaction. 'Natural categories
and forces – with instincts and desires in the foreground, which are pre-given
in human nature – constantly interact with institutions and regulation that
grow out of social consensus (*communis consensus*) or a people's spirit'.[20] 'Both
categories continuously permeate each other in perpetual interaction'.[21] This
interaction leads to a circular movement of social phenomena: 'the natural elements of technique and so forth, depending on the legal order in which they
operate, bring about specific phenomena' that demand 'changes in the existing
form of social life'; when 'the wishes and strivings for a change in regulation,
brought forth by these phenomena, are realised, then new social phenomena
arise within and due to the new social order, and they summon forth a new
desire for changes so that the play continues without end'.[22]

Stolzmann's assertion concerning the impossibility of investigating economic phenomena apart from the social form that regulates them explains to
us his relation to the two main tendencies that are struggling for predominance
in political economy: the *Austrian school* and *Marxism*. 'The study of psychological phenomena and their separate action cannot simply be excluded from
political economy';[23] as we have seen, they enter the composition of the economy's 'matter'. But the Austrian school is mistaken when it 'finds the decisive
centre of gravity of scientific-economic research in knowledge of the motivation of human actions oriented to economic behaviour'.[24] In the eyes of the
Austrian school, the study of objective factors is no more than a 'subordinate and auxiliary approach', adopted mainly when a direct study of individual
motivation is not possible.[25] But, according to Stolzmann, in reality 'the objectively given social factors are not an auxiliary means to knowledge of individual
psychological motivation; they are parts of an independent, purposive formation (*Zweckgebilde*) of regulation, with their own *inherent* definition of purpose; they *take the place* of purposive relations between individuals and 'grind
down' the latter if they dare to oppose their own will to the interests of the state,

---

19   Stolzmann 1909, p. 132.
20   Stolzmann 1909, p. 51.
21   Stolzmann 1909, p. 132.
22   Stolzmann 1909, p. 131.
23   Stolzmann 1909, p. 52.
24   Stolzmann 1909, p. 59.
25   Ibid.

to objective regulation'.[26] It is not permissible, as a starting point for research, to take the economy on its own and in isolation, in order later to add social 'contact' to it from the outside, as an external resultant of isolated individual-economic phenomena.[27] 'The social element must be present from the very beginning (*a priori*) as a *constitutive* category that internally penetrates all economic concepts and relations'.[28]

According to Stolzmann, Marx came close to a correct understanding of this social element in the economy. 'He was genuinely close to an understanding of the fundamental importance of the social category as the principle of all social regulation'.[29] He was 'one of the first to consider economic phenomena as "social" formations',[30] particularly in the theory of commodity fetishism and in the definition of capital.[31] But if Marx justifiably ridiculed those economists who 'consider social relations to be *relations between things*, Marx himself immediately turns *people, together with their products, into things*',[32] thus converting the human personality into a blind product of the development of material productive forces. 'First Marx admits the creative intervention of ideas, of human will and human purpose, and then he again pushes what is specifically human into the background by comparison with matter'.[33] Man, for Marx, appears 'as author of his own fate and at the same time as a materialistic marionette'.[34] Marx regards the development of production relations between people as a law-governed process, determined by development of material productive forces. Thus the activity of man, pertaining to the sphere of social regulation of the economy, is included in a unified process of social development that is subordinated to the law of causality. Stolzmann disagrees with both positions: first, it is not permissible to derive changes in social regulation (the production relations between people) from a 'dialectic of matter' (development of the material productive forces); and second, human actions, directed to social regulation of the economy, must be regarded as a manifestation of free moral will, autonomously setting its own rational purposes. 'The ethical moments constitute an independent, parallel cause (*Mitursache*), and *alongside* the purely economic they act with their own force. From a purely

---

26   Stolzmann 1909, p. 60.
27   Stolzmann 1909, p. 114.
28   Ibid.
29   Stolzmann 1909, p. 73.
30   Ibid.
31   Ibid.
32   Stolzmann 1909, p. 74.
33   Ibid.
34   Stolzmann 1909, p. 75.

genetic point of view, they are a manifestation of *one of the two* independent causal chains that from the very outset constitute social life; from the ethical-systematic point of view they are, in the "last instance", even solely responsible for the regulation of things. For Marx, to the contrary, they are dependent intermediate causes, and the last instance in development lies in material preconditions'.[35] Thus, from a genetic-causal point of view, social regulation acts as an independent causal chain together with the natural conditions of the economy; but from an ethical-systematic point of view, it even plays the decisive role and crowns the entire structure of the social economy as the purposeful and free ethical activity of man.

This is where the *second* level of Stolzmann's investigation begins. Up to now Stolzmann has counterposed the social to the natural, or social regulation of the economy to its matter. Now, as he puts it, we must ascend to a 'higher' level of investigation and show that the '*social*' simultaneously means the '*ethical*', that 'the essence of a national economy is founded on a social-ethical principle' consisting of two elements, the 'social' and the 'ethical'.[36] In this way, Stolzmann's 'social-organic' method becomes a 'social-organic-ethical' method.

Turning to analyse the '*ethical*' concept, Stolzmann, as when analysing the 'social' concept, begins with the 'lower' empirical, or causal, level of the investigation. He shows that ethical purposes and people's strivings find expression in a determinate type of social regulation of the economy, and thus they factually affect people's economic activity by way of social regulation. 'The setting of ethical goals is an independent cause of the historically emerged way of life and is significant as an objectively acting cause. Without this causally acting factor, national-economic life is inexplicable from both the historical and the systematic point of view'.[37] For this reason, the economist must investigate 'what ethic *is manifested* in the national economy of the past and of the present'.[38] 'Ethical factors, and "regulation" of the social-ethical system that is built upon them, namely, the entire legal and moral order', are one of several 'causal factors' that immanently characterise economic phenomena.[39] 'Social regulation is simply the expression or real sedimentation of ethical forces in their practical realisation. Ever since people first associated for life together, the ethical idea has

---

35   Ibid. 'Ethical moments', as we shall see below, mean social regulation, and 'purely economic' moments are identical to the natural.

36   Stolzmann 1909, p. 34.

37   Stolzmann 1909, p. 102.

38   Stolzmann 1909, p. 80.

39   Stolzmann 1909, p. 194.

existed and been active in the history of mankind. From the ethical-systematic point of view, the state and society have not grown up as wildflowers on the virgin soil of natural instincts; rather people have, since olden times and through an act of their will, imposed artificial constraints on what nature provides, on the primal material of wants and the striving for power – they have consciously or unconsciously subordinated them to the supremacy of some ethical ideal'.[40]

At the beginning of the comment we have just quoted, the ethical factor is regarded in its *causal* aspect, as a cause that acts alongside other causes; but by the end of the sentence the ethical factor, being created by an act of free human will, *escapes* from the world of causally conditioned phenomena. The ethical 'idea' stands opposed to empirical 'reality', which it must transform and spiritualise. In this way, Stolzmann turns from a causal investigation of social regulation, and of the ethical strivings that serve as its foundation, to an 'ethical method' of appraising all the phenomena of social regulation. The 'ethical', from being an *object* of causal study, is transformed into an ethical *method* for examining social phenomena. Now the ethical factor no longer 'marches modestly alongside all the other factors' but 'is recognised in principle as the fundamental factor'[41] of social regulation, as the motivating and moving principle of all social development. At the same time as this elevation of the ethical factor occurs, its very character also changes: from being a factor that *causally* acts on a par with others, it is transformed into the fundamental, sole and ultimate *purpose* of all social development, including that of the national economy. The latter is merely 'an instrument for the social-ethical and purposive principle',[42] and political economy is 'a science of the means for achieving ethical ends'.[43]

This investigative transition, from the *causal* method to the *teleological*, is explained by the unique character of the subject being studied, namely social regulation. The latter is a human creation, a matter of mankind's free, ethically directed will. 'The sphere of political economy is the moral work of man and of his moral freedom, which, it is true, is limited and conditioned by external nature and by the internal nature of human instincts; but within these limits, given by nature, it represents the most important, the greatest and most sacred possession that man may genuinely call his own, his participation in ongoing

---

40   Stolzmann 1909, pp. 68–9.
41   Stolzmann 1909, pp. 102–3.
42   Stolzmann 1909, p. 111.
43   Stolzmann 1909, pp. 111–12.

spiritual creativity'.[44] 'The national economy is humanly created social-ethical regulation, a positive spiritual creation that is continuously being perfected and created by legislation that mainly expresses one or another ethical ideal'.[45] Mankind's free action is simultaneously the moving and the changing element of social development. 'Unlike natural factors, which must be taken simply as given, and in that sense as constant, in the national economy the fundamental social-ethical forces create a universal *variable* element of *social* relations, which are established by people themselves and, because and insofar as they are a creation of the people, can also be altered by them'.[46]

Once social regulation is a creation of man's free, ethically oriented will, the method of causal investigation, even extended to the sphere of man's psychological experiences, is *inadequate* when applied to social regulation. 'Psychological causality' does not ascend to the 'spiritual in its highest expression – the spiritual as an idea in the sense of self-determination, in the sense of a *telos*' (purpose); it is 'insufficient for grounding moral free will'.[47] 'Although the idea can never appear in phenomena by itself, and "nature" is always the inevitable precondition for spiritual activity, it remains the case that the spiritual-ideal as such, despite all its conditioning by nature, is a separate and theoretically cognisable object that is distinguished not only by a unique psychological *causality* but also by its special *teleology* of an ethical and purposive principle, which is immanent and inaccessible to a purely natural investigation'.[48] In the realm of a science of spirit, 'the inadequate principle of causality must be replaced by the principle of purpose'.[49]

As we see, the counterposing of *natural* and *social* categories is transformed into the counterposing of the *causal* principle and the *teleological* principle. '*Natural* categories reside in 'nature' and are causes given to man from without; but when translated into the metaphysical-teleological sphere, they can also be regarded as the means to an end', and this end is not precisely known to people.

On the contrary, the *social* categories are *in the first place* purposive concepts that must be derived from human will, from the history that man

---

44   Stolzmann 1909, p. 110.
45   Stolzmann 1909, p. 111.
46   Stolzmann 1909, p. 79. Cf. Stolzmann 1896, p. 8. In his latest work, *Die Krisis in der heutigen Nationaloekonomie* (Stolzmann 1925b, p. 99), Stolzmann adds the reservation that the material content of the economy changes and develops. But the sphere of 'free' development, dictated by inherently ethical convictions, is only in the area of social regulation.
47   Stolzmann 1909, p. 50.
48   Stolzmann 1909, p. 80.
49   Stolzmann 1909, p. 157.

himself creates, from the 'category of freedom'. It is only when they are translated from the teleological to the causal sphere that they become, in the spiritual creation of social forms, independent intermediate causes that constrain the life of natural instincts within social purposes and make them serve the latter.[50]

Thus a synthesis of natural and social categories occurs in such manner that the former ascend beyond the kingdom of causality to the realm of teleology and are seen as the means for realising ethical ends; and the social categories descend for their implementation from the kingdom of teleology to the realm of causally conditioned phenomena, making the latter the means for realisation of the former. For this reason, a causal explanation of the phenomena of social regulation can only serve in a supplementary role, facilitating understanding of their teleological character.

The result of what has been said is that the national economy, when we study it in terms of its social regulation, must be regarded from the *teleological* point of view. 'The social category is the basis of the national economy; this category is founded in turn upon ethics; and therefore the national economy is an ethical purposive formation (*Zweckgebilde*)',[51] or 'an organisation of morally directed ends'.[52] From this comes the following definition of the tasks of economic science:

> The task of social economics consists of historically and systematically regarding the national economy as an ethical purposive formation, as a spiritual creation of the social ideal but one that is realised and embodied in the existing regulated matter of social life and expressed in distinct national economic institutions and phenomena.[53]

Stolzmann calls his teleological method 'social-organic-ethical' – 'social-organic' because it considers all phenomena of the national economy to be organically interconnected by the unity of the fundamental purpose of social regulation; and 'ethical' because this purpose, by its very nature, is ethical.

Summarising what has been said, we can see that Stolzmann's methodological investigation involves three stages. At the *first* stage our author counterposes the natural matter of the economy to its social form (social regulation).

---

50   Stolzmann 1909, p. 133.
51   Stolzmann 1909, p. 139.
52   Stolzmann 1909, p. 64.
53   Stolzmann 1909, p. 137.

His interest is in the antithesis of *natural* and *social* categories in the economy. At the *second* stage of the investigation, Stolzmann shows that social regulation is created by the mankind's free will and is directed to the realisation of certain ethical ideals and goals. The social category finds its basis in the *ethical* category, and in place of the aforementioned antithesis emerges a new antithesis of natural *necessity* and ethical *freedom*. Finally, at the *third* stage of the investigation, Stolzmann consequently comes to the conclusion that social regulation, as the sphere of freely realised ethical ends, can ultimately be explained in terms of *teleological*, not *causal*, moments. The social category becomes the teleological category; the antithesis between the two *aspects of the economy* (the natural-technical and the social) is replaced by the antithesis between two *methods* of investigation, the causal and the teleological.

The social category, the ethical category, the teleological category – Stolzmann's thought ascends these three stages in order to pass from the world of genuine economic reality to a world of abstract philosophical speculations. In reality, one must conclude that Stolzmann's thought moved in the opposite direction: he probably came to his study of the economy with a preconceived Kantian scheme that counterposes the world of causality to the world of teleology. In accordance with the ideas of the ethical school, which prevailed in German economic science during the latter half of the nineteenth century, Stolzmann came to a high appraisal of the role of ethical ideals and purposes as one of the causal series acting upon economic phenomena. Finally, under the influence of Rodbertus and to a lesser degree Marx, Stolzmann's thinking turned to a study of the social form of the economy. The total result, characteristic for Stolzmann, was the *social-ethical-teleological triad*.

We have followed the movement of Stolzmann's thought, which has ascended from study of the *social* categories of the economy, through the intermediate stage of investigating *ethical* categories, to the sphere of activity of *teleological categories*. In these three stages of Stolzmann's analysis, we can acknowledge scientific value only in the first. During an epoch in which German bourgeois economic science is dominated by the subjective-psychological method, Stolzmann, unafraid of swimming against the stream and remaining isolated, has raised his voice loudly in defence of the social method in economic science. He has never tired of preaching the need for study of the social form (social categories) of the economy, and he has provided a devastatingly critical analysis of the doctrine of the Austrian economists. This is Stolzmann's great and indisputable service.

In the first stage of his investigation, Stolzmann comes out decisively against a *naturalistic* study of the national economy, taken apart from any determinate *social form* of the latter; he sharply criticises the naturalistic objectivism

of the classics and of vulgar economists, as well as the naturalistic subjectivism of the Austrian school. In some places he comes close here to Marx and
– partly through [Marx's] direct influence and to some degree independently
of him – he arrives, in a whole series of partial questions, at formulations and
definitions that at times, especially from the outside, correspond perfectly with
Marx's point of view.

Stolzmann deserves particular credit for his stubborn reminders that not a
single economic phenomenon can be studied apart from a determinate social
regulation. One must not, in his words, study first the 'purely economic' or
natural-technical side of the economy and '*then* correct a one-sided and incorrectly constructed theory by subsequently adding influences issuing from the
relation of social forces. By then it would be too late, and it would be necessary to reconstruct everything anew. All that remains is to investigate matter
(*Stoff*) from the very outset in its social form (*Prägung*)'.[54] Once the subject
under study is not the technical but rather the social side of the economy, then
our attention is directed to the social relations of people. 'The national economy is not a system of equations of interdependent *quantities of products* but
an *organic* system of the interdependence of *social* relations'.[55] 'The science
of the national economy is above all a science of qualities, not of quantities'.[56]

Beginning with this general methodological principle, in his investigation
of a whole series of partial economic phenomena Stolzmann adopts a *formally* correct point of view, linking these phenomena with the social side of the
economy. Concerning value, he says that it is 'a structure of forms (*Formge-
bilde*) and not a structure of matter (*Stoffgebilde*)'.[57] He decisively rejects the
so-called 'national-economic' definition of capital as means of production that
have been made. 'Capital, "land" that furnishes land rent, or "labour", can be
understood only as social categories and not as purely technical factors of production'.[58] Stolzmann also converges with Marx when he notes the impossibility of studying the phenomena of production apart from the phenomena of
distribution. They must be investigated not 'one after the other, without any
organic connection, but *jointly*, as the connected parts of one and the same

---

54   Stolzmann 1925a, p. 70. Cf. Stolzmann 1915, pp. 203–4; 1925b, p. 135.
55   Stolzmann 1925a, p. 202.
56   Ibid.
57   Stolzmann 1925a, p. 218. As can be seen from Stolzmann's objections to Marx's theory of
      value (see below: 'Stolzmann as a Critic of Marx'), he is not aware of how much his defin-
      ition repeats – in a more confused fashion – the formulation given by Marx.
58   Stolzmann 1909, pp. 44–5.

organisation, associated by the unity of their higher purpose'.[59] These examples
show that in his initial methodological principles Stolzmann genuinely comes
close – mainly from the formal side – to the formulation of theoretical problems given by Marx.

However, even at this first stage of Stolzmann's study, which has to be
acknowledged as genuinely valuable, the weak sides of his constructions find
expression. One can say that Stolzmann persistently and tirelessly, with endless repetition on every page of his voluminous work, persuades the reader
to turn his view to the area where the most important economic problems
lie, in the area of the economy's social form. But when the reader, convinced
by Stolzmann's arguments, finally turns his eyes to the designated area, Stolzmann, instead of outlining for him a precise line or perspective of his study,
shows him only an enormous and indefinite circle of phenomena that he calls
'social regulation'. What the latter comprises, how it acts, what its source is, and
what laws govern the process of its change – to all of these questions Stolzmann
either gives no answer at all or, in passing and without any foundation, he gives
answers that point the investigation along a false road. Stolzmann is aware that
his 'social regulation' is akin to the concept of 'production relations' established
by Marx. At one point he even asserts that 'Marx just chose another name
for the same phenomenon'.[60] However, if we look more closely we find that
essentially there are more differences than similarities between these two concepts.

Even the very term 'regulation' unwittingly suggests legal regulation of relations between people that are consciously established by a specific social organ
with a specific purpose. Indeed, in the very concept of 'social regulation', as
we have seen, Stolzmann puts ethical-juridical and teleological moments in
the forefront. But much worse is the fact that Stolzmann erroneously understands the relation of this 'social regulation' to other aspects of the process of
social development. According to Marx's teaching, the sum total of the production relations between people, on the one hand, changes in dependence
on society's productive forces; and on the other hand, it forms the basis on
which grow up definite forms of legal regulation and social consciousness (the
legal and ideological superstructure). As for the latter question, that is, of the
relation between the production relations and their superstructure, Stolzmann
gives a formula that is the opposite of Marx's. He often says that social regulation of the economy is determined by 'the legal and moral system', that it is

---

59   Stolzmann 1909, p. 203. Cf. Stolzmann 1915, p. 197.
60   Stolzmann 1909, p. 540.

'founded upon ethics'. He does not develop this thought any more clearly or in any greater detail.[61] On the other hand, Stolzmann decisively parts ways with Marx on the first question, which concerns the relation between *the production relations of people and the productive forces* of society – or, in Stolzmann's terminology, between social categories (social regulation) and natural categories (economic matter). This is where the central point of disagreement lies between Stolzmann and Marxism, a disagreement that in the last analysis is based on the fact that Marx's sociological theory has a *monistic* character and Stolzmann's sociological theory has a *dualistic* one.

Marx regards the entire process of social development from a monistic point of view: people enter into 'definite relations, which are independent of their will, namely relations of production appropriate to a given stage in the development of their material forces of production'.[62] There is a close and indissoluble connection between the condition of society's material productive forces and the form of production relations. The productive forces do not belong to the sphere of nature, as opposed to society, but rather are 'social' and historically variable productive forces. On the other hand, the production relations of people do not belong to the sphere of purpose-fulfilling freedom in opposition to causal necessity; rather, the process of their establishment and change belongs entirely in the world of causally determined phenomena even though it occurs through the mediation of people's activities and their will.

Stolzmann decisively objects to the Marxist theory of dependence of the development of production relations between people upon development of the productive forces. He denies this theory not just because he thinks it contradicts the real facts but also because he knows that it is impossible in principle to derive social regulation, this conscious act of free human will, from a blind 'dialectic of matter'. This would be the equivalent of converting man from 'author of his fate' into a powerless 'materialistic marionette'.[63] Thus, in place of the Marxist theory of historical materialism, Stolzmann puts the aforementioned theory of an 'interaction' of social and natural categories as 'two independent causal chains'.[64] 'The ethical moments [social categories – *I.R.*] constitute an independent, parallel cause (*Mitursache*), and *alongside* the purely economic

---

61   This is true unless one refers to the observation, made in passing, that social regulation 'is
      created by the legislator on the basis of some prior ethical ideal', or that people, by an act
      of their will, have consciously or unconsciously subordinated their natural instincts to the
      rule of some ethical ideal, and so forth. See Stolzmann 1909, pp. 68–9; also 1925b, p. 75.
62   Marx 2010, p. 263.
63   Stolzmann 1909, p. 75.
64   Ibid.

[natural categories – *I.R.*] they act with their own force'.[65] Only the combination of these two causal series forms the social economy, and every economic phenomenon must be regarded as a result of them both. This is precisely what Stolzmann sees as the 'monism' of his theory, which, however, from our viewpoint can in no way be recognised as 'monistic', for the two series of phenomena that it joins together are of a deeply heterogeneous (differentiated) character. As we have seen above, Stolzmann associates the 'matter' of the economy with the principle of causality, and 'social regulation' with the principle of teleology. Consequently, the relation between 'matter' and 'regulation' includes within itself not only a link between two series of factors, both of which belong to the world of causally conditioned phenomena, but also something different: the relation between the world of causality and the sphere of teleology, between nature and ethical norms, between necessity and freedom of the will. Stolzmann begins his major work by saying that 'the question of whether the national economy is regarded as *a formation of nature* or *an ethical-purposive formation*' is 'only part of the great and fateful question' that asks: 'Is there causal connection and no freedom, or free self-determination and responsibility?'[66]

As we already know, in this case Stolzmann boldly makes his choice and takes as the starting point for an understanding of social life the principle of teleology and the free, morally directed will of man, which is expressed, among other ways, in the forms of social regulation of the economy that man himself creates. It is thus understandable that social regulation relates to the natural 'matter' of the economy not simply as one causal series of phenomena to another, which interacts with it, but also as the free creative activity of man that acts upon blind matter, as a world of ethical goals that realises and embodies itself through its own internal force in a world of inert matter. Therefore, while Stolzmann emphasises that social regulation without the matter of the economy is simply impossible, and that from the viewpoint of causality they are connected through 'interaction', from the 'ethical-systematic point of view' the decisive influence belongs to social regulation.[67] This is where we find the highest moving, formative and purposive principle of the economy.

Stolzmann considers his point of view to be 'organic' on the grounds that all phenomena of the economy are regarded as organically connected by a unity of purpose. But this organic unity endures only so long as we remain in the sphere of goals, or in the world of teleology. What we do not see is how

---

65   Ibid.
66   Stolzmann 1909, p. 3.
67   Stolzmann 1909, p. 75. See also p. 56.

the joining of teleology and causality occurs, how the world of goals is joined with the world of matter, or social categories with natural ones. In Stolzmann's system the connection between natural and social categories is not organic because of the heterogeneous character of the two types of categories. On the one hand, Stolzmann completely assigns social productive forces to the world of 'natural categories', or nature, thus merging the material-technical aspect of social production with its natural preconditions; on the other hand, he assigns social regulation to the world of teleology. The *material* process of production, accordingly, is deprived of all *social* attributes, and on the other hand, the *'social'* is identified with the *ethical-teleological*. In view of this fact, it is not surprising that the technical and social aspects of the economy turn out to be disconnected from each other, and the need for a synthesis of both, which Stolzmann continually emphasises, merely obscures all the more the dualistic character of his theory.[68] In fact, Stolzmann creates an unbridgeable gap between the spheres of natural and social categories: the former is ruled by nature, blind matter, immutable necessity and lifeless immobility; in the latter man prevails along with social reason, purpose and freedom, and historical variability. Purposive 'social regulation' is joined from without to the blind material-technical forces (nature, and man as part of nature); and the unity of both, created through the formative power of regulation, constitutes the economy. The material-technical forces only play a role as a boundary, or a limit that constrains rational social regulation, but within this limit the latter is the initiating and moving force.

Thus, to the Marxist formula of *historical materialism* (the social productive forces – the production relations of people – the juridical and ideological superstructure), Stolzmann counterposes an *idealistic* formula whose elements are arrayed in reverse order (the ethical and moral elements – social regulation – natural categories). With Marx, all three of the listed series of phenomena belong to the world of causally conditioned occurrences and particularly to the world of social phenomena. With Stolzmann they belong to different worlds: to the social world and to the world of nature, or – what for him corresponds to this division – to the sphere of teleology and to the sphere of causality. Marx gives us a formula of the *causal* connection of different sides of a single social process. Stolzmann gives us a formula for reconciliation of the greatest conceiv-

---

68   The degree to which these different elements are heterogeneous for Stolzmann can be seen from the following sentence, which is intended to underline their 'monistic' unification: 'The *natural-causal* elements must be seen as the matter, and the *ethical-teleological-social* elements as regulation; and the national economy as a whole must be seen as *monistic*, as "regulated matter"' (Stolzmann 1909, p. 458. My emphasis [*I.R.*]).

able discontinuity and dualism – the dualism between the world of *teleology* and the world of *causality*. Stolzmann understands a synthesis of social and natural categories to mean nothing other than a transition from what is to what must be, or realisation of the social ideal – this manifestation of the pure, spiritually free creativity of the moral will of man – in the matter of social life and in separate national economic institutions and phenomena.[69] Consequently, Stolzmann's scheme differs from Marx's not only in terms of the reverse order of its elements but also in terms of the different logical nature of the latter and the different methodological construction of the scheme itself.

Corresponding to the fundamental difference of the two schemes, their middle terms, which constitute the direct subject matter for the study of political economy (namely, the *'production relations'* for Marx, and *'social regulation'* for Stolzmann) also differ profoundly. Both Marx and Stolzmann summon us to a study of the 'social form' of the economy, but for [Marx] this form of the economy is the result of internal development of the social material process of production, whereas for [Stolzmann] it involves a force introduced from without, from the world of teleology, for purposive regulation of the blind matter of a technical process. With Marx the concept of 'production relations' is the connecting link between development of the productive forces, on the one hand, and legal and ideological phenomena on the other. With Stolzmann the concept of 'social regulation' sits at the junction of two worlds: the sphere of teleology and the sphere of causality. Intended to join the world of necessity and the world of freedom, it actually tears them apart with a dualism and becomes a two-faced Janus looking in different directions. A concept distinguished by such a dualistic causal-teleological character cannot be the basis for scientific investigation of a national economy.

We can now summarise. Stolzmann began by counterposing *natural* and *social* categories of the economy and ended by counterposing the categories of *'necessity'* and *'freedom'*. He invited us to a theoretical study of the social form of the economy, but he led us to the world of *teleology*, which excludes any strictly scientific investigation of phenomena. He began his work with a fruitful campaign against *naturalism* in economic science, but he ended with a reactionary campaign against a *purely causal* explanation of all social phenomena. He identified naturalism with causality and accused Ricardo and Marx, saying that 'both of them, in their naturalism, were unable to rise above the traditional view, according to which society and the national economy are a formation of nature (*Naturgebilde*), whose laws are similar to all other laws of nature and

---

69   See the quotation above concerning the tasks of economic science.

susceptible only to a causal investigation'.[70] By identifying the natural with the causal, and the social with the teleological, Stolzmann took a path that leads far away not just from Marxism but also from any strictly scientific and causal investigation of the phenomena of social life.

70　　Stolzmann 1909, p. 674.

CHAPTER 2

Stolzmann and the Theory of Labour Value

In the previous chapter we characterised Stolzmann's social-organic-ethical method, the main points of which are the following. The free, morally directed will of socially united people gives birth to ethical and legal views (*ethical categories*) subject to implementation in the practice of social life, especially in the form of national economic phenomena and institutions (social regulation or *social categories*). The latter regulate the 'matter' of the economy, or the technical activity of people, which at the same time also depends on the conditions of external nature and on the psycho-physiological needs of man (*natural categories*). Social regulation frames the matter of the economy, transforming it into 'regulated matter', or into a national economy as a synthesis of social and natural categories.

Stolzmann also builds his *economic* theory on the basis of these general *methodological* views. He is sharply critical of scholars who have confined themselves to a study of the natural-technical side of the economy and have attempted, for example, to explain the profit of capitalists by the technical productivity of the means of production belonging to them. Profit is a phenomenon of social regulation and is not of a technical order. It is not a portion of the product attributed to a technical factor of production, but rather the value attributed to a definite person, to the capitalist, as owner of this factor. Thus some specific magnitude of profit tells us nothing about the technical productivity of the means of production but only serves as an expression of the social fact that, on the basis of the given type of social regulation of the economy, a certain 'income' (profit) is paid to certain people (the capitalists) from the social product. Other forms of 'income' (wages and rent) are paid to other participants in production (the workers and landowners). But each of these participants in production receives his income in the form of the price or value of the factor or production belonging to him (labour power, land etc.). This means that, in order for some particular person to receive a certain income, the item belonging to him must have a corresponding value. The magnitude of the *value* of the products is determined by the magnitude of *incomes*. The value of the product must be exactly large enough to ensure a specific income to each production participant.

For Stolzmann, therefore, the links between social phenomena are drawn as follows. The given *ethical ideals* are implemented in practice in a given type of *social regulation*. To the given social regulation correspond certain *social*

© RICHARD B. DAY, 2024 | DOI:10.1163/9789004705661_013

positions of separate individuals and entire classes of society along with the magnitude of the compensation or *incomes* due to them. The magnitude of the incomes, in turn, determines the magnitude of the *value* of the products and of the factors (means) of production. Consequently, the theory of *value* must be built upon the basis of a theory of *incomes*, or of distribution.

The classics, Ricardo in particular, took the opposite route for explaining economic phenomena: they derived the incomes of various social classes from the value of the products, and the latter from labour expenditures – or in Stolzmann's view – from labour as a technical factor of production. They constructed the theory of value on a naturalistic rather than a social basis. However, if we look closely at their '*hypothesis of labour value*', then we shall see, in Stolzmann's terms, that it tacitly presupposes a certain form of social regulation of the economy and specific norms for distribution of the product between the participants in production. The theory of labour value cannot serve as the basis for an explanation of incomes, since it already presupposes a certain magnitude of incomes for members of the society. In other words, analysis of the theory of labour values must give us new evidence for the proposition that the magnitude of value of the products is determined by the magnitude of incomes, which, in turn, is ultimately explained by the given type of social regulation. It is precisely for this purpose that Stolzmann, calling himself an opponent of the theory of labour value,[1] thinks it necessary to provide a detailed critical analysis of that theory as it was formulated by the classics.

Stolzmann begins with a *critique* of how the classics posed the problem. The classics attributed operation of the law of labour value to some ancient historical period and an economy of primitive hunters. However, what interests us is not an historical question but rather the 'logical basis of the hypothesis' and its usefulness for analysis of the modern economy.[2] True, the classics understood that exchange is possible only within society, and thus the theory of value studies 'not the relation of producers to nature but exclusively the relation between producers as people'.[3] But, 'limited by the naturalistic and individualistic spirit of the time, they did not understand that the essence of labour must be derived from its organic functions within a *social system* bound together by social regulation'.[4] In their picture of a 'hypothetical society of labour', the classics committed two errors: first, they did not clarify for us the form of *social regulation* inherent in this society; and second, they did not even know how to analyse

---

1 Stolzmann 1909, p. 234.
2 Stolzmann 1909, p. 212.
3 Stolzmann 1909, p. 213. Cf. Stolzmann 1915, p. 148.
4 Stolzmann 1909, p. 213.

a 'hypothetical society of labour in its full *technical* interconnectedness and unity', founded upon an 'organic division and community of labour'.[5] Instead, they had in view 'random acts of exchange',[6] whereas 'the laws of exchange value manifest themselves only in the context of a *regular* division of labour'.[7] For this reason, Stolzmann considers it necessary to subject the classics' theory to 'revision in *both* respects, to supplement and develop it in terms of both the technical-psychological and also the social-organic aspect'.[8] What the revision leads to is that the 'primitive type of society', which played such an important role in the constructions of the classics, must be replaced by a 'social system' that is 'connected both technically, by the division of labour, and also by a defined social regulation'.[9] In other words, what must be taken as the starting point of a theory of value is a definite type of society, or a *'social system'*. Stolzmann attempts to set out such a hypothetical 'social system'.

'Let us imagine – he says – a small social union consisting of a group of ten individuals who have joined together to fulfil a single economic plan'.[10] This plan involves guaranteeing to each of these ten individuals specific consumer goods, the quality and quantity of which are determined, on the one hand, by the character of our individuals' needs and, on the other hand, by the fertility of the soil and the level of technique. Each of these ten individuals is occupied in preparing one sort of product, and the number of units of the given sort is also ten. The riches of nature are available in abundance and are equally accessible to all ten workers. Evidently each individual keeps for himself only one unit of the ten he prepares, and he must acquire nine of the other sorts of products he requires through exchange with the other producers. Thus we assume, on the one hand, that all the producers expend the same quantity of labour. On the other hand, each of them in the final analysis, and after the exchanges with the other nine producers, acquires exactly the same products as all other members of this society. And since the value of the product is determined by the quantity of other products received in exchange for it, it follows that the product of each producer's labour has exactly the same value as the product of the labour any other producer; in other words, 'the exchange value of a good is measured by the quantity of labour expended in preparing it'.[11] The labour hypothesis of

---

5   Ibid.
6   Ibid.
7   Stolzmann 1909, p. 215.
8   Stolzmann 1909, p. 214.
9   Stolzmann 1909, p. 215.
10   Ibid.
11   Ibid.

Smith and Ricardo is fully applicable to the society just described. And that is not surprising, for we have constructed our hypothetical society in advance in such a way that the law of labour value must emerge within it. The whole scientific interest of our hypothesis consists not in observing the fact that this law operates, but rather in an analysis and explanation of the reason why this occurs.[12] This analysis leads us to two conclusions, one negative and one positive. The negative conclusion is that the law of labour value does not operate in all societies; the positive conclusion explains the reason for operation of this law in the hypothetical society under discussion.[13]

Let us consider first, in technical-psychological terms, the process of production and distribution in the society we have described. Above all, according to Stolzmann, 'it is apparent that the good owes its exchange value not to labour expenditures as such'.[14] Labour expenditures serve only as the means for reaching a specific goal, namely, for receiving useful consumer goods. Utility is the 'ultimate measure of value', not just for an isolated economic individual but also for the labour community described.[15] Just as the separate individual in a natural economy apportions his labour for the purpose of best satisfying his needs, so the aggregate labour of our society is distributed according to a definite plan for the purpose of best satisfying the individual needs of the members.[16] It is only insofar as labour expenditure serves the acquisition of certain utilities that it acquires its own certain value. This fundamental proposition, which is developed in detail by the Austrian school, is also shared by Stolzmann. As distinct from the Austrian school, however, he does not consider it possible to give a precise numerical measure of the force of different needs and the corresponding utilities of products. For that reason Stolzmann suggests beginning the analysis of consumption not with the separate and incommensurable needs of man, but rather with the whole person of man as a consumer, or with the '*aggregate consumption of a person*'.[17] At a given stage of social development, a person requires a certain standard of living, a certain complex of consumer goods (in the broad sense of the word) that are necessary in order to meet his needs. Stolzmann suggests calling this complex of consumer goods a '*subsistence unit*' or a '*consumption unit*' (*Nahrungseinheit, Bedarfseinheit*). This

---

12   Stolzmann 1909, p. 216.
13   Stolzmann 1909, p. 217.
14   Ibid.
15   Stolzmann 1909, pp. 217 and 218.
16   Stolzmann 1909, p. 218.
17   Stolzmann 1909, p. 220. Cf. Stolzmann 1896, pp. 339–40; 1915, p. 151: 'Here, as everywhere else in science, the starting point of the study is man himself, the whole man'.

concept approximately corresponds to what we customarily call a 'budget set',[18] or a 'ration' in the broad sense of the word. The economic plan must ensure provision of a definite quantity of such composite 'consumption units' – not the totals of separate useful items that serve to satisfy separate needs, as the Austrian school suggests.[19]

Accordingly, the goal of the production process is a specific number of 'consumption units' or 'rations'. A certain number of 'labour units' is the means for achieving this end. As the value of any means is determined by the importance of the end it achieves, so labour expenditure has a definite value only by virtue of the fact that it is directed to preparation of useful consumption goods. However, this does not prevent us from making precisely these 'labour units' the measure of value for 'consumption units', whose composition in terms of goods may vary. The relative value of these various goods cannot be specified in view of the impossibility of providing a numerical measure of the diverse needs they satisfy. There remains only one way to measure the value of these consumption goods: it is specified according to the number of 'labour units' expended on production of these goods. But it would be a most serious error to take labour expenditures as the source of value. Value is created only through the organic connection of usefulness and costs, commensurate within a defined plan and bound together by the latter in an organically unified and purposive production process. 'It is only the economic plan that explains the *origin* of value .... Neither costs (in this case labour), nor evaluations of utility, are the original sources and determinants of value'.[20] Labour expenditures serve as a numerical indicator of the value of the products, but they are neither its basis nor its cause. They are merely 'the symptom of an equation between the levels of production and consumption, the expression of an established harmony in the economic plan', a 'symbol of value'.[21]

It is understandable, for this reason, that the *laws of value* have a different character depending on *differences in the economic plan*. The economic plan described above is distinguished by the fact that, thanks to the abundance of nature's riches, 'the satisfaction of needs depends, in the final analysis, only

---

18   [A 'budget set' or 'opportunity set' includes all possible consumption bundles that a person could afford given the prices of goods and the person's income level.]
19   Stolzmann 1909, p. 220. Cf. Stolzmann 1915, p. 151.
20   Stolzmann 1909, p. 224.
21   Stolzmann 1909, p. 226. Cf. Stolzmann 1915, pp. 152–3: 'The labour unit and the unit of consumption, as simple reflections of one and the same higher unity, namely, the unity of the consuming and toiling person, are decisive concepts upon which, in our type (of society), the definition of value is based'.

on the available quantity of labour', and thus 'the value of the goods is technically attributed only to labour'.[22] At the same time, the social regulation of the economy provides that consumption goods 'go to' or are only received by *direct participants in production* – and, since their labour expenditure is equal – in absolutely *identical measure*. The product of the labour of each producer has exactly the value that secures for him receipt of the same 'consumption unit' as goes to every other member. *Distribution* here is subject in advance to *social regulation*, and the *value* of products is established according to these socially regulated norms of distribution. Value is the *'medium of distribution'*, a means for securing to each member of society an income or 'honorarium' due to him on the basis of the given socially regulated economy for fulfilling his social functions within it. Thus, with a change in the social regulation of the economy, value also inevitably changes, even with unchanged technical conditions of production. Assume, for example, that the entire technical production plan that we described above remains unchanged, but one part of the producers, on the basis of the property they possess or their personal skills, occupies a socially privileged position and must receive a greater share of the national product. It is clear that in this case the product of each of the producers mentioned above will no longer have exactly the value of a 'consumption unit'. The consequence of a change in the social norms of distribution will also be a change in values, which serve as the 'medium of distribution'.[23]

Accordingly, in our hypothetical society the valuation of products according to labour expenditures, and their equal distribution between the producers, is the consequence of a definite social regulation of the economy and not merely of the 'nature of things' or of the natural-technical process of production. The depicted community of equals is by no means a product of the 'nature of things'; in certain circumstances it may even require stricter 'regulatory enforcement' than a society founded upon the inequality of its members,[24] for in the absence of corresponding social regulation, equality between the members of society can vanish very quickly. All one has to do is suppose that certain members of the society accumulate and begin to use a greater quantity of means of production than the others, and thus they make their labour more productive. In that case, 'equal masses of labour will already have unequal exchange values, and the integrity of the law of labour expenditures will be disrupted: the value of goods will be determined by the quantity of labour expended on production of the last units of the product that are still required for

---

22   Stolzmann 1909, pp. 218–19.
23   Stolzmann 1909, p. 228.
24   Stolzmann 1909, p. 229.

the complete satisfaction of needs'.[25] In other words, value will be regulated by socially necessary and not by individual labour; the more productive workers will begin to receive additional income, and the equal supply of all producers with means of consumption will vanish. To prevent such disruption of the law of labour value would require recourse to social-regulatory measures in order artificially to preserve the living standard of all members of society at the same level. The mediaeval guilds, for instance, resorted to such measures.[26]

Thus, the law of value begins and continues to act only in the presence of a *definite social regulation of production and distribution*. The 'symmetry' between the value of products and labour expenditures occurs due to the special 'fortuitous' conditions of the hypothesis we have constructed; namely, in the first place, a '*technical* fortuity consisting of the fact that labour is the only scarce and thus technically essential element of production; and secondly, a *social* fortuity consisting of the fact that only "workers" are recognised as participants in distribution'.[27] In sum, Stolzmann finds that the 'almost trivial truth', which is hidden in the theory of labour value and has served as the subject of investigation for more than a hundred years, consists of the following:

> *If* there existed a national economy that was 'regulated' (or more accurately, *could be* regulated) in such manner that only labour and only workers were taken into account in the production and distribution of the product, then value would be determined by labour expenditures, and this would be due to the simple truth that value, as the medium of distribution, would only have to serve the function of adjusting utilities to labour expenditures.[28]

From this also follows the reverse conclusion that in any society with different forms of social regulation of the economy (particularly in a capitalist society), the law of labour value turns out to be completely inoperative.

Such is the rationale of the 'hypothesis of labour value' that we find in Stolzmann. It is easy to see that in reality Stolzmann's reasoning does not substantiate but rather destroys the theory of labour value as the theory that must explain the mechanism of a commodity-capitalist economy. Stolzmann correctly suggests that in analysing the phenomena of value we must begin not with the technical side of production but with its *social form*. He justifiably sees

---

25   Ibid.
26   Stolzmann 1909, p. 230.
27   Stolzmann 1909, p. 233.
28   Ibid.

one of the fundamental mistakes of the classics in the fact that they ignored the latter. But Stolzmann makes a decisive mistake when he turns to the question of precisely what social form of economy ascribes the form of value to the products of labour. He wants to show us a society in which the law of labour value appears in its purest form, but in fact he describes the kind of society in which there is no value at all, that is, in which the products of labour do not have the form of value.

While Marx regarded the law of labour value as the law of an *unorganised* society of commodity producers, Stolzmann converts it into the law of an *organised* socialist community.

It is not difficult to persuade oneself that the hypothetical society described by Stolzmann, comprising ten people, is essentially nothing but a small *socialist community* with a planned organisation of the production and distribution of the products of labour. As we have seen above, the ten individuals are 'joined together to fulfil *a single economic plan*'.[29] This plan amounts to securing for the group a specific quantity of consumer goods or 'consumption units'. This means production is organised according to plan for purposes of consumption. Labour is consciously distributed between individuals in advance, and each has his own work. Each member of society knows what products the others are producing and recognises that he is producing as a member of a single production collective. Not only production but also distribution is organised in advance. Each member knows in advance what complex of consumer goods he will receive from the others. Essentially there is no 'exchange' here, only the mutual transfer of products from one to the other according to a common plan established in advance and recognised by all. If one of the producers gives nine units of product A, which he makes, and receives one unit each of nine different products B, C, D etc., then it would be strange to speak here of 'exchange', of 'exchange proportions' or of the 'exchange value' of these products. Even if these producers formally 'exchange' products, this 'exchange' does not establish a social connection between them but only realises a connection established in advance. Thus the 'exchange proportions' or 'value' of the products play no role here as regulator of production and distribution.

Indeed, let us assume that one member of society is dissatisfied with the established 'proportions of exchange'; in other words, he finds the 'ration' that he receives inadequate. In that case, as Stolzmann indicates, all he can do is threaten to leave the membership of the commune. But he cannot move from one type of labour to another that is more rewarding, since all types of labour

---

29   Stolzmann 1909, p. 215.

are allocated by plan between all members of society. If he arbitrarily moves from production of product A to production of product B, ten units of which are already being produced by another member of the group, it will be of no benefit to him since he will no doubt be boycotted by his comrades, who will properly regard him as a violator and disorganiser of the general economic plan. Equilibrium in the distribution of labour, which in a commodity-capitalist society is disrupted and restored on a daily basis, is here always fully achieved, with the exception, of course, of instances of wilful disruption by separate individuals. The actual 'exchange proportions' of products always correspond here exactly to the normal exchange proportions. Completely absent are the deviations of price from value that in a commodity society direct the outflow and inflow of labour in one branch or another. The result is that 'value' does not here play the role of *regulator of production*, since the latter is already consciously regulated and organised in advance. Nor does it play the role of *regulator of distribution*, for the latter is also consciously regulated. It is not because a given individual receives a certain quantity of consumer goods that the product he produces has a certain value; rather the opposite is true, and his product is assigned precisely the value that would allow the producer to receive a 'ration' or income that is established in advance. The share of a participant in distribution does not depend on the value of his products; on the contrary, the latter is established at a level that corresponds to the participant's share in distribution that is fixed beforehand. Value, accordingly, is not the *regulator* of production and distribution but the 'means' or '*medium*' of a distribution that is precisely fixed in advance in the form of a goal or task to be fulfilled. The link between the phenomena of value and distribution is not of a *causal* but rather of a *teleological* character. The whole of economic life is organised for achievement of a certain *goal*, and that goal is the equal *distribution* of products between members of society, while the means for achieving the goal is fixation of the comparative 'value' of the different products. Value, therefore, as with all other economic concepts, belongs to the realm of purpose-fulfilling, teleological categories.

It is obvious that Stolzmann, with his 'justification' of the theory of labour value, has not only failed to develop or make corrections to the theory of the classics but has taken a step backwards compared to them. Whatever the mistakes committed by the classics, they nevertheless, and especially in Ricardo's case, constructed a theory of value in order better to understand the phenomena of a real commodity-capitalist economy. Fixing their attention primarily upon the material aspect of economic phenomena, they saw in the latter the results of a 'natural order' and not of specific social conditions. But having clarified precisely what social structure of the economy gives things the form of 'value', 'capital', etc., they also found these forms to be present even for primitive hunters, for Robinson Crusoe and so on. Yet despite all the naïveté of such ideas, the classics still preserved in their constructions the basic outlines of a commodity-capitalist economy: they presupposed the absence of any planned social organisation of production, the presence of autonomous commodity producers striving to receive the highest possible exchange value – not use value – the deviation of market prices from value, and the resulting flow of labour and capital from some branches into others. In the system of the classics these preconditions are in part tacitly assumed, in part expressed in passing. Instead of further developing these preconditions noted in the classics, as Marx did, and instead of constructing a theory of value based on analysis of the social form of commodity economy, Stolzmann chose another route. Adopting the completely correct idea that value must be explained from the social form of the economy, Stolzmann sketches a hypothetical economy whose social structure is the opposite of the structure of a commodity economy and in fact excludes 'value' as well as the other categories of commodity economy (money, price, socially necessary labour,[30] and so forth).

Despite his expectations, Stolzmann by no means succeeded in uncovering a healthy theoretical nucleus that lies at the foundation of the 'hypothesis of labour value' and remained unknown to its authors, Smith and Ricardo. We can agree with Stolzmann in his criticism of the 'naturalistic' conceptions of the classics. And we also have to agree with Stolzmann's opinion that the basis of the law of labour value is a definite type of social regulation of the economy. On this point Stolzmann repeats the basic positions of Marx. But when the question arises as to the precise type of social regulation of the economy to which the law of value corresponds, a fundamental difference can be found between Marx and Stolzmann. For Marx, the law of labour value is an expression of the *unorganised production relations* of a society of commodity producers. Stolzmann sees in it an expression of the *organised social regulation* of a

---

30   It is characteristic that the appearance of differences in the individual expenditures of different people on production of one and the same product (due to differences in the instruments of labour), and the resulting evaluation of products according to average, socially necessary labour, is regarded by Stolzmann as a violation of the principle of labour value. Precisely where, from Marx's viewpoint, the concept of social or 'market value' (as distinct from individual value or individual labour expenditures) appears, the law of labour value is violated from Stolzmann's point of view. Conversely, where according to Stolzmann 'labour value' appears in the most pure form, Marx sees the complete disappearance of value as the social form of products of labour.

socialist community.[31] Stolzmann is inclined to understand social regulation of the economy as an economy consciously organised according to plan.

This error on Stolzmann's part is by no means fortuitous. It is closely connected with the peculiarities of his *teleological* method. The social economy is seen by Stolzmann as a teleological unity, with social regulation being consciously established through a free act of human will for the realisation of certain ethical ideals. Influenced by his teleological method, Stolzmann is inclined to exaggerate the element of organisation and planning in social regulation of the economy. Only in a planned socialist economy can Stolzmann find broad scope for the activity of his teleological categories; it is only there that the value of products (more correctly, the evaluation consciously established by social organs) genuinely appears in the role of 'medium of distribution', that is, as the means for delivering to production participants definite incomes that are fixed in advance.

As we can see, the analysis that Stolzmann gives of the idea of *labour value* is closely tied to his social-organic or teleological *method*. On the other hand, this analysis serves Stolzmann as a suitable bridge to his further studies relating to a *capitalist* economy. It is true that Stolzmann himself more than once notes the fundamental difference in principle between an unorganised capitalist economy and an organised socialist economy. Nevertheless, he persists in applying to the former the teleological categories that operate in the latter. In particular, as we shall see in the following chapter, he also attempts to find in a capitalist economy confirmation of his ideas concerning the role of value as 'medium of distribution'.

---

31   On this point it is interesting to compare Stolzmann's doctrine with the teaching of Oppenheimer. They both assert that the phenomena of a capitalist society cannot be understood on the basis of the theory of labour value. On the one hand, they both recognise the relative validity of this theory given a certain precondition. For Stolzmann, such precondition is social regulation of the economy in a socialist community; for Oppenheimer, the absolute equality of all producers. Stolzmann acknowledges the sphere of action of the law of labour value in a socialist community; and Oppenheimer does so in a 'society of equals'. With all of the opposition between their conceptions, both of these authors converge in their ignorance of the law of labour value's importance as the expression of the production relations between commodity producers.

CHAPTER 3

Stolzmann's Theory of Value and Distribution

As we have seen, Stolzmann considers the theory of labour value to be unsuitable for explaining a *capitalist* economy. 'The hypothesis of labour value' presupposes a definite type of social regulation, namely, a society consisting exclusively of direct workers. To such a type of social regulation corresponds a certain order of distribution that guarantees to all producers specific 'consumption units' or 'rations' proportional to their labour participation in production. To realise this order of distribution, the products of labour are assigned a value proportional to the quantity of labour expended upon them – a 'labour value'.

The sole conclusion that can be derived from the 'hypothesis of labour value' is that '*regulation, distribution and value* are a logically closed chain, the links of which are mutually conditioned. Distribution can be understood only as a purposeful function of regulation, and value, in turn, only as a functional-organic medium of distribution'.[1] We must also apply this conclusion to study of a capitalist economy. *Social regulation* of the latter is based upon 'free labour and inviolability of the right of property in capital and land',[2] in other words, on the presence of three social classes: workers, capitalists and landowners. And since the norms of distribution must guarantee the best fulfilment by individual actors of their social (technical and moral) functions,[3] representatives of all three of these classes must receive a specific 'socially necessary' *income* or compensation (*Abfindung*) in the form of wages, profit and rent.[4] It follows from this that the *value* of a product in capitalist society must be sufficient simultaneously to assure the three aforementioned types of incomes to the members of society; it represents only a 'numerical expression of the shares'[5] due to these three classes of society.

The magnitude of the *value* of products is determined by the magnitude of the *incomes* of the separate classes of society; and consequently the theory of value must be studied after, and on the basis of, the theory of distribution. Ricardo's mistake lay in the fact that he took the reverse route and wanted to derive incomes from the value of the product. In this case he had

---

1   Stolzmann 1909, p. 356. My italics [*I.R.*]. Cf. Stolzmann 1915, p. 197.
2   Ibid. See also pp. 335, 344, 763 et seq.
3   Stolzmann 1909, p. 353.
4   Stolzmann 1909, p. 356.
5   Ibid. Cf. pp. 764, 773 et seq.

© RICHARD B. DAY, 2024 | DOI:10.1163/9789004705661_014

to overcome an enormous difficulty in the fact that 'the *value* of products is determined exclusively by labour expenditures while *three* classes participate in *distribution*'.[6] To eliminate this difficulty, Ricardo first of all excluded rent from the product's value.[7] The value of the product (grain) is determined by natural factors, namely, by labour expenditures on the worst parcel of land that is still required in order to satisfy society's need for grain. The breakdown of this value into wages and profit is likewise subordinate to natural laws. To be precise, the physical minimum of means of existence for workers and the technical productivity of labour on the worst parcel of land are what determine the wage as a 'natural' magnitude (i.e. a magnitude determined by natural factors). Profit, as the excess of one 'natural' magnitude (the value of the product) over another (wages, as the value of means of existence for the worker), is not fixed in advance and varies according to changes in the indicated magnitudes – in particular, inversely to the change of wages.[8]

Ricardo's whole conception, according to which *incomes* are determined by *value*, and the latter by a natural factor – the productivity of the *last* expenditure of labour or capital – has its starting point in the presence of the *worst* parcel of land (among those being cultivated) as the 'theoretical microcosm that dictates its laws of value to the entire economic world'.[9] But the point is that in capitalist society there is no organ that would determine in advance the total needs of members of society and would, on that basis, decide which of the worst parcels of land must still be taken into cultivation.[10] 'This worst parcel is not something given *a priori*, and thus it cannot at all serve as a means of theoretical explanation'.[11] The worst of the cultivated parcels will be the precisely the one that can still provide a capitalist with the customary profit beyond the recovery of wages (and constant capital). 'It is only the level of wages and the profit on capital that determine precisely which parcel, providing at least these types of revenues, can still be taken under cultivation'.[12] The boundary between the natural productivity of the last of the cultivated parcels and the first of the uncultivated ones depends on purely social factors, namely, on the magnitude of incomes (wages and profits), which must also be taken for that reason as the starting point of the investigation.

---

6   Stolzmann 1909, p. 357.
7   Stolzmann 1909, p. 358.
8   Stolzmann 1909, pp. 360–1.
9   Stolzmann 1909, p. 359.
10   Stolzmann 1909, p. 366 et seq.
11   Stolzmann 1909, p. 382.
12   Ibid. Cf. Stolzmann 1896, pp. 357–8, 363; Stolzmann 1915, p. 180.

In Ricardo's theory, however, there is a very valuable feature in the fact that he determines the *'marginal'* or 'minimal' magnitude in relation to which others, which exceed this sum, yield a 'differential' surplus. But Ricardo begins with 'marginal' natural magnitudes, namely with the productivity of the marginal or last expenditure of labour and capital. Instead, Stolzmann suggests taking as the starting point the last (i.e. the least productive) worker and the last capitalist, in other words, the 'determinate income'[13] (*Grenzabfindung*) of the least competitive worker and capitalist as a *purely social magnitude*.

Let us first consider *wages*. In order that workers might exist and fulfil their socially necessary functions, the *least competitive* (i.e. least productive) must still receive a determinate *'marginal income'* or the *'socially necessary minimum'*[14] income. The need for such a precisely fixed minimum wage was also recognised by the classics, but they mistakenly saw it as the 'result of natural preconditions' and not as a 'variable socially necessary income'.[15] In fact the magnitude of the minimum wage depends on the moral and cultural level of workers and especially on the degree of their organisation as a social force.[16] The question is one of a 'socially necessary', not a 'physical', minimum. The wage of the 'last' worker cannot for long fall below this socially necessary minimum, nor can it for long rise above it,[17] for the mutual competition of the capitalists compels them to strive for the greatest possible reduction in the costs of production, including wages.[18] It is obvious that the more productive workers receive a wage above the socially necessary minimum, an additional or differential income, whose explanation involves no difficulties once a specific 'minimum' wage is established.

If the classics recognised the presence of a precisely fixed minimum wage, they treated *profit* in a completely different manner. True, Ricardo showed that profit cannot fall below a certain minimum since otherwise the capitalists will cease to invest their capital in production. But he did not recognise any *maximum* for profit. This was his fundamental error. Profit, as with wages, represents a *'socially necessary'* magnitude that is fixed in advance.

> Capital must deliver a high enough percentage of profit to secure for the smallest capitalist entrepreneur – that is, the one who is least competit-

---

13   Stolzmann 1909, p. 390.
14   Stolzmann 1909, p. 395.
15   Stolzmann 1909, p. 404.
16   Stolzmann 1909, p. 407.
17   Stolzmann 1909, pp. 399–400.
18   Stolzmann 1909, pp. 401–2.

ive given the existing conditions of property and production, and whose production is still necessary in order to supply society – with the standard of living that is customary at a given time for the given social group (*zeit- und standesgemässe Lebenshaltung*).[19]

Just as the magnitude of wages is determined by the social subsistence minimum of the last worker, so the magnitude of profit is determined by *the social subsistence minimum of the last entrepreneur-capitalist*, i.e. the one with the least – and thus with the least productive – capital.[20]

Profit cannot for long fall *below* this socially necessary minimum, for otherwise the last capitalist will not be able to fulfil his socially necessary functions.[21] But profit for the last or 'smallest'[22] capitalist cannot rise for long *above* this minimum because such a rise in profit would call forth an influx of new people and new capital into the given production. The new people will be recruited from the ranks of workers who will establish small labour enterprises: once production is sufficiently profitable so that even the very smallest entrepreneur receives a profit in excess of the minimum amount, then it is completely probable that a new petty proprietor from among the workers, even though he will work with 'fewer means and primitive tools',[23] will still, through hard work, receive the income sufficient for a modest life. Moreover, the profitability of the given production will also call forth new capitals. The sum of capitals in a country, despite the opinion of the classics, not only does not represent a precisely fixed magnitude of 'accumulated goods'[24] but, in general, can arbitrarily expand and contract depending on the need for capital. In the case of need, capitals 'grow up as if from under the ground'.[25] As a result of the influx of new capitals, profit will again fall to the socially necessary minimum. What has been said applies to the 'last' capitalist. But if, let us say, the rate of profit is established at 10 %, then it is clear that the owners of larger capitals are receiv-

---

19   Stolzmann 1909, p. 416. Cf. Stolzmann 1896, pp. 370, 384; Stolzmann 1915, p. 186.
20   It is obvious that for a capitalist this subsistence minimum is different from that of a worker. Stolzmann distinguishes the 'consumption unit (ration) of the worker' from 'the consumption unit (ration) of the capitalist'. The relation between them is determined in the first place by the relation of social forces between the two classes.
21   Stolzmann 1909, p. 422.
22   Stolzmann considers him to be the entrepreneur with the least capital, which is, however, sufficient to ensure that its owner might live exclusively on the profit from capital without resorting to a supplementary income from personal labour. Stolzmann 1909, p. 422.
23   Stolzmann 1909, p. 396.
24   Stolzmann 1909, p. 397.
25   Stolzmann 1909, pp. 399, 415.

ing revenues in the form of profits that exceed the subsistence minimum they require. This profit is of a differential character and does not require any special explanation.

We have arrived at the conclusion that both wages and profits, with a given *social regulation* (which also includes *the relation of social forces* between different classes) are of a magnitude that is fixed in advance with complete precision. Every factor of production (labour, capital) has in advance a specific evaluation or value, the magnitude of which is determined by the fact that the owner of this factor, with the given type of social regulation, must invariably receive a specific income. The sum of 'socially necessary' *wages* and 'socially necessary' *profits* (i.e. the costs of production for a product produced with participation of the least productive worker and the very 'smallest' capitalist) constitutes the *value* of the product. 'Profits and wages determine value'.[26] 'Rent does not belong among the costs of production' that determine the price or value of the product. The landowner receives rent only on condition that the individual costs of production (wages and profit) for a given product are lower than its value. Rent is always a surplus that remains after covering the 'initial shares', i.e. wages and profits.[27]

If the value of the product consists of the sum of wages and profits, then Ricardo is mistaken in the assertion that a rise in wages inevitably calls forth a corresponding decline of profits and *vice versa*.[28]

It follows from what has been said that 'it is not the rate of natural productivity but rather the law of socially necessary incomes (*Abfindungen*)' that determines the whole movement of an economy.[29] 'The given socially necessary and targeted magnitudes of income must be recognised as the final and decisive elements of a national economy'.[30] These 'teleologically given and purposively fixed magnitudes' (*Zweck-fixa*) of incomes must be taken as the starting point of the investigation.[31] Only they permit an understanding of value, which represents 'nothing but the scale of compensation for separate individuals and entire groups of people', or the 'medium of distribution' and the means for securing to each production participant the share of income due to him on the basis of the

---

26   Stolzmann 1909, pp. 383, 478–9.
27   Stolzmann 1909, pp. 381, 478–9.
28   Stolzmann 1909, p. 430.
29   Stolzmann 1909, p. 401. Stolzmann recognises that the 'natural' productivity of labour limits social regulation (because, obviously, it is not possible to distribute more products than are produced), but he does not show the direct influence on value and incomes.
30   Stolzmann 1909, p. 764.
31   Stolzmann 1909, p. 773.

given social regulation.[32] Value and incomes are bound together as means and end; they are essentially 'purposive formations and not the results of a causal connection' between phenomena.[33] A 'purely social' theory of value and distribution, constructed on the basis of the social-organic method, shows that it is not 'cause' and 'effect' but 'end' and 'means' that are the decisive, theoretical-cognitive categories of the national economy. 'Causality is the natural-born servant of teleology, a means within the limits of purposive knowledge'.[34]

Such, in fundamental and simplified terms, is Stolzmann's theory of value and distribution. The conclusions that he has arrived at, on the basis of applying his social-organic method to study of the capitalist economy, appear to us to be extremely barren and unsatisfactory. Stolzmann's economic theory leads to the following propositions: 1) The *value* of a product is determined by the *incomes* of the participants in production; 2) *Rent* is excluded from the list of incomes that determine value; 3) Wages and profits are magnitudes fixed in advance, and the fixing of both occurs on the basis of *one and the same principle* of guaranteeing the socially necessary subsistence minimum to the '*last*' worker and the '*last*' capitalist.

As for the first proposition, here Stolzmann perpetuates the old theories that entered into the so-called 'second version' of Adam Smith. As we know, in Smith we encounter two versions of the theory of value: sometimes he takes the value of the product as a given sum, and incomes (wages, profit and rent) as the parts into which it breaks down; and sometimes he begins with incomes as the original magnitudes, given at the outset, the sum of which constitutes value as a derived magnitude. From Smith's first version came the theory of labour value; from the second version, the theory of costs of production. Stolzmann essentially adheres to the second version (which he meanwhile sharply criticises[35]), but he introduces into it a change in principle. From the viewpoint of the theory of costs of production, costs are regarded as the prices or value of the separate factors of production (labour power, the use of capital and the use of land). Thus the value of the product is derived from the value of the factors of production. Stolzmann avoids this vicious circle by converting costs of production into 'anticipated income', or the 'teleologically anticipated value of items of consumption'[36] that are due to specific individuals as owners of the different factors of production. The problem of value rests upon the question

---

32   Stolzmann 1925a, pp. 210, 218. Cf. Stolzmann 1915, p. 154.
33   Stolzmann 1909, p. 773.
34   Stolzmann 1909, p. 774.
35   Stolzmann 1896, p. 50.
36   Stolzmann 1909, p. 764; 1925a, p. 219.

of incomes, and since the magnitude of incomes is determined by the relation of social forces of the different classes of society,[37] the whole problem of value, in Stolzmann's opinion, acquires a purely social character.

With his doctrine concerning incomes, Stolzmann has introduced little that is new into the theory of rent and wages. Basically he accepted Ricardo's teaching that rent does not enter into the list of production costs that determine the price of the product. As for wages, Ricardo also took them to be a precisely fixed sum determined by the minimum means of existence. Stolzmann correctly replaces a 'physical minimum' with a so-called 'cultural minimum', and he forcefully underlines the importance of the social power and organisation of workers as a factor facilitating a rise in wages.[38] There is nothing new in any of this. The new and original contribution from Stolzmann consists of his doctrine concerning *profit*. With a precise *fixing of profit*, Stolzmann wants to overcome one of the main difficulties in the theory of costs of production, which could not in any way explain the magnitude of profit since the latter does not enter into production costs but rather represents a surplus that remains after they are covered. But Stolzmann pays an extraordinarily high price to overcome this difficulty, namely, elimination of the specific social features that characterise capitalist profit as a special form of income. Stolzmann does nothing less than equate profit with wages. Such ignoring of the social nature of different types of incomes is especially inexcusable for one who supports the social method. Instead of investigating the characteristic peculiarities of capitalist profits, Stolzmann attempted to find their explanation in the idea of 'subsistence', which is characteristic for handicraft production, or in the idea of the 'subsistence minimum' of a hired worker. The idea that the social function of *profit* consists of securing the *subsistence minimum* to the capitalist entrepreneur (even to the 'smallest'[39]) sharply contradicts the nature and tendencies of a

---

37 Stolzmann 1915, p. 182.

38 True to his 'ethical' method, he also makes the magnitude of wages dependent upon how the other members of society relate to the worker, whether they fulfil, as they would to a neighbour, the injunctions of ethics and religion and so forth.

39 Recall that the small entrepreneur, investing in the effort his small capital and his personal labour, does not enter, according to Stolzmann, into the class of capitalists. Even the very 'smallest' capitalist lives only on the profit from capital. Ignoring this is one of the weak points of Böhm-Bawerk's criticism directed at Stolzmann (see his *Capital and Interest*, Vol. I, Russian edition, 1909, p. 608 et seq.). Böhm-Bawerk was also mistaken when he claimed that Stolzmann also applies to the explanation of a capitalist economy the law of labour costs with certain modifications (1909, p. 599). It must be added, however, that Böhm-Bawerk only had access to an earlier work by Stolzmann, *Die soziale Kategorie in der Volkswirtschaftslehre* (1896).

capitalist economy. There is thus no surprise in the fact that Stolzmann's theory of profit, even in its summary and basic outlines, is not free of contradictions and inadmissible exaggerations.

First of all, Stolzmann must prove that profit cannot for long remain *above* the subsistence minimum of the 'last' or the very 'smallest' entrepreneur-capitalist. He builds his argument on two assertions, the audacity of which does not correspond to the author's fluent argumentation. The first assertion says that if the profit of the last capitalist rises above the 'socially necessary minimum', and if the capitalist does not agree to share the surplus income with the workers, the latter will prefer to establish their own small enterprises. There is no need to expatiate on the point that, in the conditions of developed capitalism, such an assumption of the possibility for workers to organise their own production 'bare-handedly' (and not, as Stolzmann gently puts it, with 'fewer means and primitive tools') cannot be justified. When Böhm-Bawerk expresses similar assumptions concerning the possibility of workers beginning 'instant production' (without the aid of the instruments of labour), Stolzmann himself spitefully ridicules them as 'curious'. Stolzmann's second assertion is just as incorrect, that a rise of profit above the subsistence minimum of the last capitalist will call forth a bountiful influx of new capitals that will appear as if 'from under the ground'.

Let us assume, however, that Stolzmann has succeeded in overcoming our first difficulty and in proving that profit is really determined by the subsistence minimum of the last capitalist. But here the fundamental and decisive question emerges: just what capitalist (or group of capitalists) is the 'last'? Profit can be considered as fixed in advance only on condition that the last capitalist (which we always understand to mean the 'last' group or the stratum of capitalists with the least capital) was previously fixed. Such a condition would prevail if some central social organ, on the basis of Stolzmann's favourite 'social regulation', decided earlier that of the given population of the country, say 1,000 persons, 900 will fulfil the functions of workers and 100 the functions of capitalists. If the 'last' 10 of these capitalists each had a capital of 10,000 roubles, and if a 'decent level of existence' for the given group of 'small' capitalists required an income of 1,000 roubles per year, then profit would be established at the level of 10%. If each of the last capitalists had a capital of 20,000 roubles, then – with such a subsistence minimum of 1,000 roubles – profit would be established at the level of 5%. Fixing the group of 'last' capitalists would have the effect of fixing profit. But, as we know, in capitalist society no such fixing of the 'last' capitalists exists. On the contrary, the process of capitalist competition, thanks to the introduction of technical improvements and the cheapening of commodities, gradually severs one stratum of the 'last' or the 'small' capitalists after another from the capitalist class and throws them into the camp of wage workers (employees, salespeople, trustees and so forth) or of intermediate social groups. This phenomenon is so typical for capitalism that Stolzmann himself considers it necessary to note this squeezing out of 'small' capitalists as a 'result of well-known factors, especially as a result of the technical superiority of large enterprises'.[40] But if, by reducing the value and lowering the prices of commodities, growth of the social productive forces (in the form of growth of technically progressive large-scale production) destroys small capitalists and moves a different group of capitalists, possessing larger capitals, into the role of 'last' capitalists (whose subsistence minimum, in Stolzmann's opinion, determines the general level of profit)[41] – can one say that the value of commodities is established at exactly the level that guarantees the subsistence minimum of the 'last' capitalist? Obviously, to speak that way would mean distorting the causal linkage of the phenomena. It is not the subsistence minimum of the 'last' capitalists that determines the magnitude of the value of products; rather, changes in the value of products, conditioned by the development of labour productivity, determine which group of capitalists still proves to be competitive and will play the role of the 'last'. The movement of the incomes of different social classes cannot, accordingly, be understood without a preliminary investigation of the laws of change in the value of commodities (including labour power).

It appears that Stolzmann vaguely sensed that on this point his theory of profit risked striking a reef. He had reason for including in his formula of profit determination the observation that the 'last' capitalist is the one who is least competitive and 'whose production is still needed for supplying the society'.[42] He explains the squeezing out of 'small' capitalists by the fact that, with the introduction of technical improvements, their production is no longer needed by society. As we have already seen, however, this transfer of capitalists from the ranks of those who are 'needed' to those who are 'redundant' can only be understood as the result of a development of labour productivity and of a change in the value of products. If Stolzmann reproached Ricardo with the fact that the divide between the natural productivity of the last cultivated parcel of land and the first uncultivated one is determined by social factors (the average profit rate), then we can reproach Stolzmann by noting that his 'purely social' frontier between the 'last' active capitalist and the first to be squeezed out is determined by development of the productive forces. Apart from investigating

---

40   Stolzmann 1909, p. 417. Cf. Stolzmann 1896, pp. 391–2.
41   Stolzmann himself recognizes this. See Stolzmann 1909, p. 417.
42   Stolzmann 1909, p. 416.

the latter process, it is not possible to construct a theory of value; and without a theory of value, it is not possible to construct a theory of incomes. The fixed reference point that Stolzmann ostensibly found in the person of the 'last capitalist' turns out to be nothing more than the low point of a wave that rises and recedes in the turbulent flow of economic life.

Thus profit, as the income corresponding to the subsistence minimum of the 'last' capitalist, is not fixed in advance independently of the development of labour productivity and the value of commodities – for the simple reason that the 'last' capitalist is not fixed in advance, independently of the very same conditions. But let us suppose that Stolzmann has also overcome this *second* difficulty. Let the 'last' capitalist be known to us. But then what is the meaning of 'socially necessary' with respect to his *minimum income*? Does it mean, as we have all along assumed, and as seems to follow directly from Stolzmann's own words,[43] a 'subsistence minimum' in the narrow sense of a sum of certain *consumer items* (even if ample in number, including certain luxury items and so forth)? But, insofar as we are speaking of developed capitalism, it is obvious that a group of 'last' capitalists, whose profit only covers the needs of personal consumption, cannot possibly be competitive or, at best, will soon lose their competitive ability. This group of capitalists can preserve their competitive ability only provided that the profit they receive is sufficient not merely for satisfying the personal needs of members but also for expansion of production within the minimal limits conditioned by the level of capitalism's development. A portion of the profit, beyond the part consumed, must necessarily be accumulated. But if the concept of the 'socially necessary minimum' profit is extended to include the necessary *minimum accumulation*, the question then arises as to how the latter is determined. The minimum accumulation obviously changes along with changes in the productive forces and the value of products. But the 'socially necessary minimum' profit thereby turns from a sum fixed in advance, independently of production conditions, into a consequence of the latter. Stolzmann does all of his calculations in the governor's absence, ignoring the process of development of the productive forces: the latter avenge themselves and often become an obstacle in his way, stubbornly demanding to be included in the theoretical calculations.

The failure of Stolzmann's theory of profit simultaneously means failure of his entire theory of value and distribution. For, as we have seen, it is only by fixing the magnitude of profit, independently of the condition of labour pro-

---

43 'The customary level of existence at a given time for a given social group (zeit- und standesgemässe Lebenshaltung)'. Stolzmann 1909, p. 416.

ductivity, that Stolzmann can possibly regard incomes as original and fixed magnitudes, with value as a magnitude derived from them. Stolzmann's representation of the theoretical nature of value as the means for realising a certain goal, namely, for guaranteeing predetermined and fixed incomes to production participants, is appropriate for the socialist community that he portrays in his 'hypothesis of labour value'.[44] From there Stolzmann illegitimately carried over the concept of purposive social regulation to a capitalist economy. Determination of 'value', or the valuation of products, is not done consciously in the latter with the goal of guaranteeing definite incomes to production participants. On the contrary, the magnitude of the incomes received by the latter depends on the value of products, of labour power and of the means of production, all being spontaneously established in the process of market competition depending on the condition of labour productivity. For capitalist society, a theory of incomes can only be constructed on the basis of a theory of value.

What we have said does not mean that in a capitalist economy the incomes of production participants represent an unknown magnitude that fluctuates within indeterminate limits. With a given labour productivity, and a given value of the products and of labour power, the magnitude of incomes (wages and profits) represents a determinate magnitude. So long as the same conditions of production prevail, participants in the latter continue to receive incomes within the prevailing limits. They count in advance upon receiving the given incomes, anticipating them and refusing to take part in a production process that does not promise to provide them with an income at least within the customary limits. A definite magnitude of income, resulting from the social process of production, becomes both the precondition for every separate process of production and the subjective goal of those people participating in it. Accordingly, so long as unchanging conditions of production prevail, it is possible with equal justification to say either that the 'price of the commodity is divided into wages, profit (interest) and rent' or that 'wages, profit (interest) and rent are the constituents of the value or rather of the price'.[45] But it must be remembered that only the first proposition is theoretically correct and shows us the real, objective connection of the different economic phenomena. The second proposition is suitable only for practical purposes and proves to be practically correct only so long as the conditions of production

---

44 We leave aside here the circumstance that the 'price' of products in such a community, by its social-economic nature, would differ markedly from the 'value' of products in a commodity society. On this point see the previous chapter.

45 Marx 1972, p. 518.

remain unchanged.[46] Their change is inevitably accompanied by changes in the measure of incomes going both to separate individuals and to social classes; the preliminary calculations of separate individuals are thwarted; and in all its severe reality the dependence of the incomes of production participants upon the changing value of commodities becomes manifest, being determined in the last analysis by the development of labour productivity.

Stolzmann's economic theory essentially repeats the fundamental errors of his social-organic method. We saw above how Stolzmann transformed the scheme of objective linkage between social phenomena: *development of the productive forces – production relations* between people – *legal and ethical* phenomena. Essentially he rejected the first link of this series and took the other two in reverse order, having converted the production relations between people (or 'social regulation') into a means for realising ethical ends. On the one hand, the 'social' was detached from development of the social productive forces; on the other, it was made identical with the ethical-teleological. The causal connection between phenomena was transformed into a teleological one.

Stolzmann performs approximately the same operation with the scheme expressing the objective linkage between economic phenomena: *the productivity of labour – the value* of commodities – *the incomes* of production participants. He rejects the first link and takes the other two in reverse order, converting the value of commodities into a means for realising definite ends, specifically, into a means for guaranteeing to production participants incomes that are fixed in advance. He takes the objective result of production (incomes) as the end, and the objective precondition of this result (value), as the means. The causal connection between phenomena is inverted and interpreted to be teleological.

But for Stolzmann this is still not sufficient. The connection between social phenomena must be not merely teleological but also *ethical*. The 'value' of commodities must serve as the means for realising the ethical end of guaranteeing the income of production participants. But is it possible to prove the ethical necessity for establishing profit at a level of 10% rather than 50%? It turns out that this is possible if we presuppose that a profit of only 10% can 'feed' the very last, 'poor' capitalist. There is no need for the fact that the capitalist system routinely refuses to fulfil the ethical mission of feeding the small capitalists and mercilessly ejects them from the positions they occupy. These, apparently, are merely minor shortcomings that do not disrupt the ethical-teleological character of the entire capitalist system. To the latter is attributed

---

46   Marx 1972, pp. 517–18.

the idea of 'subsistence' adopted from handicraft production; the rabid and wasteful competition of capitalism is replaced by the ideas of price regulation by guilds for the purpose of guaranteeing a 'subsistence' level of existence to all production participants; the antagonism of class interests is denied (since a rise of wages does not entail a fall of profits) – and on this basis Stolzmann invites the capitalists not to oppose social reforms, particularly the growth of wages. The theoretical system ends in an ethical sermon in which we see a new triumph of the teleological principle: the theoretical presuppositions are chosen, as if deliberately, to lead to the ethical conclusions. But the theoretical value of Stolzmann's system suffers greatly from this fact, and it proves incapable of explaining the objective causal connection between the phenomena of a real capitalist economy.

Stolzmann as A Critic of Marx

In the preceding chapters we have considered Stolzmann's *positive doctrine* in its general methodological and also its economic aspects. But Stolzmann is interesting not only because of his attempt to construct his own scientific theory but also because of his attacks on other economic theories. The *critical* part of Stolzmann's work is extremely prominent in terms of its volume and its quality. Stolzmann comes to each of his own positive conclusions by way of severe polemical struggles with other economic schools. He always gives his own account 'through confrontations' – with the classics, the Austrian school and Marx alternating as his principal opponents.

We have more than once encountered Stolzmann's critical objections to the 'naturalism' of the *classics* in the area of method, in the 'hypothesis of labour value', and finally in the theory of distribution. Along with criticism of the naturalistic objectivism of the classics, Stolzmann criticises even more sharply the naturalistic subjectivism of the *Austrian* school. This part of his work can be acknowledged as the most brilliant and forceful. In the first chapter we observed that the most valuable part of Stolzmann's work comes at the first level of his analysis, where he persistently shows the need to investigate an economy's social form. In relation to precisely this initial and fundamental position of the social method, the Austrian school is most offensive with its 'economic subject' who is isolated from society and social relations. It is no wonder that Stolzmann aims his most crushing blows in this direction. In his criticism of the Austrian school, Stolzmann always moves within the circle of problems that arise at the first level of his analysis. Because of this fact, the weak and negative sides of Stolzmann's further constructions (the teleological and ethical point of view) are least reflected in this part of his work, and that is greatly to its credit.

In the interest of economy of space, we shall not be recounting here Stolzmann's critical objections to the Austrian school – objections that generally and on the whole correspond to those set out against Austrian economists by representatives from the Marxist camp. But that means we must spend all the more effort on Stolzmann's criticisms aimed at *Marxism*. Besides his separate critical objections scattered in the text, Stolzmann devotes to Marx's theory of value, as to the theory of the Austrian school, a special critical section (approximately 150 pages of his book *Der Zweck in der Volkswirtschaft*), which we must analyse. If, in the preceding chapters, we have given a characterisation

© RICHARD B. DAY, 2024 | DOI:10.1163/9789004705661_015

of Stolzmann from the viewpoint of Marxism, now we must acquaint ourselves with Stolzmann's characterisation of Marxism and assess its validity.

Stolzmann's critical work is interesting not just because it comes from such a major and original thinker, not simply because the author's starting points are sometimes very close to Marx's viewpoint, nor, finally, because he studies Marx with the greatest attention, often debating Marx's theories in the course of his own investigations. Stolzmann's work is interesting above all because of the unique critical position from which he proceeds when he opens fire, so to speak, on Marx's economic theory.

Marx's unique method, which examines economic phenomena as social phenomena, has remained completely incomprehensible to most of his critics. For this reason, their criticism totally misses the mark and does not strike the real Marx but rather an imaginary Marx. Stolzmann not only understands the sociological character of the Marxist method of investigation but is also himself an ardent advocate of the 'social-organic method' in political economy. He sharply criticises traditional political economy, which limits itself to study of the 'natural' (material-technical) categories of the economy while ignoring its 'social' categories. Stolzmann recognises that Marx came closer than anyone else to a correct understanding of the social categories of the economy. And if he criticises Marx, it is precisely because the latter supposedly did not apply the social method with total consistency and remained, in his theory of value, under the influence of naturalistic prejudices. If the majority of Marx's critics have not ascended to the height of his 'sociological' method, Stolzmann claims to surpass Marx with his own 'social-organic' method.

To evaluate Stolzmann's criticism correctly, it should first of all be noted that even though he, like Marx, considers it necessary to study the social form of the economy ('social regulation' in his terminology), Stolzmann understands it to mean something completely different from what Marx means. For Marx, a given social form of the economy (the production relations between people) is the necessary consequence of a definite development of society's material productive forces. Stolzmann, on the other hand, sees in it the result of a creative act of a free, morally oriented human will.[1] The latter, guided by one or another ethical ideal, strives to realise these ideals by consciously establishing a specific 'social regulation' of the economy, thus transforming the blind matter (i.e. the material-technical side) of the economy into a socially regulated economy. A given 'social regulation' of the economy must therefore be regarded as a means to realise certain ethical ends; i.e. it should be regarded

---

1   For more detail on this point see the first chapter of this work.

from the ethical-teleological point of view. And since Marx subjects the social form of the economy (the production relations between people) to a purely causal investigation, seeing the ultimate cause of its changes in development of the material productive forces of society, Stolzmann is inclined to see in this a return to the 'naturalism' that he [Marx] so despised. Identifying the social with the ethical-teleological, Stolzmann transforms his struggle against naturalism in political economy into a campaign against the purely causal investigation of social phenomena.

As distinct from other critics, Stolzmann aims not to uncover this or that individual error or contradiction in the doctrines he studies, but to criticise 'the basic views of the great systems of value'.[2] The system of labour value was created by the classics (Smith and Ricardo) and borrowed from them by the socialists (Marx and Rodbertus) with the aim of 'defeating the bourgeoisie with its own weapons'.[3] The classics did not apply the theory of labour value with sufficient consistency and did not draw socialist conclusions from it. 'It is different with the socialists. They say that if the value of *all* goods must be traced to labour, then both the profit on capital *and* ground rents represent "surplus value" or a deduction from the labour product – this is robbery, and property is theft'.[4] 'Such logic would be devastating if its foundation, the theory of labour value, were true'.[5] But the latter shares the fault of all theories that derive the value of a product from its costs of production. It is based on the 'false impression that along with the genetic-causal origin of products from the means of production, the *value* of the former [i.e. of the products] is also created together *with the latter and through their assistance*'.[6] But 'value is not at all produced like a piece of linen'. 'It is not value that is created but only its physical bearer, the material thing. It is precisely the confusion of material and value production that has generated most of the errors in our science'.[7] It is especially astonishing that this confusion of concepts should have been taken over by Marx, who rightly called fetishism the doctrine that regards the commodity as a sensual thing with extra-sensual properties. 'It is difficult to understand how Marx, "who first discerned" this fetishistic character, erects an altar to "labour" – which, in its technical-production function, is also just a natural category – as a "sensual thing", turning it into the greatest and only fetish'.[8]

---

2 Stolzmann 1909, p. 528.
3 Stolzmann 1909, p. 529.
4 Stolzmann 1909, p. 531.
5 Ibid.
6 Ibid.
7 Stolzmann 1909, pp. 531–2.
8 Stolzmann 1909, p. 533.

With his *doctrine of value*, according to Stolzmann, Marx contradicts his entire *theory of distribution*, in which he demonstrates how absurd it is to derive the three forms of income (wages, profit and rent) from the three natural factors of production (labour, the means of production and land). These forms of income express the social or production relations between people that characterise a definite social form of the economy. But if these *incomes*, which together comprise the total value of all products, result from social regulation of the economy, then it is this, and not labour, that must also explain the *value* of the product as the sum of these incomes. Marx recognises that

> the three factors of production are essentially things (or forces) of nature, and that the value people pay for them in the form of their prices is a remuneration whose character and amount derives not from nature but from the historically given 'regulation', i.e. from *distribution*. From this Marx should have drawn the only correct conclusion – that value and the function of distribution coincide, since they are *both* the consequence of a higher unity, the unity of the social organisation, and that therefore the 'total sum',[9] the value of the entire product, is *homogeneous* (the same in kind) with the 'partial sums'[10] [i.e. the incomes – *I.R.*], and that the value of the entire product and the value of these parts are *both of a social character*. But Marx avoids this conclusion by basing the value of the total product, of the entire sum, on a purely economic[11] foundation, on labour as a natural thing, while he defines the value of the partial sums from a *social* perspective – in other words, he dissolves a natural magnitude into *heterogeneous* (different), namely social, magnitudes. If Marx legitimately reproaches the vulgar economists for deriving a *social result*, namely, the three types of income, from natural agents of production, for his own part he resorts to dismembering a whole into heterogeneous parts.[12]

We have provided this long quotation because it spells out the central point of Stolzmann's criticism, which sees a deep contradiction between Marx's 'social' theory of distribution and his 'natural' theory of value. 'The socialist labour theory stopped half-way: it correctly understood the social-organic origin of

---

9   [*die 'Gesamtlinie'*]
10   [*mit den 'Teillinien'*]
11   By the term 'purely economic' Stolzmann consistently means the natural-technical aspect
      of economic phenomena as distinct from the social.
12   Stolzmann 1909, p. 536.

incomes, but in the theory of *value* it was limited to the purely economic side'.[13] After formulating this basic contradiction of Marxist theory, Stolzmann turns to proving his assertion concerning the 'natural' character of the Marxist theory of value.

It did not escape Stolzmann's attention that Marx understands value to mean not the material thing but rather its *exchange* value; and the labour he has in mind is not concrete, useful labour but rather *social abstract* labour. 'From the concept of the value of goods Marx excluded the last "atom of use value", and with it the last vestige of purely economic categories, drawing the bold conclusion that goods retain *only one property*, namely, the property of being *the products of labour*; and in the further course of his thought he attempts to strip the good, in its form as a product of *labour*, of its purely economic, natural ("useful") character'.[14] Thus, labour itself is reduced to social, abstract labour. It would seem that both value and labour appear in Marx's teaching as 'social' categories, deprived of 'all trace of purely economic categories'. However, Stolzmann manages to discover in them remnants of '*naturalism*'. It is true, he says, that Marx attributes to labour a 'social' character, but '*this* concept of the social does not coincide with the concept of a truly social category':[15] it suffers from the original sin of not completely eliminating naturalism.

Let us consider, therefore, the sense in which Marx uses the concept '*social*'. It turns out [according to Stolzmann] that we find in Marx *three* forms, or three 'stages', of the concept 'social'.[16] The first two 'stages' are found in the theory of *value*, the third in the theory of *distribution*. To illustrate the first two 'stages', Stolzmann quotes the following well-known words of Marx:

> ... the labour of the individual producer acquires a *twofold social* character. On the one hand, it must, as a definite useful kind of labour, satisfy a definite social need, and thus maintain its position as an element of the total labour, as a branch of the *social division of labour*, which originally sprang up spontaneously. On the other hand, it can satisfy the manifold needs of the individual producer himself only in so far as every particular kind of useful private labour *can be exchanged* with, i.e. counts as the equal of, every other kind of useful private labour.[17]

---

13 Stolzmann 1909, p. 539.
14 Stolzmann 1909, p. 537.
15 Stolzmann 1909, p. 539.
16 Ibid.
17 Marx 1976, p. 166.

This equality consists of reducing them both to 'abstract human labour'. In this passage Marx has in view the difference between concrete (useful) and abstract labour, from which it turns out that labour, in both of its forms, has a '*social*' character. The 'social' character of *concrete* labour means it is included in the system of social division of labour. The 'social' character of *abstract* labour consists of the equalisation of all types of labour by the act of exchange of their products.

Marx uses the concept 'social' in a *third* sense in his theory of *distribution*, when he speaks of 'social relations of production', 'a social formation' and 'historically determined production relations' between capitalists, workers and landowners.[18] Here, Marx actually has in mind a 'purely social concept' that is connected with determinate social regulation, i.e. with a given historical form of economy. But that cannot be said about the first two meanings of the concept 'social', which we encounter in his theory of value. The first concept 'social' [the social character of concrete labour] has nothing in common with a social category because the connection between different kinds of labour in a naturally emerged system of the social division of labour represents a purely technical fact.[19] Here, the concept 'social' illegitimately obscures a *purely natural* category. As for the second concept 'social', which characterises abstract, socially necessary labour that constitutes value, it is sort of mid-way between the first purely natural and the third purely social concept, and it contains a patchwork (*mixtum compositum*) of *natural and social* moments.[20] To prove this assertion, Stolzmann turns to an analysis of *the labour that creates value*.

'What is meant by the *socially necessary* labour that in Marx's opinion creates value?'[21] It means that 'labour is applied according to its average productivity, according to the "principle of the least means" and for satisfaction of the most important needs'.[22] What is involved here is a proper technical application of labour, 'purely natural expediency and the question of the technical division of labour', 'natural but not social necessity'.[23] This characterisation of labour as socially necessary[24] has no relation to the 'current social formation'.

18   Stolzmann 1909, p. 540.
19   Stolzmann 1909, p. 541.
20   Ibid.
21   Ibid.
22   Stolzmann 1909, p. 542.
23   Ibid.
24   Stolzmann does not clearly distinguish between socially necessary and abstract labour. Elsewhere, he confuses the different characteristics of labour as abstract, socially necessary and simple (see 1925a, pp. 105, 113).

In exactly the same way, the characterisation of labour as *abstract* or uniform does not imply any indicators that would point to a determinate social formation of the economy. 'This concept [of abstract labour – *I.R.*], if it is to make any sense, can only represent an aggregate concept, and it is incomprehensible how the summation of a million individual, concrete, natural labour expenditures can generate from itself the higher concept of the "social" working day; "useful" labour, that is, labour creating use values, does not lose its natural character even within the "social" division and combination of labour, which on its own simply signifies the technical interaction of natural elements of labour power'.[25]

Marx portrayed some sort of non-existent 'abstract' society of equal commodity producers, in which commodities are valued according to non-existent abstract labour. But, instead of contrasting this ideal or hypothetically postulated society with an actually existing capitalist society, he takes it for the reality and transfers his fabricated construct of labour value directly to the phenomena of a capitalist economy.[26] It is understandable that between this construct and the real phenomena a sharp contradiction should develop, since commodities are not sold in capitalist society according to labour value. Marx tries to eliminate this contradiction by pointing out that the sum of labour values of all products coincides with the sum of their prices of production.[27]

In his criticism of Marx's theory of prices of production, Stolzmann repeats in most cases the well-known arguments from Böhm-Bawerk and partially from Sombart: 'It is not the national product that exchanges for the national product, but rather individuals exchange individual products between themselves'. The theory of value must study 'exchange relations between concrete individual products'.[28] The latter are exchanged one for the other according to prices of production, and there is no need to search behind those prices for some hidden labour value. The transformation of labour value into prices of production, proposed by Marx, has never occurred in reality, as Sombart has shown.[29] Marx's indication that such transformation occurs by force of competition is not convincing because competition, as Marx himself recognises, always acts only within certain limits or boundaries, and the task of the researcher is precisely to find the inner law determining those limits.[30] In general and on the

---

25   Stolzmann 1909, p. 571. [Stolzmann claimed that 'abstract labour' is simply a 'product of the imagination'. See Stolzmann 1909, p. 543.]

26   Stolzmann 1909, pp. 543, 544.

27   Stolzmann 1909, p. 544.

28   Stolzmann 1909, p. 545.

29   Stolzmann 1909, pp. 550–1.

30   Stolzmann 1909, p. 550.

whole, Marx's efforts have not been able to eliminate the glaring contradiction between volumes I and III of *Capital*. 'It has rightly been said that publication of volume III of *Capital* amounts to suicide. Henceforth, Marx's theory of value hardly involves anything more than a pathological interest. We should, therefore, let the dead rest in peace'.[31] After burying the Marxist theory so easily, Stolzmann explains its sad fate by saying that it attempted to impose upon real phenomena an invented abstract theory instead of realistically examining the actual value of products as a result of the social regulation that characterises capitalist society.[32]

Stolzmann explains the incorrectness of Marxist economic theory by the mistaken *philosophical* and *sociological* views that underlie it. Marx's general starting point, according to which 'value and all the economic phenomena connected with it are by their essential nature social facts', is absolutely correct.[33] 'Marx was correct when he used the objectivist method, but he was mistaken in its application'.[34] He was perfectly correct to take 'society' as the starting point for his investigations, but he constructed a false concept of society in which he mixed up 'genuinely social and purely economic elements'.[35] He took the foundation of social development to be development of the productive forces – a purely technical fact that, in Stolzmann's opinion, creates only the 'possibility' for determinate social phenomena.[36] This possibility only becomes reality when a definite 'social regulation', as the conscious, purposive, constructive activity of men, is added to the fact of technical development of the productive forces.[37] Marx converts this 'social regulation' from a social-ethical 'purposive formation' into a spontaneous mechanical result of blind 'matter', of development of the productive forces, a result that emerges behind people's backs and is therefore totally incomprehensible.[38] Social life is transformed into some kind of 'hieroglyph'. Some kind of hidden, secret causes are active behind the real phenomena: the abstract society of equal commodity producers, abstract labour, the aggregate capital, and so forth.[39] As a result, the Marxist concept of 'society' (of the 'production relations' or 'social regulation') suffers from the following fundamental defects: on the one hand, it has not been freed from

---

31 Stolzmann 1909, p. 555.
32 Stolzmann 1909, p. 562.
33 Stolzmann 1909, p. 564.
34 Stolzmann 1909, p. 566.
35 Ibid.
36 Stolzmann 1909, pp. 567, 595.
37 Stolzmann 1909, pp. 595, 596, 606.
38 Stolzmann 1909, p. 574.
39 Stolzmann 1909, pp. 566, 614.

elements of naturalism; on the other, it has an unreal, invented and 'abstract' character. Indeed, Marx's many unreal and fantastic constructions can only be understood if we assume that they are based upon a scrupulously concealed 'ethical' tendency that he denies: the striving for a just social system, and a violent protest against the inequality prevalent in capitalist society.[40]

For example, the concept of 'equal' and 'abstract' labour expresses nothing but the striving for a just social equality. The concept of 'simple' labour was constructed by Marx with the goal of obscuring the deep differences between various types of labour and between the different strata of the proletariat in order to contrast the latter all the more sharply, as a whole, with the class of capitalists.[41] The concept of 'productive' labour amounts to denial of the useful role of the organisational labour of the entrepreneurs.[42] The 'ethical' categories that Marx banished from his economic system stealthily creep back into it in the form of theoretical categories. Marx would have done better if he had directly and openly posed the 'ethical' problem of the reconstruction of society. Then he would have seen, in Stolzmann's opinion, that introducing social reforms within the framework of the capitalist economy is a better way of removing its evils than the realisation of socialism.

From the whole complex of critical arguments that Stolzmann directs against Marx's economic doctrine, we must leave aside those of a partial character that require no special analysis and refutation by Marxists. These include: 1) arguments based upon an obviously *incorrect understanding* and sometimes on a direct misunderstanding of Marx; 2) claims that Marx replaced the theoretical study of phenomena with their *ethical* appraisal; and 3) arguments that simply repeat those advanced previously by other critics of Marxism, in particular by Böhm-Bawerk.

Stolzmann, unfortunately, did not escape the usual fate of the opponents of Marxism, in whose critical arsenal we can find arguments based on a simple lack of understanding of Marx. For example, inclusion of Marx in the same group as the utopian socialists, who deduced from the theory of labour value the right of workers to the full product of their labour, cannot be regarded as anything other than a misunderstanding. As an example of arguments of the second kind, we can mention the opinion that Marx put forth the theory of the reduction of skilled labour to simple labour in order to represent the entire working class as a homogeneous, undifferentiated mass. This opinion requires no rebuttal: it is perfectly obvious that a theoretical economist, regardless of

---

40   Stolzmann 1909, p. 577.
41   Stolzmann 1909, pp. 580–1.
42   Stolzmann 1909, p. 627.

his own positive or negative attitude towards the actually occurring process either of differentiation or levelling of the different strata of the working class, can and must begin his theoretical analysis with the fact of the equalisation of various types of labour that are distinguished by their different qualifications.[43] Finally, we include in the third group Stolzmann's critical objections to the Marxist theory of the prices of production, which repeat Böhm-Bawerk's well-known conclusions and have already been appraised in the Marxist literature.[44]

Leaving aside these groups of arguments, we can deal with Stolzmann's fundamental and central argument that is most characteristic of him. As we have already mentioned, Stolzmann's critique is interesting for us insofar as it is based on the author's unique 'social-organic' viewpoint and thus differs in principle from the critical arguments of other opponents of Marxism. The latter usually ignore the sociological method that Marx applies to the study of economic phenomena. Stolzmann not only acknowledges Marx's great service in this respect but also himself emphatically follows a 'social-organic' method, ruthlessly and thoroughly exposing all remnants of naturalism in political economy in both of their forms – the material-technical and also the subjective-psychological. Being a zealous supporter of the 'social-organic' method, Stolzmann reproaches Marx for not having applied it with sufficient consistency, especially in the theory of value. The uniqueness of Stolzmann's critical position lies precisely here, and it deserves the attention of Marxists.

Stolzmann ultimately traces the errors of Marx's economic theory to the fallacies of his sociological constructions. That Stolzmann should take such an attitude towards Marx's sociological theory is not surprising. In reality, Marx's 'sociological' method, which is aimed at a purely causal investigation of social phenomena, is profoundly different from Stolzmann's teleological 'social-organic' method, which identifies naturalism with causality and accuses Ricardo and Marx of naturalism because they confined themselves to a causal analysis of economic phenomena. Once Stolzmann takes causality to be naturalism, he quite readily finds traces of this 'naturalism' also in Marx, whose entire effort was aimed at revealing causal conformity to law in the changes

---

43   Even the theorists of the Austrian school, who have frequently reproached both the classical economists and Marx for inadmissible 'simplification' of the problem of skilled labour, are obliged in their analysis to turn to the same method of simplification. 'In the theory of a simple economy we can omit all these obstacles (delaying the passage between types of labour with different skills – *I.R.*) and adopt the idealised condition of full equalisation.' (Wieser 1914, p. 187).

44   See Rudolf Hilferding, *Böhm-Bawerk's Criticism of Marx*, 1904 [republished in Böhm-Bawerk 1949, pp. 119–95.]

of social phenomena. For Marx, a given type of production relations between people is not the manifestation of a free spiritual creativity, expressing the moral will of men, but rather the necessary, causally conditioned result of a determinate condition of society's productive forces. Marx's efforts to establish a close connection between the condition of society's productive forces and the corresponding social form of the economy provoke reproaches of 'naturalism' from Stolzmann.

Stolzmann knows very well that Marx always takes the object of his investigation to be the 'social' or 'public' form of the economy. But, he says, it is only in his theory of distribution that Marx really uses the concept 'social' in a purely social sense, having in mind the social relations between people (workers, capitalists and landowners) that characterise the given social form of economy. In his theory of value, he uses the same concept in two different senses: labour is called 'social' first because it is included in the system of social division of labour; second, because it is equalised with all other kinds of labour. In the first case we have a purely natural concept; in the second, a mixed, natural-social concept. Let us see whether these accusations from Stolzmann are justified.

We begin with the *first* concept. Marx calls labour *social* because it is included in the system of *social division of labour*. Was Marx content with this characterisation of labour? No, in the same sentence he speaks of a 'twofold social character', namely, of the specific social form that the social division of labour assumes in a commodity society based upon exchange of the products of labour of independent commodity producers. Marx speaks not only of *the material connection* between different kinds of labour but also of the *social form* (exchange) in which that connection reveals itself. The social division of labour is

> a necessary condition for commodity production, although the converse does not hold; commodity production is not a necessary condition for the division of labour. Labour is socially divided in the primitive Indian community, although the products do not thereby become commodities .... Only the products of mutually independent acts of labour, performed in isolation, can confront each other as commodities.[45]

To accuse Marx of confusing the social division of labour, as such, with its specific social form in a commodity economy is all the more strange because it was precisely Marx who taught us to distinguish between those two aspects

---

45   Marx 1976, p. 132.

and who severely stigmatised those economists who described the capitalist economy as a system of social division of labour while saying nothing about its contradictory, antagonistic social form.[46]

But, if Marx did not confuse the social division of labour with its specific social form in a commodity economy, did he not err in the sense that he devoted primary attention in his investigation to the former while ignoring the latter? This question, too, can only be answered in the negative. Marx was not interested in those features that commodity society has *in common* with the ancient Indian community (i.e. the social division of labour), but in those features that *distinguish* them. Marx derived value and the other economic categories not just from the fact of a social division of labour but precisely from the latter's given social form. The fact that 'as soon as men start to work for each other in any way, their labour also assumes a social form' still does not create value.[47] The latter only appears where the social division of labour has assumed the special social form of a commodity economy. By characterising labour in two ways: 1) as *materially connected* with other kinds of labour and 2) as *socially commensurable* with any other kind of labour through the exchange of their products in the market, Marx turned his whole attention to the *second* aspect, to the social form of labour (i.e. according to Stolzmann's classification, to the concept 'social' in its second sense).

But if that is the case, why did Marx use the concept 'social' in the first sense at all; why did he have to refer to the material connection between all types of labour, which served as the grounds for accusing him of 'naturalism'? Here the specificity of Marx's method, as distinct from Stolzmann's, comes to light. Marx investigates a *given social form* of the production process, but he never forgets that it is precisely a question of the social form of the *production process*. The social relations between autonomous and formally independent commodity producers can only be properly understood on the basis of the material unity of the social process of production. Reference to the latter is necessary from the standpoint of Marxist doctrine concerning the connection between the productive forces and the production relations between people. When Marx characterises 'social' labour as being included in the system of division of labour, he still tells us nothing about its social form, provisionally indicating only the preconditions necessary for his analysis. But they are the preconditions required

---

46   Marx more than once charged Smith with the error of which Stolzmann now accuses
        Marx, namely, trying to explain the transformation of concrete labour into value-creating
        labour from the *single* fact of the existence of the social division of labour, independently
        of its specific commodity form. [Marx 2010, p. 263.]
47   Marx 1976, p. 164.

for an analysis of the social form of labour. Stolzmann's accusation that Marx took, as the basis for his theory of value, the fact of a material connection of socially divided labour (using the concept 'social' in the first sense) thereby collapses. Let us now proceed to the concept 'social' *in the second sense*.

In the passage cited above, Marx sees the 'social' character of labour (in the 'second' sense, according to Stolzmann's classification) in the fact that 'every particular kind of useful private labour can be exchanged with, i.e. counts as the equal of, every other kind of useful private labour'.[48] Here Marx notes the organisation of social labour as a totality of private economic activities that are carried out by autonomous and equal commodity producers and are connected by the mutual exchange of all the products of labour. In other words, Marx speaks here of value and abstract labour, and he characterises the social form assumed by the social division of labour in a commodity economy. This concept of 'social' (in the second sense) is central to Marx's theory of value, and against it Stolzmann directs his main objections. He finds that this concept, too, does not have a purely social character, and thus it differs in principle from the purely social concepts of capital, profits, wages and rent that Marx uses in his theory of distribution to analyse the social or 'production relations' between people (the concept of 'social' in the third sense).

Stolzmann's view here is absolutely mistaken. None of the methodological differences that he alleges between the concept 'social' in the '*second*' sense (the concepts of abstract labour and value) and in the '*third*' sense (the concepts of capital, profits, wages and rent) exist. In methodological terms, the categories that Marx employs in the theory of *value* (more accurately, in the analysis of a simple commodity economy) do not differ from the categories he uses in his theory of *distribution* (more accurately, in the analysis of a capitalist economy). Both of them are expressions of determinate *social* or '*production relations*' between people. The category 'value', like the category 'capital', expresses a determinate type of production relations between people, and Stolzmann's basic error consists precisely in ignoring that fact. Stolzmann does not see that in a commodity-capitalist society, besides the production relations between capitalists, workers and landowners, there exists a special type of production relations between people as sellers and buyers (or as equal commodity producers). This most abstract type of social production relations between people is the historical and logical precondition of more concrete types of social production relations between people in capitalist society. Analysis of the latter is impossible without a prior analysis of the social production relations that con-

---

48   Marx 1976, p. 166.

nect independent commodity producers in a single economic system. Marx's theory of value is precisely an analysis of these social relations between commodity producers as such (i.e. the analysis of a simple commodity economy). The products of labour do not acquire the social form of 'value' by virtue of the technical fact of the labour expended upon them – Stolzmann attributes this idea to Marx – but by virtue of the fact that their producers are connected through determinate social relations as private commodity owners. It is only the specific and historically transient social form of the organisation of social labour, according to the principles of a commodity economy, that imparts to the products of labour the specific social form of value. Notwithstanding Stolzmann's view,[49] Marx therefore has in mind 'social production relations', a 'social formation' and 'historically determinate relations of production' not only in his theory of distribution (or of a capitalist economy), but also in his theory of value (or of a simple commodity economy).

Thus, the category of 'value' has a 'purely social' and not a mixed 'social-natural' character. Of course, full development of the category of value has as its material precondition a specific condition of the productive forces – or of 'social technique', which also changes in the course of social development and therefore does not deserve the label of a 'purely natural' economic element – which prepares and accompanies the development of exchange. But the category of 'value' shares this specificity along with all the 'social relations of *production*', including capital, profits, etc. If this circumstance does not, in Stolzmann's opinion, prevent the latter categories from retaining their 'purely social' character, there is also no basis for seeing an unwarranted mixture of natural and social moments in the category of value. Stolzmann is deeply mistaken when he accuses Marx of not wanting to acknowledge that 'the value of the total product and the value of its components [wages, profit and rents – *I.R.*] are both distinguished by their social character'.[50] This is precisely what Marx claimed in the strongest possible terms, and Stolzmann's opinion that Marx dissolved the value of the total product (after deducting the part that replaces constant capital) into individual types of income, breaking up 'a natural magnitude into heterogeneous (diverse), namely social magnitudes',[51] is without foundation. The relation between the value of the product and the types of income is portrayed by Marx as a relation between different magnitudes of a social character. Marx proves the absurdity of the vulgar economists' doctrine – according to which the means of production (or 'capital' in their terminology) create profits, and the earth produces rent – precisely by showing that profit and rent are parts of the value of the product; and value, as the social form of the product, cannot be derived from the material factors of production that contributed to preparation of the product in question.[52]

Stolzmann seeks to substantiate his assertion regarding the mixed natural-social character of Marxist value theory by analysing the abstract, socially necessary labour that creates value. He believes that the concept of *abstract* labour can only mean 'the summation of a million individual, concrete natural labour expenditures', or 'the technical interaction of natural elements of labour power'.[53] In other words, by abstract labour Marx understands, in Stolzmann's opinion, the union of different concrete types of labour in the single system of the social division of labour – a fact that, as we saw before, concerns the material side of the production process but not its social form. Such a union of labour occurs in both the ancient Indian community and also in socialist society. The concept of abstract labour, therefore, tells us nothing [in Stolzmann's view] regarding the social form of the economy, not to mention [his claim] that for Marx this concept has an unreal and fantastic character.

Stolzmann's objection is based on an incorrect understanding of abstract labour that is widespread among Marxism's critics and sometimes even among its supporters. The characterisation of labour as abstract not only implies its union with other types of labour in a single, materially connected economic system; it also reveals to us the specific *social form* in which this union takes place in commodity society. In the ancient Indian community, the given labour, of a blacksmith for instance, was directly included in the social economy as a special *concrete* labour, with all its special features that distinguish it from other kinds of labour and, for exactly that reason, make it their material complement. In commodity society, the inclusion of a specific concrete labour in the general system of the national economy takes place only by means of market exchange of the products of the given labour for a specific product (gold), or a universal equivalent possessing *abstract* purchasing power with respect to all other products of labour. The act of market exchange results in equalisation of the given product of labour (through money) with all other products, and of the given type of labour with any other type of labour; that is, in the transformation of *concrete* labour into *abstract* labour, and simultaneously in the union of the totality of all the concrete types of labour into the single system of *the social*

52   See, e.g. Marx, *Capital*, Volume III, Part 2, pp. 359, 360 ff. [The reference is to the 1908 Russian translation by V. Bazarov and I. Stepanov.]

53   Stolzmann 1909, p. 571.

division of labour. Presupposing the union of the labour of private commodity producers through multilateral exchange of the products of their labour as values, the concept of abstract labour characterises a fact that is actually occurring in reality and that, at the same time, is typical only of a given social form of economy.

Stolzmann's objection to the concept of *socially necessary* labour may, at first sight, appear to be more valid. In his opinion, socially necessary labour means that 'labour is applied according to its average productivity, according to the principle of the least means'[54] – a fact that holds for all forms of economy. In a socialist society, of course, the fact of different productivity of equal labour expenditures in one and the same branch of industry likewise does not disappear. The labour day of different agricultural workers supplies an unequal quantity of grain depending on the personal traits of the workers, the character of the means of production they use (if they are different), and the fertility of various parcels of land. On the other hand, a social organ probably assigns a specific average evaluation to a pood of grain regardless of the amount of individual labour expended on any given pood of grain. It seems, therefore, that the concept of the average socially necessary labour holds not only for a commodity economy but also for a socialist one.

In reality, however, the concept of socially necessary labour has another meaning in the Marxist theory of value. It signifies not only the fact that identical units of a given commodity are produced with the aid of unequal individual labour expenditures, but also the fact that, as a result of the equalisation of unequal labour expenditures, 'socially necessary' labour is determined at precisely the level that *regulates the equilibrium between one branch of production and the others*: any deviation of the market price above or below the value of the commodity, which corresponds to the specified level, inevitably gives rise in the given branch to an influx or outflow of social labour. This concept of socially necessary labour, as determining the magnitude of the value of products that corresponds to a condition of equilibrium between the different branches of production, is connected with the social form of commodity economy in which the distribution of social labour takes place spontaneously through market exchange of the products of labour as values.

From this point of view, there is a fundamental difference between a *commodity* economy and a *socialist* one. Let us assume that socialist society will want to evaluate grain exactly in accordance with the average amount of labour expended on its production. Through accounting, it is determined that this

---

54   Stolzmann 1909, p. 542.

average labour will be specified as 2 hours per pood of grain, and the evaluation of the latter will be established as 2 roubles. Let us assume that this latter figure coincides fully with the exchange value of grain in commodity society. Nevertheless, the average socially necessary labour plays a completely different role in regulating the exchange value of grain in a commodity society as opposed to the case when it is the basis for the evaluation of grain in a socialist society. In the former case it regulates, through the value of the product, the actual process of distribution of social labour between the various branches of production; in the latter case, such a distribution of labour is brought about by social organs according to a plan and is not directly changed with an alteration in the evaluation of a pood of grain. The *social function* of socially necessary labour, as a *quantitative regulator* of production, is absent in a socialist society – in the same way as the products of labour, however they are appraised in this case, have no 'value'. Therefore, '*average*' labour, which is calculated in a socialist society through special social organs, is fundamentally different from '*socially necessary*' labour, the concept of which was developed by Marx.

Our supposition in the above example – that the magnitude of 'average' labour in socialist society coincides with 'socially necessary' labour in commodity society (with the condition of completely identical technique in the production processes of the two societies) – is not very probable. In the first place, it is quite possible that in a socialist community the exact average labour expenditure required for production of a given product will not be taken as a guide when evaluating it, or else this criterion may be combined with others. [A socialist community] could decide to reduce the evaluation of grain, as an article of prime necessity, say from 2 roubles to 1.5 roubles per pood. But let us leave this suggestion aside and assume that the socialist community will evaluate a product exactly according to average labour expenditures. Nevertheless, even in this case, evaluation of the product may differ in magnitude from the exchange value of the product in a commodity economy.

Suppose that a total of 300 poods of grain are produced, of which 100 poods are cultivated on more fertile land with the expenditure of 1 labour day per pood of grain; 100 poods on soil of average quality with an expenditure of 2 labour days per pood of grain; and 100 poods on the poorest soil with an expenditure of 3 labour days per pood of grain (the other personal and material factors of production, except for the quality of the soil, being the same). If socialist society deemed it necessary to evaluate grain exactly according to the 'average' labour expended in its production, it would make the following calculation. Altogether, 600 labour days were expended and 300 poods of grain were produced. The evaluation of each pood of grain is equal to 2 days of labour, or 2 provisional labour units that we will call 'roubles'. Given exactly the same technical conditions of production, the exchange value of grain in a commodity economy is established at 3 roubles per pood, i.e. at the level corresponding to the 'socially necessary' labour expenditure on the poorest soil. The total value of all the grain will be equal to 900 roubles, with an actual expenditure of 600 labour units. The excess value of 300 roubles, for which there are no corresponding labour expenditures in the given branch of production (agriculture), constitutes, in Marx's words, the 'false social value' that landowners appropriate in the form of differential rent. 'This is determination by a market value brought about by competition on the basis of the capitalist mode of production; it is competition that produces a false social value. This results from the law of market value to which agricultural products are subjected'.[55]

The 'labour value' of the product in a commodity economy does not quantitatively coincide with its labour evaluation in a socialist society,[56] just as the 'socially necessary' labour of the former does not quantitatively coincide with the 'average' labour of the latter. Thus, we come to the conclusion that in a socialist society: 1) evaluation of a given product can be totally *detached* from the labour expenditures required for its production; 2) even with an evaluation based on labour expenditures, the *quantitative* formula of the relation between the former and the latter is different from the formula of 'labour value' in a commodity economy; and 3) even if there is a quantitative correspondence between the two formulae, the *qualitative* character of this link between labour and evaluation (or the social function of 'average' labour) will be different. Therefore, while recognising that the organs of a socialist economy must reckon with 'average' labour in one form or another, we must not confuse the latter with the 'socially necessary' labour that characterises the social form of commodity economy.

With this we can conclude the analysis of Stolzmann's critical objections to the theoretical aspect of Marxist teaching, leaving aside his arguments challenging the ethical merit and practical possibility of realising socialism. Stolzmann's attempts to draw a sharp distinction between Marx's *theory of value*, which is allegedly an improper mixture of 'natural' and 'social' elements, and the remaining parts of the Marxist system, [allegedly] built on a 'purely social' basis (in particular the *theory of distribution*), are radically mistaken.[57] The charge concerning Marx's 'naturalism' originates, on the one

---

55   Marx 1991 p. 799.

56   In the same place Marx described as false 'the assertion that the value of the products remains the same if capitalist production were replaced by association'. [Marx 1991, p. 800.]

57   This counterposing of Marx's 'naturalistic' theory of value to his 'sociological' theory of

hand, from ignoring the 'social' character of the basic concepts of the Marxist theory of value (value, abstract labour, socially necessary labour), and on the other hand, from Stolzmann's own *incorrect construction* of the concept of the 'social' (the teleological point of view, social-ethical categories, the separation of social relations from development of the productive forces). The failure of Stolzmann's criticism is extremely significant. It would seem that it is precisely from Stolzmann – who claims the title of the most consistent representative of the sociological method – that Marxism would have to expect the most forceful and dangerous criticism. In reality, Stolzmann's critique is not only unable to shatter in any way the basic foundations of Marx's economic theory, but it is also unable to make any corrections to it whatever. This can justifiably be regarded as one of the most promising symptoms of Marxism's rich possibilities for development. Even the most progressive trends of bourgeois economic thought have been unable to rise to the level of scientific perspectives opened up by Marx's doctrine. In this respect, the new offshoots of the sociological trend in political economy that have recently emerged, sometimes under Marx's direct influence (Stolzmann, Petry[58]) and sometimes independently of him (Amonn[59]), are no exception. Despite the fact that more than half a

---

capital has almost become the *communis opinio doctorum* [the general opinion of professionals] in bourgeois economic literature. We give two examples singled out at random. Odenbreit, who considers Marx one of the founders of comparative historical economic research, makes an exception for Marx's theory of value. 'In the important question of the formation of value, we do not find in Marx an application of the comparative method'. 'Marx's doctrine of value, the basis of the theory of surplus value, is distinguished by its thoroughly ahistorical character' (Odenbreit 1919, pp. 41, 90). In Gottl's opinion, Marx, in his critique of the contemporary economy, goes far beyond the traditional limits of political economy as a 'science of goods'. But where he touches upon fundamental questions of the economy and society, Marx himself limits the scope and force of his criticism by basing it on the 'hypothesis of value', thus reverting to the narrow framework of a 'science of goods' (Gottl-Ottlilienfeld 1923, p. 108).

58 Petry 1916. See our essay on Petry in this volume.

59 See Amonn 1911. It is one of the most striking examples of the truly phenomenal ignorance concerning Marx's theory that the work of bourgeois scholars often exhibits. Amonn, who comes very close in many parts of his book to the problems of Marxism, does not mention the name of Marx even once, and he is evidently not even familiar with Marx's definition of capital, which won mainstream fame and even partial recognition in bourgeois academic circles. He even believes that Komorzhynski – who wrote after Marx – is the author of the sociological theory of capital: 'The idea that the essence of capitalism lies in a social power relationship is already found in Komorzhynski' (Amonn 1927, p. 410). On the other hand – what an irony of fate – Amonn dedicates his book, which leaves no stone standing in the building of the Austrian School's subjective method, to his teacher, Professor Philippovich, and he thanks the main representatives of that school, Böhm-Bawerk, Wieser and Philippovich. Sombart already remarked, in his article on Amonn's book published in the

century has elapsed since the first volume of *Capital* appeared, Marxism is still
at the forefront of economic thought and is the most consummate scientific
instrument for investigating the laws of social development.

Archiv für Sozialwissenschaft und Sozialpolitik, Vol. 383, that the utter ignorance of bourgeois scholars concerning Marx's system depresses the theoretical level of their works.
They often discover Americas that had long ago been discovered and better researched
by Marx. [This footnote appears in the German translation of this chapter but not in the
original Russian edition of *Contemporary Economists in the West*.]

PART 3

Alfred Amonn and the
Social Method in Political Economy

∵

Introduction by the Editor

Like most Central European economists of his day, Alfred Ammon was a student of both law and economics, studying at the Universities of Innsbruck and Vienna and then becoming an associate professor at the University of Freiburg in 1910. In 1912 Amonn took a position at Czernowitz University (1912–20), after which he taught in Prague (1920–26), Tokyo (1926–29), and Berne (1929–53). Although he was a prodigious writer with a very distinguished academic career, Amonn's work never gained significant currency among English-speaking economists, few of whom were interested in the epistemological and philosophical issues that captured Amonn's attention.[1]

The book that Isaak Rubin analyses in the following essay, *Objekt und Grundbegriffe der theoretischen Nationaloekonomie* (*The Object and Basic Concepts of Theoretical Economics*, 1911) was Amonn's Inaugural Dissertation and has seen 27 editions from 1911–96. In his preface, Amonn called for 'a new conception of the nature and prerequisites' of economic knowledge, which must begin by answering 'the purely logical question' of the relation between the object, task, and method of political economy.[2] Amonn approached this undertaking with the famous *Methodenstreit* in mind – the debate over methodology between the German Historical School and the Austrian theorists of marginal utility.[3]

By the mid-1800s most German economists had turned from classical discussions of value and income distribution to concentrate on economic history and statistics for purposes of practical policy. But in 1871 the Austrian Carl Menger published the first edition of his *Grundsätze der Volkswirtschaftslehre* (*Principles of Economics*) with the intention of disclosing the logic of general economic laws. Menger claimed that 'the phenomena of economic life, like those of nature, are ordered strictly in accordance with definite laws' that 'condition the economic activity of men and are entirely independent of the human will'.[4]

In 1883 Menger launched a vigorous critique of the German Historical School in his *Untersuchungen über die Methode der Socialwissenschaften und der Politischen Oekonomie insbesondere* (*Investigations into the Method of the Social Sciences with Special Reference to Economics*). He argued that 'the contrast

---

1 For biographical information on Amonn see Winterberger 1983, pp. 387–96. Readers may also be interested in the following *Festschrift* in honour of Amonn: Wagner and Marbach 1973.
2 Amonn 1911.
3 For a survey of the *Methodenstreit*, see Louzek 2011, pp. 439–63.
4 Menger 2007, p. 48.

© RICHARD B. DAY, 2024 | DOI:10.1163/9789004705661_016

between the investigation and description of *the individual* and the *general* aspect of human phenomena is always what distinguishes the historical sciences from the theoretical'.[5] To move beyond empirical-historical studies, Menger thought science must first distinguish two paths forward.

The first was a *realistic-empirical orientation to theoretical research*, in which the investigator must sort through empirical data to establish which phenomena are exemplified in 'typical relationships', thereby discerning laws that are valid in relative terms, depending upon the phenomena being observed. This would be the approach of an economic historian looking for theoretical conclusions. But beyond this investigation of 'real types' and 'empirical laws' lay an *exact orientation to theoretical research*, in which the investigator abstracts from history and focuses upon a particular aspect of phenomena while assuming that all other circumstances remain constant.[6] In the latter approach, invoking the *ceteris paribus* assumption, the object of economic theory is predictability through 'the determination of laws of phenomena which commonly are called "laws of nature", but more correctly should be designated by the expression "exact laws"'.[7]

Menger said the 'exact laws' of economic theory are discovered through replacing the 'one-sided collectivism'[8] of historical studies of a national economy with a methodological individualism that focuses upon constituent singular economies and ultimately upon individual decisions. Individuals act according to '*individual* economic aims' and '*individual* interests'.[9] 'National' economies are fictional; reality involves the interaction of a multitude of individual economies. To understand the whole, therefore, the theoretical economist must ascertain the exact laws that govern individual economic behaviour. Menger regarded his approach as being analogous to the natural sciences, the difference being that, in place of *imagining* 'atoms' and 'forces', the exact social sciences have the advantage of studying the observable behaviour of 'human *individuals* and their efforts'.[10]

Alfred Amonn had no dispute with Menger's theory of marginal utility when explaining individual choices and price determination in conditions of relative scarcity. Since he rejected the labour theory of value, he also did not share Stolzmann's concern to reinterpret income distribution in terms of any ideal

---

5   Menger 1985, p. 37.
6   Menger 1985, p. 58.
7   Menger 1985, p. 59
8   Menger 1985, p. 93.
9   Menger 1985, p. 194.
10   Menger 1985, p. 142n.

social purpose. The problem, for Amonn, was that Menger clarified methodological differences between the historical and the theoretical study of economics but neglected the 'striking historical conditionality' that necessarily distinguishes economics from 'many other fields of knowledge, especially the Natural Sciences'.[11] In his *Objekt und Grundbegriffe der theoretischen Nationaloekonomie* (*The Object and Basic Concepts of Theoretical National Economy*), Amonn undertook to specify political economy's historically conditioned 'object of knowledge' as the *social form* of an economy mediated through exchange.

Amonn asked: '*What is it that conditions the exchange relation between people*, or what are its prerequisites?' He answered that exchange relations presuppose

> a specific external order ... of social intercourse, which is given by or through the society, is precisely established or implicitly acknowledged, and is imposed (with either a legal or purely conventional character) upon the individual independently of his will. On the basis of this external order of social relations of intercourse, social will and behaviour assume specific forms, and social relations of a definite character emerge ...[12]

> [The social relation of exchange] is characterised by ... four essential moments: 1) recognition of the *exclusive* power of *an individual* in a particular relation ... to dispose of *external* objects ... 2) recognition of the *free ... exchange* of this power of disposal ... 3) the *freedom ... to determine the quantitative proportions* of the objects being exchanged (since this is the root of all economic problems, particularly the problem of price); 4) recognition of a *universal social measure of value* and means of exchange ....[13]

Political economy's 'object of knowledge' turned out to be the formal conditions of a *capitalist* economy. Rubin comments that Amonn's book immediately propelled him 'into the ranks of the brightest and best representatives of the "social" method in the latest economic literature'. He also concludes, however, that Amonn still ended up 'halfway between the Austrian school and a genuinely sociological method', for he never considered *how forms of social*

---

11   Amonn 1911. Menger had briefly referred to this issue when he acknowledged in a footnote 'the immense vagueness about the true field (the object) of research which political economy had to deal with'. See Menger 1985, p. 198.
12   Amonn 1911, p. 170.
13   Amonn 1911, p. 181.

order are themselves objectively determined by social relations of production.
'The "social organisation" of exchange, which Amonn considered apart from
any connection with the social process of production, turns out to be an empty
form devoid of any content'. By focusing on the *'formal-qualitative* side of economic phenomena' at the expense of the *'material-quantitative* side', Amonn
overlooked 'the problem around which the whole of theoretical economics
revolves', namely, the role of labour expenditure in the determination of value,
profit, and the distribution of social income.

Isaak Rubin on Alfred Ammon

Amonn's book *Objekt und Grundbegriffe der theoretischen Nationaloekonomie*
(*The Object and Fundamental Concepts of Theoretical Economics*) appeared in
1911 and immediately attracted attention from a wide audience of scholars and
people interested in methodological problems. With a forceful logical analysis,
the author of this book pursues the idea that theoretical economics is a social
science, whose subject matter is investigation of a definite form of social relations between people. Starting from this general point of view, the author clev-
erly and convincingly criticises traditional notions of political economy as a
science that studies the economic activity of people aimed at acquiring 'goods'.

    This book immediately propelled Amonn into the ranks of the brightest and
best representatives of the 'social' method in the latest economic literature.
This fact is all the more noteworthy, since Amonn emerged from the bosom
of the Austrian school and in his other works was unable to free himself completely from the influence of that school's ideas.[14] In this respect, Amonn's
scientific activity is an interesting example of the kind of Babel of languages
that can often be seen in the work of contemporary West-European economists
– this being one of the symptoms of the crisis that modern economic science is
experiencing. A couple of brief comments will give the reader an impression of
this Babel. In the work that we are considering, Amonn develops methodological views that sharply diverge from the individualistic-psychological method

---

14   In his article 'Liefmanns neue Wirtschaftstheorie' (in *Archiv für Sozialwissenschaft und
     Sozialpolitik*, 46, II.2), Amonn comes out in defence of the Austrian theory against Lief-
     mann's attacks. In his most recent book, *Ricardo als Begründer der theoretischen Nation-
     aloekonomie* (1924), Amonn subscribes to the 'theory of scarcity' developed by Cassel. It
     would never enter the head of a reader of these two books that they were written by the
     author of a well-known methodological study and a supporter of the social method in
     political economy (on this issue see below, at the end of this article).

of the Austrian school. On every page of his book, Amonn calmly and persistently, directly or implicitly, undermines the methodological foundations on which the entire edifice of the Austrian school is erected. Yet this by no means prevents him, at the beginning of his work, from expressing his sincere gratitude to the highly esteemed teachers, professors and shadow counsellors – Böhm-Bawerk,[15] Wieser,[16] and Philippovich[17] – who [built upon Menger's work and] are the three pillars of that school.

On the other hand, in many parts of his book – like Molière's hero who spoke prose without being aware that he was doing so – Amonn comes close to the problems of Marxism without once mentioning Marx's name or referring to his works, with which he apparently has no familiarity.[18] This striking example of the truly phenomenal ignorance of Marx's teachings, which is often evident in the works of bourgeois scholars, has already been noted by Sombart.[19] Citing the example of Amonn's book, Sombart quite correctly pointed out that the complete lack of familiarity with Marx's system on the part of bourgeois scholars lowers the theoretical level of their works: they often discover new 'Americas' that were long ago discovered and were much better investigated by Marx. An examination of Amonn's book will convince us that the author even of this superb, and in a certain sense exemplary, methodological investigation has yet – as a result of its purely formal framing of the question – to take even the first timid steps along the road that was long ago explored by Marx.

---

15   [Eugen von Böhm-Bawerk (1851–1914), Austrian economist and prominent critic of Karl Marx.]

16   [Friedrich von Wieser (1851–1926), one of the principal members of the Austrian school.]

17   [Eugen von Philippovich (1858–1917), Austrian economist and university professor.]

18   We can even assume that the Marxist definition of capital, which has become widely known and even partially recognised in bourgeois scholarly circles, remains unknown to Amonn. At the very least, he considers the author of the sociological theory of capital to be Komorzhinsky, whose work came after that of Marx: 'The idea that the essence of capital lies in a social relation of forces can be found in Komorzhinsky' (Amonn 1911, p. 410).

19   Sombart devoted an article to Amonn's book in *Archiv für Sozialwissenschaft und Sozialpolitik*, 38, pp. 647–61. Karl Diehl, in his review of Amonn's book, also could not help expressing surprise that Amonn did not once mention his predecessors: Marx and Rodbertus, Stammler and Stolzmann (see *Jahrbücher für Nationaloekonomie und Statistik*, 1915, 104, p. 835). Liefmann, a constant opponent of Amonn, pointed out with glee – in response to similar charges from Amonn – that the latter is himself guilty of an 'unparalleled' ignorance of his predecessors. [See Amonn 1918–19, pp. 367–421; Liefmann 1920–21, pp. 500–22; and Amonn 1920–21, pp. 523–41.]

CHAPTER 1

Amonn's Doctrine on the Subject Matter of Theoretical Economics

Amonn takes as the starting point for his entire analysis the assertion that *political economy is a social science.* He recognises that this claim is far from novel and can be found in the work of numerous economists. Among them he includes the names of Knies,[1] Wagner,[2] Dietzel[3] and Schmoller,[4] yet he says not a word about Marx, the true founder of the sociological method in economic science. However, Amonn is justifiably dissatisfied with the way the question has been posed by previous economists, who have recognised political economy in words as a social science but have not attributed to this position 'any importance in principle for understanding the essence and basic methodological problems' of this science.[5] Amonn, quite properly, puts this thesis in the forefront of his entire study.

As a social science, political economy must group together and investigate phenomena from a special, social point of view, and it must correspondingly formulate its special subject matter or its 'object of knowledge'. The *'object of knowledge'* (*Erkenntnissobjekt*) has to be differentiated from the *'object of observation'* (*Erfahrungsobjekt*).[6] The latter includes the totality of empirical facts from which a given science directly acquires its material for observation and study. But science works upon this material logically and separates (abstracts) from complex and diverse phenomena the particular features that are essential from its own point of view, and thus it transforms the concrete 'object of observation' into an abstract 'object of knowledge'.

---

1 [Karl Gustav Adolf Knies (1821–1898) was a German economist of the Historical School of economics, best known as the author of *Political Economy from the Standpoint of the Historical Method* (1853).]

2 [Adolf Heinrich Gotthelf Wagner (1835–1917) was a German economist and politician.]

3 [Karl August Dietzel (1829–1844) was an early economist of the German Historical School.]

4 [Gustav Friedrich von Schmoller (1838–1917), was leader of the 'younger' German Historical School.]

5 Amonn 1911, p. 151.

6 A literal translation of the word *Erfahrungsjobjekt* would be 'object of experience'. [In Russian, the word used is '*опыт*', which means either 'experience' or 'experiment'.] But in this context the meaning is not to be narrowly understood as an experiment, but rather in a broad sense that embraces both observation and experiment.

As its 'object of observation', political economy takes the world of economic phenomena in all is complexity and concreteness. But in order to form its special subject matter, its 'object of knowledge', it must examine these phenomena from a distinct, social point of view. Everyday thought regards economic phenomena 'from the individualistic point of view of psychological relations between purposes, or as natural-technical relations between things'. Economic activities are seen either as being conditioned by the psychological experiences and motivations of separate individuals, or as being directed to the acquisition of material goods required for the satisfaction of needs. Both of these points of view, the psychological and the natural-technical, have thus far been prevalent in the science. On the one hand, economists have directed their attention to 'the material and qualitative characteristics of goods', considering the object of their study to be all activities aimed at acquiring material goods; on the other hand, they have taken the criterion of economic activity to be its correspondence to 'the psychological principle of rational behaviour (the economic principle)'.[7]

It is clear that such prevalence of the individual-psychological and natural-technical points of view contradicts the character of political economy as a social science. Indeed, 'purely economic activity' in the sense described (i.e. as activity aimed at acquiring material goods or guided by the so-called 'economic' principle of expediency) is possible in any social conditions and even for an individual living apart from society. In order to remain a social science, political economy must investigate not individual-psychological or technical phenomena but rather those that are 'socially conditioned'.[8]

By 'socially conditioned facts' we understand 'facts that are conceivable and possible only with the presupposition of people who are living a social life together and interacting, i.e. of a social community that exists in some form or other'.[9] It is true that these facts originate from individuals, but when we take into account 'the interdependence and mutual conditioning of their individual wills and behaviour' we must look for explanation of the facts not in the individual motivations of separate individuals but rather in the 'social relations that in turn condition the will and behaviour of individuals (and thus affect them in a causal manner)'.[10]

It follows from what has been said that 'the object of the theoretical social sciences involves social relations or their socially conditioned lawfulness and

---

7   Amonn 1911, p. 151.
8   Amonn 1911, p. 143.
9   Amonn 1911, p. 159.
10   Amonn 1911, p. 160.

propriety'.[11] And since political economy is a social science, it too has *social relations* for its 'object of knowledge' (exactly which ones, we shall see later) and not, as economists assume, 'the economy' in general. It investigates 'not what is common to *all* economic activity, but a determinate social form and structure of the economic, i.e. exactly what distinguishes one kind of singular economic facts from others'.[12]

Thus far, Amonn's reasoning has to be recognised as exemplary in terms of its clarity and methodological correctness. Amonn quite properly takes up arms against the prevailing inclination among bourgeois economists to convert political economy into a science of the relations of people to things – relations that are regarded either from the standpoint of the subject (the individual) or from that of the object (the things). Given all the seeming contradictions between the subjective-psychological and objective-technical points of view, they converge in making the subject matter of their investigation the relations of people to things and not the social relations between people. The convergence in principle between these two viewpoints is aptly underlined by Schumpeter in the following words: 'The elements (of economic theory) are either some quantity of goods or else individual-psychological value magnitudes, since it is generally only a question of expediency as to whether we put the terminological emphasis on the former or the latter – i.e. whether we define our system of elements as a system of quantities of goods or as a system of individual-psychological value magnitudes: in both cases we do essentially one and the same thing'.[13] Amonn successfully polemicizes against both of these traditional points of view, showing that political economy ceases to be a social science when regarded either as a science of 'goods' or of economic 'motives'. Amonn must be given credit for coming to the correct view that political economy is a science of social relations between people. But if we continue the analysis further and pose the question of precisely which relations between people political economy investigates, we find in Amonn a number of very serious errors and omissions. All of these errors and omissions have their source in a *fundamental error* that the author makes by severing all connection between *the social relations of people and the material process of production.*

As we have seen, Amonn rightly rejects the view that political economy studies *'economic activity'* in general. He should then have concluded that this science studies a particular social form of economy, or the definite social relations into which people enter in the process of material production. However,

---

11   Amonn 1911, p. 161.
12   Amonn 1911, p. 144.
13   *Archiv für Sozialwissenschaft und Sozialpolitik*, 42, p. 5.

Amonn goes much further and asserts that political economy studies definite social relations between people completely *independently* of whether they
occur *within the process of production* or apart from it. In Amonn's opinion, our
science studies a certain *form* of social relations between people; as we shall
see below, this means the form of exchange between independent counter-
parties (or commodity owners in Marx's terminology). If a given social relation
between people, in terms of its *formal characteristics*, belongs to same type of
social relations that are the subject matter studied by political economy, they
are then economic relations even if they are not in the slightest degree connected with the sphere of 'the economy' or with 'production'. Political economy has
no relation to 'the economy' or 'production'. True, Amonn acknowledges that
the social relations between people that interest us (exchange, for example)
occur 'mainly' and 'primarily' 'in connection with the production and circulation of material goods'.[14] But this 'concrete form of manifestation' of the given
social relations, their 'empirical connection' with the sphere of production,
involves only 'insignificant modifications' without essentially changing their
formal or social nature, which is of primary interest to us.[15] 'It is true that an
empirical connection exists between economic and social facts, but there is
no *logical* connection between these two concepts'.[16] Logically, therefore, we
must study a given social relation between people (exchange, for example) as
'something that exists completely independently of production activity and for
the most part is connected with it only fortuitously'.[17] 'Political economy is not
interested in "economic" facts in the usual sense, but in *a certain form of social
relations* – a form which, it is true, is expressed mainly in economic facts but is
not generally characteristic of *all* economic facts as such, and which, moreover,
does not exist *only* in the sphere of economic facts (if we understand the latter
in the sense of activity directed to the acquisition of *material goods*)'.[18]

Thus, the social relations between people that are studied by political economy have only a *fortuitous empirical* connection with the process of production and must be investigated apart from any link with the latter. Amonn converges with Marxism in the sense that he makes social relations between people
the subject matter of political economy. But Marxists add that political economy studies the social relations that people enter into directly in the process

---

14   Amonn 1911, pp. 144, 157, 239 ff.
15   Amonn 1911, pp. 156, 157 *et passim*.
16   Amonn 1911, p. 156.
17   Amonn 1911, p. 239.
18   Ibid. We italicise the last two words in order to draw the reader's attention to them. Their
      meaning will be clarified below.

of social production, in other words, 'production relations' (and besides that, only production relations of a definite type that characterise a commodity-capitalist economy). Amonn refuses to recognise the subject matter of political economy to be precisely the 'production' relations between people. While Marxists study a definite *social form of economy*, Amonn takes the subject matter of his investigation to be social relations between people *divorced* from their basis – the social process of production. We shall see below the kind of unfortunate theoretical consequences that result from such a complete rupture between the social form and the material content of the economy. But for now, let us continue following Amonn.

Thus far, all we know is that political economy studies *social relations* between people. Amonn rejects all attempts to define these social relations more closely as those of 'production'. But, in that case, the central question arises: *precisely which* social relations does *political economy* study? After all, it is only one of many social sciences, and obviously it does not study all the social relations between people but only certain ones.[19] Precisely which are they? Unlike Marx, Amonn is not in a position to move by a synthetic route from the general concept of 'the social relations of people' – precisely because he refuses to define them more closely as production relations – to the genuine object of political economy, to social relations between people as commodity producers. But, at the same time, Amonn recognises the pressing need to erect a bridge from 'social relations' in general to the social relations of commodity producers (i.e. to exchange). There is, consequently, no other way for him but to adopt an analytic type of study. Once we are unable to descend from the concept of 'social relations', detached from the process of production, to the concept of exchange (since exchange can only be understood as a special form of social-production relations that has emerged between people at a definite stage in the development of the productive forces), can we not then try to find a path of logical ascent to the concept of exchange, beginning with analysis of the problems that modern political economy actually does study? From the countless multitudes of diverse social relations, we shall select as the subject matter of our investigation only 'the kind of social relations that lie at the basis of the fundamental problems of political economy'.[20]

The fundamental problems of political economy are logically connected and array themselves around a single centre, '*the problem of price*', to which all the other more complex problems can be reduced.[21] It follows from this that of all

---

19   Amonn 1911, p. 164.
20   Amonn 1911, p. 171.
21   Ibid.

the social relations between people, the economist is interested only in social relations of a specific type, namely, those that lie *at the basis of the phenomena of price*, in other words, *the relations of exchange* between people. From the concept of price we have ascended to the concept of the exchange relation.[22]

Thus, we have now taken a step forward in defining the object of our science. Previously, we saw it as social relations in general, but now we recognise definite social relations between people as our object, namely, the exchange relations that lie at the basis of the phenomena of price. But do not the concepts of 'price' and 'the exchange relation' lead us back to the sphere of the economy, from which Amonn wanted to banish us with the help of his abstract, purely formal concept of social relations? No, answers Amonn, for we regard 'price' and 'the exchange relation' in terms of their *formal-social* and not their *economic* aspect. 'The economic problem of price is not covered by the concept of the economy': it does not arise wherever there is an economy (for instance, it is absent in the primitive natural economy), and on the other hand it is present even when there is no mention of an economy[23] (for instance, personal services and entitlements have a definite price; in this case there is no mention of material items or, therefore, of an economy in the sense of acquiring *material* goods). The same applies to the concept of 'exchange relation'; this is a definite type of social relations, which, it is true, also includes instances of economic exchange (i.e. the exchange of material products), but it is by no means inherent in every social economy and, on the other hand, it is found outside of the sphere of economy[24] (including, for example, the exchange of services, entitlements and other such nonmaterial objects). The object of political economy is not 'the exchange *economy*', as many economists believe, but a purely formal '*exchange relation*' between people that is not necessarily connected with the sphere of the economy or with social production.[25] Thus, we study the exchange relation as a determinate form of social relations between people. But the social relations between people take on a uniform and regularly recurring form only

---

22 The gaping abyss that separates the concept of 'exchange relation' from the concept of social relations in general is hidden in Amonn's work by the several meanings of the German term '*Verkehr*' (signifying 'intercourse' (*общение*) and 'exchange' (*обмен*) along with other meanings). At the outset Amonn always operates with the concept of 'social relations of intercourse' (*Verkehrsbeziehungen*) [Rubin translates this word as '*социальное общение*']. Then suddenly appears the combined concept of 'social relations of intercourse or exchange in the broad sense of the word' ('*Verkehrs- oder Tauschbeziehungen*', on page 175), and this creates a word-bridge from social relations in general to the exchange relation.

23 Amonn 1911, p. 174.

24 Amonn 1911, p. 175.

25 Ibid.

thanks to 'the uniform and identical conditioning of the will and behaviour of individuals in social intercourse'.[26] This raises the question: *What is it that conditions the exchange relation between people*, or what are its prerequisites?

The will and behaviour of individuals in the process of exchange is conditioned in two ways, by both *individual* and *social* factors: on the one hand, by the personal motives that convince people to enter into exchange and to pay a certain price for commodities and so forth; on the other hand, by the social organisation of the community that imparts to exchange one or another social form. If there were only individual conditioning of exchange acts, then the latter could not serve as an object for social research in general. And if, on the other hand, there were only social conditioning of exchange (for example, those entering exchange acted only upon orders from social organs), then there would not arise the problems that are studied by political economy and presuppose a regime of free competition.[27] Insofar as we are interested precisely in the kind of exchange relation that lies at the basis of the problems of political economy (particularly the problem of price), what we have in view is an exchange relation that involves the dual influence of individual and social factors, or the so-called '*individualistic exchange relation*'.

However, despite the existence of a dual (individual and social) conditioning of the social relations that interest us (i.e. exchange relations), the subject matter of our research is solely the *social conditioning* of exchange relations. Insofar as exchange occurs because of the attempt by individuals to satisfy their needs better, there is no place here for social research. 'From the *purely individual* conditioning of human behaviour, for instance, from the economic principle, we cannot derive specifically economic problems'.[28] 'The character of *social* relations is constituted not by the character of their individual conditioning but by the character of their *social conditioning*'.[29] Consequently, the exchange relations between people interest us only in terms of their social conditioning, i.e. their dependence upon specific social phenomena.

The social conditioning of exchange relations involves the fact that the character of exchange relations between people is determined by *the structure of the society* whose members enter into mutual exchange. 'The social relations, with which fundamental economic problems are associated, emerge on the basis of a fully determined (positive) social order or organisation of intercourse (*Verkehrsordnung – oder Organisation*), and specific economic problems arise

26   Amonn 1911, p. 166.
27   Amonn 1911, pp. 166, 167.
28   Amonn 1911, p. 170.
29   Amonn 1911, p. 169.

only *given the precondition of this determinate social organisation of intercourse and are even inconceivable apart from it*.[30] Social relations of exchange presuppose a determinate 'organisation of intercourse', i.e. a social structure. The character of exchange relations is conditioned by '*a specific external order* (which we refer to as *the organisation*) *of social intercourse, which is given by or through the society, is precisely established or implicitly acknowledged, and is imposed (with either a legal or purely conventional character) upon the individual independently of his will. On the basis of this external order of social relations of intercourse, social will and behaviour assume specific forms, and social relations of a definite character emerge'[31] that lie at the basis of economic problems. Thus, on the basis of a given 'organisation of social intercourse' (i.e. the structure of society), people enter into definite social relations (namely exchange relations), which, in turn, lie at the basis of economic problems (particularly the problem of price). Conversely, *economic problems* (the problem of price) presuppose definite *social relations* between people (exchange relations), which in turn presuppose a determinate *structure of society*. Thus, the investigation of economic problems leads us, in the final analysis, to a study of the *social structure*, on the basis of which arise definite social relations between people and the corresponding economic problems. 'What are the most general features of this specific social conditioning, of this specific order or organisation of the social relations of intercourse? That is the final and conclusive formulation of our central question and the only correct formulation of the problem'.[32]

In summary, Amonn comes to the following conclusion:

The economic problem of price and all the specific social-economic problems connected with it arise *only* in the presence of *social* exchange, i.e. exchange occurring between a number of people on the basis of mutually conditioned and corresponding wills, and *only* given the precondition of a specific external social *order* (or *organisation*) of exchange intercourse – an order that conditions *a specific form of exchange*.[33]

What are the characteristic features of this external social order or social structure?

---

30   Amonn 1911, p. 169.
31   Amonn 1911, p. 170.
32   Amonn 1911, p. 171.
33   Amonn 1911, pp. 180–1.

It is characterised by the following four essential moments: 1) recognition of the *exclusive* power of *an individual* in a particular relation (i.e. demanding respect on the part of other individuals but also not completely without limits) to dispose of *external* objects, i.e. objects that are not inherent in the person of one of the exchanging parties (this is the precondition for exchange); 2) recognition of the *free* (i.e. completely independently of the individual will of the subjects of social intercourse) *exchange* of this power of disposal (*Verfügungsmacht*) by individuals (this is the purpose of exchange) together with a lasting obligation to respect the disposals once made; 3) the *freedom* (i.e. depending exclusively on the individual will of the exchanging parties) *to determine the quantitative proportions* of the objects being exchanged (since this is the root of all economic problems, particularly the problem of price); 4) recognition of a *universal social measure of value* and means of exchange (as the condition for the possibility of comparing these social acts of exchange).[34]

The *four conditions* listed must be recognised as the most general preconditions for the statement of economic problems. In the absence of a social organisation distinguished by these four features, the problems investigated by political economy are also absent; 'with this specific organisation, these problems *necessarily* appear'.[35] In truth, one cannot conceive of the phenomenon of exchange and the problem of price without the first condition, namely, without 'social recognition of the *exclusive* power of individuals to dispose of objects of exchange'.[36] This refers to 'external objects that are not entirely and directly tied to a single individual' and that include not only material things but also personal services that may be transferred to the use of another person.[37]

On its own, the *first* condition 'signifies merely the general possibility of social relations of exchange'.[38] The *second* condition must also be joined to it – free exchange, or free transfer of the right of disposal over objects from one individual to another at the discretion of the exchanging parties. Furthermore, the *third* condition must also be present, namely, the free discretion of the exchanging individuals in determining the quantitative proportions of the objects being exchanged.[39] If these quantitative proportions were compulsor-

---

34   Amonn 1911, p. 181.
35   Ibid.
36   Amonn 1911, pp. 181–2.
37   Amonn 1911, p. 182.
38   Amonn 1911, p. 183.
39   Amonn 1911, pp. 187–8.

ily established by a social authority, we could not speak of the problem of price. But even these three listed conditions are insufficient for posing the problem of price in the form studied by political economy, namely, in the form of a problem that embraces 'not the separate concrete phenomena of price but rather all prices independently of their particular concrete existence'. 'What this necessarily requires is the possibility of a uniform mental objectification of all prices', specifically, the possibility of comparing them with the aid of an (at least mentally) abstract unit that serves as the universal social *measure of value* (i.e. the monetary unit).[40]

Thus, economic problems have as their precondition the presence of a determinate social organisation that is distinguished by the four listed features. But this social organisation must not be confused with a particular *legal system*. What is involved is 'a factual social order' that in some cases is also sanctioned by law and in other cases has a purely conventional character (i.e. is founded upon social customs) and may even contradict 'the legally established order'.[41] For this reason Amonn objects, for instance, to any understanding of the first of the four listed conditions in the sense of the presence of 'private property' as a definite legal institution.[42] It is sufficient to have 'social recognition' of the exclusive power of individuals to dispose of external objects, but it is not necessary that this recognition be cast in the legally complete form of the institution of private property. The logical precondition for posing the economic problems is the presence of specific *social*, but not *legal* conditions.

Now, finally, we can define precisely the *preconditions* and the *object* of economic science. The economic problems have as their *precondition* the presence of a determinate '*social organisation*' (or structure) that is characterised by the four listed features. 'The *object* of knowledge for theoretical economics is the *social relations* that have as their common and necessary precondition the aforementioned organisation of social intercourse, which is characterised by the four listed features'.[43] At last, we have now learned *precisely which* social relations between people are the object of political economy: they are *social relations of exchange* between individuals, who have exclusive *power of disposal* over external objects and transfer them to one another at their discretion while freely determining the *quantitative proportions* of the objects being exchanged and comparing them with the aid of a common *abstract unit*. Translating this

---

40   Amonn 1911, pp. 188–9. The difference that Amonn sees between this 'social measure of value' and 'money' in the precise sense is not of concern to us here.
41   Amonn 1911, pp. 217, 167, 170, 185–7.
42   Amonn 1911, pp. 184–5.
43   Amonn 1911, p. 191.

definition into more conventional language (although Amonn insists upon his own terminology), we could say that political economy studies only the *social relations of exchange* between *commodity producers* – an exchange in which the products have a specific *price* (and *value*) expressed in a certain quantity of *monetary units*. Every exchange relation that is distinguished by the social features described is studied by political economy, regardless of whether it is a case of the exchange of material things, of personal services and so forth, and even regardless of whether the given act of exchange can generally be ascribed to the sphere of the economy or reaches beyond the limits of the latter. Contrariwise, not a single act of the production or exchange of goods, in the absence of the social form described, is studied by political economy even if it has all the features of an 'economic' act directed to the acquisition of 'economic goods'. Political economy studies not 'economic' but 'social' phenomena – and not all social phenomena, but only those *social relations of exchange* that are distinguished by the four listed formal features.

Following his doctrine concerning the 'object' of political economy, Amonn turns to analysis of the 'basic concepts' of this science, by which he means concepts that are the necessary logical elements of the object described above, namely, the 'individualistic relation of exchange'. The following four 'basic concepts' necessarily emerge from the concept of exchange that is being analysed: 1) the *subject* of exchange, 2) the *object* of exchange, 3) the *price*, and 4) the *universal measure* (or *money*, although Amonn makes a distinction between them). We shall not follow Amonn in the analysis of these concepts, limiting ourselves to a critical analysis of his aforementioned general doctrine concerning the 'object' (or subject matter) of political economy.

CHAPTER 2

A Critique of Amonn's Doctrine[1]

Amonn's teaching represents an enormous step forward compared with the generally accepted doctrines of bourgeois economists, who consider the subject matter of political economy to be any 'economic activity' aimed at the acquisition of 'goods' – regardless of the social form of the economy. Amonn, by contrast, tirelessly stresses on every page of his book – and in the process does not shy away from numerous repetitions and verbosity – that political economy does not study just any economic activity so long as it involves a relation of man to things, but rather social relations of a definite type. Amonn's first thesis is

---

1 [This section of Rubin's commentary on Amonn was republished in 1929 in *Unter dem Banner des Marxismus*, 3, no. 1, pp. 128–49. In the introduction to that version, Rubin added the following comments:

In 1927 the second edition appeared of the famous book by Alfred Amonn: *Objekt und Grundbegriffe der theoretischen Nationaloekonomie*. In the preface to the new edition, the author notes that he upholds completely the theoretical views that he first expressed fifteen years ago: 'I was ... unable to find any evidence, either critical or positive, that would induce me to change my outlook, either in general or in specific cases. My views have, on the contrary, been progressively strengthened and deepened'. (Alfred Amonn, *Objekt und Grundbegriffe der theoretischen Nationaloekonomie*, zweite Auflage (Leipzig: F. Deuticke, 1927, p. v.))

In the new edition of his book, Amonn was compelled to offer a short response or anti-critique of the articles by his critics (Sombart, Oppenheimer, Diehl), who had investigated his work more closely when the first edition appeared. The author concludes the anti-critique by summoning his critics to probe more deeply into his book: 'So I hand over this book to criticism for the second time, with no other desire than that my critics *examine thoroughly* which of these arguments are tenable and which should be discarded'. (Amonn, *Objekt und Grundbegriffe der theoretischen Nationaloekonomie*, p. 422.)

Amonn's desire is well-founded. He enjoys a great authority in German economic literature. Whatever one's opinion about *Objekt und Grundbegriffe der theoretischen Nationaloekonomie*, we must recognise that it is one of the best works in German literature dealing with the methodological questions of theoretical economics. Anyone wanting to deal seriously with methodological issues must take a stand on Amonn's book and answer the questions that he raises.

In this paper we set ourselves the goal of giving a thorough and detailed analysis of Amonn's basic methodological views. We will limit ourselves to a critique of his methodological teachings and leave aside his attempt to give a positive exposition of political economy (see Alfred Amonn, *Grundzüge der Volkswohlstandslehre* (Jena: Fischer, 1926)). It is in the area of methodology that Amonn is most original, and it is precisely here that he wants to offer something new. As the subject of the present paper, we have therefore chosen Amonn's basic methodological views, namely, his theory of the object of theoretical economics.

that all economic *problems*, which revolve around the problem of price, presuppose the presence of certain *social relations between people* (namely, a special exchange relation). His second thesis is that this social relation between people presupposes in turn a certain *structure of society*, namely, a 'social organisation' characterised by the four features he describes (or in Marxist terminology 'a society of commodity producers'). Pursuing these theses with the greatest consistency in the methodological part of his book, Amonn may rightly be regarded as one of the clearest and best representatives of the 'social' tendency in contemporary bourgeois political economy.

To his credit, Amonn differs from other supporters of the social tendency by his rigorously theoretical, scientific-causal point of view. In Stammler, Stolzmann, and Petry, the 'social' study of economic phenomena is reduced, in the final analysis, to an investigation of the latter from a special 'social' point of view that is in fact teleological and has nothing in common with the scientific-causal research method. Amonn defends the need for the 'social' method, but he does so within the framework of a purely theoretical, causal exploration of phenomena, and he rejects any attempt to introduce a teleological point of view into science.

These positive aspects of Amonn's constructions entitle us to conclude that the author is on the correct methodological path, which promises to open before him a broad scientific horizon. If, despite that fact, Amonn has taken no more than the first few steps along that path, the fault lies with a fundamental defect of his system that also characterises the views of other supporters of the social tendency in bourgeois political economy: the abrupt severance of *social relations* between people from the social process of *material production*. Amonn is absolutely correct when he says that political economy does not study the economic or production process apart from the social form in which it occurs; but this by no means implies the reverse conclusion that he draws, namely, that political economy studies social relations between people characterised by certain formal features regardless of whether they occur within the sphere of the social production process or apart from it.[2] In fact, political economy does study a determinate *social form* of economy, but it must not be forgotten that this refers precisely to a social form of *economy*, which is closely connected with the material content of the social production process and changes along with changes in the conditions and requirements of

---

2   This basic error of Amonn's system was already noted by Werner Sombart (in his article in *Archiv für Sozialwissenschaft und Sozialpolitik*, 38). See also the book by S. Solntsev, *Vvedeniye v politicheskuyu ekonomiyu* (1922, p. 24).

the latter. If the subject matter of political economy is taken to be social relations between people independently of their connection with the process of
production, the result is, in the first place, to convert political economy from
a science of economic phenomena into a science of *purely formal* features of
the social connection between people, and secondly, to block the path even to
a correct understanding of the *origin and development* of these purely formal
features of human intercourse. In other words, it means no economics at all
but a purely formal and, even in this domain, unsatisfactory sociology.

Amonn regards the above-mentioned deficiency – i.e. restricting his horizon
to the pure form of social relations between people – as his special accomplish-
ment, and he consistently retains it throughout his entire work. We know that,
in Amonn's opinion, the subject matter of political economy involves definite '*social relations*' between people that presuppose the presence of a specific,
objective '*social order*', namely, the 'individualistic relation of exchange'. All the
concepts that follow logically from this definition, according to Amonn, have
a purely formal character. He sees 'social relations' as being *independent* of the
production process. The 'social order' consists of the recognition of a particular
form of relations between people. Finally, by 'exchange' he understands only a
specific *form* of social relations. Let us see whether Amonn has succeeded in
demonstrating the purely formal character of these concepts or whether such
an idea leads him into a series of contradictions and misunderstandings.

We begin with the concept of '*social relations*' between people. Amonn
converges with Marxists insofar as the subject matter of political economy is
'social relations between people'. But the whole profound difference between
Marx's system and Amonn's becomes evident by comparing the two following
schemes.

Marx's scheme	Amonn's scheme
Social relations between people	Social relations between people
Production relations between people	A specific type of social relations between people ('individualistic exchange relations')
A specific type of production relations between people (exchange between commodity producers)	

Among the social relations between people, Marx singles out the special group
of economic or *production relations* that people enter into in the course of

material production. These 'production relations' between people, which directly organise the process of production and thus constitute the social form of the economy, differ from other types of social relations, for instance, political relations. Furthermore, from among the production relations between people Marx singles out a special group characterising the contemporary commodity-capitalist economy, namely, the production relations of exchange between commodity producers (and the 'class' relations between capitalists and workers, and between capitalists and landowners, that arise from them). It is precisely this type of production relations between people, emerging at a certain stage in development of the material productive forces, which constitutes the object of political economy.

Amonn's scheme is different. Beginning his analysis with the general concept of 'social relations' between people, he refuses to highlight relations of production that are distinguished by the direct character of their link with the material production process. As the criterion for classification of social relations between people, he does not take material features (the character of their connection with the process of production) but rather purely formal features (the form of relations between people). If people enter into social relations with each other that are characterised by the above-mentioned formal features, we have the 'individualistic relation of exchange' that constitutes the object of study for theoretical economics. There are no intermediate links between the concept of 'social relations' in general and the concept of 'individualistic exchange relations'. But how, in that case, do we classify production relations between people that do not fall within the concept of commodity exchange, for instance, the production relations between people in a feudal-manorial economy? Of course, these production relations between people are profoundly different from the production relations of commodity producers, and for that reason they do not constitute an object of study for modern theoretical economics. But what they do have in common is the fact that in both cases we are concerned with the 'production' relations between people, i.e. with social relations that fulfil the special function of organising the material process of production (which in the one case is feudal, in the other capitalistic).

An economist who claims to employ the sociological method cannot manage without the concept of 'production relations' between people. It is true that his attention has to be concentrated more on the diversity of forms between the different types of production relations than on their correspondence. It is not what is common between feudal and commodity-capitalist relations of production that constitutes the immediate subject matter of the economist's study, but rather what characterises and distinguishes the latter from the former.

But if the economist takes a specific *form* of production relations between people as the subject matter of his investigation, he must not forget that they are *production* relations between people. When Amonn claims that political economy examines social relations between people that are distinguished by certain formal features (namely, the relations between people as participants in the exchange described above) and have nothing in common with the production process, he simply ignores the real content of modern economic science. If we do not have in mind some fantastic science of the 'pure forms' of human society, but instead the real content of economic theories (the theories of value, money, capital, profit, etc.) – and Amonn himself recognises the need to begin with the content of theoretical economics as this science has emerged in the course of historical development – then the claim that economic relations between people are not dependent on the material production process is absurd. Amonn himself realises the paradoxical nature of his claims and therefore repeatedly feels obliged to acknowledge the existence of 'an empirical connection' between the social relations of people and the process of production.[3] The social relations between people, in which we are interested, 'appear empirically'[4] precisely in the sphere of material production. Amonn often says that the social relations between people (exchange, for example) are, 'under certain conditions', connected with the production process.[5] Elsewhere he affirms that we are interested in a 'specific form of social phenomena that become visible *mainly* (*hauptsächlich*) in economic facts'.[6] In a third place it turns out that this social form is '*fortuitously* associated *primarily*' (*zufällig vorzugsweise*)[7] with production activity. Thus, the social relations between people that political economy investigates (for instance, between commodity owners, capitalists, workers, etc.) are encountered 'mainly' in the realm of production. But, in that case, can we agree with Amonn that this only occurs 'fortuitously', that there is no necessary connection between a given state of the productive forces and a given form of social relations between people? Apparently, Amonn does not recognise how much the appeal to 'fortuity' signifies the theoretical bankruptcy of his purely formal constructions.

We must say in Amonn's defence that it is certainly impossible to imagine, after the following paradoxical claim, anything but an appeal to chance:

---

3   Amonn 1911, p. 156.
4   Amonn 1911, p. 157.
5   Amonn 1911, p. 237 and elsewhere.
6   Amonn 1911, p. 144.
7   Amonn 1911, p. 239.

The economic problems are essentially connected only with the relations between producers, traders and consumers, between employers and
workers, and between employers and (money) capitalists. But not only
are these phenomena not necessarily connected with 'economic production activity'; they are even completely autonomous and independent of
it. They also occur where there can be no question of 'economic production activity'. 'Economic production' can occur apart from these social
relations,[8] and conversely, these social relations are conceivable in the
absence of production[9] and quite independently of any production activity.[10]

Thus, it turns out that the social relations between employers and workers exist
in complete independence of the production process. If a connection between
them is usually ('mainly') to be observed, that is explained by pure 'fortuity'.
This claim is so paradoxical that it requires no criticism.

But, the reader may ask, how can a thoughtful and talented economist
defend the idea that the social relations between people that political economy
studies (for instance, those between employers and workers) are not connected
with the process of production? To be fair to Amonn, the following two circumstances must be borne in mind: 1) by the economy, or production, Amonn
has in mind the production of *material* things; 2) he denies any *purely logical*
connection of social relations with the sphere of production while recognising the existence of a 'casual', 'empirical' link between them. Let us examine
whether, as a result of these two limiting conditions, his assertion turns out
to be more correct. Amonn devotes considerable space to debates between
economists over whether the sphere of the 'economy' should be restricted to
the production and exchange of *material things*, or whether it also includes,
for example, the exchange of personal services, shares, entitlements and similar non-material objects. Amonn rightly suggests that political economy studies definite social relations between people even if they appear beyond the
immediate sphere of the production and exchange of *material things*. Usually,
Amonn substantiates his paradoxical ideas concerning the independence of
people's social relations from the production process by pointing out that a
given type of social relations (e.g. exchange) can exist, for instance, in cases

---

8   On this point Amonn is correct, since production can occur in other social forms.
9   Here Amonn is mistaken, because the social relations of production among people cannot
        arise otherwise than on the basis of some kind of production process.
10   Amonn 1911, p. 239.

involving the exchange of *non-material objects* (in the sphere of material production, for instance, the purchase of labour power by the employer), or even in the sphere of *non-material production* (as in the case of hiring teachers).[11] But what do those examples prove? Only that production must not be understood in the narrow sense of direct production of physical goods but rather in the broad sense of the production of use values in general. The economist must not forget: 1) that the relations of production he studies originated in and mainly occur in the sphere of material production; and 2) that from there they also gradually spread out into the sphere of non-material production. Even if 'capitalist production is only applicable to a very limited extent'[12] in the sphere of non-material production, to the extent that social relations of a capitalist type (such as the relations between employers and workers) are established in this sphere they are included within the purview of political economy. But it by no means follows that political economy also investigates social relations that have a 'non-production' character. All that follows is that *production relations* are understood in a *broad* sense; they include social relations of a given type that have formed in the sphere of material production (even if it is not directly a question of material things) and have partially spread out from there into the sphere of non-material production. But instead of broadening the concept of 'production', Amonn employs it in the narrow sense of the direct production of material things and thus inevitably comes to the paradoxical conclusion that theoretical economics studies social relations with certain formal features, regardless of whether they have any connection with the production process (in the narrow sense) or not.[13]

Therefore, Amonn's idea that theoretical economics studies social relations that are 'unrelated to production' and have a purely formal character cannot be justified by reference to the fact that such social relations are also observed outside the sphere of direct production of material things. Nor can this idea be substantiated by Amonn's constant references to the lack of any '*inner*', '*logical*' *connection* between the given type of people's social relations and the production process. What do such references mean? Only one thing: that if we think

---

11   Amonn 1911, pp. 158, 240, ff.

12   Marx, *Theorien über den Mehrwert*, [*Theories of Surplus Value*] 1905, Bd. I., S. 425. In the Russian translation of Volume I, *Теории прибавочной стоимости*, edited by G. Plekhanov and published in 1906, see p. 333. [Marx 1969, pp. 410–11.]

13   Judging by the arrangement of Amonn's book, one might even conclude that it is precisely his wish not to limit the field of economic research to the sphere of direct production of *material things* that led him to a purely formal definition of the object of our science as social relations that are generally independent of the *production process*.

of a given type of social relations in purely formal terms, our concept will not include any features indicating their link with the process of production. It is self-evident that if the concept of social relations is independent of the process of production, then it has no 'logical' connection with the concept of production. But the question is precisely whether our science proceeds correctly if it does not establish a 'logical' connection between the concept of the given social relations and the concept of production. Take, for example, the social relation between capitalist and worker, which consists of the exchange of labour power for money. Is this social relation 'logically' connected with the process of production? Seen from a purely logical, or more precisely from a purely formal point of view, this social relation is not necessarily connected with the production process. One can imagine that the capitalist, after the act of purchasing the labour power, does not send the worker to toil at the factory but instead takes a stroll with him and passes the time in friendly conversation. In this case there is no production process at all, and nevertheless, from a purely formal point of view, Amonn could recognise here the existence of social relations between the capitalist (the person who bought the right of disposal over labour power) and the worker (the person who sold the labour power). Does theoretical economics study such a purely formal 'social relation'? Yes, replies Amonn, for we have before us a social relation between people that exhibits definite formal features. No, we reply, for in this case the 'production relations' between people are absent. Does the social relation described above belong to the class of social relations between capitalists and workers that theoretical economics investigates? Yes, says Amonn, for it has the required formal features, and the presence of the production process introduces only 'minor modifications' to our formal definition without changing its essence. No, we reply, for belonging to the sphere of production is an integral feature of the social relations studied by political economy: the aforementioned fantastic relation between capitalist and worker, for all of its formal similarity to production relations of a capitalist type, is in essence profoundly different from them.

The sharp contrast introduced by Amonn between the *'logical'* connection of concepts and the *'empirical'* connection of phenomena results from his tendency to pose the problem in a *formal-logical* way. Amonn abuses the contrast between a 'logical' and 'genetic' analysis, between *'posing* the problem' (*Problemstellung*) and '*solving* the problem' (*Problemklärung*).[14] The connection of the social relations between people with the process of production, in

---

14   Amonn 1911, p. 208 *et passim*.

his opinion, can certainly be taken into account when *'solving* the problem' but not at all in *'posing* the problem'. It is as if Amonn forgets that a particular posing of the problem leads to a particular way of solving it, and that the latter, conversely, presupposes the former. From a formal-logical point of view, of course, the researcher is entitled, when posing the problem, to create logical concepts at will out of any features he selects. For example, he is free to establish a formal-logical concept of the social relation between the capitalist and worker, including also the fantastic case described above. But the question is precisely whether such a 'posing' of the problem leads to its 'solution', and thus whether, on the basis of the given concept of social relations (i.e. beginning with the given object of knowledge), we can build a scientific theory. In other words, can we formulate a series of interconnected theses that relate equally to cases of a 'production' relation between capitalists and workers and to the aforementioned fantastic case of a 'non-production' relation between them? Must we not recognise that the economic theories of wage, profit, etc., apply only in the first case and do not relate directly to the second? But this is tantamount to acknowledging that the object of economic knowledge is precisely 'production relations' between people and not social relations in general, independent of their connection with the process of production.

The inconsistency of Amonn's view is revealed most vividly in the transition from the formal-logical posing of the question to its 'genetic' investigation. For the moment, let us agree with Amonn that theoretical economics studies definite social relations between people regardless of their connection with the production process. But then the question quickly arises: How does the given *form* of social relations between people emerge, and how does it *develop*? Amonn has only one answer to this question: the given *form of social relations* between people is the result of a given *'social organisation'* of society.[15] But this

---

15   Amonn sees in a particular 'social organisation' of society the *logical* precondition for the given form of social relations between people. But in order to explain the real, 'genetic' conditionality of these social relations – for instance, of exchange relations – he is forced to refer to facts that are, in his opinion, outside the field of theoretical-economic research, namely, the individual motives of the persons involved in exchange and their quest for the best possible satisfaction of their needs. While he defends the social method within the realm of 'logical' analysis, in that of 'genetic' investigation he actually surrenders the battlefield to the individualistic-psychological method (1911, p. 327 and elsewhere). He assigns the field of preparatory, methodological disquisitions to the social method, but when turning to study of the economic problems as such it is the psychological method that comes to the fore. It is only by taking into account this delimitation of the two methods that one can explain the strange fact that Amonn, who in the methodological work that we are

answer immediately leads to a new question: How does the given *form of the 'social organisation'* of society emerge and develop? To this question Amonn can give no answer whatsoever, for he regards the social organisation of society in the same formal-logical terms as the social relations between people. Let us briefly consider this 'social organisation' of society.

By the *'social organisation'* of society (insofar as it serves as the logical precondition for the social relations between people that are studied by theoretical economics), Amonn understands 'social recognition' of the four formal features of the social relation of exchange that were set out above (the individual's exclusive right of disposal over objects, the free transferability of that power of disposal over objects, the free determination of quantitative exchange proportions, and a universal measure of value). Does Amonn have in view the social organisation of the *process of production*? No, he speaks only of the formal recognition by society – apart from any dependence on the course and requirements of the production process – of a definite type of social relations between people (for instance, the 'individualistic relation of exchange' or the relation between capitalists and workers). But how does such 'social recognition' of specific relations between people occur? According to Stolzmann, 'social regulation' (i.e. the social form of the economy) also emerges independently of the needs of the material production process and is brought into it from without.[16] But Stolzmann at least says where it comes from: 'social regulation' is established by the free will of man and is directed to the realisation of ethical objectives. The sharp separation of the social form of the economy from its matter is transformed by Stolzmann into the antithesis of teleology and causality. Amonn, apparently, is not inclined to recognise such a profound and irreconcilable dualism of the social process because he wants to stay within the limits of causal-theoretical research. But how does a given form of the 'social organisation' of society come about?

On this matter Amonn remains completely silent. He gives us only scanty information on how this social organisation does *not* arise; specifically, it does not arise by the force of laws or rights. Social organisation must not be confused with legal organisation, or 'social recognition' with juridical recognition. The precondition of the given social relations between people, as we have seen, is a specific 'factual social order'[17] that sometimes even contradicts the law-

---

considering actually leaves no stone of the Austrian School's method unturned, appears in his other works as a defender of the latter. (See for instance Ammon 1918–19, pp. 367–421).

16   [See Stolzmann 1909. See Rubin's work on Stolzmann in this volume, Essay 3.]

17   Amonn 1911, p. 217.

fully established legal order and, in a struggle with it, proves to be stronger. The 'social recognition' of a given type of social relations between people can be 'purely conventional' – not reinforced by law[18] but based exclusively on the 'power of social opinions'.[19] In this regard, Amonn notes in one place that the forms of social organisation between people are 'not initially created or artificially constructed by the legal order, but, on the contrary, they develop organically from *the requirements of social intercourse*'.[20]

Had Amonn not restricted himself to these general formulae but instead seriously posed the question of precisely which 'requirements of social intercourse' cause the appearance of a given form of society's 'social organisation', along with its corresponding social relations between people, he would have convinced himself that it is a question of the requirements of the material process of production. The growth of these requirements evokes a change in the 'social organisation' of the economy. The 'social organisation' of society, which Amonn considers apart from any connection with the social process of production, turns out to be an empty form devoid of any content. Amonn regards this 'social organisation' of society merely as the given, formal-logical *precondition* of economic phenomena; but he forgets that it is simultaneously the result of a certain development of the productive forces. The dialectical process of connection and interaction between the social process of production and its social form – a process in which certain forms of production relations between people are simultaneously both the *result* of previous development of the productive forces and also the *precondition* for their further development – remains unknown to Amonn. Although Amonn claims on every page of his book that he takes the subject matter of his investigation to be the relations between people and the social organisation of society, as a result of his purely formal method he can tell us nothing concerning the laws of *the origin and development* of this social organisation.

As we see, a formal posing of the question has closed off for Amonn the road to a genuine study of '*social relations*' between people and the '*social organisation*' of society that underpins them. The sterility of the purely formal method appears even more clearly when we turn to analysis of those concrete social relations that Amonn does recognise as the object of theoretical economics, namely, '*individualistic relations of exchange*'. How did this specific

---

18   Amonn 1911, pp. 167, 170 *et passim*.

19   Amonn 1911, p. 185.

20   Amonn 1911, p. 219. In this way Amonn attempts to avoid confusion of social with legal regulation – a confusion that is to be found most forcefully in Stammler and in a more diluted form also in Stolzmann.

form of social relations between people, namely, the exchange relation, emerge and develop? Is it not a consequence of a specific development of the productive forces? Is not commodity exchange a determinate social form of the production process? No, answers Amonn, we study the relation of exchange in its purely formal aspect, apart from any connection with the process of production. True, when Amonn has to explain the fact of the mediaeval natural economy's dissolution and the appearance of exchange relations, he can offer nothing better than reference to a series of changes occurring in the social process of production ('improvement of production thanks to the division of labour, the differentiation of products and needs, a rise in productivity, the appearance of surplus products'[21] and so forth). But he evidently considers this historical connection between development of the productive forces and the appearance of social relations of exchange to be only 'fortuitous' and 'empirical'; from a theoretical or logical point of view, Amonn studies the relation of exchange apart from any connection with the process of production.

Accordingly, 'individualistic relations of exchange' are the object of our investigation as a special form of the social relations between people. The question of how these exchange relations emerged and developed remains beyond the field of study. Likewise, Amonn is not interested in the connection between these exchange relations and the process of social production. In that case, what is it about 'individualistic exchange relations' that interests us? Only their *formal* features. It is a matter of complete indifference to us whether exchange involves *products of labour* or *labour power*, purchase of *commodities* or purchase of *slaves*. Provided this exchange occurs in the form of 'individualistic exchange', characterised by the four features mentioned above, it is a subject for our investigation without any regard to the material properties of the objects being exchanged (things, labour power, slaves, rights, etc.). 'The object of individualistic exchange relations includes everything that is being bought and sold, lent or rented, etc.'[22] The concept of the '*object of exchange*' has a purely formal character and can include any empirical objects. In this purely formal character of the concept, Amonn sees its special merit.[23] Depending upon the society's concrete social structure, the circle of 'objects of exchange' expands or contracts (for instance, the purchase of human beings is prohibited, purchase of labour power commences, etc.), but this is of no consequence for a theor-

21   Amonn 1911, p. 218.
22   Amonn 1911, p. 285.
23   Amonn 1911, p. 284.

etical study of 'individualistic relations of exchange', which in all these cases retain unaltered their social or purely formal nature.[24]

Now we can clearly see the profound difference between Amonn's concept of the 'individualistic exchange relation' and Marx's concept of 'commodity exchange'. At first sight it might seem that Amonn, like Marx, takes the subject matter of his investigation to be the social relations of exchange that characterise a commodity economy. But Marx regards exchange relations as a special social form of *economy* or the *process of production*. Since Marx investigates the social relations of people in the *process of production*, or the *production* relations of people, it is understandable that he makes a distinction between cases of the exchange of *products of labour* and those involving sale of *labour power*. He studies the first group in terms of the theory of value and the second in terms of the theory of capital. For all the purely formal similarity between the two cases (both labour power and the products of labour are bought and sold, each has a specific price that sometimes rises and sometimes falls, etc.), they differ profoundly from each other because of the different *social positions* of exchange participants in the social *process of production*. Exchange of the products of labour presupposes that the exchange participants are independent commodity producers who own all the means of labour required for production. Sale of labour power presupposes that the seller does not possess his own means of production and is therefore deprived of the opportunity to act as seller of the products of labour. Despite all the purely formal similarity of exchange relations between people in the two cases, hidden behind them are entirely different production relations. In other words, persons who occupy a formally identical position in the process of exchange, as formally independent buyers and sellers (the independent craftsman, the wage worker and the capitalist), occupy totally different positions in the social process of production. This difference in their social position also finds expression in the object of exchange, which in one case is a product of labour and in the other is labour power. To mix together the sale of products of labour and the sale of labour power means to confuse different types of production relations between people on the basis of their formal similarity.

While Marx makes exchange of labour products the object of investigation in his theory of value, from the very outset Amonn extends his concept of 'individualistic relations of exchange' to every instance of exchange, regardless of whether it is a question of products of labour, of land, labour power, transfer of rights, etc. Amonn objects to singling out products of labour from all

---

24   Amonn 1911, pp. 286 ff., 311.

other objects of exchange: 'It is not the natural individual fact – that acquiring a thing costs labour – that makes it the subject matter of a specifically economic study, but the completely independent social fact that this thing is intertwined within a certain *nexus* of social exchange relations of a definite type'.[25] Amonn's objection misses the point. Obviously, it is not simply the fact of labour expenditure in producing the thing that confers upon it the character of 'value'. Also required is a definite social organisation of labour, which must be divided between independent commodity producers. But, given this social organisation of labour (i.e. in a commodity society), the production relations between commodity producers and the interconnection of their labour activities are only established through market exchange of the products of their labour as values. Therefore, in order to reveal the mechanism of the social labour process in conditions of a commodity economy, we must: 1) distinguish exchange of the *products of labour* from all other cases of exchange; 2) analyse the *social form* of this exchange, which establishes the *production relations* between independent commodity producers; and 3) investigate the *material connection* of the processes of exchange with the process of the *distribution of social labour* between the different branches of production and the individual commodity producers.

Severing the connection between people's *social relations* and the social *process of production*, Amonn is far from any understanding of 'individualistic relations of exchange' as a social form within which, at a certain stage of development, the social process of production occurs. He is interested only in the social form of acts of exchange, regarding them as 'completely independent' of the process of production. When the question is posed this way, the fact that social labour is expended and distributed through the process of production loses any interest for Amonn. The last of the above-mentioned three points falls totally outside his field of investigation. Amonn focuses all of his attention solely on the second point, concerning the social form of relations between the persons taking part in exchange, while these relations are viewed not as those of production but rather as purely formal social relations. It is perfectly understandable, from this point view, that Amonn should place the exchange of labour products in the same category with the exchange of labour power, land, etc., provided only that all these cases of exchange satisfy the above-mentioned four formal features. However, Amonn does not stop there but goes much further. His point of view, if consistently followed, requires the widespread slave trade of the ancient world to be included in the concept of 'individualistic

---

25　　Amonn 1911, pp. 281n.

relations of exchange'.[26] The slaves were bought and sold in the market and evaluated in terms of money – therefore, these acts of selling slaves did not formally differ from acts of selling the products of labour. Moreover, to judge from one of Amonn's footnotes, one might think that corruption in the form of buying votes, which is widespread during election campaigns, must also be included in the concept of 'individualistic relations of exchange'.[27]

From the formal-social viewpoint, therefore, there is no difference between the purchase of labour products, labour power, slaves and votes. Differences between the objects of exchange in all these cases have no essential signific-ance and involve only 'insignificant modifications' in the act of exchange. In all of these cases, identical formal-social relations are established between sellers and buyers, entitling us to discern the presence of the 'individualistic relations of exchange' that are investigated by political economy. Amonn does not notice that the variety of objects of exchange in our example conceals a difference in the social-production relations between people. The purchase of slaves char-acterises a slave economy; the purchase of products of labour, a commodity economy; and the purchase of labour power, a commodity-capitalist economy. To mix together all of these instances of exchange means not to notice the profound difference of *social-production* relations behind the uniformity of *formal-social* relations between people.

As we can see, his formal posing of the question has taken cruel revenge upon Amonn. It has led him to absurd conclusions that contradict his own methodological presuppositions. Indeed, we have seen that Amonn himself insisted that, in constructing the object of theoretical economics, we must take as our starting point those problems that our science in fact studies, particu-larly the problem of price. This means that the concept of the 'individualistic relation of exchange' must coincide with the concept of exchange from which present-day theoretical economics proceeds. The concept of exchange con-structed by Amonn diverges sharply from that concept. There is no need to demonstrate that the problem of price, as it appears in modern theoretical eco-nomics, has not the slightest connection with the slave trade or vote buying. This problem of price – although economists are often unclear on the matter and thus make numerous mistakes – presupposes a definite type of *production relations* between people as independent commodity producers. The produc-tion relations that characterise a different mode of production (for instance, the slave trade) cannot be taken by the economist as his point of departure for

26   Amonn 1911, pp. 290–1.
27   Amonn 1911, pp. 285n.

the theory of value or price, even though, in purely formal terms, they did not differ from the production relations of a commodity economy.

Amonn's investigation has been rendered sterile by his *purely formal* framing of the question. As long as it is a matter of the most general methodological issues, this error of Amonn's system remains concealed. But as soon as the author comes closer to defining his 'object' (the individualistic relation of exchange), and to analysis of the resulting 'basic concepts' of our science (the subject of exchange, the object of exchange, value and price, and the universal measure of value), this flaw appears most forcefully. Taking an example of one of these 'basic concepts' (specifically, the 'object of exchange'), we have already seen the absurd results to which the purely formal method leads. Amonn's remarks concerning the other 'basic concepts', namely, value and the measure of value, are equally formal in character. These remarks amount to nothing more than criticism of other theories – occasionally quite justified and to the point – and purely formal definitions. Likewise, Amonn's attempts to pursue his own 'sociological' path to the theory of value and money remain merely attempts that result in no further development. After Amonn expounded his methodological views in his extensive work – in which a correct sociological kernel was present, although it was sterilised by a purely formal approach to the problem – one might have expected him to continue his projected attempt to apply the 'social' method to the theory of value, money and capital. Those expectations, however, were not justified. Equipped with the formal-social method, Amonn became stranded in an awkward position that offered no prospects, halfway between the Austrian school and a genuinely sociological method. Amonn was prevented from advancing further by a purely formal approach to economic problems and, possibly, by the traditions of his own scientific education and the accompanying academic environment – traditions that were more likely to pull him backwards.

There are reasons to fear that Amonn's new work, *Ricardo als Begründer der theoretischen Nationaloekonomie* (*Ricardo as the Founder of Theoretical Economics*, 1924),[28] represents a step backwards from the social method and towards the traditional naturalistic-psychological theories of bourgeois economists. Much of the book is dedicated to a critique of Ricardo, particularly his theories of value and rent. Amonn's general conclusion, of course, states that the theory of labour value is untenable in every respect. His critical arguments, set out with Amonn's typical logical clarity and even logical elegance, essentially contain little that is new. They partly reveal genuine contradictions and

---

28   [See also Amonn 1926.]

weak points in Ricardo's teaching that have already been noted by his previous critics, most notably by Marx (the theory of profit, the teaching on wages), and they are also partly based on a confusion of value and price (his criticism of the theory of rent).

Despite his scathing criticism of Ricardo's doctrines, Amonn praises him as the true founder of theoretical economics and calls upon modern economists to return to Ricardo. 'The task for our epoch is not to replace Ricardo but to understand and further develop his thoughts',[29] to 'reconstruct' his theory in a new way. What should this 'reconstruction' of Ricardo's theory involve? We have to drop Ricardo's ideas on labour value and develop his thoughts concerning the dependence of the price of commodities on their scarcity. These thoughts, which Ricardo mentions in passing and which refer to absolutely rare objects (old pictures, statues, etc.), must be generalised and taken as the basis of the theory of value. It is necessary to build the theory of value on the consistently held principle of the dependence of the value of commodities on their 'scarcity'. The 'principle of scarcity' is the key that unlocks all the secrets of the theory of value. It readily explains to us the value of all objects of exchange: reproducible and non-reproducible objects, material things and labour services, simple labour and skilled labour, etc.

Bordering closely upon Cassel's theoretical constructions, in the last twenty pages of his new book Amonn lays out the basic ideas of this 'theory of scarcity'.[30] Compared with the work by Cassel and the Austrian economists, Amonn's brief exposition provides us with nothing original. We mention this new work by Amonn only to note the interesting fact that the author does not make even the slightest attempt to reconcile the 'theory of scarcity', adopted from Cassel, with his own social method as developed in his earlier work. With a few examples we can demonstrate the divergence between the former Amonn and the new Amonn.

Consider the concept of *value*. In his earlier work Amonn stressed that 'objective exchange value has a social character and is essentially conditioned by social facts'.[31] We learn from his new work that 'the value of a good (*eines Gutes*) *increases with the increase* of its relative *scarcity*, which may be due either to an increase in our needs or to a reduction of the available quantities of this good'.[32] The earlier concept of value presupposed a certain 'social organisation' of society. Now the author has in mind a 'value' that products

---

29   Amonn 1924, p. iv.
30   See Cassel 1921.
31   Amonn 1911, p. 325.
32   Amonn 1924, p. 107, Amonn's italics.

possess in any social form of economy. Previously Amonn sharply criticised the concept of a 'good' (*Gut*) and excluded it from the field of theoretical economics. Now he himself operates with this term. Previously he objected to naturalistic-psychological theories; now he sees the ultimate basis of value in the urgency of 'needs' (more accurately, of wants – *Begehr*) on the one hand, and in the number of available goods on the other – that is, in purely psychological and technical factors.

The difference between the present and the former Amonn can be illustrated even more pointedly with the example of the concept of *labour*. In his earlier book, Amonn sharply criticised the conventional definition of 'labour' as an activity distinguished by certain purely technical or psychological features (for instance, its purpose is to acquire material things, or it is driven by the so-called 'economic principle'). This psychological-technical concept of labour is alien to political economy as a social science. 'The criterion for the concept of labour in the *economic* sense must not be sought in a specific technical property or psychological direction of human activity, but only in the special position that human activity occupies in a specific social intercourse',[33] namely, in the exchange turnover. 'Labour' can only interest us as an object of social relations of exchange, and as such it differs from other objects of exchange (commodities, for example) only in the presence of a capitalist economy, i.e. in the form of 'wage labour'. It is only the concept of wage labour, not the concept of labour in general, that has a social character and belongs within the research field of theoretical economics.[34] 'Labour, in the sense of theoretical economics, is *an activity performed for a third party for a specified remuneration*'.[35] To our bewilderment, this formal-social definition of labour gives way in Amonn's new book to a technical definition that does not significantly differ from the traditional definitions of labour that the author so aptly criticised in his earlier work.

---

33   Amonn 1911, pp. 375, 376.

34   On this question, as on so many others, Amonn converges with Stolzmann, although we
      are surprised to see that he makes not a single reference to him. Like Stolzmann, Amonn
      overlooks the fact that in addition to the two concepts of labour that he describes [1] the
      technical concept of 'labour in general', and 2) the social concept of 'wage labour' that
      is characteristic of a capitalist economy] it is also possible to construct the concept of
      'abstract labour' or the 'labour of commodity producers' – the concept that characterises
      a commodity economy and is the basis for the theory of labour value. Both Amonn and
      Stolzmann confuse this social concept of 'the labour of commodity producers' (which pre-
      supposes a specific social form of the economy and specific production relations between
      people) with the technical concept of labour in general, and on this basis Amonn mis-
      takenly concludes that the theory of labour value is built upon a technical concept of
      labour.

35   Amonn 1911, p. 414.

'Labour, in the sense of theoretical economics, is any activity whose purpose is an artificial change of the relative quantities of goods objectively provided by nature'.[36] Here, in a new and more concealed form, we encounter the traditional reference to the psychological goals and technical results of labour, while its social form is completely ignored.

Finally, let us also compare Amonn's former and current views on *capital*. In his earlier work, Amonn showed that for the transformation of 'individualistic exchange relations' into 'capitalist relations' one further condition must be added to the four described above: 'inequality of the individual power of disposal in social intercourse, i.e. the social superiority of some individuals over others'.[37] Because capitalism presupposes the existence of certain social relations between people, the technical (or so-called 'economic') definition of capital, as the totality of produced means of production, cannot be considered correct.[38] 'The property of capital is not constituted by the technical nature of objects (for instance, their character as moveable things or products, or their industrial purpose etc.), which here remains completely constant, but only by the social factor'.[39]

Amonn tells us something completely different in his new book. There we learn that 'capital is anything in which labour and the productive services of land (*Bodennutzung*) are accumulated, i.e. any product. It is not the character of a good as means of production that makes it capital but rather its character as a product'.[40] Whereas Amonn previously said that the character of an object as a product (*Produkteigenschaft*) does not make it capital, now we learn exactly the opposite. Every finished 'product' (provided only that it has exchange value) is capital, as distinct from labour that still has to be performed and from the productive services of lands that are not yet in use. A 'product' contains within itself both of these elements (labour and the productive services of land) in already 'accumulated' form, and therefore it 'always has a higher value' than these two elements that compose it. It is this difference of value that forms the 'percentage' [rate of return] on capital.[41] What Amonn gives us, in slightly altered form, is Böhm-Bawerk's theory of profit and his division between 'present' and 'future' goods.[42] The property of capital is derived

---

36   Amonn 1924, p. 108.
37   Amonn 1911, pp. 387, 388.
38   Amonn 1911, pp. 393, 395.
39   Amonn 1924, p. 406.
40   Amonn 1924, p. 116.
41   Amonn 1924, p. 115.
42   Amonn 1924, pp. 111–12. [In this volume see the appended essay by Rubin on the Austrian school.]

from the material-technical characteristics of a 'product', and social elements are meticulously etched from capital's definition.

As we see, the same sad fate has befallen Amonn as happened with the other supporters of the 'social' tendency (for instance, Stolzmann and Petry), who detach the social relations of people from the social process of production. With this separation they have sterilised their 'social' method and transformed their 'social' concepts into empty schemes that are unsuitable for explaining real economic phenomena, which are closely connected with the process of production. These authors operate more or less successfully with their 'social' concepts as long as they limit themselves to general methodological discussions of the way to pose a problem. But, as soon as it is a question of actually solving economic problems (the theory of value, money, capital, etc.), the formal-social concepts, being divorced from the production process, fail to work. If the phenomena of value, capital, profit, etc. are viewed exclusively as expressions of certain formal-social relations between people, apart from any connection with the process of material production, then the whole *material content*, and especially the *quantitative determination* of these fundamental economic phenomena, remains completely unexplained. Indeed, quantitative changes in value, wages, profit, etc. fulfil certain functions in the process of material production, and once the latter is omitted from the field of investigation the lawful pattern of these changes remains inexplicable. The one-sided interest of the economists of the social tendency in the *formal-qualitative* side of economic phenomena, together with their complete disregard for the *material-quantitative* side, exacts a bitter revenge. It forecloses any possibility for these economists to explain quantitative changes of value and incomes, i.e. to resolve the problem around which the whole of theoretical economics revolves. In order to surmount this difficulty, supporters of the social tendency have no choice but to take refuge in one of two options. One possibility is to ascribe to formal-social regulation the miraculous property of determining a given magnitude of incomes as well as of value. Thus Stolzmann, for instance, argues that in both a capitalist society and in a socialist community social regulation determines in advance the 'socially necessary' magnitude of incomes (wages and profit), which in turn determines the magnitude of value.[43] Stolzmann obviously conceives social regulation of a capitalist economy in terms of the model of a consciously acting teleological unity. Amonn is not inclined to take refuge in such a risky and arbitrary construction. The result is that he, like Petry,[44] has no other way out but to acknowledge that all

43   [In this volume see Rubin's essay on Stolzmann, Chapters 2–3.]
44   [Petry 1916. The next chapter of this volume is Rubin's essay on Franz Petry.]

quantitative changes of value and incomes can only be explained by the motivation of individual economic actors. After recapturing a specific, narrow sphere of research for the social method, Amonn and Petry are compelled to capitulate to psychological theories in the sphere of research that involves real economic phenomena. The social method, rendered sterile by its purely formal point of view, has turned out to be too weak an instrument for reconstructing the edifice of theoretical economics.[45]

---

45   [In the German translation of this essay, which appeared in *Unter dem Banner des Marxismus*, 3, no. 1 (1929), pp. 128–49 and was published after *Contemporary Economists in the West*, Rubin slightly revised his conclusion as follows:

... Stolzmann obviously conceives the social regulation of a capitalist economy in terms of the model of a consciously acting teleological unity. Amonn is not inclined to take refuge in such a risky and arbitrary construction. The result is that he, like Petry, has no other choice but to forego explaining real economic phenomena by means of the social method, and to capitulate in that area to the traditional theory that looks for the explanation of economic phenomena in technical and psychological factors. This explains the duality in Amonn's doctrines, as we have shown above with the examples of his definitions of value, labour and capital. In his new book *Grundzüge der Volkswohlstandslehre*, Amonn strives to turn this dualism into a principle. In his opinion, the science of theoretical economics consists of two different parts: 1) *theoretical political economy* [*Volkswirtschaftslehre*], which studies the process of the *economy* insofar as it depends upon specific conditions, and 2) *theoretical economics* [*Nationaloekonomie*], which studies specific social relations between people regardless of whether they take place in the economic sphere or not.

In this essay, whose purpose has been a critical analysis of Amonn's methodological views, we cannot offer a criticism of this new positive system, which is also characterised by dualism. We only stress that this new system of Amonn indirectly testifies to the fact that he has given up his methodological principles. Amonn's social method, rendered barren by its purely formal point of view, has turned out to be too weak an instrument for reconstructing the edifice of theoretical economics.]

PART 4

Franz Petry and His Attempt at a Social Interpretation of Marx's Theory of Value

∴

Introduction by the Editor[1]

When Rubin turns in this chapter to Franz Petry's social interpretation of Marx's theory of value, he describes Petry as 'a faithful student' of Heinrich Rickert, a leading philosopher of the Baden school of neo-Kantianism. Since Rubin explains Petry's work in terms of Rickert's influence, it is appropriate here to comment briefly on Rickert's view of the social sciences and particularly the study of history. As a philosopher committed to the autonomy of reason, Rickert taught that all knowledge involves *values* – as opposed to Menger's concern with economic *goods* – that ultimately belonged to an 'irreal' realm.[2] Whereas natural sciences claim to be value-neutral (apart from their obvious commitment to the value of truth), Rickert saw cultural sciences, including history, as necessarily value-relative. He rejected historicism because it denied ultimate values; he rejected naturalism because it implied a determinism that is indifferent to values.

If reason were to provide true knowledge of human action, Rickert believed the study of history must be a science. Unlike natural sciences, which abstract from particulars to discern universal laws of nature, history must be an *individualising* science that distinguishes what is value-significant from an endless stream of otherwise incoherent and disconnected experiences.[3] Historians do not record events; they analyse meanings. They do not posit values; instead, they determine what to study on the basis of generally acknowledged cultural values, and they pursue the object of their study in terms of the values of the historical periods and agents they are examining. The historian may approve or disapprove of those values, but historical science in all cases relates to values rather than to any natural causality.[4] The science of history, therefore, ulti-

---

1 There is very little secondary literature on Petry. Paul Sweezy briefly mentions the significance of Petry's distinction between the quantitative and the qualitative interpretation of value theory in *The Theory of Capitalist Development* (Sweezy 1946, pp. 25–8); there is a review by Rudolf Hilferding in *Archiv für die Geschichte des Sozialismus und der Arbeiterbewegung* (1919, pp. 439–48; reprinted in 15 volumes by Graz Akademische Druck- und Verlagsanstalt. Verlagsanstalt, 1964–66); another review by Rudolf Stammler in *Jahrbücher für Nationalökonomie und Statistik* (1917, pp. 237–41); and a brief foreword by Karl Diehl in Petry 1916, pp. iii–v.

2 Beiser 2015, pp. 415–16. For a comprehensive commentary on neo-Kantianism, see Heis 2018; also Kim 2015, pp. 39–58; in the same volume, Wagner and Härpfer 2015, pp. 171–85.

3 Rickert 1962, p. 21.

4 In *The Limits of Concept Formation in Natural Science* (1986, p. 93), Rickert gives the example of Martin Luther:

We can regard the personality of Luther as either a good thing or a bad thing. In other words, we can believe that it was a stroke of luck for the cultural development of Germany

mately requires a philosophy of history to determine what is culturally significant in universal terms, including the values of truth, beauty, happiness and morality in a community of free people.[5]

The connection that Petry finds between Marx and Rickert is the centrality of the *labour theory of value* in Marx's analysis of capitalism. Interpreting Marx in terms of Rickert, Petry imposes upon Marx what Rubin calls a preconceived idealistic viewpoint, 'an alien, Rickertian view of social science as an operational method for the *evaluative* arrangement of phenomena and not for their *causal* explanation'.[6] As a result, it seemed to Petry that Marx was engaged in an internally contradictory enterprise:

> From one direction Marx provides a causal study of the phenomena of capitalist economy; from the other, he wants to understand their 'social content' or 'cultural significance' .... Thus, what is original in Marx's sociological method ... is not the fact that Marx opened new paths for a *causal* explanation of economic phenomena, but rather that *alongside* a causal investigation of these phenomena he endeavours to reveal their 'social content' or '*meaning*'.

Petry thought Marx provided nothing new in terms of the theory of price determination; like all previous economists, he explained prices through competition. The true novelty of Marx's work concerned the qualitative rather than the quantitative results of competition, that is, 'the significance for separate social classes of the given state of prices, incomes and the corresponding distribution of products'. Petry thought the labour theory of value provided Marx with 'an *a priori methodological point of view* ... [that] makes it possible to regard things "as culturally significant objects"'[7] connected with the development of human personality.

Petry interpreted Marx's movement in *Capital* – from the specific, concrete labours of individual commodity producers to the universality of abstract labour – to imply Marx's acknowledgement of an equality of *rights* between market participants: the '*equality* of [abstract] labour signifies for Marx not the

---

or that it brought misfortune. On this point, the opinions of historians will probably always be in disagreement. But no one who knows the facts will doubt that Luther had some sort of *significance* with reference to generally acknowledged values, and it can never occur to a historian to claim that Luther's personality is historically *unimportant*.

5   Rickert first set out his view of ultimate values in 1913 in his essay on *The System of Values*, later elaborated in his *System of Philosophy* (1921). See Staiti 2018, section 4.

6   Italics added.

7   Petry 1916, p. 60.

common *natural* character of various human labours, rooted in their identical organic fundamentals, but an *ideal, legal* equality'. In Petry's view, Marx at times misunderstood his own method; he thought he was analysing dialectical causality, but in reality his theory of value functioned as 'a means to analyse ideal production relations between autonomously valued "subjects of rights" as "abstract" human personalities'.

Petry's idealism had clear affinities with the original works of Immanuel Kant, who had written in his *Idea for a Universal History with a Cosmopolitan Purpose* (1794) that 'The history of the human race ... can be regarded as the realization of a hidden plan of nature to bring about ... [a] perfect political constitution as the only possible state within which all natural capacities of mankind can be developed completely'.[8] For Kant, empirical history culminated in the coercive force of an external state of laws, wherein the lawful rights of each can coexist with the equal rights and duties of all others. But Kant believed that empirical history also pointed beyond itself to an ideal purpose, namely, an ethical commonwealth on earth and a noumenal kingdom of ends, or a rational whole of self-determining wills, each of which determines itself in accordance with the categorical imperative never to treat others merely as means to one's own ends.

Interpreting Marx's work through Rickert's neo-Kantian theory, Petry's study amounted, in Rubin's words, to 'a unique – and unsuccessful – attempt at a convergence of Marx's *sociological* method with Rickert's *teleological* method'. Rubin demonstrates how Petry mistakenly entangled Marx in neo-Kantian teleology, yet he also applauds Petry's understanding of the sociological character of Marx's work compared to 'the objective-technical point of view of vulgar economists' or the subjective individualism of the Austrian school. Rubin never undertook his own independent study of Marxist ethics, but his obvious respect for Petry's effort implicitly accords with Marx's conviction that the objective causality of dialectical contradictions points beyond commodity fetishism towards a real – not merely ideal – prospect of self-determination in which social individuals, embracing a humanist ethic, will rationally determine production relations through their own universal economic plan.

---

8   Kant 1990, p. 50.

Isaak Rubin on Franz Petry

Petry is not one of today's well-known German economists, such as Oppenheimer, Stolzmann, and Liefmann. Unlike them, he did not manage to publish numerous works and establish his own 'system'. The scientific career of this especially promising young scholar was cut short very early. Petry only submitted his doctoral dissertation in May 1914. He was called to the front a few months later, when the world war began, and within a year, in September 1915, he died in a Vilnius hospital at 26 years of age. His entire literary legacy consists of a brief doctoral dissertation of 70 pages, which was posthumously published in 1916 with the title *Der Soziale Gehalt der Marxschen Werttheorie* (*The Social Content of the Marxist Theory of Value*), including a foreword by Karl Diehl.

Although Petry's scientific activity remains unfinished, finding expression only in an attempted interpretation of Marx's theory of value, we nevertheless think it useful to familiarise the reader with his book. The work interests us first as a conscientious and thoughtful effort to interpret the Marxist theory of value – even though it begins with an incorrect point of view – and second, as one of the typical symptoms of the strong urge that can be seen among supporters of the 'social' tendency (Stolzmann and Amonn, for instance) to bring political economy closer to sociology.

Since 'the true founder of the social method of research is Karl Marx'[1] – according even to such a zealous opponent of Marxism as Liefmann – it is quite understandable that the most recent supporters of this method are somewhat influenced by Marx and are compelled, to one extent or another, to determine their relation to his economic theory, whether positive or negative. It is no coincidence that Stolzmann, the most important representative of the social method, considers himself in this respect to be continuing and 'correcting' Marx. Nor is it a coincidence that Petry tries, on the one hand, to provide a sociological interpretation of Marx's theory, while apparently attempting, on the other hand, to reach a sociological understanding of economic phenomena through a study of Marx.

Supporters of the sociological tendency (e.g. Stolzmann and Amonn) deserve recognition for their severe criticism of the traditional doctrines of contemporary bourgeois economic science, especially those of the Austrian school.

---

1 Liefmann 1920, p. 33. Rubin will turn to Liefmann in the next chapter of this book.

© RICHARD B. DAY, 2024 | DOI:10.1163/9789004705661_020

But notwithstanding all the promise of this critical work and all the validity of the sociological method as such, in the hands of today's bourgeois economists the latter takes on a sterile and at times even dangerous form for scientific research, appearing in close combination with an idealistic philosophy and neo-Kantianism in particular. The most important trend in contemporary bourgeois philosophy, *neo-Kantianism*, endeavours with all its strength to erect a high wall separating the social sciences from the strictly scientific and purely causal method of research that has achieved such splendid successes in modern natural science. In the opinion of neo-Kantians, social phenomena cannot become fully known to us solely by means of the causal method of investigation, that is to say, by clarifying their causes and consequences. In their view, it is also necessary to reveal the meaning of a given social phenomenon, its importance as a means for realising certain purposes and as a link in a series of phenomena that are connected with other phenomena not causally but teleologically. In this respect, neo-Kantians sometimes have in view an evaluation of the given phenomenon as a means, promoting (or hindering) the realisation of moral purposes and ethical norms. In that case, we have an attempt to subordinate social science to an obvious *ethical teleology*. Other neo-Kantians, from the school of Windelband and Rickert, attempt to disguise ethical tendencies and to give a narrower formulation to the teleological principle. They claim that in order to have a complete understanding of social phenomena the researcher must, of course, make a strict selection of those facts and phenomena to be studied from among a multitude of observations. And such selection, in their opinion, is possible only from the viewpoint of a definite *'purpose of the research'*. For example, a scholar who aims to study the Great French Revolution includes within the scope of his investigation only those phenomena that promoted (or hindered) dissolution of the aristocracy and the monarchy in France. The 'purpose of the research' provides the researcher with the key for selecting and classifying phenomena: he assembles and groups facts according to their importance for realising specific cultural-historical results, or their 'cultural significance'. The phenomena that serve as means for realising one and the same set of historical purposes, or social 'values', are assembled in one group. The result is that knowledge of social phenomena, independently of the ethical leanings of individual researchers, is necessarily distinguished by its teleological character. As distinct from the previously mentioned 'ethical teleology', in this case one can speak of *'gnoseological teleology'*,[2] as if it results from the very nature of the cognition of social phenomena.

---

2   [See note 6 in the preface to this volume regarding 'gnoseology' and 'epistemology'.]

As we have already mentioned, it is no coincidence that among bourgeois economists the sociological method frequently appears hand in hand with philosophical idealism. Stolzmann begins his investigation by counterposing 'natural' to 'social' categories in economic science, and he ends by counterposing the causal method of research to the teleological. With him, the 'social' is transformed into the 'ethical-teleological', and the campaign against 'naturalism' becomes a campaign against a strictly scientific and causal investigation, free of ethical teleology. While in Stolzmann's work the social method converges with the ethical-teleological, Petry presents us with teleology in a narrower form: he is a true student of Rickert, a supporter of 'gnoseological teleology'. He makes a unique – and unsuccessful – attempt at a convergence of Marx's *sociological* method with Rickert's *teleological* method.

In Petry's opinion, the entire Marxist system is penetrated by methodological *dualism*: it is founded upon an 'unnatural combination' of Hegel's idealistic philosophy with the 'materialistic and natural-scientific tasks of thinking'.[3] In the theory of value, this dualism is expressed in a contradiction between 'the causal, natural-scientific explanation of the phenomena of value and price', originating with Ricardo, and a 'cultural-scientific tendency that aspires to analyse the phenomena of value and price in terms of their social content and to introduce the "social" point of view'.[4] Elsewhere Petry counterposes 'the *explanatory*-causal mode of research' to a type of investigation that 'concerns the meaning and *understanding* of social relations';[5] that is, 'a purely theoretical investigation of price phenomena' to a 'social understanding' of them.[6] The implication of these rather unclear expressions is explained when Petry counterposes the Austrian school – which limits 'its task merely to an *explanation* of exchange phenomena, not evaluating them but viewing them solely in their natural connection' – to Marx, who wants 'to understand the same exchange phenomena in terms of their *cultural* significance, and who connects these exchange phenomena with special social values and thus highlights their social significance and makes their meaning understandable'.[7]

Thus, what we have here is a certain division, following Rickert, between 'the science of nature' and 'the science of culture' – a contrast between the natural-scientific method, which arranges phenomena in their *causal* connection, and the cultural-historical method, which organises phenomena according to a def-

---

3 Petry 1916, p. 2, all italics provided by Petry.
4 Ibid.
5 Petry 1916, p. 31.
6 Petry 1916, pp. 31–2.
7 Petry 1916, p. 59.

inite *evaluative* criterion. It is true that Petry, as a faithful student of Rickert, recognises that at the basis of his investigation Marx has not an ethical but a gnoseological criterion; Marx's theory of labour value is founded not upon a 'practical ethical demand for equality' but upon 'the formation of concepts that serve the pure goals of knowledge'.[8] 'In the Marxist concept of value there is no positive evaluation whatever, yet within it the *theoretical* principle of evaluative relations does find expression': and it is precisely with the help of this concept that Marx wants 'to understand the social value content' of the capitalist economy.[9] Marx's doctrine is 'a two-faced Janus',[10] with one face turned to the genetic (causal) method and the other face to the critical method[11] (in the sense of critical philosophy, i.e. the teleological method). From one direction Marx provides a causal study of the phenomena of capitalist economy; from the other, he wants to understand their 'social content' or 'cultural significance'. Petry limits his own task in advance: leaving aside the genetic or causal aspect of Marx's method, he assumes the task of illuminating the hitherto overlooked 'critical', cultural-historical, or social aspect of his method. Petry understands that such a presentation of Marx is one-sided and may even 'seem to be arbitrary',[12] but he stipulates beforehand that he does not want to elucidate Marx's theory of value as a whole, only the character of his method as critical or social.[13]

Thus, what is original in Marx's sociological method, despite the opinion of Hilferding and other Marxists, is not the fact that Marx opened new paths for a *causal* explanation of economic phenomena, but rather that *alongside* a causal investigation of these phenomena he endeavours to reveal their 'social content' or '*meaning*'. Insofar as the question involves a purely causal study of the economy, Marx did not introduce anything that was new in principle by comparison with other economists. In this respect, one can discern no difference in principle between the individualistic-psychological method of the Austrian economists and the sociological method of Marx: the former do not deny the presence of 'supra-individual ties that condition the separate individual', just as Marx, on the other hand, according to Petry, does not deny that 'analysis of empirical social life always leads to single individuals as its final elements'.[14]

---

8   Petry 1916, p. 32.
9   Petry 1916, pp. 32–3.
10   Petry 1916, p. 28.
11   Petry 1916, p. 21.
12   Petry 1916, p. 3.
13   Petry 1916, p. 6.
14   Petry 1916, p. 55.

Likewise, the uniqueness of Marx's sociological method must not be seen in the fact that he looks for inner causes concealed behind the external phenomena of competition. It is true that Marx himself, due to his admixture of the sociological (cultural-historical) and causal methods of research, is often inclined to interpret his sociological constructions in the sense of causal laws. For example, he often speaks of the importance of labour as 'the cause of the level of prices';[15] and with this causal interpretation he transforms labour value into some sort of 'supra-empirical causal series that operates over the heads of separate individuals'.[16] But such a causal understanding of labour value, which Marx adopted from Ricardo, in fact has nothing in common with the real ideas of Marx himself, for whom, as we shall see below, labour is an indicator of social relations of dependence between people and not at all the cause for the level of prices. Insofar as Marx is concerned with a purely causal investigation of price phenomena and exchange value, he sees the moving force of their real empirical changes in the same way as other economists do – not in labour but in competition. 'In reality, for him too (Marx), the moving forces are competition and separate individuals'.[17] 'Never thinking of excluding competition from his investigation, Marx, to the contrary, turns to competition for help in explaining every concrete phenomenon in the distribution of the aggregate value; it is not simply that the initial distribution of all values between capitalists and wage workers results from competition, but the distribution of surplus value and formation of the average level of profit are also explained exclusively by the motives of individual capitalists'.[18] Thus, when it is a question of a purely theoretical or *causal* study of the *empirical* phenomena of price, exchange value and distribution, together with their *quantitative variations*, Marx, in the same way as other economists, must assign the role of active cause to *competition* and the motives of *individual producers*.

In Petry's opinion, the whole novelty of Marx's method, in social terms, only appears with full force after a purely causal study of the real phenomena of price formation *has been completed*. The Austrian economists, whose sole task is a theoretical or causal study of the phenomena of exchange, take their research to be concluded at that point. Not so with Marx, who only now begins his 'social' analysis. We have seen that the process of market competition, directed by the motives of separate individuals, operated in the form of active cause for the real phenomena of price formation and resulted in a certain level

---

15   Petry 1916, p. 42.
16   Petry 1916, p. 55.
17   Ibid.
18   Petry 1916, pp. 44–5; See also p. 49 *et passim*.

of prices and incomes (since the wage is the price of labour power, rent is the price for using land, etc.). Up to this point we have looked only at the movement of things (prices and incomes) in the market. But now Marx proposes – and it is only here that his 'social' formulation of the problem begins – 'to analyse the finished results of capitalist competition in terms of their social content'.[19] In other words, Marx takes the given condition of prices and incomes as the 'finished results' of the competitive process, for which a causal explanation is no longer the issue that interests us, and he poses this question: *What is the 'social meaning' of these results of competition*, what is the significance for separate social classes of the given state of prices, incomes and the corresponding distribution of products? In this case, therefore, Marx wants to disclose not the 'cause' of the phenomena of price formation and distribution but rather their 'social meaning'. 'The causal mechanism of competition, which brings about the entire process of distribution through price formation, remains outside the scope of Marx's investigation; what he wants to understand, in terms of "*social meaning*", is the result of the forces that operate in competition'.[20] Marx's formulation of the problem has a '*social*', not a '*causal*', character.

This 'social' formulation of the problem consists of the fact that Marx wants to disclose the *relations between people* behind the movement of things in the market. 'The categories of political economy must be social, they have to express not the relations between things but the relations between people',[21] or the social relations of production. Here Petry – apparently influenced by Hilferding, whose work he cites – comes very close to a correct understanding of the sociological character of the Marxist theory of value. However, he quickly turns away from the proper path under the influence of his mistaken initial point of view, namely, the erroneous way in which he counterposes the social method to the causal. For Marx, the study of production relations between people belongs entirely within the scope of a causal examination of economic phenomena. That is precisely why, in order to understand the causes of the phenomena of price formation and distribution correctly, a preliminary analysis is required of the social structure of the economy or the production relations between people. Marx studies the production relations between people as a real phenomenon that enters into the causally conditioned mechanism of social development. Marx demonstrates that with the determinate type of production relations between people that characterises a commodity economy,

---

19   Petry 1916, p. 31.
20   Petry 1916, p. 30.
21   Petry 1916, p. 5.

with relations between commodity producers, the products of labour necessarily assume the social form of value (the form of value or exchange value in qualitative terms). Subsequently, Marx studies the various types of production relations between commodity producers (relations between independent commodity producers, relations between capitalists and workers, and relations between capitalists in various branches of industry). For each of these types of relations between people there is a corresponding special relation of exchange proportions between things as values in the market (exchange according to labour values, exchange of labour power for wages, and exchange according to prices of production). Although these formulae of exchange regulate the real process of price formation and distribution only through competition and the motives of individual commodity producers – determining a stable midpoint for the fluctuations and deviations of market prices – they also indicate the general direction for the motivations of producers and determine the general limits of the competitive struggle. Consequently, the presence of a determinate type of production relations between people is the precondition for the operation of definite 'economic laws' (in this case the formulae of exchange), which are the regulators of the process of market competition. Despite Petry's view, there are no 'economic metaphysics' involved, and there is no 'supra-social economic necessity upon which competition depends'.[22] All that is involved is the fact that in a causal explanation of phenomena we cannot, following Petry's example, regard competition and the motives of separate individuals as the ultimate moving cause of the phenomena of price formation and distribution. In the very process of competition we discern a lawful pattern in which the conditioning of competitive struggle and the motivation of producers is expressed in specific 'economic laws'; we look for explanation of the latter in the social structure of the economy, or in the specific features of the production relations between people. From Marx's standpoint, the production relation between people is a real social phenomenon, study of which is necessary for a causal explanation of the movement of things as values in the market.

For Petry, such understanding of the production relations between people and of the corresponding social form of things (exchange value) is alien. He looks for the ultimate explanation of exchange value and prices in competition and in the motives of individual producers, and at that point he considers the task of purely causal research to be completed. Consequently, in Petry's view, Marx turns to consideration of the production relations between people without any intention of giving a causal explanation of economic phenomena.

---

22   Petry 1916, p. 43.

Marx applies the sociological method of research in *parallel* with the purely theoretical and causal method, and he does so independently of the latter, even though Marx himself is not free from mistakenly confusing the two.

Independently of a causal explanation of the phenomena of exchange, Marx wants to uncover their 'social meaning', specifically, the production relations between people that are hidden behind them. In this context, however, Petry understands production relations as

> relations between people who relate to each other not as objects but as free, purposeful subjects. These are not the real-causal relations between things or people as elements of an external world; they express an ideal relation between people as *subjects*, a mutually recognised delimitation and correlation of their free spheres of action. In formal terms, the social production relation must be conceived as a legal relation and not as a real relation of dependence.[23]

There is no need to show in detail that Petry is completely mistaken in attributing to Marx this definition, which suffers from two fundamental errors: 1) *the production relation in general* is confused here with the production relation of *commodity producers*, since the relation between 'free, purposeful subjects', in possession of their own 'free spheres of action', is in fact an idealised relation between independent commodity producers; and 2), whereas Marx understands production relations to mean precisely a *'real* relation of dependence' between people, Petry has in mind an *'ideal* relation between people as subjects'.

This definition from Petry fully corresponds to his general understanding of Marxist theory: in Petry's view, Marx uses the concept of 'production relations between people' not for a causal explanation of economic phenomena but instead for *a social evaluation* of them. Viewing prices and the distribution of products as the 'finished result' of the process of competition, requiring no causal explanation, Marx is interested in the 'social meaning' of this result, in its significance for 'free, purposeful subjects' and its influence upon human per-

---

23 Petry 1916, pp. 7–8. It is true that on the material side Petry distinguishes the production relation from the legal one and provides a 'material' definition of the production relation that is closer to Marx's understanding: 'this is a unique social relation, established between participants in the process of production, based upon the division of labour, thanks to the real legal classification of the technical conditions of the labour process' (Petry 1916, p. 9). But subsequently the decisive role in Petry's constructions is played by the 'formal' definition of the production relation that we have cited in the text.

sonality. In order to understand this production relation (as 'an ideal relation between people as subjects'), which is concealed behind the given exchange proportions and the given distribution of products (e.g. the production relation between capitalist and worker), Marx must turn from the market movement of *things* to the human *personality*. And such a transition requires that all things or commodities be seen as *products of human labour*: the concept of labour serves Marx as the transitional link in moving from things to the human personality. 'How can the exchange relation, which seems to be a quantitative relation of one thing to another, be understood as a *social* production relation between *people*? Here we come to the decisive point where the *a priori* character of the principle of labour, as the measure of value, is revealed'.[24] What is involved is not a study of the empirical phenomena of exchange, but rather establishment of the kind of *a priori* point of view that would give us the possibility of moving from the *things* being exchanged to the human *personality*. Marx's labour theory of value is just such an *a priori* point of view. 'In use value, as the product of labour, a part of the human personality is embodied; whoever acquires such use value as property – regardless of how this occurs – also has indirect disposal over the product of human activity and thus over the man himself'.[25]

> The commodity has only one property that makes it possible to recognise it as the bearer and expression of social relations, namely, the property of being *the product of labour*, for in terms of that quality we can see it already not from the point of view of consumption but from the point of view of production, as embodied human activity; hence, the fate of that commodity in the process of circulation is in fact the fate of the human personality standing behind it and embodied in it through the process of production.[26]

The labour point of view transfers us

> ... from the sphere of circulation to the sphere of production; in the factories and workshops we see how a man embodies his personality in the product; and this product, entering into exchange, is no longer a natural thing but wholly the creation of a man, the congealed reality of living labour power, and though it is dead and mute its fate expresses the fate of

---

24   Petry 1916, pp. 17–18.
25   Petry 1916, p. 18.
26   Petry 1916, p. 19.

the man standing behind it, its direct producer. With such an understanding of the unity of the *process of production and circulation*, the process of commodity exchange is transformed from a purely external relation between products, having no effect on the social structure of society, into a social relationship between the personalities of producers.[27]

In order to pass from the exchange proportions between things to the personalities of the producers, Marx *a priori* regards commodities as products of human labour, as labour 'values', and the aggregate distribution of products as distribution between workers and capitalists of the aggregate value created by labour. The value separates into wages and surplus value, which in turn is divided into different types of revenue (entrepreneurial profit, interest, rent).[28] The purpose of all these constructions by Marx is not to provide a causal explanation of the real phenomena of production and distribution, nor do they aim to discover 'deeper, causally acting motive forces';[29] Marx simply wants to understand the 'social' significance of the already established process of product distribution for the *personalities* of the producers, and thus he *a priori* sees in products only the value created *by labour*. Only such an *a priori methodological point of view*, concerning labour as the measure of value, makes it possible to regard things as 'goods, i.e. as culturally significant objects'[30] connected with the human personality.

Petry endeavours, so to speak, to attribute an *idealistic* character to this '*apriority* of labour' that distinguishes Marxist theory. In his opinion, the exclusive significance that Marx assigns to labour, his 'accentuation' (underlining) of labour, reflects the 'exceptional evaluative emphasis that German philosophical idealism attaches to man as a willing subject in contrast to material nature'.[31] The presupposition of Marx's theory of labour value is 'Kant's doctrine concerning the primacy of practical reason, which, with an incomparable and special evaluative emphasis, distinguishes man and human relations from the whole of nature'.[32] Under the influence of German idealistic philosophy, which counterposes the human personality to material nature, Marx wants to pass from the movement of things in the market to the living personality

---

27   Petry 1916, p. 20.
28   Petry 1916, p. 30.
29   Petry 1916, p. 31.
30   Petry 1916, p. 60.
31   Petry 1916, p. 18. Here Petry comes close to the ethical teleology developed by Stolzmann. On the counterpoising of the free will of man to nature, see the first chapter of my essay on Stolzmann in this volume.
32   Petry 1916, pp. 20–1.

of the producers, and for that purpose he must first, so to speak, spiritualise the things themselves, regarding them as the products of labour or labour values.

Obviously, this entire 'social' construction of labour value on Marx's part differs sharply from Ricardo's causal construction of labour value. With the help of the '*law of value*' (*Wertgesetz*), Ricardo wants to give a causal explanation for the phenomena of exchange and distribution; with the help of an *a priori* 'value analysis' (*Wertbetrachtung*),[33] Marx aims to reveal the 'social meaning' of these phenomena completely apart from their causal explanation. Using labour value, Ricardo wants to explain exchange proportions or the exchange value of things; 'for Marx, representation of the good as a "value" says nothing concerning the concrete exchange relation or the exchange value of goods'.[34] The distinction that Marx draws between 'value' and 'exchange value' is mistakenly interpreted by Petry to mean that for Marx these concepts are separated from each other by an impassable divide; in his opinion, when Marx speaks of exchange value he has in view a causal investigation of quantitative changes in the empirical phenomena of exchange, whereas he uses the concept of 'value' to express only the *a priori* conditions for analysing the 'social meaning' of the same phenomena.[35]

Marx's 'social' method, according to Petry, means a complete and decisive turnabout both in terms of the general methodological formulation of the entire problem of value (a social rather than a causal posing of the question) and also in constructing the concept of 'value' (its difference in principle from 'exchange value'). Hence, it is clear that the concept of 'labour' also plays a completely different role in the Marxist theory of value than it does, for example, in Ricardo's theory. Claiming that the value of a product is determined by the quantity of labour (e.g. 20 days of labour), Marx has no intention of saying that the magnitude of labour expenditure causally determines the price level or exchange value of the product. He only wishes to define the social significance of the given product for the producer, to characterise the degree of 'social relations of dependence' expressed in the transfer of a given 'value', or of the product of (20 days of) the worker's labour, into the hands of the capitalist. Accordingly, in the Marxist theory of value 'labour is the measure of social relations of dependence; it is not the substantive cause of the level of price but

---

33   [Rubin translates '*Wertbetrachtung*' as '*точка зрения стоимости*'. When he subsequently refers to the '*точка зрения стоимости*', it will be translated here as 'value analysis'.]

34   Petry 1916, p. 27.

35   Petry 1916, pp. 27–8.

rather an indicator of the social content of the phenomena of price'.[36] It is true that in Marx, 'together with the idea that labour is an indicator of social relations, there also appears the idea, borrowed from the Ricardian theory of value, that labour is the indicator of exchange proportions, the *cause* of the level of prices'.[37] But such conceptual confusion only results from the fact that Marx himself did not clearly grasp the uniqueness of his social method and sometimes confused the latter with a causal method of research. To the extent that Marx remains true to his own social point of view, freed from the foreign impurities of causal research, he sees in labour not *'the cause' of the level of prices but an indicator of the social relations* between people.

Once labour plays a completely different role in the Marxist theory of value than it does in Ricardo's doctrine, it is natural that the very concept of 'labour' means something different for Marx than for the classics. Petry understands that for Marx the concept of *'abstract-universal'* labour differs markedly from 'the technical concept of labour as useful labour';[38] he emphasises – and this is his contribution – that this concept has a social, not a technical, character.[39] Yet Petry is unable to say just what this means. He does not understand that with the concept of 'abstract-universal' labour Marx generalises the real phenomena of a commodity economy (the equalisation of various types of labour through the market exchange of labour products as values), which is conditioned by the social structure of the latter, i.e. by its characteristic type of production relations between people as commodity producers. For Marx, the concept of abstract labour serves as the means to analyse the real production relations of commodity producers; for Petry, it is a means to analyse ideal production relations between autonomously valued 'subjects of rights' as 'abstract' human personalities. In 'abstracting' from various types of labour (through the exchange of their products), Marx sees the characteristic specificity of a 'concrete' economic structure (namely, a commodity economy), whereas for Petry 'abstract' labour is a manifestation of the activity of 'abstract' man.

> Universal labour is not a natural-scientific concept that includes only a common physiological content; rather, particular labours are abstract-universal and thereby also social as manifestations of the activities of subjects of rights. And just as the concept of a subject of rights is indiffer-

---

36   Petry 1916, p. 29.
37   Petry 1916, p. 42.
38   Petry 1916, p. 22.
39   Petry 1916, pp. 36–7.

ent in its *a priori* universality to the individual particularities of people, so also the concept of abstract-universal labour, which results from it, is foreign to all the individual differences of concrete useful labour.[40]

In exactly the same way, the '*equality* of labour signifies for Marx not the common *natural* character of various human labours, rooted in their identical organic fundamentals, but an *ideal, legal* equality'.[41]

As we see, in his doctrine of labour Petry also remains true to his general understanding of Marx's 'social' method, the purpose of which, in his view, is not to explain the real empirical phenomena of the labour activity of people but to know their 'social meaning' and 'cultural significance'. 'The investigation of economic phenomena from the point of view of labour is an *a priori methodological* device, the subjective condition for knowing', not the 'reflection of a real process in the object'.[42] The idea of labour value, which for Ricardo served as a causal, natural-scientific explanation of the phenomena of exchange, is transformed by Marx – although it is confused with the causal point of view that he adopted from Ricardo – into the 'subjective condition for knowing, which alone constitutes the social point of view'.[43] The latter involves not a causal study of social phenomena but a social evaluation of phenomena independently of their causal investigation. 'The social consists of a uniquely directed *purpose of knowledge* – not the peculiarities of the *object* but the initial formal, methodological point of view, which is characterised by the *subjective* mode of investigation'.[44] The social must be sought in a special *gnoseological point of view*, not in the 'particulars of the causal link' between phenomena.[45]

It follows that the goal of Marx's social method, if implemented consistently and freed from all elements of a causal explanation of phenomena, is not to find the causes for price changes. Insofar as it is a question of finding the *cause* for price changes, it must be sought in competition and in the motives of separate producers, not in labour value. Likewise, it is only competition that can explain for us the real distribution of incomes. But, in order to reveal the '*social meaning*' of prices and incomes that have already *emerged*, we must apply the *a priori scale of labour value* to them and consider them as specific 'shares of the aggregate value, as forms of the disposition of human labour, and thus as

---

40 Petry 1916, pp. 23–4.
41 Petry 1916, p. 24.
42 Petry 1916, p. 50.
43 Ibid.
44 Petry 1916, p. 59 (Rubin's italics).
45 Petry 1916, p. 59.

social relations'.[46] If it was possible in Volume I of Marx's *Capital*, given the condition of correspondence between prices and labour values, to interpret the *a priori* social 'value analysis' (*Wertbetrachtung*) mistakenly in the spirit of Ricardo's causal 'law of value' (*Wertgesetz*), in Volume III of *Capital* the discrepancy between them is striking. Here, prices clearly deviate from labour values, and it would be incorrect to assign to labour the role of 'cause' or final regulator of prices of production in the way that Marxists attempt to do. Prices of production, in Petry's opinion, are determined solely by competition and not by labour value. But does this mean that Marx's opponents are correct when they see in Volume III of *Capital* a collapse of his entire theory of labour value? No, replies Petry, such an opinion would be correct only if the goal of Marx's theory of labour value were a causal explanation of price phenomena and discovery of their 'cause'. In reality, Volume III of *Capital* represents abandonment of a causal 'law of labour value', although Marx fully retains his social 'value analysis',[47] because only with its help can he reveal the 'social meaning' of the phenomena of price formation and distribution that characterise a capitalist economy. The collapse of the 'law of value' in Volume III of *Capital* does not prevent consistent implementation of the 'value analysis', and the characteristic features of Marx's 'social' or 'critical' method, with its fundamental distinction from the method of causally explaining phenomena, appear even more clearly.[48]

The counterposing of *causal* to *social* methods, on which Petry builds his entire attempt at a 'social' interpretation of the Marxist theory of value, condemned the effort in advance to complete failure. Marx's entire system is built on a strictly implemented method of *causal explanation of real phenomena*, and it is therefore totally incorrect to counterpose his method – as being 'critical' (in the sense of Kant's critical philosophy) – to Ricardo's causal or 'genetic' method. Marx himself counterposed his method, as 'genetic', to the analytical method of the classics.[49] Marx strives, just as Ricardo does, for a causal explanation of phenomena. But Ricardo limits his investigation to quantitative

---

46   Petry 1916, pp. 29–30.
47   Petry 1916, p. 48.
48   Petry 1916, p. 45.
49   ['Classical political economy occasionally contradicts itself in this analysis. It often attempts directly, leaving out the intermediate links, to carry through the reduction and to prove that the various forms are derived from one and the same source. This is however a necessary consequence of its analytical method, with which criticism and understanding must begin. Classical economy is not interested in elaborating how the various forms come into being, but seeks to reduce them to their unity by means of analysis, because it starts from them as given premises. But analysis is the necessary prerequisite of genet-

changes in the value of the commodity, looking for an explanation in development of the material process of production and in the rising technical productivity of labour. Marx is interested not only in quantitative changes but
also in the qualitative, in the social 'form of value' that the products of labour
acquire in the presence of a determinate social structure of the economy.
Beneath the external form of the 'value' of commodities, Marx finds social-
production relations between people as commodity producers; beneath the
quantitative changes of value, he finds the process of distribution of social
labour. It is precisely here that we find the sociological character of the Marxist
theory of value. In Petry's attempt to interpret 'the social content of the Marxist theory of value' (the title of his book), he makes two fundamental mistakes.
First, he severs all ties between the phenomena of *value* and the process of
material production and distribution of *social labour*; the result is an impassable gulf between value, on the one hand, and exchange value and prices on
the other. Secondly, although he acknowledges the connection between value
and the production relations between people, Petry portrays this connection
in a *purely idealistic* way. He understands production relations not as real relations between producers, which require a causal explanation, but as 'ideal relations' between abstract human persons as 'the subjects of rights'. These 'ideal
relations' (actually representing relations between formally independent commodity producers in an idealised manner and translated into philosophical
language) are constructed *a priori* by the researcher, or the knowing subject,
who in so doing begins not with the real features of the phenomena being
investigated but with his own 'ideal', gnoseological and essentially evaluative
criteria, specifically, with the wish to reveal their 'social meaning' or to give a
social evaluation of these phenomena. Hence, characterisation of the social
relation as one of 'labour' (the *a priori* methodological principle of labour) is
not derived by the researcher from the real phenomena themselves but is introduced into them from without, being 'invented'[50] by the knowing subject. In
fact, it turns out from Petry's point of view that a purely theoretical or causal
investigation applies only to the phenomena of competition or the movement
of things in the market. But since the 'social', *a priori* point of view demands
an 'evaluative emphasis on personality', which is counterposed to the whole
of nature, the researcher must turn away from things to the living human personality, and he accomplishes this transition by considering things as products
of human labour. The concept of 'labour' serves the transition from things to

---

ical presentation, and of the understanding of the real, formative process in its different
phases'. Marx 1972, pp. 920–1.]

50   [The word that Rubin uses is 'примышляется'.]

human personality. One can say that for Petry the thing is the *object* of the investigation insofar as the latter has a causal character; personality is the *goal* of the research; and labour is the *'means* of analysis',[51] i.e. the means for the investigation. For Marx, the *object* of the study is labour relations between persons as members of society (not the 'human personality' in general). But since the labour connection between people in a commodity-capitalist economy only occurs through the transfer of things, it follows that the production-labour relations between people take the form of the value of things. The connection between value and labour results from the social form of the commodity economy, not from an *a priori* concept 'invented' by the knowing subject in order to construct a bridge from things to 'personality'. The labour relation between people and the movement of the value of things are closely intertwined and interact with each other in real economic activity; the theoretical connection between values and labour in the Marxist scheme is a reflection of this real connection between phenomena, not the result of *a priori* gnoseological requirements.

Petry's basic errors are not unique; in a certain sense they are common both to him and to other economists who combine the 'social' method of research with philosophical *idealism*. Given all the differences between Petry's constructions and those of Stolzmann, one can still see in them certain lines of convergence. They both recognise the fruitfulness of Marx's 'social' method, which saw in economic categories an expression of the social production relations between people. Yet Stolzmann and Petry both understand these relations in an idealistic sense. Both of them tear apart the close connection that exists between the production relations of people and the development of material productive forces, resulting in a rupture between changes in the value of things and the growth of labour productivity. Stolzmann and Petry transform the production relations of people into purely formal, ideal relations between the 'subjects of rights' (Petry) or the participants in 'social-ethical regulation' (Stolzmann). Insofar as the purely formal aspect of production relations is emphasised, the result is an inclination to merge social-economic with legal relations.[52] And to the extent that production relations are conceived as 'ideal' relations, constructed by the knowing subject according to his gnoseological mission (Petry), or constructed by society according to its ethical mission

---

51   Petry 1916, p. 21.
52   Petry recognises their formal similarity, although he notes the material difference between them in a commodity society. A more striking inclination towards an ethical-juridical understanding of social relations appears in Stolzmann. See the first chapter of my essay on Stolzmann in this volume.

(Stolzmann), the social method of investigation is converted into a *teleological* method and counterposed to the *causal* method.

While it is true that Petry's idealistic point of view condemned his original attempt at a sociological interpretation of the Marxist theory of value to complete failure, it must still be pointed out that it is precisely in the sociological understanding of economic phenomena that Petry correctly saw the special value and characteristic feature of Marx's method. In several places throughout his book Petry emphasises Marx's interest in the social relations between people – which are concealed by the movement of things in the market – and the difference between Marx's sociological point of view and the objective-technical point of view of vulgar economists. Petry clearly understands that for Marx many concepts (the concept of abstract labour, for instance) have a social and not a technical character, yet Petry is not in a position to explain that character correctly because of his erroneous general methodological point of view. In reading Petry's book one occasionally gets the impression that this young scholar, who was foreign to Marxism in terms of his education and separated from it by a wall of philosophical idealism, persistently endeavoured to break through those barriers into the world of Marxist ideas. The barriers proved sufficiently strong to restrain Petry's thoughts within the enchanted circle of philosophical idealism. Nevertheless, the author's conscientious and sincere effort to grasp the flow of Marx's ideas deserves special recognition.

PART 5

The Economic Theory of Robert Liefmann

..

Introduction by the Editor[1]

One of the most obvious failures that Rubin saw in Austrian theory was its inability to move beyond individual economic judgements. Although in the classical period of political economy writers such as Smith, Malthus, and Ricardo had considered the market system as an integrated whole, today macroeconomic theory is generally said to have originated with Keynes' *General Theory of Employment, Interest and Money*. It is a fact, however, that long before Keynes' *General Theory* Marx's *Capital* systematically moved from simple commodity production and individual exchange to the law of value, social classes, the periodic occurrence of business cycles, and even the beginnings of a theory of capitalist imperialism.

In the essay that follows, Rubin explains his interest in Robert Liefmann's work by reference to its attempt to impart more 'realism' to marginalist theory. Liefmann's theory represented 'a new attempt to justify the psychological method' by deriving all the most important phenomena of the exchange turnover, namely, the processes of price and income formation, from 'evaluations of utilities and costs that originate with consumers':

> [Liefmann] wants to provide an 'empirical-realistic' version of the psychological theory. Whereas the Austrian economists have focussed their attention mainly on elaborating the basic psychological premises of their theory, making only passing reference to 'modifications' introduced by capitalist reality, from the very outset Liefmann wants to include in his psychological theory features adopted from the capitalist economy.

Like most economists of the time, Rubin considered Liefmann to be a disagreeable person and an even more mediocre economic theorist.[2] Readers who fol-

---

1   Robert Liefmann was educated in law and economics at Freiburg University. At the suggestion of Max Weber, a personal friend, he completed his *habilitation* in business organisation and antitrust law, became associate professor in 1904 and later full professor. He acquired a substantial reputation for his early work on cartels and trusts, which, as Rubin notes in this essay, 'provided valuable material for understanding the latest forms of monopoly capitalism'. Liefmann was murdered by the Nazis in 1941.

2   A typical assessment came in a review of Liefmann's work by G.A. Kleene (1921, pp. 461–8):
    On the whole there is little reward for the pain-cost of going through [Liefmann's] fifteen hundred pages. His understanding of the existing body of economic theory is astonishingly superficial. It is conceivable that a vigorous mind unhampered by what others have accomplished might attain to new and valuable ideas. But when a writer with all the prestige that

low the labyrinthine reasoning of Liefmann's *Grundsätze der Volkswirtschafts-lehre* (*Principles of Economics*, 1924), will find remarkably little that is, in fact, either empirical or realistic. On the contrary, there is almost no connection between Liefmann's theory and empirical-technical, let alone social, ethical or political issues. Liefmann's system is based entirely upon personal introspection and economic psychology. After examining each of Liefmann's claims to 'modernise' the doctrines of the Austrian school, Rubin finds few substantial differences and concludes that Liefmann ended with 'a series of insurmountable contradictions and arbitrary constructions'.

Isaak Rubin on Robert Liefmann

A polemic for and against Liefmann has attracted considerable attention in the latest German economic literature, especially since Liefmann published his copious two-volume work *Grundsätze der Volkswirtschaftslehre* in 1917–19.[3] Liefmann is not a newcomer to the economic literature. He emerged on the literary scene as early as the late nineteenth century with a whole series of works of a concrete-descriptive character. Liefmann became most widely known for his books on cartels and trusts[4] and on financial societies, which provided valuable material for understanding the latest forms of monopoly capitalism.[5] But Liefmann has not limited himself to observing and describing the concrete phenomena of modern capitalism. He always felt 'compelled' to investigate purely theoretical problems, a calling whose force was not quite matched by the author's talents. From 1907 onwards, Liefmann wrote numerous articles that subjected the theory of modern economists, and primarily the theory of price and distribution, to sharp and often warranted criticism. Subsequently,

---

goes in Germany with academic position puts forth such vast claims to originality as does Professor Liefmann, he should have informed himself conscientiously of what has already been done in the field. A long catalog could be made of his misconceptions of other writers and of his reckless generalizations in regard to prevailing theoretical tendencies.

3   [For the dispute between Alfred Amonn and Robert Liefmann, see Amonn 1918–19, pp. 367–421; Liefmann 1920–21, pp. 500–22; and Amonn 1920–21, pp. 523–41. For Franz Oppenheimer's commentary on Liefmann, see Oppenheimer 1919c. Also Steinberg 1922; Stolzmann 1922. See also Kleene 1921, pp. 461–8, and Robert Liefmann's reply (1922, pp. 335–42).]

4   [There is a Russian translation: Liefmann, *Karteli i tresty* (Izdatel'stvo 'Ekonomicheskoi zhizni', 1925). A short popular work by Liefmann was also published in Russian: Liefmann, *Formy predpriyatii* (Moscow: Izdatel'stvo VSNKh, 1924).]

5   The book *Kartelle und Trusts und die Weiterbildung der volkswirtschaftlichen Organisation* appeared in 1905. The book *Beteiligungs- und Finanzierungsgesellschaften, eine Studie über den modernen Kapitalismus und das Effektenwesen* appeared in 1909.

Liefmann became interested in the problem of money; in his book *Geld und Gold* (*Money and Gold*, 1916) he emerged as one of the most extreme representatives of the nominalist theory of money. Finally, in *Grundsätze der Volkswirtschaftslehre*, Liefmann summarised his theoretical works and attempted to provide a complete 'theoretical system', embracing all the basic problems of theoretical economics. In the first volume, the author develops in detail his psychological conception of economy, built upon the concepts of psychological utility, psychological costs, and psychological yield. In the second volume, Liefmann attempts to use his psychological conception of economy to explain the most important phenomena of the turnover of commodities; here we find his teaching on money, the theory of prices, and the theory of incomes.

Liefmann appears in the proud pose of a reformer, reconstructing the entire building of theoretical economics. With the greatest of self-esteem, bordering on self-promotion, he never tires of emphasising on every page the novelty and originality of his own views on the one hand, and the stupidity and mediocrity of his opponents on the other. Liefmann claims the title of a new Ricardo, revealing new paths and perspectives for science.

This limitless pretension, however, is not matched by the quality of Liefmann's 'theoretical system'. Even against the background of today's European economic literature, which is far from glittering with a profusion of theoretical talents, Liefmann cannot claim first place. It is easier, perhaps, to agree with the opinion of one of his critics, Esslen, who has called Liefmann a poor economist and a bad writer.[6] Unlike Oppenheimer, Liefmann does not impress the reader with any clarity of thought and sparkling presentation; and unlike Stolzmann, he does not attract the reader with a well-intentioned pursuit of the truth and profound critical analysis. Upon reading Liefmann's book, readers are unpleasantly struck by a confusion of concepts, inconsistent terminology, forced analogies and endless repetitions, captious criticism and clamorous self-promotion. True, the reader will also be struck by Liefmann's strong point: the perseverance and stubbornness with which he tries to develop his ideas through an unfolding series of complex phenomena and problems. But, with the help of an uncritical confusion of concepts and terms, Liefmann only manages to create the appearance of triumph for his ideas.

If, despite these theoretical and literary shortcomings, we consider it necessary to familiarise readers with Liefmann's works, it is mainly because of the importance that Liefmann's theory assumes as a new attempt to justify the

---

6 [Esslen 1918, p. 1075; see also Liefmann's 'Abwehr' and Esslen's 'Erwiderung' in *Schmollers Jahrbuch für Gesetzgebung, Verwaltung und Volkswirtschaft im Deutschen Reiche*, Vol. 44 (1920). See also Kleene 1921, pp. 461–8, and Liefmann's reply (1922, pp. 335–42).]

psychological method. Liefmann is a supporter of the individualistic-psychological method in political economy, which has been so strikingly developed in
the works of the Austrian economists. As a quite knowledgeable observer of the
real phenomena of modern capitalism, however, Liefmann cannot be unaware
of how far the psychological constructions of the Austrians depart from actual
reality. In place of the abstract and lifeless psychological theories of the Austrian economists, Liefmann wants to provide a new psychological conception
of the economy that is much more suitable to the phenomena of modern capitalism. He wants to provide an 'empirical-realistic' version of the psychological
theory. Whereas the Austrian economists have focussed their attention mainly
on elaborating the basic psychological premises of their theory, making only
passing reference to 'modifications' introduced by capitalist reality, from the
very outset Liefmann wants to include in his psychological theory features
adopted from the capitalist economy. For that reason, Liefmann's theory bene-
fits from a sense of realism and an approximation to reality when compared to
the teaching of the Austrian school, although it loses in terms of logical clarity and coherence compared to the Austrian school. In the following chapters
we shall try to reveal the arbitrary constructions and strained analogies with
which Liefmann hopes to bring his psychological theory closer to actual capitalist reality. The arbitrariness and failure of these constructions and analogies
can justifiably be regarded as evidence of the collapse not just of Liefmann's
theory, but also of the psychological method in political economy in general.

The Psychological Conception of the Economy

Liefmann is an extreme representative of the individualistic-psychological-method in political economy. He accuses all former and contemporary schools of political economy of a 'technical-materialistic' or 'objective-materialistic-quantitative' bias. Economic phenomena appear to us primarily in the form of prices or the monetary expression of goods. The classics stripped this 'monetary veil' from economic phenomena and revealed beneath it the technical process of the production of material products. But that way of thinking led them from the economy to technique. In order to remain within the limits of the economy or economics, we must direct our attention elsewhere. Behind the 'monetary veil' we must uncover the *psychological experiences* of individual economic actors, which in the final analysis explain the entire process of exchange along with its characteristic problems of money, prices and incomes.

Economy must be strictly distinguished from *production*. The distinguishing attribute of economy is not some specific feature of the technical process of production, not the 'relation of man to the external things of nature', but instead 'something *psychological, a special type of judgements and decisions*'.[1] Economic activity occurs whenever individuals have a certain psychological experience, which consists of comparing the utilities they are striving for with the costs necessary to attain them. 'Economic activity means *comparing utility (Nutzen) with costs (Kosten) – a sense of pleasure and displeasure*[2] – *on the basis of the economic principle*',[3] which prescribes striving to achieve the greatest utility with the least costs.

The psychological concept of economy leads us, therefore, to two basic concepts: *utility (Nutzen)* and *costs (Kosten)*. Both of these concepts must be understood in a strictly psychological sense. 'Utility' refers to the psychological condition of pleasure that the individual experiences with fulfilment of a given need. 'Costs' refer to the sense of displeasure that an individual experiences due to the burdens or sacrifices that he must take upon himself in order to acquire the

---

1   Liefmann 1920, p. 67.
2   [The word that Rubin uses is '*неудовольствие*'.]
3   Liefmann 1920, p. 276. There are significant difficulties in translating into Russian the term '*Kosten*' in the sense used by Liefmann. S. Solntsev (1922) translates this term as '*stoimosti*' (p. 140). A. Sokolov (1923, p. 28) uses the word '*zatraty*'. It seems more appropriate to us to use the term '*izderzhki*', which P. Struve used in *Khozyaistvo i tsena*, part 2 (1916, p. 99).

utility that he desires. To acquire the utilities, an individual must make a sacrifice in the form of: 1) his labour, 2) material things, or 3) money. Hence labour, material things and money can be regarded as bearers or 'factors of cost' (*Kostenfaktoren*), although it would be totally incorrect to confuse them with actual costs (*Kosten*).[4] *Costs* do not involve labour, things or money in their material form, but rather the *psychological feeling of displeasure* that the individual experiences due to the need to sacrifice labour, goods or money. 'Costs do not consist of a quantity of things; this is a concept involving feeling or evaluation, a psychological category'.[5] Of the three factors of cost that we have mentioned, it is usually the case (although not always) that labour is the basic and ultimate one to which the others are reduced. For now, therefore, we shall simplify and assume that the only factor of cost is labour. In this case, the costs themselves consist not of labour as such (for example, the expenditure of 10 hours of labour), but rather of the individual's psychological evaluation of the burden of the labour, or his 'labour efforts'.[6]

Neither the sum of utilities nor the sum of costs is *fixed* in advance, i.e. the individual cannot know beforehand (except from previous experience) either the total sum of his needs that can be satisfied – in accordance with the economic principle – or the total costs he must pay.[7] Both of these magnitudes are determined only after our individual performs the psychological act of *comparing utilities and costs* (as psychological sensations) and, on the basis of this act, prepares for himself a concrete economic plan that precisely specifies both the sum of needs to be satisfied and the sum of costs to be expended.

A comparison of utilities and costs enables the individual to determine: 1) *the general sum* of costs to be expended in his economic activity, and 2) the sum of costs being expended for the satisfaction of each *individual need*. The first task is relatively easy to solve. It is obvious that the individual will continue his economic activity only as long as the utility exceeds the costs, i.e. as long as the pleasure from fulfilment of needs exceeds the displeasure connected with 'labour efforts'. But, according to Gossen's[8] famous law of the 'satiation of needs', to the extent that needs are fulfilled the resulting pleasure diminishes. Conversely, each additional hour of labour causes the individual greater

---

4 Liefmann 1920, pp. 309, 387.

5 Liefmann 1920, p. 303.

6 Liefmann 1920, pp. 387–8.

7 On this point, we cannot agree with the opinion of Liefmann's critics (Amonn and Esslen), who claim that the sum of costs (*sredstv*) must always be pre-given and precisely fixed (see Amonn 1918–19, p. 48; Esslen 1918, p. 274).

8 [The reference is to Hermann Heinrich Gossen (1810–1858), whose first law was that of diminishing marginal utility.]

displeasure, i.e. represents to him a greater sum of (psychological) costs. This means that a moment must inevitably arrive when any further expenditure of costs for the satisfaction of needs will come to an end.

For example, suppose that our individual has only a single need, bread for instance. The first pound of bread yields him a psychological utility that may be numerically expressed[9] by the figure 12, the second pound by 11, and so forth. On the other hand, the first hour of labour represents for him psychological 'costs' equivalent to 1, the second hour 2, etc. Each hour of labour brings him one pound of bread. During the first hour of expending costs equal to 1, our individual acquires bread whose utility equals 12. He receives a net psychological benefit or psychological 'yield' (*Ertrag*) of 11. This 'yield', as we see, is what Liefmann calls the '*surplus of utility over costs*' or the *relation* between utility and costs.[10] In this case, we can say that for his unit of costs our individual has received a utility equal to 12, or a yield equal to 11.

The concept of 'yield' (*Ertrag*) plays a central role throughout Liefmann's theory. It is derived from the concepts of 'utility' (*Nutzen*) and 'costs' (*Kosten*), and like those two concepts it has a *purely psychological* character. The 'yield' of which we are currently speaking is a psychological sense of the difference (or relation) between utility and costs. This purely psychological yield we call the '*consumer yield*' (*Konsumertrag*), insofar as our individual realises it in the process of consumption.

Our individual, having worked for one hour, not only senses a 'yield', as the difference between the utility he has received and the costs expended; he also senses a *magnitude of yield*.[11] He cannot measure it and give it a numerical expression, yet he can compare this yield to some other yield and say which is greater. For example, our individual clearly feels that during a second hour of labour his psychological or consumer yield is less than during the first hour. In fact, if we come to his assistance and provisionally assign numbers to his utility and costs, we shall see that during the second hour of labour his yield is only 9 (namely, 11–2), during the third hour 7, the fourth hour 5, and the fifth hour 3. During the fifth hour, our individual has received a utility equal to 8, he has expended costs equal to 5, and his return is 3. Let us assume that our

---

9   Liefmann realises that psychological sensations of pleasure and displeasure cannot be measured but only compared. The individual may say that one sense of pleasure is greater than another, but no number can be attached to this feeling. Nevertheless, in the interest of clarity of exposition, Liefmann allows himself to use figures to denote the magnitude of utility and costs.

10   Liefmann 1920, p. 395.

11   Ibid.

individual works no more than 5 hours. It is true that from a purely theoretical point of view our individual, in accordance with the economic principle, must continue working until his utility corresponds to the costs, i.e. until the yield approaches *zero*. However, Liefmann avoids this conclusion and assumes that the psychological yield always involves a certain positive sum,[12] in our example, 3.

Accordingly, our individual works a total of 5 hours. Each hour provides him with a different psychological yield, and the final hour of labour provides the least, or the '*marginal yield*' (*Grenzertrag*) equal to 3. 'The return from the last unit of costs, expended on each need, we call the marginal yield'.[13]

The concept of the 'marginal yield' is extremely important. Only with its help is it possible to solve the *second* of the tasks mentioned earlier, which is the central task of all economic activity: 'an expedient and correct distribution of expenditures on the most diverse needs based upon the principle of the max-imum'[14] (i.e. the maximal satisfaction of needs). Our individual has not just one need but many different needs.[15] The question is *how to distribute* costs, labour expenditures for example, between them. Costs must be distributed in such a way that for all needs the 'marginal yields' (i.e. the yields furnished by the last unit of costs) *will be equal*. If, in the sphere of satisfaction of one need (clothing, for example), the 'marginal yield' is higher than in another sphere (e.g. food), it is to the individual's advantage to transfer one or several units of costs (e.g. labour) from the latter sphere to the former as long as the marginal yields are not equal in both. That is the great, fundamental economic '*law of the equalisa-tion of marginal yields in the consumer economy*', the law that Liefmann sees as the principal key to the explanation of all economic phenomena.

'The law of the equalisation of marginal yields', as is evident from its formula-tion, represents nothing more than the theoretical combination of three basic ideas: 1) the idea of '*yield*', 2) the idea of the '*margin*', and 3) the idea of '*equal-isation*'. Liefmann ascribes to himself the exclusive honour of combining these ideas, although he acknowledges that they were also individually developed by previous economists. Thus, the idea of the 'margin' is found in its infancy even

---

12   Liefmann 1920, pp. 416, 417.

13   Liefmann 1920, p. 404.

14   Liefmann 1920, p. 281.

15   In Liefmann's opinion, we can only speak of economic activity when the individual must choose between the satisfaction of various needs, i.e. when costs are compared with *differ-ent* utilities. Insofar as the individual is concerned with selecting the least costs (*sredstv*) for acquiring a previously given and determinate utility (*tseli*), what is involved is a tech-nical but not an economic act.

in the classics (in Ricardo's theory of rent and in Thünen's[16] theory of wages) and was most forcefully developed in the doctrine of marginal utility by the Austrian economists.[17] The idea of 'equalisation' is also found in Ricardo (in his teaching on the equalisation of the rate of profit on capital) and also in the work by Austrian economists, who adopted Gossen's famous law, which says the satisfaction of needs for different types of goods continues until the marginal yield of the different types is equalised.[18] Yet Liefmann insists that the idea of 'yield', understood in the psychological sense as a surplus of (psychological) utility over (psychological) costs, is found in none of the previous economists.

Asserting the complete originality of his theory, and knowing meanwhile that an impartial reader cannot fail to be struck by the numerous similarities between this theory and the doctrine of the Austrian economists, Liefmann painstakingly seeks to differentiate between the two theories. He finds differences between them where in fact there are virtually none, and he enormously exaggerates their importance where they do exist.

In general terms, the basic lines of difference between the doctrine of the Austrian economists and that of Liefmann can be reduced to the following three:

1) The Austrian economists assume the *prior* existence of a determinate *supply of goods*.[19] Liefmann justifiably reproaches them for ignoring the fact that the quantity of goods is itself simply a result of the economic activity of individuals who act on the basis of a preliminary comparison of utilities and costs.

2) Beginning from a pre-existing supply of goods, the Austrian economists come to the conclusion that the subjective value of a given good depends not only upon its usefulness but also upon its *scarcity* (i.e. the quantity available). The magnitude of a particular good's supply determines its marginal utility and thereby also its value. All units of a given supply of goods have the same 'value' (*Wert*), which corresponds only for the last unit to its individual 'utility' (*Nutzen*). Liefmann harshly condemns the Austrian economists for introducing into their theory, along

---

16 [The reference is to Johann Heinrich von Thünen (1783–1850), a representative of the German geographical school in economics and one of the predecessors of marginalism.]

17 Liefmann 1920, p. 440.

18 Liefmann 1920, p. 443.

19 Liefmann 1920, pp. 652, 312 *et passim*. We leave aside the question of whether the Austrian economists start from a given supply of 'consumer' goods, an assertion that we encounter sometimes in Liefmann (e.g. p. 651 of Volume I) and that is disputed by supporters of the Austrian school. In any case, the latter also recognise that their theory presupposes a given supply of productive goods (which include labour).

with the concept of individual utility, also the concept of 'value'. Recognising the dependence of a good's value upon such an objective factor as the quantity (scarcity) of the good is tantamount to abandonment of subjective-psychological theory. 'The modern concept of economic value, as a function of utility and scarcity, means nothing but the introduction of objective-materialistic-quantitative notions, pretending to be subjective, into the theory of value'.[20]

Since the Austrian economists did not know how to free themselves from the influence of objective-materialistic ideas, Liefmann claims for himself alone the honourable title of consistent defender of the subjective-psychological theory. He completely banishes from political economy the concept of 'value' (Wert), concurring in this respect with several of the most recent economists (Cassel)[21] who begin from other points of view. In Liefmann's opinion, economic theory must operate solely with the concept of the individual 'utility' (Nutzen) of a given good, based upon the purely subjective 'valuation' (Schätzung) of it by a particular individual.[22] Specific units of a given good satisfy different needs of the individual and for that reason have different 'utility', regardless of the volume of their current supply.[23] For instance, in our earlier example the first pound of bread represents a utility of 12 for our individual, the second pound 11, etc. Regardless of whether our individual has five pounds of bread, as we assumed, or some other quantity – in all circumstances the first pound of bread provides him with a utility of 12, the second 11, etc. The Austrian economists are mistaken when they assume that, in a case where our individual has five pounds of bread, each pound of bread will have an identical value of 8 (i.e. the utility of the marginal, fifth pound of bread).

3) Finally, the Austrian economists – and this is the third, most significant failing of their theory – who begin with a previously given supply of goods and erect upon this basis an erroneous concept of 'value', completely overlook the psychological concept of costs (Kosten), without which economic understanding is impossible.[24] The Austrian school 'does not counterpose purely subjective appraisals of utility to equally subjective appraisals of

20   Liefmann 1920, p. 211.
21   [The reference is to Karl Gustav Cassel (1866–1945), a Swedish economist and professor of economics at Stockholm University.]
22   Liefmann 1920, pp. 652–3 et passim.
23   Liefmann 1920, p. 512.
24   Liefmann 1920, p. 654 ff.

cost, and therefore it does not arrive at the concept of yield in the sense of a comparison of utility with costs'.[25]

Liefmann's claims that the Austrian economists, who developed the psychological concept of utility and value, considered costs from a mathematical-quantitative point of view (as a specific sum of means of production and labour), cannot be seen as fully valid. Certain Austrian economists, especially Wieser,[26] paid considerable attention to the problem of costs of production and tried to include them in their general psychological conception of the economy. They also considered costs (means of production and labour) as having subjective value for the individual and being subject to psychological 'valuation' from that direction. But they assumed – and this, in our view, is the main point of difference between them and Liefmann – that the psychological *valuation of costs* is entirely determined by the psychological *valuation of the utilities* that can be obtained with their use. In the example that we gave earlier, each pound of bread, in the opinion of the Austrian economists, has a value equal to 8. This value of consumer goods is transferred to 'productive goods', which play the role of necessary costs to acquire consumer goods. In our example, the individual expends 'costs' in the form of 5 hours of his labour. In the view of the Austrian economists, each hour of labour has, in this case, a subjective value for the individual of 8, i.e. the value of the good acquired by applying the last hour of labour. The valuation of costs is nothing more than a *reflection* of the valuation of utilities; the magnitude of the former is determined by the magnitude of the latter. Liefmann disputes that view. In his exposition, the process of evaluating costs appears as an *independent* psychological process that is *counterposed* to the process of evaluating utilities. The 'utilities' of the five pounds of bread, being different for each individual pound, are expressed by the figures: 12, 11, 10, 9 and 8. Meanwhile, the psychological valuation of the 'costs' required to obtain them (i.e. the displeasure associated with labour efforts), was 1 for the first hour of labour, 2 for the second, 3 for the third, 4 for the fourth, and 5 for the fifth. Each unit of costs is given its own psychological valuation, which does not depend upon the valuations of utility (bread) and is counterposed to them. It is precisely this *counterposing* of two psychological valuations (utilities and costs) that produces the resulting psychological sensation of 'yield' (*Ertrag*), as the *difference* between utility and costs.

---

25   Liefmann 1920, p. 656.

26   [The reference is to Friedrich von Wieser (1851–1926), professor of political economy at the University of Vienna.]

However, if the valuation of utilities (of the bread) does not influence the valuation of costs (labour efforts), the reverse also applies: *the valuation of costs does not influence the valuation of utilities*. If the first of Liefmann's claims differentiates him from the *Austrian* school, the second claim separates him from the *theory of subjective labour value* (the so-called disutility theory) widely used by the Anglo-American economists. The latter acknowledge, as does Liefmann, the psychological act of evaluating labour efforts (as costs) that are independent and primary. But, in their view, the valuation of costs is transferred to the valuation of utilities acquired through their expenditure. In our example, the psychological valuation of the burden of labour is expressed for each of the five hours of labour by the figures: 1, 2, 3, 4 and 5. According to the theorists of subjective labour value, the value of one hour of labour is determined by the burden of the final, marginal hour of labour, i.e. it is psychologically expressed by the figure 5. Each pound of bread also has that same subjective value. Although the 'utility' of the final pound of bread is 8, if that pound is acquired with the help of 'costs' that equal 5, then the value of each pound of bread drops to 5. If the Austrian economists assumed that the valuation of utilities determines the valuation of costs, and the theorists of subjective labour value have connected phenomena in the opposite direction, Liefmann affirms a mutual independence of the two psychological acts of valuation. We shall not subject the aforementioned general psychological foundations of Liefmann's doctrine to a detailed critique, since they do not interest us in themselves but only as the starting point for explaining the phenomena of an exchange economy. We shall only briefly note that already, in this introductory and purely psychological part of Liefmann's theory, there are many debatable propositions and contradictions.

Liefmann says that economic activity consists of the psychological act of comparing sensations of pleasure (utilities) and displeasure (costs). Acknowledging that psychological sensations and feelings are *immeasurable*, Liefmann insists on the possibility of *comparing* them: an individual knows, more or less clearly, that one experience of pleasure is greater than another. But can the individual compare his sense of *pleasure* (e.g. from the possibility of replacing a linen shirt with a cloth jacket) with the sense of *displeasure* resulting from the need to incur determinate costs for this purpose (e.g. an additional hour of labour)? Knowing the explicit impossibility of such psychological comparisons, in some places Liefmann modifies his formulation and says that economic activity comprises two *sensations of displeasure*: 1) one is connected with costs and 2) the other with inability to satisfy a given need.[27] But, in order to demon-

---

27   Liefmann 1920, p. 284.

strate the identity of this formula with the one developed above, which sees economic activity as a comparison of 'utilities and costs, feelings of pleasure and displeasure',[28] it must be assumed that the 'desired utility' (*erstrebter Nutzen*), i.e. the sense of pleasure for which our individual is striving, is equal in terms of magnitude and precision to the sense of displeasure experienced in the case of not satisfying the given need. Such an assumption is far from being demonstrated. Moreover, it is not at all clear how a comparison of two negative magnitudes (feelings of displeasure) produces the result of a positive sense of surplus utility or 'yield' (*Ertrag*).

But let us move beyond this area of contentious psychological questions. Let us agree with Liefmann that, as a result of psychologically comparing utilities and costs, the individual has a psychological awareness of 'yield' as the excess of the former over the latter. After the first act of comparison (of utilities with costs), the individual turns to a second act of comparison: for different needs he compares 'the surpluses (i.e. the yields, *I.R.*) acquired with each expenditure of costs'.[29] Only through such a 'dual comparison' can the individual, as we have already seen, correctly distribute his costs between all of his needs in accordance with 'the law of the equalisation of marginal yields'. But the separate psychological 'yields', acquired through satisfaction of different needs, could only be counterposed to each other and subject to comparison if they had psychologically crystallised as independent sensations or feelings. Yet Liefmann himself has to admit that 'the magnitude of surplus (i.e. yield, *I.R.*) is sensed by the individual ... not as an independent magnitude side by side with utility and costs, but together with the sensation' of the latter.[30] And if that is the case, is there any possibility of the psychological act of *comparing different yields*, an act that is central to Liefmann's constructions?

But let us assume, together with Liefmann, that the individual can psychologically compare the 'yields' that he acquires from the satisfaction of different needs. But has it been proven that the individual distributes his costs on the basis of 'the law of equalisation of marginal yields', i.e. satisfying all the groups of needs up to one and the same level of satiation? If that were actually so, every reduction of the general sum of costs spent by the individual would have to be directly reflected in each group of the needs he is satisfying. But that contradicts the well-known fact, for example, that reduction of an individual's income is frequently accompanied by a decision not to satisfy one group of needs (e.g. the need for entertainment) without having any reflection on the

---

28   Liefmann 1920, p. 276.
29   Liefmann 1920, p. 284.
30   Liefmann 1920, p. 395.

degree of satisfaction of other so-called 'essential' needs (for bread etc.). That fact has caused considerable difficulty for Austrian economists with their 'law of the equalisation of marginal utilities',[31] and it also contradicts Liefmann's law of 'the equalisation of marginal yields'.[32] As Liefmann himself recognises, if '*most* consumers', in '*most* of their consumption, acquire yields that exceed *by far* their marginal consumer yield',[33] then what remains of the illustrious 'law of the equalisation of marginal yields'?

We shall not insist that the exceptions we have mentioned completely undermine operation of the 'law of the equalisation of marginal yields'. We shall assume that this law fully operates. In that case, it must be expected that our individual will work until his marginal costs reach the same level as marginal utility; i.e. until the *marginal yield approaches zero*. Liefmann himself knows that this conclusion is theoretically mandatory: 'Theoretically, the most perfect satisfaction of needs in the consumer economy is reached when the marginal yield for all needs is almost zero and the last units of utility and costs are almost the same'.[34] Liefmann tries to avoid this conclusion, by the way, with the argument that 'often labour efforts cannot be continued at will up to the limit determined by the economic actor's own sense of satisfaction, and the labour or hours of labour is externally determined'.[35] But that argument surely overturns all of Liefmann's constructions. If the number of hours of labour is externally limited, by factory legislation for example, that means that the entire mechanism of people's labour activity cannot be explained by processes of 'comparing utility and costs' within their own psyche, but instead it is determined by objective conditions of the social surroundings to which the will of particular individuals is subordinated. To use Sombart's famous expression, 'motivation' is here replaced by 'limitation'. The entire conception of economy as a psychological process of comparing utilities to costs turns out to be groundless. Insofar as Liefmann has no wish to give up his psychological conception of economy, he must acknowledge that marginal consumer yields have a tendency to approach zero.

Aware of how precarious his arguments are, Liefmann hastens to insure himself in the event that they should be seen to be incorrect: 'Even if the marginal

---

31   To explain this fact, Wieser had to turn to a very subtle and convoluted construction. See
       Wieser 1914, pp. 164–5.
32   Although Liefmann insists upon the complete originality of his 'law', the latter essentially
       corresponds to the law of the equalisation of marginal utilities provided we start with calculation of a *unit of costs* (e.g. 1 hour of labour or 1 rouble).
33   Liefmann 1919, p. 343. Rubin's italics.
34   Liefmann 1920, p. 416.
35   Liefmann 1920, p. 417.

yields were always zero, that fact would not diminish the importance of yield as the regulator of economic activity in the consumer economy'.[36] That is an argument with which we can agree: if marginal yields are equally zero, that does not mean that the individual gets no yield whatever (all units of costs, except for the last one, bring him positive yields), nor that he does not know how to distribute his costs (he will direct them to satisfaction of those needs where the marginal yield has yet to decline to zero). Nevertheless, recognition of the equality of marginal yields at zero has unpleasant consequences for Liefmann's theory that we shall consider later. For now, let us remember that the 'law of the equalisation of marginal yields' in consumer economy can also be formulated as a *tendency for marginal consumer yields to approach zero*.

As we can see, even in the introductory and purely theoretical part of his study Liefmann already encounters several difficulties. The psychological 'comparison of utilities with costs' is impeded by the impossibility of comparing feelings of pleasure with feelings of displeasure. The psychological comparison of different 'yields' is complicated by the lack of any autonomous psychological experience of yield. The different qualitative features of various groups of needs are an obstacle to the 'equalisation of marginal yields'. All of these difficulties can be circumvented only with the aid of contentious and artificial assumptions. But does Liefmann succeed – at least with the help of these artificial assumptions – in erecting a *purely psychological* conception of economy, freed from all objective moments? This question must be answered in the negative. Apart from the fact that the conception of economy that we have been discussing is not suited for an explanation of economic phenomena (something we shall look into in subsequent chapters), it is not completely free from objective factors.

As distinct from the Austrian economists, who were compelled to recognise the influence of objective factors (namely, the quantity of goods) on the marginal utility and value of goods, Liefmann has constructed a purely subjective concept of 'utility' (*Nutzen*). But the *objective economic factors*, banished by Liefmann from the concept of utility, break back in, against his will, in the concept of '*costs*' (*Kosten*). True, Liefmann also understands 'costs' in a psychological sense: they mean the sense of displeasure caused by the need for expenditures of labour (or of material things and money, which we shall consider in the following chapters). But why is it that in the economic sphere – as distinct, for example, from the sphere of aesthetic enjoyment – a sense of satisfaction or utility is purchased with the aid of a sense of displeasure or

---

36   Liefmann 1920, p. 689.

labour efforts? It is solely due to the objective fact that the products required for the satisfaction of human needs are acquired with the help of expenditures of labour in the process of production. Despite all efforts to separate completely the psychological concept of economy from the objective process of production, Liefmann is compelled to retain a bridge between them in the concept of costs (insofar as labour efforts are concerned). Every change in labour productivity necessarily brings a change in psychological 'costs' (i.e. in labour efforts or the sense of displeasure that accompanies the expenditure of labour). Change in the magnitude of 'costs' automatically alters the magnitude of 'yield', thereby requiring a complete redistribution of all costs and a change of the entire economic plan. Accordingly, the psychological process of comparing utilities with costs undergoes profound change under the influence of changes in *the technical process of production*. True, up to this point it still occurs independently of any influence from social aspects of the economy. But that is merely explained by the fact that until now we have been considering an isolated economic actor like Robinson Crusoe. As soon as we include him in a society of other people, we shall be assured that the psychological process of comparing utilities with costs is to a much greater extent determined and 'limited' by *conditions of the social environment*.

CHAPTER 2

Money Economy

The psychological conception of economy that we have been presenting serves Liefmann merely as an introduction, or a methodological instrument, for understanding the modern *monetary and commodity-capitalist* economy. It would not be entirely fair to reproach Liefmann for depicting merely an isolated Robinson Crusoe economy. Although Liefmann begins with a description of natural economy, where, in his view, 'economic activities can be studied in their simplest forms', he quickly turns to a 'consumer economy', which is woven into the exchange turnover'.[1] It can even be said that in his portrait of a pure (natural) consumer economy Liefmann already introduces features that characterise money economy; and conversely, for an explanation of the latter he appeals to the psychology of an isolated, individual economic actor. On these grounds, Liefmann claims that his theory is simultaneously 'pure' – and thus suitable for explaining any economy – and also 'capitalistic', explaining in particular the phenomena of money-capitalist economy.[2] In reality his theory, due to a motley mix up of imaginary-psychological givens with the concrete phenomena of a capitalist economy, is neither 'pure' nor 'capitalistic'.

Nor would it be entirely appropriate to accuse Liefmann of studying only the psychological *feelings* of people while totally ignoring their economic *activities* and *objective social-economic* phenomena, for instance prices and incomes. Liefmann's main objective is an explanation of 'the phenomena of an exchange economy, such as prices, incomes, capital, credit, crises, and so on'.[3] But, in his opinion, these phenomena are simply the result of the activities and 'interactions of individuals'. Thus, the 'final cause' of the phenomena of exchange (above all prices and incomes) must be sought in the 'economic judgements of individual people',[4] i.e. in the psyche of economic subjects. We have already familiarised ourselves with the basic mainsprings of the psychology of an economic subject. The subject makes a psychological comparison of utilities (*Nutzen*) with costs (*Kosten*) and strives to acquire the greatest surplus of the former over the latter, or the greatest consumer yield (*Konsumertrag*). Now, let us situate our individual within the context of an exchange or money economy.

---

1 Liefmann 1920, p. 362.
2 Liefmann 1920, p. 187.
3 Liefmann 1920, p. 122.
4 Liefmann 1920, p. 119 *et passim*.

The psychological process that we have been describing now becomes significantly more complex, since our individual no longer produces 'utilities' for his own consumption and therefore cannot *directly* compare his utilities with costs. Our individual can acquire the 'utilities' (commodities) that he requires only by purchasing them, and for that purpose he must first have something to sell. The activity of our individual occurs in the form of two separate actions: sale and an ensuing purchase, or in Marx's famous formula, C–M and M–C_1. The individual first *acquires* money (C–M) in order to be able to purchase items for *consumption* (M–C_1). The formerly singular and indivisible economic individual now decomposes into two stages, or in Liefmann's terminology, two economies: the 'acquisition economy' (*Erwerbswirtschaft*) and the 'consumer economy' (*Konsumwirtschaft*). For example, the worker sells his labour power, receiving for it a certain 'money yield' (the wage); the businessman organises a factory and sells finished products, also receiving a certain 'money yield' (a profit). In both cases we have before us 'acquisitive activity' or an 'acquisition economy'.[5]

The worker (or the employer), having received in his acquisition economy a money yield, uses it to purchase items of consumption or 'utilities'.[6] The 'money yield' (*Geldertrag*), received by the worker or employer in the acquisition economy, comes to him in the form of 'income' (*Einkommen*) in his household or consumer economy, where it is spent to purchase 'utilities'. The ultimate goal of economy – the satisfaction of human needs – is reached only in the consumer economy. The acquisition economy only supplies monetary means for this purpose. 'Acquisition economies are all those that are directed towards receiving a *money yield* (*Geldertrag*), and consumer economies are those that *spend the money yield as a means for satisfying the needs of their owners*'.[7]

As we can see, in an exchange economy the psychological process of directly comparing utilities with costs cannot occur, for the worker, with the aid of his costs (labour efforts), obtains no direct utilities but instead just money to make purchases. Accordingly, the psychological comparison of utilities with costs is possible only indirectly, through the medium of *money*. If, for an 8-hour working day, our worker receives a money wage of 80 kopecks, he can psychologically compare the feeling of displeasure incurred during the last (the eighth) hour of labour with the feeling of pleasure that he derives from the utilities being purchased with his last ten kopecks. But for such psychological comparison to be possible, the worker must know the sum of money that he will receive

---

5   The difference between these terms will be explained below.
6   We assume here that the employer spends his entire profit on personal consumption.
7   Liefmann 1920, p. 356. Also Liefmann 1919, p. 28.

for an hour of labour and the sum of utilities (commodities) he will be able to purchase with that money. In other words, he must have prior knowledge of: 1) the magnitude of his *income*, which depends upon the *price of labour power*, and 2) *the prices of articles of consumption* that he requires. With every change of the worker's income (his wage) or of prices for articles of consumption, the results of our individual's psychological comparison of costs (labour efforts) and utilities will turn out to be different.

In an exchange economy, the separate individual finds an *objective social system of prices and incomes* that is historically formed, independent of his will, and within whose limits he must act. Our worker receives the same wage as other workers, regardless of how he subjectively evaluates his costs (labour efforts). He pays the same price as other purchasers do for items of consumption, regardless of how he subjectively evaluates their utility for himself. A psychological comparison of utilities and costs can only be done by an individual within the limits of a system that consists of objective social magnitudes (prices and incomes), and changes of the latter give completely different results. We can understand, therefore, the utter futility of Liefmann's attempt to build a theory of money, prices and incomes on the basis of his doctrine of economy as a psychological comparison of utilities and costs.

The hopelessness of such attempts is fully understandable if we call to mind the profound difference between an exchange economy and Crusoe's natural economy. In the latter, the individual confronts only nature, and his economy aims directly at satisfying his needs. The given, *concrete* character of the individual's economic activity is explained by the given, *concrete* character of his needs (and costs, which depend upon the technical conditions of production). In exchange economy, the commodity producer does not work directly for himself but for the market. It is true, as Liefmann constantly reminds us, that although the commodity producer *technically* creates products for other members of society, he *psychologically* (and for him this also means economically) endeavours thereby to satisfy his own needs. There can be no objection on that score. The condition for any commodity producer's economic activity is, of course, the existence of his own definite needs. But the *concrete* character of our commodity producer's economic activity (in both technical and social terms) is determined not by the *concrete* character of his needs, but instead by the *concrete* objective conditions of the social economy and the market conjuncture. If Liefmann's psychological conception is applicable to the natural economy of an individual, working for himself in isolation (and within limits imposed by objective aspects of the technical process of production), it is not in the least suitable for explaining a commodity economy, within which the particular individual accounts only for a miniscule and subordinate part of a single social process of production. In commodity economy the conditions of *social production* determine those of *individual production*, and the conditions of *individual consumption* are dependent upon the latter. This means that a number of *objective social conditions* determine the scale, direction and results of the individual's *acquisition* activity, and those results, in the form of a definite sum of money (income), enter into his *consumer* economy and determine its scale and character.

Liefmann is inclined, of course, to interpret the causal connection between acquisition and consumer economies in reverse order. That is also why he elaborated this division of economy into two stages, so that in the household or *consumer* economy there is a 'tranquil household' or 'quiet corner' that is protected from the stormy tides of market spontaneity and governed by the will of the individual. Indeed, the consumer economy may at first glance appear, with reservations, to fit a psychological concept of economy such as the natural economy of Robinson Crusoe. The goal of this economy is to acquire 'utilities' for the isolated Crusoe. The other economy's goal is the acquisition of 'utilities' for an individual who is entwined in a web of exchange relations. Crusoe compares the utilities he wants with the costs (labour efforts) needed to obtain them. In the same way our individual, in his consumer economy, compares the desired utilities with the costs (in money) needed to purchase them. Just as Crusoe expends his labour only to acquire utilities that he subjectively evaluates more highly than the costs involved, so also our individual spends his money (income) only on the purchase of utilities that he evaluates more highly than the sum of money spent on their purchase. And this means that our individual, as in the case of Crusoe, receives a certain 'consumer yield', an excess of utilities over costs.

True, there is the following profound difference between the natural economy of Crusoe and a consumer economy that is entwined in the net of the exchange turnover: in the former the role of costs is fulfilled by labour efforts, in the latter by sums of money being spent on the purchase of items of consumption (utilities). The concept of costs divides and appears at one time in the form of a *psychological feeling*, at another time as a *sum of money* (psychological costs and money costs). But if the sums of money spent by our individual in his consumer economy are obtained with the help of his own labour (e.g. if we are speaking of a peasant or worker), these money costs are simply *surrogates for psychological costs* (labour efforts). Comparing the utility of the commodity being purchased with the sum of money required to obtain it, our individual (for example, a worker) essentially compares a psychological utility with the psychological costs (labour efforts) that he must spend to acquire the given sum of money. Money only plays the role of an intermediary in the psychological act of comparing utilities with costs.

Thus, in the sphere of consumer economy, our individual acts at his own discretion: he does a comparison of his costs (his income) with utilities (items of consumption); with each unit of expenditure (i.e. for each rouble being spent) he seeks to acquire the greatest possible utility or the greatest possible consumer yield (*Konsumertrag*). He distributes his costs between individual needs in such a way that for all needs the marginal consumer yields are equal. In short, events in the consumer economy proceed as if in conformity with the previously developed law of psychological *comparison of utilities and costs* and with the law of *equalisation of marginal yields*.[8] But the problem is that our consumer economy operates with a previously established sum of costs (incomes) that it receives from the acquisition economy. As a result, the economist cannot limit himself to study of the *consumer* economy but instead must turn from there to the *acquisition* economy, especially since it is precisely in the latter sphere that *prices and incomes* are formed and we thus encounter the central problems of political economy. We are thereby thrown once more from the quiet harbour into the stormy sea of market spontaneity, and we might again lose sight of our psychological conception of economy. In order to rescue the latter, we have no alternative but to regard the consumer economy as the basic and primary phenomenon and then add to it the acquisition economy as subordinate and providing auxiliary functions in relation to the former. The consumer economy must find within itself the strength to take the acquisition economy in tow, as it is being buffeted by the tempests of market spontaneity, and lead it to the serene quay of the individual psyche and subjective evaluations. Liefmann's entire system can be reduced to solving this complicated task.

What *method* does Liefmann hope to use in solving this task? The last thing to look for in Liefmann is methodological clarity. Liefmann does not attach much importance to purely methodological research and makes fun of those who do. That is his right. But in his own research he hopelessly mixes the most diverse methodological viewpoints and thus violates the first duty of any serious scientific researcher. In Liefmann's reasoning one can trace *three* different methodological approaches to the question of the relation between objective economic phenomena and the psychological experiences of the individual.

The first approach, which is methodologically the only one suited to solving the task that Liefmann sets for himself, consists of the following. Lief-

---

8   The error involved here will be explained in the following chapter.

mann would have to show that the phenomena of the acquisition economy are *causally dependent* upon phenomena of the consumer economy, which are explained by the psychological feelings of the individual. Thus, the entire sphere of economic phenomena would be subordinate, so to speak, to the laws of psychological causality, and the applicability of the subjective-psychological method in political economy would be solidly established. For the sake of brevity, let us call this kind of argumentation the method of *'psychological causality'*.

Later we shall see that all attempts by Liefmann in this direction come to a very deplorable end. Yet, in his general declarations, Liefmann never tires of repeating that the psyche of the individual, as a consumer, must be taken as the starting point for explaining economic phenomena.

> Behind every consumer economy are its proprietors, one or several people, and the *economic* task of the acquisition economy, its task as an *economy*, consists exclusively of delivering to its proprietors (i.e. to their consumer economies) the most complete satisfaction of needs, albeit in a roundabout way through the medium of money. Consequently, all economic phenomena originate in the consumer economy, occur because of it, and must be reduced to it.[9]

The error of most economists is that they have limited themselves to investigation of the acquisition economy, ignoring its subordinate and auxiliary role in relation to the consumer economy. Only through beginning with the latter is it possible to explain the phenomena of exchange. 'A psychological economic plan must always remain the foundation for an investigation of exchange processes as well; in order to explain the whole mechanism of exchange, it is always imperative, in the final analysis, to turn to evaluations of utilities and costs on the part of consumers'.[10]

Along with the method of 'psychological causality', Liefmann turns to a completely different method that might be called the method of 'analogies'. He attempts to show that phenomena of the acquisition economy are *analogous* to phenomena of the consumer economy, i.e. that they can be summed up with concepts and formulae analogous to the psychological concepts and formulae that we saw earlier. We have seen that the psychological conception of economy is founded upon the concepts of utility (*Nutzen*), costs (*Kosten*) and yield (*Ertrag*). Liefmann also tries to reduce phenomena of the acquisition economy,

---

9   Liefmann 1920, p. 362. Also pp. 358, 408 *et passim*.
10   Liefmann 1920, p. 473.

occurring in objectified money form, to these same concepts. Indeed, every subject of the consumer economy must expend 'costs' (the worker, his labour power; the employer, a sum of materials and money called capital). They do so only if, with the help of these expended costs, they hope to acquire 'utilities' that exceed costs (e.g. for the worker, items of consumption that he subjectively evaluates more highly than the labour expended; for the employer, a sum of money that exceeds the expended capital). Consequently, in 'both (i.e. in the consumer and acquisition economies, *I.R.*) a comparison occurs between utilities and costs, in which we have discerned the essence of economic activities'.[11] It is true that in a natural economy two psychological impressions are compared, and in the acquisition economy of the factory owner, two sums of money.[12] But, despite this 'dualism',[13] Liefmann still considers it possible to speak in both instances of 'costs' and 'utilities'.

Once comparison of utilities with costs occurs in both the consumer and the acquisition economy, it is then obvious that in both cases we can speak of a 'yield' (*Ertrag*) as a surplus of utility over costs. 'We differentiate *consumer yield (Konsumertrag)*, the surplus of utility over costs in the consumer economy, from *acquisition yield (Erwerbsertrag)*, the surplus of utility over costs in the acquisition economy, a surplus that is expressed here as a sum of money'[14] and thus is also called a *money yield (Geldertrag)*.[15] It is true that here, too, the consumer yield means a psychological sensation, and the acquisition yield a sum of money. But, despite that fact, Liefmann combines them in the concept of 'yield' and assigns analogous roles to both of them. 'The prospect of a higher money yield is also the goal of the acquisition economy, just as the prospect of a higher consumer yield, a surplus of utilities over costs, is the regulator of the consumer economy'.[16]

Therefore, the structure of the acquisition economy is *analogous* to the structure of the consumer economy, and at the basis of both are the identical concepts of utility, costs and yield.[17] 'The principles of economic behaviour in

---

11   Liefmann 1920, p. 358. See also p. 355.

12   Liefmann 1920, p. 358.

13   Liefmann 1920, p. 466.

14   Liefmann 1920, p. 465.

15   In what follows, the terms 'consumer yield' and 'money yield' will be used in one and the same sense.

16   Liefmann 1919, p. 33.

17   Later, in an analysis of the theory of prices, we shall see that the analogy is extended still further: in the acquisition economy there are also marginal yields, and the law of equalisation of marginal yields is in operation.

both cases are identical, and it is important to establish this homogeneity'.[18] That is the conclusion Liefmann comes to with the help of the method of analogies.

Liefmann himself apparently recognises that not every phenomenon of the acquisition economy can be explained as causally conditioned by phenomena of the consumer economy (the method of psychological causality) or by analogy to them (the method of analogies). Consequently, along with these two methods of argument, we very often find in Liefmann a third approach to the problem. Frequently Liefmann takes a certain phenomenon of the acquisition economy, for example price or income,[19] to be the primary and given magnitude. Sometimes, following the classics, he even recognises that this magnitude is conditioned by objective social phenomena; for instance, the magnitude of the worker's income (i.e. wage) depends upon the price of conventional means of subsistence. But Liefmann hastens to add that a given money income, the result of a combination of objective conditions, upon entering the sphere of the consumer economy, is refracted there in the psyche of the subject and undergoes a unique, purely individual 'psychological evaluation' that depends upon its importance for satisfying the needs of the particular subject. For example, 'money, like all costs, is *evaluated in consumer economies* and enters into the *psychological* comparison of utilities and costs'.[20] Every monetary unit (the rouble, for instance) is subjectively evaluated differently by different individuals depending upon the size of their income: the higher the income, the lower the valuation of each rouble.[21] The money income of the individual, being the result of his acquisition economy and entering his consumer economy as a precisely defined sum, receives in the latter a definite subjective valuation depending upon the extent of satisfaction of the given individual's needs.[22]

As we can see, there are three different methodological approaches in Liefmann's argumentation that are intertwined and mixed together; they can be called the method of *psychological causality*, the method of *analogies*, and the method of *psychological evaluation*. The conclusions to which these three methods might lead are far from identical. In the first case, objective phe-

---

18   Liefmann 1920, p. 362.
19   Liefmann speaks of income (*Einkommen*) only with regard to consumer economy, although he recognises that this income is not different from money yield received in the acquisition economy.
20   Liefmann 1920, p. 467.
21   Liefmann 1919, pp. 114, 159, 160 *et passim*.
22   Liefmann 1920, p. 471; 1919, p. 160 *et passim*.

nomena of the acquisition economy are recognised as *secondary* and derivative compared to psychological phenomena of the consumer economy; in the second case, they are considered to be *analogous* to the latter; and finally, in the third case, the author is compelled to acknowledge the *primary* character of objective economic phenomena.

It goes without saying that the *final* method cannot possibly lead Liefmann to his goal. In order for objective economic phenomena (prices and incomes) to undergo an ensuing 'psychological evaluation' by the subject, they must be given for him in advance and can in no way be explained as coming from his psychological valuations. Insofar as Liefmann resorts to the third method, he effectively relinquishes any consistent implementation of his psychological concept of economy.

The *second* method, likewise, cannot serve Liefmann's purpose. Whereas the method of psychological evaluation contradicts what Liefmann would like to prove, the method of analogies proves nothing at all. True, the reader may think at first glance that we have unjustifiably called Liefmann's second method that of analogies. Is it not the case that what Liefmann is using here is the common method of generalising or summarising, combining various concepts (for example, the psychological consumer yield and the monetary acquisition yield) into a single higher and more abstract concept (of yield in general)? Our answer to this question is unflinchingly in the negative. Liefmann does not even attempt to construct an abstract concept of 'yield' that includes characteristics common to both psychological yield and money yield. Such an attempt would be completely futile: what is there in common between a psychological feeling and a sum of money, apart perhaps from the fact that they are each a 'phenomenon' or 'magnitude' (and the latter is already dubious in relation to a psychological feeling)? Liefmann himself acknowledges a 'dualism of fundamental economic concepts, with one part essentially psychological – the concepts of evaluation and feeling – and the other part essentially monetary expressions'.[23] This 'dualism' makes it impossible to construct abstract concepts of utility, costs and yield that would equally embrace both a psychological feeling and a sum of money. Liefmann himself, with all of his diligence, cannot find anything in common between a psychological yield and a monetary yield except for the fact that they both represent a difference between two magnitudes (the magnitude of utility and that of costs).[24] In reality, that too is false

---

23   Liefmann 1920, p. 466.
24   In one place Liefmann takes utility and costs to mean psychological sensations of pleasure and displeasure, in another they mean sums of money (acquired and spent).

because only a monetary yield can be measured or calculated, whereas a psychological yield is not measurable. Liefmann himself has to admit that 'pure sensations and numerical expressions are so different that there is no common term that is suitable for them'.[25] The best common term he can find for them – often more unsuitable than suitable – is one such as 'utility', 'costs' and 'yield'. But nothing follows from this purely terminological association. If we ask what a 'yield' is, Liefmann will give us two definitions: a 'yield', on the one hand, is a surplus of one psychological feeling (the sense of satisfaction) over another; on the other hand, it is a surplus of one sum of money over another. It is true that Liefmann suggests that we consider the latter yield by analogy to the former. But apart from the fact, as we shall later demonstrate, that Liefmann's analogies cannot withstand criticism from his own point of view, even the most apt analogies neither prove nor explain anything. We need only recall the history of the organic school in sociology, which discovered numerous and sometimes even clever analogies between social and biological phenomena. That school collapsed because its analogies proved nothing. It is the same with the analogies that Liefmann draws between social-economic and psychological phenomena, the one difference being that his are not distinguished by any cleverness.

Thus, of the three methods that Liefmann uses, only the method of *psychological causality* could lead him towards his goal. Any validity of the psychological method in political economy could only be recognised if Liefmann demonstrated that objective phenomena (prices and incomes), which arise in the sphere of the acquisition economy, are causally dependent upon the psychological experiences of a subject concerning the sphere of his consumer economy, and that they can therefore be explained by analysing those psychological experiences. In what follows, our main goal will be to assess how far Liefmann has succeeded in proving this proposition. Along the way we shall more than once encounter analogies provided by Liefmann and have frequent opportunities to subject them to critical analysis.

---

25   Liefmann 1920, p. 471.

CHAPTER 3

Capitalist Economy

The essence of economy, according to Liefmann's teaching, consists of a psychological comparison of utilities with costs. Neither the sum of costs being expended by the individual nor the sum of utilities that he receives is known in advance. 'The main problem of economy'[1] is their determination. Let us recall that both the *scale* of an individual's economic activity (i.e. the sum of his expenditures) and its *results* (i.e. the sum of utilities he receives) can only be determined on the basis of a psychological comparison of utilities with costs.

In order to bring this psychological conception into proximity with economic reality, Liefmann introduces into it features drawn from 1) *money* economy in general and 2) *capitalist* economy in particular. In so doing, Liefmann tries to portray the matter in such a way that these features are packed without difficulty into the confines of a psychological conception of economy, and their principal goal is to assist the individual in the psychological act of comparing utilities with costs.

In the preceding chapter we have already characterised in general terms Liefmann's attempt to subordinate the acquisition economy to the consumer economy and thus to prove the applicability of the psychological conception to the phenomena of a money-exchange economy. In this chapter, our task is a more detailed analysis of the acquisition and consumer economies in the more complex form that they assume in capitalist economy. In the first chapter we considered as *one whole* the singular economy of the individual. We learned in the second chapter that in conditions of monetary exchange the singular economy of the individual divides into two stages or two economies: that of *acquisition* and that of *consumption*. In this chapter we shall see that in capitalist economy the singular economy of the individual appears in two completely different forms: the singular economy of the *worker* and the singular economy of the *employer-capitalist*. We shall undertake to demonstrate to the reader that the psychological conception of Liefmann is not applicable to either of these forms of economy.

Readers need not be surprised by the fact that we pay so much attention to analysis of the singular economy. We are compelled to do so by Liefmann

---

1   Liefmann 1920, p. 300 *et passim*.

© RICHARD B. DAY, 2024 | DOI:10.1163/9789004705661_024

himself, who takes investigation of precisely a singular economy as his point of departure. The individual's endeavour to satisfy his needs explains to us the structure of a *singular economy* – that is Liefmann's first proposition. The interaction between singular economies explains the structure of the *exchange turnover* (or the national economy, a term rejected by Liefmann). That is his second proposition. Both of these propositions must be subjected to critical examination. In the present chapter we shall analyse the extent to which the psychological conception is applicable to a singular economy (of the worker and of the capitalist). In the following chapter we shall assess the extent to which the phenomena of the exchange turnover, and particularly the process of price formation, can be explained from the viewpoint of the same psychological conception.

We have already learned in the previous chapter that with the appearance of money exchange the singular economy of the individual has split apart into two stages. A separation has occurred between the acquisition economy and the consumer economy. Now we must turn our attention to the fact, acknowledged by Liefmann himself, that in capitalist society this separation appears in two forms. The factory owner, for example, has an '*acquisition economy*' that is completely detached from his consumer economy. The worker, who toils in someone else's 'acquisition economy', does not have one of his own; as far as he is concerned, we can speak only of '*acquisition activity*' that is not completely separated from his consumer economy.[2] The same also applies to the peasant and the craftsman. What we have, therefore, is nothing short of a contradiction between a 'labour' economy (of the worker or petty commodity producer) and a 'non-labour' economy (of the employer or capitalist).[3]

The main distinction between a labour economy and a capitalist one lies in the sphere of the acquisition economy. The consumer economy is organised in approximately the same way for the worker and the employer; they both spend their money yield (wage or profit) on the purchase of consumer items in accordance with the law of 'equalisation of marginal consumer yields'. Both of them, in their consumer economy, spend their money (income) as a 'cost' and receive utilities or 'consumer yields'. Yet there is a profound difference in the structure of the two consumer economies. That difference can be illustrated with the following scheme:

---

2 Liefmann 1919, p. 33. There is also a third 'acquisition' going to rentiers and landowners: they 'acquire' (interest and rent) without any specific 'acquisition activity'.
3 Liefmann does not use these terms.

Acquisition activity of the worker		Acquisition activity of the employer	
Costs	Yield	Costs	Yield
Labour efforts	Money yield (wages)	Money or goods (capital)	Money yield (profit)

Although there is an important difference between the yield of the capitalist and the yield of the worker, about which we shall have to say more later, both of these yields appear in the form of a definite sum of money (the wage or profit), and in that sense they are homogeneous. But there is a completely *heterogeneous* character in their two *costs*: for the worker, costs are *labour efforts*; for the capitalist, they have the form of a determinate *sum of money* (or goods that are priced in money). In the economy of the capitalist, costs (capital) and yield (profit) appear in the form of two sums of money that can be directly compared to one another. In the acquisition economy of the capitalist, a *purely monetary* or *purely quantitative* comparison of costs and yields occurs, while the worker, in his acquisition economy, cannot manage apart from a psychological comparison of utilities with costs.

Since the worker does not have his own acquisition economy in the proper sense of the word, the entire production activity of capitalist society occurs in the acquisition economies of employers. From there certain sums (the part of profit being consumed) pass into the consumer economy of the capitalist, while other sums (wages) flow into the acquisition economy[4] of the worker, whence they proceed into his consumer economy in the form of income. Since the centre of gravity of the whole of capitalist economic life lies in the economies of the employers, this is where we must direct most of our attention. But before turning to that task, we think it necessary first to examine the question of the extent to which Liefmann's psychological conception is applicable to the economy of the *worker*. Much more than the economy of the employer, that of the worker serves the purposes of its owner's personal consumption, and for that reason we can expect that here, at least, the psychological conception of economy will fully apply.

---

4 Here and in many other places below, we use the term 'acquisition economy' – following Liefmann's example – in a broad sense that includes not only the acquisition economy of the capitalist but also the acquisition activity of the worker.

Using the method of 'analogies', Liefmann wanted to convince us that a comparison of utilities with costs, whether in the psychological or the money form, occurs in both the acquisition and the consumer economies. Let us analyse separately the processes occurring in each of them. In the acquisition economy of the worker there are *psychological costs* (labour efforts), but 'utility' or benefit has the form of a *sum of money* (the wages). Therefore, so long as we remain within the limits of a single acquisition economy of a worker, a psychological comparison of utilities with costs cannot occur. But, on the other hand, comparing them in money terms is also impossible because, in Liefmann's words, the worker does not calculate his labour efforts in the form of a sum of money, i.e. from the purely monetary point of view he considers his costs to be zero and on that basis regards the entire sum of wages as a pure yield.[5] Accordingly, from the *psychological* viewpoint *utility* is missing in the acquisition economy of the worker, while *costs* are likewise missing from the *money* point of view. This means that we cannot speak of any comparison of utilities with costs, nor consequently of any yield as a surplus of the former over the latter. In fact, Liefmann has no right to call the wage a 'monetary yield', because there is here no deduction of costs from utilities.[6] The term 'yield' is employed here by Liefmann simply for the purpose of creating an appearance of analogy with his psychological conception of economy.

Let us turn now to the consumer economy of the worker. Here, psychological utilities (consumer goods) are counterposed to money costs, which in Liefmann's opinion are also subject to psychological evaluation on the part of the individual: the higher the latter's income, the lower is the psychological valuation he attaches to every rouble spent on the purchase of items of consumption. Let us examine the magnitude of the psychological valuation of each rouble. In the consumer economy, the general sum of costs has a determinate magnitude in advance that depends upon the results of the individual's acquisition activity. But wherever the magnitude of costs is determined in advance, a unit of costs is psychologically evaluated up to the utility

---

5 Liefmann 1920, pp. 499, 500; 1919, pp. 469, 505, 640.

6 Likewise, there is no deduction of costs – if they are missing – from money interest that is received by the money capitalist (Liefmann 1919, pp. 519, 659). Consequently, both wages and rental receipts – in Liefmann's own words the most typical 'sums of money' – in fact must not be called 'yields' in the sense in which Liefmann uses this term. We can only speak of a yield with reference to an industrialist or merchant, who receives a gross income (money utility) from which money costs are deducted.

provided by the last unit of costs (as the Austrian economists believe) or a new additional unit of costs (as Liefmann thinks). 'In the consumer economy money, as a factor of cost (*Kostengut*), is evaluated according to the utility that can be received with the use of an additional unit of money'.[7] If the consumer economy of the worker disposes of an annual income of 1,000 roubles, the owner will evaluate each rouble by the utility that an additional rouble – rouble 1,001 – would procure for him. The evaluation of costs (money) in this case is nothing more than a reflection of his evaluation of the marginal utility he is receiving. Thinking about whether he should buy a certain item at the price of 1 rouble, our worker in fact compares not utility with costs but rather one utility (from the given item) with another utility (delivered by the marginal or additional rouble). In Liefmann's own portrayal, an *independent psychological evaluation of costs* has no place in the consumer economy, and there can be no talk of any *psychological comparison of utilities with costs*.[8]

Accordingly, we have not found, either in the acquisition or in the consumer economy of the worker, the feature that Liefmann regards as characterising any economy in general – a comparison of utilities with costs. But, Liefmann may object, the psychological comparison of utilities with costs can easily be found if we consider the worker's economy as a *whole*, including both stages. We need not remind Liefmann that he promised to show a comparison of utilities with costs at each of the two stages of the economy: in both the acquisition and the consumer economies.[9] Let us now take a look at the worker's economy as a single whole.

The economy of the worker as a whole can be represented in the form of the following scheme:

---

7   Liefmann 1919, p. 114.

8   Agreeing with the position of the Austrian school, that with a given magnitude of costs all units of costs receive an identical evaluation that is equal to the marginal utility provided by the last (or marginal) unit of costs, Liefmann himself makes an irreparable breach in his conception of economy as a psychological comparison of utilities with costs. If costs are taken to be a given magnitude (which very often occurs, namely, in all consumer economies and in the acquisition economy of the capitalist), there is no independent psychological evaluation of costs as such. The whole difference between Liefmann and the Austrian economists on this point is that in the opinion of the former, the evaluation of each rouble, with a sum of costs equal to 100 roubles, is equal to the utility that would be provided by the 101st rouble, whereas in the view of the Austrian economists, it is equal to the utility provided by the last, the 100th rouble.

9   Liefmann 1920, p. 358.

Acquisition economy		Consumer economy	
Costs	Yield	Costs	Utilities
Labour efforts	Money yield (wages)	Money income	Consumer goods

As in natural economy, the starting point here is labour efforts, ending with items of consumption. But the link between them is only formed through a definite sum of money (wages), which in the worker's acquisition economy plays the role of *yield* (or utility) and in the consumer economy is spent as *costs*. Unlike in the natural economy, where he distributes his labour efforts between different sorts of work with the goal of acquiring different items of consumption, our individual, having received a sum of money (the yield), spends it in his consumer economy to purchase consumer items according to the 'law of the equalisation of marginal consumer yields'. In the consumer economy, money serves as the universal and sole *'unit of costs'* (*Kosteneinheit*),[10] although in the final analysis the real psychological 'costs' of the individual are his labour efforts. Ultimately, the worker undertakes a psychological comparison between his labour efforts and the utility furnished by consumer articles. In this psychological budget of the individual, money only plays the role of a 'transitory item',[11] involved identically in income and expenditure but not determining the final psychological sum. It is a matter of complete indifference to the worker whether his money yield (the wage) is expressed in 10 roubles or 100 roubles, provided that in both cases he acquires, with the same expenditure of labour efforts, an identical quantity of utilities. Money serves only as an 'abstract accounting unit', or a 'means of accounting and comparing costs in the consumer economy'.[12]

Transforming money into the intermediate link or 'transitory item' of a psychological comparison of utilities with costs, Liefmann leaves the most important question in the shadows: What is the *sum of utility* that is being counterposed to the given *sum of costs*? Without an answer to that question, there is no possibility of comparing utilities and costs. In natural economy, this ques-

---

10 Liefmann 1919, p. 115; also Liefmann 1916, p. 75.
11 Liefmann 1920, p. 313.
12 Liefmann 1919, pp. 120–1, 130 *et passim*. Detailed analyses of Liefmann's theory of money and his theory of capital are beyond the theme of this essay.

tion was decided by the *technical productivity of labour*: a given sum of costs (labour efforts) was counterposed to the utility of the product created with the help of a unit of labour. In exchange economy, the link between costs and utility is not created directly by the technical process of production, but instead by the mechanism of social exchange. For a unit of his labour (e.g. 1 hour of labour), our worker receives a determinate money yield (the wage, e.g. 10 kopecks), and with that sum he buys a determinate amount of consumer items (e.g. 2 pounds of bread) that provide him with utility. The psychological counterposing of utility (2 pounds of bread) to costs (the sense of displeasure associated with the hour of labour), can only be done by the worker on the basis of two previously given and objectively existing equations of social exchange: 1) 1 hour of labour = 10 kopecks, and 2) 1 pound of bread = 5 kopecks. The psychological comparison of utilities with costs presupposes, as we have seen earlier, an objectively existing system of prices and incomes (wages). We cannot frame the issue as if there were pre-given and autonomous psychological sensations (costs and utility), so that the whole question merely amounts to whether a comparison between them will occur directly (in natural economy) or indirectly (through the medium of money as abstract accounting units). In money economy the magnitude of these psychological sensations depends upon the level of prices and incomes. It is a mistake, therefore, to see in money economy only a modified and more complex form of the same psychological process of comparing utilities with costs that characterises natural economy.

We can see that a psychological comparison of utilities with costs cannot be taken as the starting point of the investigation, since it already assumes an existing system of *objective prices and incomes* upon which it rests, so to speak. But perhaps a psychological comparison of utilities with costs, although operating with the help of prices and incomes that are given for the worker in advance, has a decisive influence in turn upon the character of the worker's economic activity. Let us also examine that question.

As we outlined in the first chapter, Crusoe is an isolated economic actor who determines for himself, on the basis of his own psychological comparison of utilities with costs, both the *scale* of his economic activity (the sum of labour expended) and also the *results* (the sum of utilities received). Liefmann assumes that in capitalist economy, too, it is the worker himself, on the basis of a psychological comparison of utilities with costs, who decides how many hours he will work and thus what general sum of wages he will receive. With an hourly wage of 10 kopecks, he will work as long as the utility he receives from the last ten kopecks of wages exceeds the sense of displeasure resulting from the last hour of labour. Liefmann often repeats that workers who are employed in piecework are able to determine, according to their own wishes, the duration of their labour and the general sum of their wages.[13] But need it be pointed out that such cases are only a rare exception? Usually the worker's hours of labour are fixed in advance either by a collective agreement or by the unilateral will of the employer. Joint work by numerous workers in a single factory is impossible without establishing a uniform working day for all workers that is not left to the discretion of individual workers. Our worker cannot choose whether he will work 5 hours a day and receive 50 kopecks for his work, or instead work ten hours for pay of 1 rouble. The fact is that he must work 8 hours for pay of 80 kopecks even if, on the basis of a psychological comparison of utilities with costs, he would prefer to work less (if he tires quickly and has few needs) or more (if he does not tire and has elaborate needs). A psychological comparison of utilities with costs, even if carried out by the worker, cannot have any decisive influence on the scale and results of his economic activity. The worker has but one choice: either accept the objectively determined combination of costs and utilities (8 hours of labour and pay of 80 kopecks), or turn it down under penalty of hunger.

Perhaps Liefmann will reply that once the worker has agreed to accept the given combination of utilities and costs, we must assume that he has made a psychological comparison and determined that the former exceed the latter. But that would be an empty assumption, for the threat of hunger compels a worker to accept work on generally established terms and thereby predetermines the result of his psychological comparison. But while such an assumption would be empty, it would be directly false to assume that all cases of turning down work are explained by a negative sum resulting from the worker's psychological comparison of utilities and costs. If the capitalist attempts to reduce wages below the customary level, e.g. to 70 kopecks, the worker will refuse to work and would prefer hunger even if a psychological comparison showed him that the utility he might acquire for 70 kopecks exceeds the sense of displeasure associated with labour. Perhaps Liefmann will say that in this case the latter sense of displeasure is augmented by the sense of displeasure connected with possible censure from his comrades for strikebreaking. But would it not then follow that the behaviour of the worker cannot be explained by the psychological experiences of the *individual as such*, but rather by the objective social position of the *individual as a worker*? Moreover, even in the absence of reproof from his comrades, the worker will not agree to a reduction of wages until the heavy burden of struggle proves to him that it is impossible, with the given objective condition of the market, to preserve wages at the former level. On

---

13   Liefmann 1920, pp. 473, 497.

the basis of previous experience, the worker attributes in advance to his labour power a determinate normal exchange value or price – independently of the subjective burden of labour efforts that he experiences. The existing objective system of prices and incomes is not only the *precondition* for an economic subject's psychological experiences; it also entails a determinate *content and direction*.

We have come to the conclusion that Liefmann's psychological conception does not apply to the economy of the *worker*. Neither in the acquisition nor in the consumer economy of the worker do we find a psychological comparison of utilities with costs. A psychological comparison of utilities with costs may occur if we consider the economy of the worker as a whole, but it presupposes a system of objective prices and incomes that already exists, and it cannot, in itself, have a decisive influence upon the worker's economic behaviour.

If analysis of the worker's economy has revealed the futility of Liefmann's psychological constructions, analysis of the *employer* economy, to which we now turn, will demonstrate to us that they are false in principle. Even the very structure of the employer (capitalist) economy appears to overturn completely all of the positions that Liefmann has presented to us in his psychological conception of the economy. We were told earlier that labour efforts are the final factor of costs and that the essence of economy consists of comparing feelings of pleasure (utilities) with feelings of displeasure (costs). Now we learn of the existence of a 'countless' multitude of economies in which 'costs cannot be reduced to labour efforts'[14] and, as a result, there can be no talk of a feeling of displeasure due to economic activity. Previously we were told that the sum of costs to be spent in the economy is not fixed in advance. Now we are told of an economy that starts from a precisely fixed sum of costs (capital).

Liefmann, of course, is not inclined to look to the class structure of society for an explanation of the phenomena of a capitalist economy. On the contrary, he emphatically rejects that method of investigation. In his view, economic theory

> studies the exchange acts of people independently of the fact that sociology divides people into classes. The latter would be important for economic theory only if belonging to a class were a direct consequence of special exchange phenomena, or if the grouping of people into classes were a decisive factor for explaining the exchange mechanism. That is not the case. The whole doctrine of social classes does not take us one whit

---

14   Liefmann 1920, p. 471.

beyond what is explained by a correct economic theory with the help of both of the factors of costs (*Kostenfaktoren*): labour efforts and the sacrifices incurred in the form of material goods.[15]

Liefmann is not interested, therefore, in society's class structure. He hopes to give us an explanation of capitalist economy on the basis of a psychological conception of economy. He considers it enough for that purpose to provide a more detailed analysis of the 'factors of costs', to which we shall now turn.

Until now we have been assuming that the individual's psychological 'costs' consist of his labour efforts, and the 'factor of costs' is labour. But, while Liefmann assigns to labour the honorary title of 'ultimate factor of costs', it turns out that it is not always so in reality. 'There are three factors of costs that are sacrificed in economic activities: *labour, quantities of goods* (*Gütermengen*) and *sums of money*'.[16] Of course, it often happens that an outlay of goods or money ultimately comes down to an expenditure of labour, e.g. if a worker spends money that is earned with the help of his own labour, or if a peasant uses seed that results from his own labour. In such cases, goods and money are not independent factors of cost. But, along with these cases, there are others in which the quantity of goods or money, spent in the form of costs, is pre-given and precisely fixed without regard to the labour of any particular person (e.g. the sum of capital invested in an enterprise). Those cases involve a *pre-given and determinate sum of costs* (in material things and money).[17]

These positions of Liefmann cannot fail to cause confusion. Was it not Liefmann himself who taught us that to start from a previously given sum of costs is to ignore 'the main problem of economy'?[18] Was it not he who severely criticised the Austrian and other economists who, referring to the 'limitation of external nature',[19] started from a determinate quantity of goods? Finally, did he not argue that the quantity of money, spent in the form of costs, also must not be taken as given but instead is entirely determined by the sum of the 'ultimate' costs (i.e. labour efforts) that the individual considers it necessary to spend on the basis of his psychological economic plan?[20] What is the origin of money and goods that cannot be reduced to the 'ultimate factor of costs', to labour? Liefmann's reference to the fact of the social division of labour, which

15   Liefmann 1919, p. 598.
16   Liefmann 1920, p. 387.
17   Liefmann 1920, p. 390.
18   Liefmann 1920, pp. 269, 318, 390 *et passim*.
19   Liefmann 1920, p. 286.
20   Liefmann 1920, p. 313.

causes the emergence of 'goods that are no longer reducible to the labour of the person who uses them economically',[21] is of no help whatever. That argument is nothing more than a tribute that Liefmann pays to the 'technical' manner of presentation that he finds so abhorrent. With the existence of the social division of labour, a multitude of goods (more accurately, all goods) used by a particular person in the form of costs are not *technically* created by him, although *economically* they can be reduced to his labour insofar as they are purchased with money that he earns with the help of his own labour. To explain the emergence of 'goods that no can longer be reduced to the economic subject's own labour',[22] it is not enough to refer to the fact that goods and money exist alongside of labour. What is also required is that goods and money be converted into an independent source of non-labour income, into *capital*, and such conversion presupposes a definite class structure of society. Despite all his efforts to ignore this class structure, Liefmann inevitably runs up against it.

As we can see, the concept of 'costs', which originally and from a purely psychological point of view were understood in the sense of the displeasure that accompanies labour efforts, is also expanded by Liefmann to include sacrifices incurred in the form of goods and money. Since the latter cannot be reduced (economically, not technically) to the labour of their owner, they appear in the role of capital (or the income from this capital, i.e. profit). In fact, with his concept of '*costs*' Liefmann wants to combine the concepts of '*labour*' and '*capital*' and erase the profound difference between them. Liefmann himself makes no effort to hide the fact that this is his purpose. In his words, the concept of costs includes 'everything that has conventionally been covered until now by the concepts of *labour* and *capital*'.[23] Both of these concepts must be 'combined in the psychological concept of costs'.[24] Accordingly, we can now replace Liefmann's three-sided division of factors of costs (labour, goods and money)

---

21   Liefmann 1920, p. 390.

22   Liefmann 1920, p. 481.

23   Liefmann 1920, p. 466. To characterise the logical contradictions and terminological confusion that distinguishes Liefmann's investigation and severely hampers an accurate presentation of his ideas, we can point out that in another place Liefmann expresses himself differently: 'By costs we understand the *greater* part of what the materialistic theory calls *labour and capital*' (p. 385, Rubin's italics). Finally, a third definition says: 'The concept of costs includes everything that previous theory usually treated with the concepts of *labour, land and capital*' (p. 692). The third definition does not contradict the first insofar as Liefmann includes land, evaluated in money, as capital. But there is a clear contradiction between the first and the second definitions.

24   Liefmann 1920, p. 466.

with one that is two-sided. The factors of costs are either *labour* or *money* (that is advanced in the form of *capital*).[25]

In this case, as in those mentioned earlier, we witness Liefmann's vain attempts to use a common term to cover up the gaping contradiction between psychological sensations and the objective phenomena of money-capitalist society. Liefmann constructs the concept of 'costs', but it disintegrates before our eyes into the two heterogeneous concepts of labour and capital, a psychological sense of displeasure and an objective sum of money.[26] He develops the theory of economy as a comparison of costs with utilities, but he is himself compelled to recognise that two types of economy exist – the labour and the capitalist – which develop according to two different formulae. The first formula is one of *'costs – utilities'* (i.e. psychological costs and psychological utilities). The second formula is one of *'money costs – money yield'*.[27] The first formula, if we include in it a number of objective aspects resulting from the nature of money economy (namely, a definite system of objective prices and incomes), can be loosely applied to the labour economy of a small commodity producer (or of a worker), who expends his labour with the aim of acquiring

---

25   Liefmann also tries to give a two-sided division of the factors of cost, and he tumbles
      as usual into numerous contradictions. We have already quoted his definition on p. 387:
      'There are three factors of costs that are sacrificed in economic activities: *labour, quantit-
      ies of goods (Gütermengen)* and *sums of money'*. On page 309 of that same first volume, we
      read that 'costs are embodied in two factors of costs: *labour and Kostengüter'*, i.e. things
      that are spent in the form of costs (meaning goods and money). On pp. 598–9 of the
      second volume Liefmann forgets the sharp distinction he drew between psychological
      costs (labour efforts or sacrifices) and the factors of costs (labour or goods) and unexpec-
      tedly calls the factors of costs '*labour efforts and sacrifices* offered up in the form of things'.
      Finally, on p. 285 of the first volume Liefmann acknowledges that either *labour efforts*
      or *money* can serve as the 'unit of costs' (*Kosteneinheit*). See also Liefmann 1919, p. 115 *et
      passim*. This is where Liefmann comes closest to the essence of the matter. From his own
      point of view, things cannot serve as an independent factor of costs because they cannot,
      as such, be expressed in terms of a single unit; to reduce costs to a single unit is necessary
      and possible only with respect to labour efforts or money (Liefmann 1920, pp. 285, 294).
      Things, which cannot be reduced to labour efforts, must be reduced to money. In view of
      that fact, the factors of costs can only be either labour efforts or money. In the acquisition
      economy, things are also expended (machinery, materials, etc.), but evaluation of them
      occurs in terms of money (1920, p. 508). 'It is not the cost of goods themselves (*Kosten-
      güter*) but the sums of money in which they are calculated that are called capital' (1920,
      p. 575).
26   We shall look later at Liefmann's attempt to replace an objective sum of money with a
      subjective evaluation of the same sum of money.
27   Liefmann, of course, simply speaks of the 'formula: costs – utilities, or money costs –
      money yield' (p. 459), but it is obvious that this involves combining two different formulae
      into one.

items of consumption through the medium of money (in Marx's terminology, this is the circuit $C–M–C_1$). The second formula is suitable for the economy of an employer-capitalist, who invests in the business a determinate money capital for the purpose of receiving a money yield or profit: here we have the circuit $M–C–(M + m)$.

In these two economies, the phenomena flow in completely different directions. In the first economy, the sum of costs (labour efforts) is *not determined* in advance and, in Liefmann's view, is only determined as a result of the psychological comparison of utilities with costs. The second economy begins with a *definite sum of money*, or money capital.[28] In the first case, labour is actually *expended*; in the second case, capital is only *advanced* and is not spent at all.[29] An expenditure of labour is directly connected with a *sense of displeasure*; in the case of an advance of capital, it would be ridiculous to speak of any accompanying psychological sensation of displeasure. With regard to labour, we can speak of an *independent psychological evaluation* of costs (labour efforts) that depends upon accompanying feelings of displeasure. As for money costs: 1) in the acquisition economy they appear in the role of capital and are not subject to any psychological evaluation at all,[30] only to a *purely quantitative* comparison with money yield, i.e. profit; 2) in the consumer economy money costs – even if we accept Liefmann's views concerning their psychological evaluation – are evaluated in terms of the *utility* they can provide, i.e. there is no independent psychological evaluation of costs as such.[31] All of the features that Liefmann took to be characteristic of costs in general (the absence of any previously given quantitative determination, and the connection with a sense of displeasure, based upon the latest independent psychological evaluation) are inapplicable to money costs.

While the first components of both of our formulae (costs and money costs) differ so profoundly, there is no less of a difference between their second components (psychological utilities and money yields). Liefmann at least attempted, although unsuccessfully, to combine the first components of both formulae with the single concept of 'costs'. As for the second components, he had to

---

28   Liefmann 1920, p. 481.
29   Even the old James Steuart, writing in the eighteenth century, was quite clear concerning the difference between money advanced and money expended (see the quotation that Marx provides in *Capital*, Vol. 1, Ch. IV, footnote 3). But Liefmann – and this is the central idea of his system – mistakenly wants to equate the case of *advancing* money, with the goal of acquiring *a greater sum* of money, with cases in which money is *being spent* with the goal of receiving *utilities* (use values).
30   Liefmann 1919, p. 167.
31   Liefmann 1920, p. 512.

give up even on such a terminological combination. While the goal of the consumer economy, of a worker for example, is to acquire a certain sum of *gross utility* embodied in items of consumption (and not merely a surplus of utility over costs, i.e. the feelings of displeasure that accompany labour efforts), the goal of the employer's acquisition economy is precisely to obtain a *net yield*, i.e. a surplus of gross utility over costs (capital).[32] While the worker (or peasant), as described by Liefmann, psychologically compares the *utility* he receives with the *costs* incurred, the capitalist makes a purely quantitative comparison of *net yield with costs* (capital), with the goal of determining the *percentage* relation between the yield (profit) and the costs (capital)[33] – a method that is specifically characteristic of a capitalist economy and beyond the limits of a psychological conception of the economy. While the peasant, in exchange for the product of his labour (and the worker, in exchange for his labour power) receives an *equivalent* utility (i.e. a product with the same exchange value but a different natural form), for the capitalist both costs and utilities are nothing but sums of money that merely have *different magnitudes.*

An attempt to include in one abstract formula: 1) cases of the expenditure of individual *labour* for the purpose of *direct* production of products that are required (natural economy); 2) cases of the expenditure of *labour* by a commodity producer for the purpose of *exchanging* finished products for products of *equivalent value* but with a different natural form (simple commodity production, or the circuit $C–M–C_1$); and 3) cases of the capitalist advancing a definite *sum of money* (capital) in order to acquire a *greater* sum of money or net profit (capitalist economy or the circuit $M–C–M_1$) – cannot but end in failure.[34] Liefmann's psychological conception inevitably leads him to ignore the

---

32   Liefmann 1920, p. 514. This fact fundamentally undermines the importance of analogies between the two types of economy. For that reason, nothing remains to Liefmann but to obscure as much as possible the points of difference under the guise of analogies, mentioning them only in passing. On p. 33 of Volume II we read: 'It is possible that a higher money yield is also the *goal* of acquisition economy, just as it is possible that a higher consumer yield is the *regulator* (*Richtschnur*) of consumer economy' [Rubin's italics]. Liefmann is counting upon an unperceptive reader who will not notice that the analogy is lame; the first half of the sentence speaks of an economy's *goal*, while the second half speaks of a *regulator* [or guiding principle]. Liefmann again counts upon such a reader when he writes on p. 34 of the same volume: 'A maximal money *yield* is the goal of acquisition economy just as maximal *utility* or maximal satisfaction of needs is the goal of consumer economy' [Rubin's italics]. In this case, both halves of the sentence speak of an economic goal, but in the first half it is *yield* and in the second half (gross) *utility*.

33   Liefmann 1920, p. 703.

34   Liefmann himself recognises (see 1920, p. 463) that the distinction he is making between psychological and purely quantitative (or monetary) comparisons of utilities with costs is

specific feature of capitalist economy, namely, the *objective self-expansion of value as capital* (as opposed to the subjective increase of feelings of pleasure in the psychology of an individual due to psychological utility exceeding psychological costs). This is why Liefmann, in his pursuit of imaginary-psychological constructions, loses sight of the real specificity of employer psychology; it is not the best satisfaction of personal needs but rather the most rapid possible expansion of capital that constitutes the subjective purpose of the capitalist.

> The objective content of the circulation we have been discussing, the valorization of value – is his [the capitalist's] subjective purpose, and it is only in so far as the appropriation of ever more wealth in the abstract is the sole driving force behind his operations that he functions as a capitalist, i.e. as capital personified and endowed with consciousness and a will. Use-values must therefore never be treated as the immediate aim of the capitalist ....[35]

As we already know, Liefmann portrays the scheme of capitalist economy in the following form:

Acquisition economy		Consumer economy	
Costs	Yield	Costs	Utilities
Money or Goods (capital)	Money yield (profit)	Money income	Consumer goods

The starting point of the economy, as can be seen from the scheme, is a determinate sum of capital (money or goods evaluated in terms of money). *Psychological costs* (feelings of displeasure), as the starting point of economy, are in this case completely *absent*. Why is it that in this case money costs, whose

---

close to the distinction that Marx made in his famous formulae of C–M–C₁ and M–C–M₁. But Marx, at the same time, sees in these formulae the expression of *different* objective social-production relations between people. Liefmann sees them as nothing more than different ways of realising *one and the same* psychological process of comparing utilities with costs. That is why Marx, with the help of these formulae, actually succeeded in clarifying the *specific* features of capitalist economy, while Liefmann tries with all his power to *smother* these specificities with the help of a universal psychological conception.

35 Marx 1976, p. 254.

advancement is not connected with any sense of displeasure, must invariably provide a yield (profit), while on the other hand the craftsman or worker, who is expending labour efforts (psychological costs), does not evaluate them as a specific sum of money costs, i.e. regards costs as zero from a purely monetary point of view? Nowhere does Liefmann directly pose this question, which is fatal for the psychological conception. Evidently he does not even see any question here and considers it perfectly natural for labour efforts, as a feeling of displeasure, to be subject to a psychological evaluation, while goods and money are calculated in the form of a certain sum of money costs that must provide profit. But that sort of assumption is refuted by the facts, which are not completely unknown to Liefmann. There are cases when a producer (e.g. a craftsman) does not regard his money expenditures (for material, instruments, etc.) as costs that must provide a profit; he is limited to deducting this sum from the gross yield, and the remainder, in the form of net yield, is attributed entirely to his 'costs', which are expended in the form of labour efforts.[36] On the other hand a manufacturer, who has invested in the business not just his capital but also his personal labour, quite often evaluates the latter as a certain sum of money (e.g. as the compensation received by a factory director); this sum is subject to deduction from the gross yield, and the net yield (profit) is entirely attributed to capital.[37] Even more often, the manufacturer completely omits any inclusion of his personal labour in the list of costs.[38] Thus, even an individual's personal labour is sometimes subject to psychological and at other times to money evaluation (or else is not evaluated at all). On the other hand, money expenditures are not always regarded as 'costs' that have to provide a 'yield' (profit). The psychological conception of economy is completely unable to explain these profound differences, which are due to different social types of economy and the social characters of economic subjects (employers, workers, craftsmen).

Thus, the starting point of an entrepreneurial capitalist economy is objective money costs, not psychological costs. Here, as in many other places, the method of 'analogies' fails to serve Liefmann. But can we not, in place of the capitalist's money costs, substitute his psychological evaluation of them? In other words, might it not be possible for Liefmann to get more favourable results with help from the 'method of psychological evaluation'? Leaving aside the fact that this method, as we clarified earlier, cannot lead Liefmann to any final confirmation of the psychological conception of economy, let us examine the

---

36   Liefmann 1920, p. 472.
37   Liefmann 1920, pp. 472, 507; 1919, p. 573.
38   Liefmann 1920, p. 507; 1919, p. 573.

question of what *psychological evaluation* the capitalist in fact attaches to the *capital* he advances. We learn from Liefmann that in the sphere of acquisition economy the capitalist does not subject his capital to any psychological evaluation whatever, considering it only from the purely quantitative perspective as a certain sum of money units counterposed to another sum of the same the same units (i.e. profit).[39] But, Liefmann continues, we must examine the capitalist's acquisition economy together with his consumer economy, since the former serves the interests of the latter. In that case we shall be convinced that the capitalist psychologically evaluates his *capital* as a means of delivering *utilities*[40] (i.e. consumer articles that are purchased with the sum of profits).

Let us suppose that Liefmann is correct, that the capitalist evaluates each hundred [marks] of his capital in terms of the marginal utility provided to him by the last hundred [marks] of capital (in the form of profit that is being spent on items of consumption). But, is it not obvious that the evaluation of money costs (capital), in that case, is nothing more than a reflection of the evaluation of the marginal utility they provide? What is *missing* is any *autonomous psychological evaluation of costs* that is independent of the psychological evaluation of utilities. We may speak here of a psychological comparison of different utilities obtained with the help of capital, but there is no *psychological comparison of utilities with costs* – which, in Liefmann's opinion, is a necessary feature of any economy. It is a fact that once the employer economy has no psychological costs (feelings of displeasure connected with labour efforts), there can also be no place for an independent psychological evaluation of the costs (of capital).

Let us take a step further and ask ourselves whether the capitalist in fact subjectively evaluates his capital according to the marginal utility of the items of consumption he receives. That could happen in the event that the entire profit was spent only on the purchase of consumer goods. However, a part of the profit, and often a very significant part, is accumulated by the capitalist, i.e. it becomes capital. Suppose that from his annual profit of 40,000 marks the capitalist spends 30,000 marks on his personal consumption and accumulates 10,000 marks, i.e. converts them into capital providing him with 5% profit. It is obvious that in this case the capitalist 'evaluates 10,000 marks *as capital* (i.e. of course, not only its money interest but also the possibility of disposal at any given moment over capital itself) more highly than any expansion of his *consumption*'[41] beyond the specified sum of 30,000 marks. Each hundred marks from the sum of profit can be directed into either the fund of consumption

---

39   Liefmann 1919, p. 167: 'Acquisition economy does not generally evaluate money'.
40   Liefmann 1920, p. 481.
41   Liefmann 1919, p. 282 [Rubin's italics].

or the fund of accumulation. And this means that in relation to each hundred marks two evaluations compete: 1) an evaluation of the given sum of money (as costs) according to the marginal utility it delivers, and 2) an evaluation of the same sum of money as *capital*, i.e. as a constant source of profit (in the sense of money interest). Instead of what Liefmann expects – an evaluation of capital according to the utility delivered by the profit on capital – our employer evaluates his profit according to the 'utility' that it acquires in the form of future potential capital.[42] Consequently, in capitalist economy there is a unique evaluation of *money as capital* that does not correspond to the evaluation of money according to the utility it provides for satisfying the personal needs of its owner. This means that alongside 'natural' economic motivation, arising from the personal needs of the individual, in capitalist society there is an 'artificial' economic motivation that originates in capital's need for unlimited expansion. The individual, as *a capitalist*, has purely 'social' needs (for example, the growth of capital and the expansion of production) that are not covered by the 'natural' needs of the capitalist as *an individual* (for food, clothing, etc.).[43] Any attempt to explain the movement of capital beginning with 'natural' needs of the individual – and this is what Liefmann's theory comes down to – is condemned in advance to failure.

As we see, capital must deliver not just the sums intended for satisfaction of the personal needs of its owner, but also sums necessary for the expansion of capital itself. In other words, the profit delivered by capital, or the 'money yield', does not enter as a whole into the consumer economy, and the phenomena of the acquisition economy must not, therefore, be explained exclusively by the needs of the capitalist's consumer economy. And since phenomena of the acquisition economy are also essentially the same phenomena investigated by political economy (money, prices, incomes), it follows that Liefmann's psychological conception must be recognised as unsuitable for explaining a capitalist economy.

In moments of reflection, Liefmann himself comes to the idea that the only possible refuge for his psychological conception of economy remains the *consumer* economy (of the worker and the capitalist). 'Since acquisition activity becomes increasingly separated from the consumer economy, and most economic actors appear as dependent workers in the acquisition economy of

---

42   This 'utility' of money, as a source of capital formation, has nothing in common with its
      utility in the sense of its suitability for satisfying the personal needs of the individual.

43   It is obvious that the latter needs of the individual are social in the sense that the forms
      they assume and the ways of satisfying them change, depending upon changes in the sur-
      rounding social environment.

other people, the economic judgements of a majority of people, strictly speaking, are increasingly dislodged into the sphere of the consumer economy'.[44] Accordingly, the sphere of operation for the psychological laws of economy revealed by Liefmann is not in factories and shops, not in joint-stock societies and trusts, but rather in the modest kitchens of workers and the luxurious dining rooms of millionaires' mansions. If Liefmann had succeeded in proving a causal dependence of phenomena in the acquisition economy upon the needs of the consumer economy, the uncharacteristic modesty that he shows on this point would be rewarded according to merit: from his kitchen or dining room he would easily conquer the entire world of economic phenomena. But since Liefmann has not solved this task, the words that we have cited from him amount to the bankruptcy of his theory.

We could easily leave Liefmann within the four walls of the kitchen or dining room, but truth requires us to recognise that even in the sphere of the consumer economy, where the individual has greater freedom of individual choice than in the sphere of acquisition activity, there is no place for a psychological comparison of utilities with costs. And that is simply because, in conditions of money economy, all costs of the consumer economy appear in money form and not as psychological costs. Even if we agreed with Liefmann that a unit of money costs in the consumer economy is subject to psychological evaluation, that evaluation of costs, as we have seen above, is no more than a reflection of the evaluation of the marginal utilities they procure. There is no *independent psychological evaluation of costs*.

Analysis of Liefmann's teaching cannot fail to provoke a question from the reader: What goal was Liefmann pursuing with his complicated constructions, which are not suitable at a single point for explaining capitalist society? After all, Liefmann spent considerable psychological efforts or costs on these constructions.[45] One must think, in agreement with his own theory, that he hoped his work would provide utility and a surplus (or 'yield' in Liefmann's terminology) covering the sum of his costs. What 'utility' did Liefmann hope to get from his work? We believe that the main utility that he was seeking involved a solution, or more accurately an elimination of the *problem of profit*. Liefmann cannot understand why bourgeois economists rack their brains so much over this problem. In his opinion, it presents no difficulties: it goes without saying that the capitalist is unwilling to 'sacrifice' his 'costs' (capital) unless he receives a corresponding 'yield' (profit). In this respect, the capitalist is no different from

---

44   Liefmann 1920, p. 500.
45   It is enough to point out that the first volume of *Grundsätze der Volkswirtschaftslehre* has 708 pages and the second, 858 pages.

the worker or craftsman, who exchanges the product of his labour according to the formula C–M–C₁. In a debate with Böhm-Bawerk, who recognized all the difficulties concealed in the problem of profit, Liefmann writes:

> Is there any surprise in the fact that an economic actor only agrees to 'consume' some goods for the production of other goods if he benefits from doing so? Indeed, what might persuade him to relinquish goods, to sacrifice them, if he is not hoping to receive, in exchange for this loss, a surplus in other goods (*ein Mehr an anderen Gütern*)? Why does Böhm not pose such a question for any exchange of goods, in which a person gives one good and expects to receive some yield for it? ... If Böhm also asked the same question here, he would come to the fundamental principle of all economy, the striving to receive a surplus utility or yield, in short, to the *psychological* conception.[46]

So now we know the end that Liefmann's psychological conception must serve. It must eliminate the specific problem of profit and equate the latter with the psychological yield of Crusoe or the craftsman. Both Crusoe and the craftsman receive utility that exceeds the sum of their psychological costs (labour efforts); they receive a psychological 'yield'. What is surprising about the fact that the capitalist also receives a profit as a surplus of utility over costs? The specific characteristic of capitalist economy is not at all the fact that capital (costs) deliver profit (a yield) – in that respect this economy does not differ at all from natural or simple commodity economy – but merely that the capitalist, wishing to make a more accurate comparison of his money yield with costs, does all the calculations of costs in the form of sums of money.[47]

Drawing a parallel between natural and simple commodity economy on the one hand, and capitalist economy on the other, what Liefmann forgets is nothing more nor less than the cardinal fact that in the former case the issue is a *subjective increase in feelings of satisfaction*, whereas in the latter case it is the *objective increase of sums of money* (or more accurately, of exchange value). It is perfectly understandable that Crusoe, giving his labour in 'exchange'[48] for the products that he obtains with the help of that labour, receives a benefit consisting of the opportunity to satisfy his needs. The craftsman receives the same benefit when exchanging the product of his labour, through the medium

---

46   Liefmann 1919, p. 558.
47   Liefmann 1920, pp. 567 ff., 572, 586.
48   Bourgeois economists love to portray the production process as an 'exchange' between man and nature.

of money, for some other product that has the same exchange value but a different use value (the circuit C–M–C_1). The capitalist, in the circuit M–C–M_1, gives and receives money, and thus his benefit or yield cannot consist of anything other than the objective expansion of sums of money (or more accurately, sums of value) at his disposal. If previously the issue was the subjective increase of feelings of satisfaction, which accompany the exchange of equivalent products and are experienced by both parties to the exchange, now we see before us the objective expansion of sums of money (or values), which at first sight is impossible with the exchange of equivalent values. Whence comes the surplus sum of money (profit) – that is the question that Liefmann does not even raise apart from endlessly repeating that this profit is paid by consumers. With the help of the most crude and naïve methods, Liefmann attempts to *occlude* this specific problem of capitalist economy. In the passage cited above, he has the capitalist hoping to receive a 'surplus in other goods'. This vague expression must identically characterise the behaviour of both the capitalist and the craftsman. In fact, it does not fit either one of them. The craftsman does not receive any 'surplus' (*ein Mehr*) in the exchange of his products for 'other goods': his psychological 'surplus' or benefit consists of the very possibility of exchanging his products for 'other (consumer) goods' of equivalent value. The capitalist really does acquire a 'surplus' (profit), not in 'other goods' but rather in the very same goods in which his costs are expressed, i.e. in the form of money.

As might be expected, Liefmann's attempt to eliminate the problem of the *objective self-expansion of capital*, with the help of psychological concepts of utility and costs, could not succeed. We can easily explain how all members of society (working in the capacity of isolated Crusoes in natural economy, or as commodity producers in conditions of simple commodity economy) *simultaneously* experience a subjective increase in feelings of satisfaction (psychological yields). But we cannot even imagine a situation in which all members of society, not expending their own labour, might *simultaneously* use expenditure of a determinate sum of exchange value (money) to acquire a greater sum of exchange value. The possibility of receiving *that sort* of 'yield' is conceivable only with regard to *one part* of society that is exploiting another part. The problem of capital and profit cannot be solved without an analysis of the class structure of society – the analysis that Liefmann wanted to dismiss with his universal psychological concepts of economy.

CHAPTER 4

The Theory of Prices

We concluded our previous chapter by pointing out that Liefmann, with the help of his psychological conception of economy, hopes to cut the Gordian knot of the problem of profit, which is the most difficult part of the problem of *incomes* in general. But Liefmann's claims extend further. He suggests that an integral *theoretical system*, embracing all the phenomena of economic life, can only be constructed on the basis of his psychological conception. With his characteristic sense of unlimited self-importance, Liefmann does not tire of repeating on every page that he is the first since the time of the classics to create a comprehensive theoretical system, in relation to which all other economists are nothing but unsuccessful and pathetic precursors.

Since all economic phenomena in capitalist society appear in the form of prices, it is understandable that the problem of prices and value are at the centre of political economy. Liefmann, as we have noted in passing, considers it necessary to discard from our science the concept of 'value' (*Wert*) in both the subjective and objective sense. In the world of an individual's psychological experiences, we never encounter 'subjective value' as distinct from the concrete *psychological valuations*' of the subject. Likewise, in an analysis of the mechanism of exchange, we never encounter any objective 'exchange value' of products that is separate from their concrete *prices* or monetary expressions. Political economy must begin with the psychological evaluations of the subject in order to arrive at the explanation of market prices. Although Liefmann sees the *basis* of our science in the theory of the subject's psychological evaluations, he regards its ultimate *purpose* as an explanation of the mechanism of exchange, in which the formation of prices and incomes occurs. Liefmann sees the ultimate justification of his psychological conception of economy precisely in the fact that it is the basis for providing the first satisfactory theory of prices (which is closely tied to the theory of incomes).

Hitherto we have been occupied mainly with the *private* economic individual (the worker and capitalist) and have been attempting to show that even the behaviour and psychological experiences of the individual, occurring in the sphere of his private economy, cannot be summed up in Liefmann's formulae. We have often been persuaded that the psychological evaluations of the individual already presuppose existence of a social-objective system of prices and incomes. But perhaps this objective system of prices and incomes in turn, as Liefmann claims, can only be understood as the result of an interaction and

© RICHARD B. DAY, 2024 | DOI:10.1163/9789004705661_025

encounters between the subjective evaluations of separate individuals? In that case, we would revert once more to the theory that Liefmann advocates concerning the primacy of the subjective-psychological aspects of economy over the objective-social, or at the very least we would be compelled to acknowledge their equality. We must now examine the extent to which Liefmann has really succeeded in grounding his theory in an analysis of the *general-economic processes of exchange and price formation*.

We have already seen that in his attempts to derive objective-social economic phenomena from subjective-psychological ones, Liefmann hopelessly confuses three different methods that we have provisionally called the method of *psychological causality*, the method of *analogies*, and the method of *psychological evaluation*. We need not be surprised by the fact that in his attempt to derive objective prices from individual psychological evaluations Liefmann resorts to the same three methods without differentiating one from the other. In some places Liefmann claims to show, in accordance with the first of these methods, a *causal conditioning* of the exchange mechanism by the psychological evaluations of individuals. He extols his theoretical system as 'the only one that really explains the mechanism of exchange economy from the psychological sensations of needs'.[1] 'In order to explain the whole mechanism of exchange economy, it is ultimately necessary to return to evaluations of utilities and costs that originate with consumers'.[2]

In other places, however, Liefmann's claims are more modest. 'One of the most important results of my theory is that it shows *how the organisational principle of a singular economy, regulating the economic behaviour of a particular individual, and the organisational principle of exchange turnover are completely identical*'.[3] These words, which Liefmann italicises and often repeats, in fact contain merely a promise to reveal *an analogy* between the sphere of subjective evaluations by a subject and the sphere of objective exchange phenomena. It is as though Liefmann never guesses that even if he succeeded in establishing an analogy between these two spheres of phenomena, he would not move a single step forward in understanding a causal connection between them.

Finally, when Liefmann has to turn to the essence of price phenomena, he is compelled to restrict his claims still further and to operate solely with the method of *psychological evaluations*. An objective price exists in the market and is the same for all purchasers, e.g. the price of a pair of shoes is 20 marks.

---

1   Liefmann 1920, p. 430.
2   Liefmann 1920, p. 478.
3   Liefmann 1920, p. 318 [Rubin's italics].

This price does not correspond with the subjective evaluations of individual purchasers or even, as we shall see, of the marginal purchaser (on that point Liefmann disagrees with the Austrian economists). 'Price is not an expression of subjective evaluations but is itself evaluated in the consumer economy (namely, as a share of income).'[4] One and the same objective price of a pair of shoes, 20 marks, is subjectively evaluated differently by different consumers, depending upon the size of their income. A rich man would be willing to pay 100 marks for a pair of shoes, and therefore his subjective evaluation of the utility of the shoes far exceeds his evaluation of the costs (i.e. 20 marks). A poor man, to the contrary, subjectively evaluates each mark that he is spending so highly that he decides against buying a new pair of shoes; therefore, the subjective evaluation of the utility of shoes in this case is less than the subjective evaluation of costs (20 marks). From this viewpoint, the entire problem of prices is formulated as follows:

> That a pair of shoes of a definite quality costs 20 marks is a universal phenomenon, the same kind of objective expression as 100 centners.[5] The problem of prices consists of *how this objective monetary expression is connected with subjective evaluations of utility on the part of consumers*. And the answer to this problem must be that these objective monetary expressions or prices *are subjectively evaluated as a share of money income by the consumer economy that is paying these prices*.[6]

In the first half of the passage Liefmann wants to find the 'connection' between objective prices and subjective evaluations. There is no doubt that such a 'connection' exists, but the whole question concerns its nature. From the second half of the passage we learn that this connection consists of the *ensuing psychological evaluation* by each singular consumer economy of prices that are given to it in advance and objectively exist. And from this we can justifiably draw the conclusion – unexpected by Liefmann – that objective prices are primary and subjective evaluations are secondary.

Now we can turn to an exposition and criticism of Liefmann's theory of prices, without forgetting for a moment that his reasoning erratically confuses and interweaves all three of the viewpoints that we have mentioned.

Liefmann begins with an analysis of *demand* and *supply*. In order to connect this starting point of the theory of prices with his psychological conception of

---

4 Liefmann 1919, p. 204.
5 [A centner is a unit of weight, usually understood to be about 110 pounds.]
6 Liefmann 1919, p. 211. Liefmann's italics.

economy, Liefmann turns to his favourite method of analogies. It turns out that demand and supply conceal the concepts of *utility* and *costs* with which we are already familiar:

> We shall come to a correct understanding of supply and demand only if we recognise that demand and supply in the exchange turnover are essentially the same as utility and costs within the confines of a singular economy. What in a singular economy is *need*, or a *desire for gratification*, in the exchange turnover is *demand*; what in the former are *costs*, are here called *supply*.[7]

Later we shall analyse the extent to which this analogy is correct, but for now let us carry it further. Just as utility and costs are not fixed in advance in a singular economy, so it would be incorrect to consider the dimensions of supply and demand in the exchange turnover to be fixed in advance – on this point Liefmann is totally correct. 'The problem is how, with a demand that is unlimited in itself but of steadily declining intensity, supply emerges, i.e. the outlays of costs'.[8] To solve this question we have to examine demand and supply separately.

Final demand originates in the *needs* of the individual,[9] but only in those needs that the individual 'calculates in the exchange turnover',[10] i.e. those on which the individual, beginning with his economic plan of consumption (i.e. his comparison of all his needs with his aggregate income), agrees to spend the *costs*. The consumers' projected or 'calculated costs (*Kostenanschläge*) become demand'.[11] What is the measure of demand, i.e. of costs, that our individual agrees to spend on the satisfaction of a particular need? That depends not only upon the intensity of the given need but also upon the size of a given individual's money income.[12] 'Each consumer economy anticipates a money income, the size of which is known with near certainty'.[13] Our individual 'projects' all of his needs onto his money income, the size of which determines the scale of his demand, i.e. the costs that he can spend on the satisfaction of

---

7   Liefmann 1919, p. 43.
8   Liefmann 1920, p. 318; also 1919, p. 45.
9   Demand originating from consumer economies, e.g. demand for cotton on the part of the fabric manufacturer, ultimately depends, according to Liefmann, on the demand for fabric originating from final consumers.
10 Liefmann 1919, p. 43.
11 Liefmann 1919, p. 220.
12 Liefmann 1919, p. 219.
13 Liefmann 1919, p. 215.

different needs. However, for the determination of a correct (consumer) economic plan, it is not enough for our individual to know the intensity of his
needs and the size of his income. His economic plan will be better compiled,
the more accurately he knows 'previous prices of the most important goods'.[14]
In order to determine what sum of money he can spend on the purchase of
clothing, our individual must have foreknowledge of the prices of products that
satisfy his most imperative needs (bread, meat, etc.). In general, it is only with
knowledge of prices for the most important products that our individual will
know the extent to which his needs can be satisfied with a given income, and
consequently how highly he must subjectively evaluate each rouble (which is
determined by the utility of the last or marginal rouble).

Now, when our individual knows in advance the amount of his *income* and
the *prices* on products, he can compile an appropriate consumer plan on the
basis of the familiar 'law of the equalisation of marginal consumer yields':[15]
he allocates his costs (income) to purchases of different products in such a
way that, in all spheres of the satisfaction of needs, the last unit of costs (i.e.
the last rouble) provides the identical 'consumer yield' (or subjective utility).
Now our individual enters the market with a determinate demand: he determines in advance the maximal sum of costs that he is willing to spend for each
unit of each good, and thus his 'estimate of costs (*Kostenanschläge*) becomes
demand'.[16]

From the analysis of demand given by Liefmann, we can already draw certain conclusions that speak against his theory. To begin with, we can be certain
of the total inconsistency of the *analogy* that he undertakes between demand
and supply. After all, demand does not involve needs alone but needs compared
to costs and calculated in money. Demand essentially means a sum of costs
that consumers, given existing conditions of incomes and prices, propose to
incur on the purchase of various products. And these *costs* for the purchase of
products – costs that Liefmann himself acknowledges do not express the subjective utility of these products for consumers – are what Liefmann proposes
to call *utility*! This example clearly demonstrates what terminological abuse
the method of analogies generally leads to, and especially in cases when they
are used with the theoretical off-handedness in which Liefmann indulges. At
first Liefmann defined utility as the sense of satisfaction connected with consumption. After that he extended the concept of utility to the sums of money

---

14   Liefmann 1919, pp. 216, 219.
15   Liefmann 1919, p. 219.
16   Liefmann 1919, p. 220.

received by workers (wages), on the grounds that these sums will be expended on the purchase of utilities. We further learned that the sums of money acquired by the capitalist are also covered by the concept of utility, although only a portion of them is spent on the purchase of articles of consumption. But hitherto, at least, we have been dealing with sums of money that are possessed by *a single subject* and therefore enter into his sphere of psychological evaluations. Now it is proposed that we call the costs – projected by *different* individuals who evaluate them differently in psychological terms – utility.

Our second, and much more important, conclusion is that this analysis of demand completely overturns the method of *psychological causality*, which aspires to explain the mechanism of exchange economy (especially the formation of prices and incomes) from the subjective evaluations of consumers. The psychological evaluations of consumers, or the psychological comparison of utilities and costs, on the basis of which they compile their consumer plan, already presupposes, as we have seen, the existence of *given objective prices and incomes*. The system of objective prices and incomes has to be examined by us as something primary, and the subjective evaluations and consumer plans of separate individuals – as something derivative.

Liefmann himself knows that an analysis of demand alone does not solve the problem of prices, and that is why he turns to an analysis of *supply*. We know that each individual enters the market with his demand. The wealthy man agrees to pay up to 100 marks for a pair of shoes, and the poor man – no more than 5 marks. Why is it that a *uniform, general price* is established in the market, namely 20 marks for a pair of shoes? What is it that determines the *level of an objective price* and the volume of the *real supply* of a particular commodity (and thereby the extent of the actual *satisfaction of demand*)? For these central questions, Liefmann must search for an answer in the analysis of supply. 'The problem of exchange consists precisely of explaining how supply emerges and the scale of costs that are expended,[17] or according to the materialist conception, what volumes of goods are entering the market. To explain the emergence and the scale of supply is the main task of the theory of prices'.[18]

The answer to these central questions of the theory of prices consists of the following:

---

17   The reference here is to costs that are expended by industrialists and merchants on the production and supply of goods to the market, i.e. costs determined by the supply of commodities.

18   Liefmann 1919, p. 45. Liefmann justifiably rebukes the Austrian economists who start from a given supply of goods, i.e. a given volume of supply.

The supply of different goods, for which consumers experience a need, occurs in exchange economy exactly according to the law of the equalisation of marginal yields, which, as we have already seen, regulates the economic behaviour of a single economic actor. The individual economic actor satisfies each need only to the point where the marginal yields for each type of good are equal, and the whole aggregate of sellers (*Anbieter*) in exchange economy do exactly the same. Sellers provide each good to the market only in such quantity that the marginal yield, i.e. the yield acquired in each branch by the most expensive supplier, is approximately equal for all branches.[19]

'With free competition and the greatest possible mobility of capital and the workforce, the supply and the prices of goods offered by numerous individuals must in fact be established at the level where the most expensive provider, on average, receives the same (marginal) yield as the most expensive provider receives in other branches'.[20] Otherwise, capital and labour power will move to those branches of production where the marginal yield is higher. 'That is how the equalisation of marginal yields occurs between different branches of the economy, along with the formation of a *common marginal money yield*'.[21]

At last, we have now found the 'organisational principle' of commodity turnover, which corresponds with the organisational principle of a singular economy, namely, the famous 'law of the equalisation of marginal yields'. This law gives us the answer to both of the questions that we have posed: first, it regulates the *volume of supply* and thereby also the extent to which demand is satisfied,[22] and secondly, the *level of price*. 'With free competition, price tends to be established at a level equal to the marginal money yield plus the costs of the supplier who still receives this marginal yield'.[23] If we call the costs of this most expensive producer the 'marginal costs', then we get the following abbreviated formula of price: '*The price of a good is determined by its marginal costs plus the marginal money yield*'.[24]

---

19   Liefmann 1919, p. 228 (Liefmann's italics). The most expensive seller refers to the marginal or least competitive seller, e.g. the producer who works with the least advanced means of production. Such a producer, expending the greatest sum of costs, receives only the 'marginal yield' (e.g. the customary rate of profit), which is higher for each producer the lower are his individual costs (e.g. due to using the best machinery).

20   Ibid.

21   Liefmann 1919, p. 229.

22   Ibid.

23   Liefmann 1919, p. 232.

24   Ibid.

To give the reader a clearer view of this central point in his theory of prices, we have tried to use Liefmann's own words to outline his reasoning with regard to the law of the equalisation of marginal yields as regulator of the supply and prices of products. Reading these quotations from Liefmann must have raised a number of puzzling questions from the reader: 1) Does Liefmann not repeat in his theory of prices, which he proclaims to be a great scientific discovery, exactly the same theory of *costs of production* that was formulated by the classics; and 2) does this objective theory of prices not overturn Liefmann's entire *psychological conception*? In order to answer these questions, we shall first sort out the points of similarity and difference between Liefmann's formula of prices and the theory of costs of production, and then we shall turn to Liefmann's attempts to connect his theory of prices with the psychological conception of economy.

As we know, supporters of the classical theory of costs of production defined the price of a commodity as the sum of costs spent on its production in the least favourable circumstances, plus the average profit. It is obvious, without any need for proof, that Liefmann's 'marginal costs' correspond to the costs mentioned by supporters of the classical theory. What remains for us is to demonstrate that Liefmann's 'marginal money yield' cannot mean anything other than the general rate of profit.[25]

It is true that Liefmann would like to attach a wider significance to his concept of the marginal money yield: for him it includes not only the minimum rate of profit but also the minimum interest rate and the minimum wage rate.[26] However, Liefmann himself senses that in fact we have *three different rates* towards which the incomes of three different classes of the population gravitate: industrial capitalists, money capitalists, and workers. 'It might have seemed that we should speak not of one marginal money yield but of three marginal yields'.[27] Liefmann too readily dismisses this difficult question by pointing

---

25 With the difference that Liefmann, in accordance with economists from the Austrian school and the American school, understands the normal rate of profit to be the minimum or the marginal profit received by the capitalist who works with the highest costs.

26 Since there are no deductions of money costs from interest or wage payments, the minimum wage is nothing but 'the wage of the common worker' (p. 468), i.e. the average pay of simple workers, while the minimum rate of interest is nothing but 'the customary rate of interest in the country' (p. 824), i.e. the average rate of interest. Later we shall discuss average profit, wages and interest, but we ask the reader to keep in mind that Liefmann is speaking of the marginal or minimum level of these incomes.

27 Liefmann 1919, p. 260. Liefmann shamefully refers to profit, wages and interest as 'three forms of the appearance of marginal money yield' (p. 250).

out that profit and the wage rate (and still more, profit and interest) move in parallel: when the former rise, so do the latter.[28] We shall not dwell on criticising this assertion.[29] Let us even suppose that Liefmann is correct – which in fact he is not. But surely a tendency for parallel change of profits and wages does not eliminate their *different levels* at any given moment. What exactly are we to understand by the 'marginal money yield' in the previously mentioned formula of prices: is it the average profit or the average wage? There is no doubt that it is the former, since: 1) the sum of wages is already included in the sum of 'marginal money costs'; and 2) it is precisely the equalisation of the average rate of profit (and not wages) that plays the role of regulator of the supply of commodities, i.e. the role that Liefmann attributes to his 'marginal money yield'.

We have arrived at the conclusion that what is concealed by the 'marginal money yield' is nothing more than the *normal rate of profit* with which we are already quite familiar in the classical theory of costs of production. But, in that case, Liefmann faces the fateful question that is not resolved from the viewpoint of a vulgar theory of costs of production: What is it, in turn, that determines the *normal rate of profit*? It is for exactly that reason – to avoid answering this direct question – that Liefmann has attempted to present us with the normal rate of profit in the form of a novel and mysterious stranger, namely, the 'marginal money yield'. The magnitude of the latter is determined by Liefmann in the following way. Our marginal (minimum) money yield is also the '*minimum income*' that enters the consumer economy. But the minimum income must ensure the consumer economy's ability to purchase 'such a quantity of means of livelihood and consumption as is necessary for the satisfaction of needs in accordance with normal living habits'.[30] In other words, the 'minimum income must be high enough to support purchase of the *necessary means of subsistence* that correspond to the given cultural level'.[31] Our *marginal money yield* must also equal this *minimum income*. Since the magnitude of the

---

28   Liefmann 1919, p. 261.

29   The claim that there is a tendency for wages and profits to change in parallel (e.g. upwards) could only be taken as correct, with great reservations, in the event that both of these forms of income are understood in the sense of a mass of consumer goods – an interpretation that Liefmann himself sharply opposes. Insofar as the *rate* of money wages and profit are at issue – and this is precisely how Liefmann understands his marginal yield – historical experience shows that there is a tendency for money wages to rise simultaneously with a tendency for the rate of profit to fall.

30   Liefmann 1919, p. 262.

31   Liefmann 1919, p. 467. [Rubin's italics.]

minimum income depends upon prices for items of consumption, our 'marginal money yield is [also] the resultant, or an extraction, so to speak, from *all the former prices*'.[32]

It seems that Liefmann has not only determined the magnitude of the marginal money yield – this most important component of the prices of all commodities – but has also made it closely dependent upon the needs of the consumer economy. The entire objective system of commodity prices revolves around a previously given and uniform magnitude of marginal yield, and the magnitude of the latter is determined by the needs of consumer economy. Liefmann's entire construction seems to confirm his thesis concerning the primacy of consumption in the economy. But the trouble is that this construction has two significant shortcomings: it revolves in a *vicious circle*; and it is based, in fact, upon a *confusion of concepts*.

In his formula of prices, Liefmann claimed that the *price* of a product is determined by the marginal costs plus the *marginal yield* (or minimum income). Now we learn that the magnitude of the *marginal yield* is determined by the *prices* for articles of consumption. Are Liefmann's critics not correct when they argue that he falls into the *vicious circle* of deriving prices from prices? Liefmann himself is compelled to recognise that he 'explains incomes by prices and prices by income'.[33] Liefmann attempts to deny the charge of a vicious circle on the grounds that he assigns the decisive influence on formation of prices not to income in general, but rather to the income limit (*Einkommensgrenze*).[34] However, the limit of income is none other than the marginal or minimum income, and the question is precisely whether the marginal income depends upon commodity prices or, to the contrary, prices depend upon the marginal income. A second argument that Liefmann uses in justification refers to actual economic reality, in which there is constant conversion of prices into incomes (the acquisition economy obtains a yield from the selling prices, which is transferred into the consumer economy as income) and incomes into prices (the consumer economy spends income on the purchase of articles of consumption, paying certain prices for them). But this argument cannot save Liefmann either. Of course, in economic reality there is a very close interdependence and interaction between the level of prices and the level of incomes. But the task of the economic theorist is not to stop with an observation of the interaction between two series of phenomena, but rather to disclose the causal connection between them. Liefmann ultimately abandons this task, with the result

---

32   Liefmann 1919, p. 264. [Rubin's italics.]
33   Liefmann 1919, p. 265.
34   Ibid.

that the two most important parts of his system – the theory of prices and the theory of incomes – taken together, portray an enormous vicious circle. Liefmann considers his most important contribution to the theory of prices to be his recognition that the regulator of the entire process of price formation is the pre-given magnitude of the minimum income (the marginal money yield).[35] In the theory of incomes he recognises that all incomes are essentially nothing but prices, and thus the process of income formation is completely explained on the basis of the theory of prices.[36]

We can see that Liefmann's price theory, even it provoked no essential objections, could still not escape the vicious circle. It further suffers, however, from an internal logical contradiction and is based upon a confusion of concepts. The level of prices is regulated by the marginal money yield, and the latter must be sufficient to assure to the consumer economy a minimum of the means of subsistence.[37] One could only agree with the latter claim on condition that the marginal yield in this case is understood to be the wage, whose magnitude Liefmann sees, in agreement with the classics, as being closely connected with the minimum means of subsistence. But in the previously mentioned formula of prices, the marginal money yield in fact meant, as we have seen, a sum of profit – not of wages. And to say that the level of profit is determined by the minimum means of subsistence for the capitalist is to ignore completely the specific social nature of profit, as distinct from wages. Liefmann could only reach such an absurd conclusion because he has committed a crude, double confusion of concepts. In place of profit, in the formula of prices he has used the wider concept of the marginal money yield, which includes not only profit (and interest) but also wages. To determine the magnitude of the marginal money yield, he then attributes to it features that are characteristic only of wages, namely, a close connection with the minimum means of subsistence. Thus, Liefmann initially refers to the whole in place of a single part, in order then to attribute to the whole features borrowed from one of the parts. The result is that one part of the whole (profit) is assigned features that are completely foreign to it and instead characterise another part of the whole (the wage).

It is possible that on this issue Liefmann did not escape a certain influence from Stolzmann.[38] Stolzmann puts forth the view, with perfect consistency, that the magnitude of profit is regulated by the same laws that regulate the magnitude of the wage: the rate of profit is established at a level that allows

---

35   Liefmann 1919, pp. 265, 266 *et passim*.
36   Liefmann 1919, pp. 428, 837 *et passim*.
37   Liefmann has in mind, of course, a cultural and not a physiological minimum level.
38   Liefmann 1919, p. 262.

the most 'marginal' or the most 'diminutive' capitalist still to acquire an income guaranteeing to him the standard of living that is customary for the given social group.[39] In the excerpts quoted above, where Liefmann speaks generally of the marginal money yield as the minimum income of the consumer economy, he is essentially repeating the same ideas. However, he cannot support them through to the end. When he turns from general discussions concerning the marginal yield to its different 'forms of manifestation', he is unable to conceal the difference in principle between profit and wages. Here, he must acknowledge that in terms of 'the minimum *income*, the marginal money yield appears only with wages'. 'Other forms of marginal money yield appear not as income, but for the most part only as interest rates that can be applied to any sum of money'.[40] The marginal money yield, received by the last employer, still exceeds the 'minimum income that is just sufficient for a subsistence that corresponds to the cultural level of a people'.[41]

As we can see, Liefmann is now abandoning his previous claims. Earlier he said that the marginal yield is at the same time the minimum income of the consumer economy; now he recognises that none of the forms of marginal yield, apart from the wage, appear in the form of the minimum income. Earlier we were persuaded that the level of the marginal yield must be sufficient to provide a minimum of subsistence; now we learn that the rate of profit exceeds that level. And since the issue in the formula of prices is precisely profit, we feel justified in drawing the following conclusion: Liefmann's entire attempt to portray the marginal yield, which figures in his pricing formula as a *previously given magnitude*, determined by a *minimum of means of subsistence*, has completely collapsed. After taking a lengthy detour, Liefmann has again found himself back where he started, and his formula of prices continues to hang in the air. He faces once again the fateful question for a theory of costs of production: What is it that determines the *normal rate of profit*? Liefmann has no answer to this question, and he is left with no alternative but to follow the example of many supporters of the cost of production theory and of the Austrian school – first to derive the rate of profit from the interest rate, and then to derive the latter from the former. Thus we learn, for example, that 'the minimum expected yield from employers' capital depends to a certain extent upon the rate of interest for loans'.[42] And how is

39 Stolzmann 1896, p. 384; 1909, p. 416. See our earlier essay for discussion and criticism of Stolzmann's theory.
40 Liefmann 1919, p. 469. Liefmann's italics.
41 Liefmann 1919, p. 470.
42 Liefmann 1919, p. 258.

the interest rate for loans determined? In one place Liefmann has the interest rate depending upon the rate of profit, obviously lapsing into a vicious circle.[43] In another place we learn that the rate of interest is determined by the scale of accumulation and the supply of capital.[44] And how is the scale of capital accumulation determined? Liefmann answers: by the level of the interest rate.[45]

So, where is the 'originality' of Liefmann's theory of prices compared to the classical theory of costs of production? Liefmann personally sees the original feature of his theory of prices, and of his psychological conception of economy, in the law of the equalisation of marginal yields, which is based upon a unique combination of three ideas: the idea of 'yield', the idea of 'equalisation' and the idea of the 'margin'. We shall not debate the degree of originality involved in applying this law to the sphere of a subject's psychological sensations, i.e. in replacing the concept of marginal utility, developed by Austrian economists, with the concept of the marginal psychological (consumer) yield. We suggest that Liefmann's doctrine in this area adds little that is new to the stock of ideas he has borrowed from the Austrian school. We must all the more decisively reject Liefmann's claim to originality concerning the objective sphere of price formation. Here the law of the equalisation of marginal yields has long been known in the form of the law of equalisation of the rate of profit. There are times when Liefmann acknowledges this fact, at least when the issue concerns the idea of yield and the idea of equalisation. 'That the idea of yield explains supply – this is an observation for which we do not claim the slightest novelty'.[46] This idea is found already in the classics, who Liefmann justifiably believes had a better understanding of actual reality than the latest economists such as those who support the Austrian school.[47] Likewise, the idea of 'equalisation' is already found in the teachings of the classics and also in Marx's theory concerning formation of the general average rate of profit.[48] True, Liefmann rebukes the classics for studying different incomes and for discussing equalisation of the profit rate separately from the equalisation of wages; they did not get so far as the idea of the overall equalisation of money yield.[49] But we are already convinced as to how far Liefmann's attempt to combine profit and

---

43   Liefmann 1919, p. 255.
44   Liefmann 1919, pp. 280–1.
45   Liefmann 1919, pp. 259, 841.
46   Liefmann 1919, p. 227.
47   Liefmann 1919, p. 239.
48   Liefmann 1920, p. 443.
49   Liefmann 1919, p. 243; 1920, p. 443.

wages, in a single concept of marginal yield, meant regression rather than any improvement of the theory of costs of production.

Recognising that applying the idea of yield and equalisation to prices occurred already in the classics, Liefmann still insists that his contribution consists of introducing into the theory of prices the idea of the 'margin', which was developed by the Austrian economists with reference to marginal psychological utility. The classics supposedly ignored the fact of the existence of differential profits and assumed that the equalisation of profit applies to *all* employers involved in one and the same branch of production. Liefmann thinks it necessary to emphasise that the tendency towards equalisation extends not to the profit of *all* employers, but only to *marginal* profits (i.e. the profits of employers working with the highest costs) in the different branches of industry.[50] Unfortunately, on this point too Liefmann's claims to originality are not well founded. Apart from certain modern economists (e.g. Marshall),[51] who examined this question earlier and better than Liefmann, we can, for example, find in Marx a clear indication that the law of equalisation of the rate of profit extends only to *similar* capitals[52] employed in *dissimilar* branches of production, and not to *dissimilar* capitals[53] employed in one and the same branch of production. Marx points out that two laws operate in capitalist economy: the law of the existence of different rates of profit and the law of the equalisation of the rate of profit. 'The first law applies to the various independent capitals invested in *the same sphere of production*. The second applies to capitals in so far as they are invested *in different spheres* of production'.[54]

Insofar as the issue concerns laws that regulate the objective process of price formation, Liefmann's claims to originality are without foundation. Liefmann has discovered no new theory of prices. But perhaps Liefmann's originality lies in the fact that he was able to shed new light on the theory of costs of production, or to give a new *interpretation* by connecting it with the psychological

---

50   Liefmann 1919, pp. 256, 243.
51   [In the English-language literature, Alfred Marshall (1842–1924) was one of the most prominent economists of his time. His *Principles of Economics* was published in several editions and integrated the issues of supply and demand – marginal utility and marginal production costs – into a single comprehensive theory.]
52   We understand 'similar' capitals to mean capitals of approximately the same size and using technically equal means of production. Larger capitals, or those operating with especially productive means of production, receive, in Marx's words, a surplus or differential profit. See Marx 1991, p. 279.
53   By 'dissimilar' we mean capitals that differ in size or the technical productivity of their means of production.
54   Marx 1969, Vol. II, pp. 206–7.

conception of economy? Thus we turn to the second of the questions posed above: To what extent is Liefmann's theory of prices consistent with the psychological conception of economy?

At first sight, Liefmann's theory of prices has a completely objective character. The entire process of price formation is determined by a previously given, objective magnitude of the marginal yield (the rate of profit). *'It is not supply and demand that determine price, but rather the marginal money yield*, which is a component of every price. This is an *external, objective magnitude* that must be given in order to explain the emergence of supply'.[55] Elsewhere, the marginal yield is characterised as a 'universal, to some extent objective magnitude', or as a 'social factor'.[56]

But if the entire process of price formation is made dependent upon an objective, social factor, does that not contradict the psychological conception of economy? In order to eliminate this contradiction, Liefmann tries to connect the marginal yield, this 'objective magnitude', with psychological evaluations of the subject as consumer. He attempts to establish such a connection from two directions: from the direction of *supply* and from the direction of *demand*. On the supply side the marginal yield, as we have seen, must guarantee the minimum income to the last producer. Liefmann makes the magnitude of the marginal yield dependent upon the needs of the consumer economy of the last producer. We have already convinced ourselves of the insolvency of this attempt, which even its author was ultimately compelled to abandon. Following that failure, Liefmann has no way out but to turn again to the analysis of *demand*.

In his theory of prices, Liefmann has up to now discussed sellers or producers. Now he recalls that buyers, or consumers, are the counterparts of sellers. If the *marginal producer* figures on the supply side, on the demand side can be found the *'marginal consumer'*. In search of salvation for his subjective theory, Liefmann turns for help to this marginal consumer, who plays, as we know, the central role in the constructions of the Austrian school.

Let us position all the consumers in a row, beginning with the most competitive, i.e. those who would not decline to pay even more than the existing price for a given commodity. The last purchaser of the given commodity is the 'marginal consumer', who is willing to purchase a given unit of the commodity at the existing price (e.g. a pair of shoes for 20 roubles) but would refuse to purchase them in the event of the slightest rise in price (e.g. to 21 roubles).[57] As we know, the Austrian economists see the price of a commodity as dependent upon the

---

55   Liefmann 1919, p. 266.
56   Liefmann 1919, pp. 250, 118.
57   Liefmann 1919, p. 273.

subjective evaluations of the marginal consumer: the price of a commodity cannot exceed its marginal utility for the marginal consumer, who would otherwise refuse to buy it. In accordance with his general psychological conceptions, Liefmann here enters a correction. The price of the commodity (e.g. 20 roubles for the pair of shoes) expresses not the utility received by the marginal consumer, but instead the costs he is expending. For each unit of costs, our consumer wants to receive, at the very least, the 'marginal consumer yield', i.e. a certain minimum surplus (which is different for each consumer) of utilities over costs. For that reason, he will never agree to pay for the pair of shoes a price that he subjectively evaluates as being higher than the marginal utility of that pair of shoes minus the marginal consumer surplus that he might receive by spending the same sum of money on his other needs. Therefore, *the upper limit of the price* of a commodity *is the marginal utility of the commodity for the marginal consumer minus the individual marginal consumer yield for this consumer.*[58]

Now we already have *two* formulae for price. From the viewpoint of supply, price cannot be lower than *marginal costs plus the marginal money yield* for the last producer. From the viewpoint of demand, price cannot be higher than *marginal utility minus the marginal consumer yield* for the last consumer. With numerous sellers and buyers, the upper and lower limits to price correspond, and we reach a 'uniformly applicable price for all',[59] which depends simultaneously upon objective factors of supply and subjective factors of demand. Marginal consumers from the demand side determine price in the same way as marginal producers do from the supply side.[60]

However, Liefmann is not satisfied with these two formulae. He realises that the two formulae, the objective and the subjective, are not integrated and consistent. He cannot fail to realise that a theorist will no doubt prefer the first formula of price, which includes a 'universal', objective, generally valid and measurable factor (the marginal money yield), compared to the second formula, which 'consists of two purely psychological, individual factors'[61] that differ for particular individuals and even change over time for one individual. In order to give a more generally valid character to his second formula, Liefmann would like to include in it the 'universal' factor that figures in the first formula, namely, the marginal money yield, which would thereby create a bridge between the formula of objective price formation and the formula of subjective evaluations.

58   Liefmann 1919, pp. 277, 280.
59   Liefmann 1919, p. 289.
60   Liefmann 1919, p. 273.
61   Liefmann 1919, p. 279.

In order to create such a bridge, Liefmann resorts to a very complex and artful construction. Let us assume, he says, that among marginal consumers there are some who do not spend their whole income on personal consumption but instead accumulate part of it and convert it into capital.[62] Once the most essential needs have already been satisfied, our marginal consumer asks himself, with respect to each rouble of his income, whether to put it into the consumption fund or the accumulation fund. In the first case, this rouble will provide him with a 'marginal consumer yield', and in the second case with a 'marginal money yield' (understood here as the rate of interest on loan capital).[63] If the marginal consumer yield is subjectively evaluated by our individual more highly than the marginal money yield in the form of interest on loan capital, he increases his consumption fund at the expense of the accumulation fund, and vice versa. Our individual reallocates his income between the two funds until he subjectively evaluates the marginal consumer yield just as highly as the possibility of receiving a marginal money yield (interest on capital). To the two laws with which we are already familiar – the 'equalisation of marginal *consumer* yields' in the consumer economy and the 'equalisation of marginal *money* yields' in the exchange turnover – a third law is added: 'equalisation between the marginal *consumer* yield and the marginal *money* yield' (or the yield on capital, i.e. interest), which operates for consumer economies that transfer part of their income into the accumulation fund.[64]

This equalisation allows us to modify our second formula of price, according to which the price of a commodity is equal to its marginal utility minus the marginal consumer yield (for the marginal consumer). We can now, on the basis of the equalisation we have discovered, replace the marginal consumer yield with the marginal money yield. We then get the following complete formula of price: *'Price is simultaneously: 1) marginal utility minus marginal money yield, and 2) marginal costs plus marginal money yield'*.[65]

---

62   Liefmann 1919, p. 280.

63   Liefmann 1919, p. 283.

64   Liefmann 1919, p. 287. Liefmann's first equalisation is essentially nothing but a psychological interpretation of the fact that the individual is free to spend a given rouble on satisfying any one of his needs. The second equalisation rests on the fact that the individual can invest a given rouble as capital in any of the branches of industry (e.g. by purchasing shares). Finally, the third equalisation is a conclusion – a false one, as we shall see – from the fact that the individual can either spend the given rouble on personal consumption or convert it into capital.

65   Liefmann 1919, p. 289. For the sake of clarity, we have provided the figures in the formula.

Liefmann has now finally reached his goal: the concept of 'marginal money yield' figures in both formulae, not just in the formula of the producer but also in the formula of the consumer.

> For that reason the *marginal money yield*, which at first sight is a totally objective magnitude and, as we have discovered, determines the size of supply and thereby the extent of satisfaction of demand, *has been connected* with needs and with evaluations of utility issuing from the consumer. This is the final task that the theory of price formation had to resolve, namely, to *derive* marginal money yield from consumers' evaluations of utility ... . The sums of money, representing marginal money yield, are also subject to *evaluation*, they are income, and since the consumer can either consume his income or release it again into the exchange mechanism in the form of money capital, the marginal money yield is directly *included* in the comparison of utilities and costs that occurs within the singular economy.[66]

We draw readers' attention the fact that in the excerpt quoted, as in all of Liefmann's statements, there is a confusing tangle of very different points of view. In the first sentence, marginal money yield 'has been connected' with subjective evaluations of utility; in the second sentence it is 'derived' from the former (the method of psychological causality); in the third sentence it is subject to ensuing psychological 'evaluation' (the method of psychological evaluation).

Liefmann himself understands that 'identification of individual marginal consumer yield with marginal money yield' might be called 'too bold a construction'.[67] He reassures the reader, who complains about the difficulty of understanding these ideas, by referring to the existence of 'endlessly more difficult and arbitrary constructions in the Marxist theory of surplus value or the average rate of profit'.[68] However, there is a 'minor difference' between Marx and Liefmann. The difficulty of understanding Marx's ideas is explained by his profound insight into the concealed mechanism of capitalist economy; the only source of the difficulty of understanding Liefmann is the chaotic confusion of concepts and terms and the unparalleled sloppiness of the exposition. In the interest of economy of space, let us note only the most important errors and contradictions that Liefmann admits into his 'bold', or more accurately arbitrary, construction.

---

66   Liefmann 1919, pp. 287–8 (Rubin's italics).
67   Liefmann 1919, p. 281.
68   Ibid.

Liefmann assumes that some marginal consumers have the opportunity to accumulate capital. But how can marginal consumers have that opportunity? Liefmann himself acknowledges, in accordance with common opinion, that marginal consumers are people with the least income,[69] i.e. the poorest group of the population. In another place we learn that 'currently a very large part of the population does not accumulate capital'.[70] It would seem that only one conclusion can be drawn, namely, that marginal consumers do not accumulate capital but instead spend their whole income on personal consumption (apart from savings intended for future consumption or for personal belongings, which Liefmann recognises do not enter into the process of capital formation).[71] At any cost, however, Liefmann must find people who are accumulating capital amongst marginal consumers, and he decrees their existence despite the direct evidence.[72]

However, let us agree with Liefmann for the moment that the price of a commodity really is determined by the evaluations of a fantastic marginal consumer, who refuses to purchase a given commodity if there is the slightest rise in its price and who, at the same time, manages to accumulate capital. In other words, two kinds of opposing motivations operate in the psyche of this consumer: a motivation to satisfy personal needs, and a motivation to accumulate capital – which is a purely 'social' motivation and, in terms of its character and intensity, is entirely determined by the objective social structure of the economy. But this already means that the behaviour of our consumer cannot be explained entirely by a comparison of 'utilities' and 'costs' in the sense initially

---

69   Liefmann 1919, p. 260.
70   Liefmann 1919, pp. 764–5.
71   Ibid.
72   Liefmann 1919, p. 280. Liefmann's wish to attribute accumulation of capital to marginal consumers leads him to even more striking contradictions, as shown in the following example. We have already seen that marginal consumers are the poorest consumers. On page 420 of the first volume and p. 764 of the second, we learn that impoverished consumers have a *marginal* consumer yield that is *higher* than that of the wealthy (at the same time as the general sum of their consumer yield is less) because, having a smaller income, they interrupt the satisfaction of their consumer needs sooner. It seems that from this we are to conclude that for marginal consumers the marginal consumer yield is *higher* than for other consumers (and that is why, with each rise in prices, they refuse to purchase the commodity, for the consumer yield from purchase of the given commodity turns out already to be lower than the general level of their marginal consumer yield). But Liefmann is trying to transform the marginal consumer into a capitalist. To our amazement, this is what we read on p. 827: 'The last consumer will always be the one whose marginal consumer yield is so *low* that he wavers between receiving this consumer yield or receiving the marginal money yield, i.e. between consumption and the formation of capital'.

implied in the psychological conception of economy: utility now means not just a psychological sensation of satisfaction of personal needs but also the possibility of acquiring non-labour income; on the other hand each rouble, in terms of expenses, is now considered not just as representing articles of consumption but also as a source of interest on money. We suggest that Liefmann has not strengthened but instead weakened his general position by introducing an imaginary capitalist in the form of last consumer: the pure consumer has now been divided into a 'natural' and a 'social' being, and a purely capitalist motivation has invaded the sphere of demand itself.

But, Liefmann will object, the accumulation of capital in our scheme is subordinated to the needs of personal consumption: it comes to a halt at precisely the point where the subjective evaluation of marginal money yield (i.e. interest) is equal to the marginal consumer yield. Is it even possible, however, to speak of a comparison of these two yields – of an equality between the benefit that I derive from 100 roubles by purchasing this sum of articles of consumption, and the benefit presented to me by the possibility of receiving 5% annually on this same sum? The possibility of such a comparison is complicated not just by the heterogeneous character of the two series of motivation, but also by the circumstance that in the first case my goal is not just a single consumer yield but the entire (gross) utility that I might obtain for the 100 roubles, while in the second case my goal is acquisition of a money yield (interest on money). Furthermore, in the first case the entire sum of 100 roubles is a cost to me; in the second case they are only advanced and at some time I can receive them back. Finally, equalisation of the two yields must be complicated by the fact that one of them, the marginal consumer yield, has a tendency to approach zero, as Liefmann reluctantly had to acknowledge.

But let us put aside all these doubts and accept the whole of Liefmann's arbitrary construction. Let us suppose that the marginal consumer really does accumulate capital, and that the marginal money yield is equalised in the sphere of his psychological evaluations with the marginal consumer yield. What is the result? Only that in place of the formula of demand – 'Price is equal to marginal utility minus the individual marginal consumer yield' – we would be able to say: 'Price is equal to marginal utility minus *the individual psychological evaluation of the marginal money yield*'. Instead of that formula, Liefmann gives the following: 'Price is equal to marginal utility minus the *marginal money yield*'.[73] It is as if the objective sum of interest money and the subjective evaluation of the same sum – which differs between individuals and even for a single indi-

---

73   Liefmann 1919, p. 289.

vidual over time – are one and the same thing! Liefmann himself understands that in his formula both factors of price formation (marginal utility and marginal money yield) have the same subjective character, for the issue concerns not the objective money yield but its individual subjective evaluation.[74] Nevertheless, before our eyes he commits the inadmissible substitution of objective concepts for subjective ones.

The reason why Liefmann had to make this substitution is obvious. Only in this way can he create the false impression for a credulous reader that the most significant objective factor (the marginal money yield), which figures in the formula of supply and determines the entire process of price formation, is also included in the formula of demand and can be derived from the subjective evaluations of the consumer. If Liefmann gave us the formula: 'Price is equal to marginal utility minus the *individual psychological evaluation* of money yield', then the reader would quickly surmise, first of all, that this 'evaluation of money yield' is just as much an immeasurable, indeterminate and fluctuating magnitude as the 'marginal consumer yield' that Liefmann wants to replace, and secondly, that the marginal money yield must pre-exist as an objectively given social magnitude in order that it might be subject to an ensuing psychological evaluation on the part of the individual. And that means the impossibility of 'deriving' the marginal money yield, the determining factor of price formation, from the individual's subjective evaluations. In order to conceal his failure, Liefmann also offers us the formula that we mentioned previously: 'Price is simultaneously: 1) marginal utility minus *marginal money yield, and* 2) marginal costs plus *marginal money yield'*. Speaking in the terms of criminal law, this formula represents nothing but a scientific forgery: one and the same term covers an objective sum of money in the second half of the sentence and a subjective evaluation of that sum in the first half of the sentence.[75]

---

74 Liefmann 1919, p. 284.

75 Liefmann not only substitutes an objective magnitude for a subjective one, but from the resulting false formula he also draws a further series of conclusions. Instead of saying that the 'evaluation' of marginal money yield has the same subjective-individualistic character as does the marginal consumer yield, Liefmann draws the opposite conclusion. It turns out that for everyone who is capitalising a part of their income, 'the marginal consumer yields are approximately equal to the marginal income from capital', and therefore 'in the whole national economy an equalisation of marginal (consumer, *I.R.*) yields can be observed' (1919, p. 764). Accordingly, it turns out that for Rothschild and for his poor servant, who once a year buys a stock or bond, the marginal consumer yields are equal because they are both equal to the 'marginal money yield' – although, with regard to the servant and the worker, who are spending their entire income on personal consumption, Liefmann considers it 'likely' that they do not succeed in reducing their marginal consumer yield to the same low level as Rothschild does. At this point Liefmann abandons his usual self-

After a long detour, Liefmann comes to the following final formula of price: 'Price is a sum expressed in a *universal accounting unit* and thus determined by all the *comparisons of utilities and costs* coming from all the economic subjects in relation to all the goods of the exchange turnover – the sum with which the most expensive *seller* and the least solvent *buyer* on average (*auf die Dauer*) still receive the *marginal money yield*'.[76] The only thing that we can agree with in this formula is that the price of the commodity is always expressed in money and has a tendency to be established at the level where the producer (and not always the most expensive one, as Liefmann thinks) receives the average rate of profit (the marginal money yield). The incorrect parts of the formula are those that bear the mark of Liefmann's own theory and that we have already outlined, namely: 1) the assertion that price is determined by *comparisons of utilities and costs* on the part of consumers, and 2) the assertion that the marginal consumer and the marginal producer both receive the 'marginal money yield'. The first assertion revolves in a vicious circle because a psychological comparison of utilities and costs on the part of consumers already presupposes, as we have often concluded, an existing objective system of prices and incomes. The second assertion is based, as we have seen, on the erroneous identification of an objective sum of money with its subjective evaluation.

Liefmann's theory not only suffers from errors and contradictions that are the author's own inalienable property; it also shares the theoretical shortcomings of economists from the Austrian school. The attempt to derive the price of a commodity from subjective evaluations of the marginal consumer cannot withstand criticism, not only because evaluations are completely subjective

---

confidence and has serious doubts: 'It is virtually impossible to establish the extent to which a national economy approaches this ideal condition' (1919, p. 764) of the complete equalisation of marginal consumer yield on the part of people who are not capitalising any of their income with those who are capitalising part of their income. But Liefmann has no doubt that for all people in the latter group, marginal consumer yields are equal.

The absurdity of these conclusions is magnified when they are compared with other claims by Liefmann. On p. 419 of the first volume we are told that there is *no measure* for comparing the marginal consumer yields of two people. On p. 420 we learn that, assuming an equal intensity of needs on the part of the rich and the poor, this yield is *lower* for the first group. Now Liefmann suggests that regardless of differences in the material position of the two groups (so long as the poor accumulate a part of their income), their marginal consumer yields are of *one and the same positive magnitude*, namely, the marginal money yield. Finally, remember that Liefmann himself acknowledges on page 416 of the first volume that the marginal consumer yield must 'theoretically' always be equal to *nil*. Not a bad bouquet of claims for illustrating the applicability and fruitfulness of the psychological method in political economy!

76   Liefmann 1919, p. 294. Rubin's italics.

and immeasurable, but also because *which consumer* (or group of consumers) *turns out to be last is only determined by the commodity's conditions of production and supply*. It is not the marginal consumer who determines the price of the commodity; rather, which consumer turns out to be the last depends upon the price of the commodity. A rise in labour productivity and a fall in the commodity's costs of production, in conditions of free competition, inevitably brings a reduction of the commodity's price and makes it accessible to less solvent groups of the population: with a change of the commodity's price, the role of 'last consumer' moves to other people or other groups of the population. Liefmann knows this process of the shifting last consumers. If, he says, the evaluations of utility on the part of consumers 'are not high enough to pay the necessary costs plus all the yields, the current marginal consumers drop out, supply declines, and the price is determined by other marginal consumers with higher evaluations of utilities'.[77] But, if that is the case, would it not be more correct to say that the level of a commodity's price is determined by its costs of production plus the average profit, not by the evaluations of the last consumer?

In another place Liefmann is compelled to recognise that the level of prices is much more dependent upon supply factors than upon demand factors. 'With mass products the marginal consumer, with his marginal utility, has, of course, far less importance than the most expensive seller, who alone sells perhaps a million times more than what the marginal consumer buys'.[78] Even if we assume that the marginal consumer is not one person but a group of people, the price of mass products 'is more determined by factors on the side of costs. This is reinforced by the circumstance that with such products the evaluations of utilities on the part of consumers, their needs, are usually quite stable and, in the absence of significant income changes, fluctuate very little'.[79] Here we come to the Achilles' heel of any consumer conception of economy. The latter can barely defend its positions in the investigation of a *static* economy, referring to the undoubted fact of correlation between supply and demand. But it is completely unable to explain economic *dynamics. The moving forces of economic development* can be found only in the sphere of *social production*, not in the sphere of *individual consumption*. And Liefmann himself must once again recognise this fact. Emphasising the stability of the exchange process as a whole, he finds that 'its disruptions currently come much less

---

77   Liefmann 1919, p. 578.
78   Liefmann 1919, p. 314.
79   Liefmann 1919, pp. 314–15.

from the side of consumers – almost always involving only items of fashion – than from the side of external, technical circumstances, fluctuating harvests of the most important natural products, and changes in production due to technical progress'.[80] Likewise, Liefmann finds that 'technical progress' is 'the final and most profound' cause of crises.[81] Moreover, even the appearance of new needs is caused on the one hand by changes in consumers' *incomes*, and on the other hand by changes in the conditions of *commodity supply*.[82] The dynamic of needs obediently follows the dynamic of prices and incomes, not the reverse.

What we have been saying also applies in full measure to the theory of prices. In Liefmann's view, this theory has two tasks: it must first of all explain the *'formation of prices'* (i.e. 'show how, from the subjective needs of a multitude of people, we get what at first sight are completely objective, universal monetary expressions that we call price)', and secondly, *'changes in prices'* (i.e. 'examine and systematically demonstrate the causes that lead to changes in prices').[83] All of the reasoning from Liefmann that we have been considering refers only to the first task of the theory of prices. As for the theory of price changes, which he recognises as 'the most difficult part of all economic theory',[84] here Liefmann must acknowledge the bankruptcy of his psychological conception of economy. From the viewpoint of the latter, the fundamental cause of price changes should be sought in changes of people's needs. But the hopelessness of this line of investigation is also obvious to Liefmann: indeed, he himself recognises the 'stable' character of people's major needs unless changes are caused by a change in prices and incomes. Accordingly, our author has no recourse but to explain a change of commodity prices by a change in their costs of production – and thus capitulate to the objective theory of costs of production – or else completely give up their explanation and thus directly confess the bankruptcy of his theory. Liefmann is compelled to resort to both of these escape routes, unpleasant as they are for him. On the one hand, at the beginning of his chapter devoted to the theory of price changes he is forced to declare, with uncharacteristic modesty: 'I believe that in this area, too, my economic theory, with its general foundations, will be able to help prepare the way to great progress, but I am aware that in this area I can still suggest relatively little myself'.[85]

---

80   Liefmann 1919, p. 401.
81   Liefmann 1919, pp. 760–1.
82   Liefmann 1919, pp. 338, 314–15.
83   Liefmann 1919, p. 198.
84   Liefmann 1919, p. 327.
85   Liefmann 1919, p. 327.

And when we are interested in this 'relatively little' that Liefmann promises, we shall only find commonly known truths, taken from the arsenal of the cost of production theory, such as 'a rise in costs, as a general rule, finds expression in a rise of the price for products'.[86]

Summarising, we can note the complete failure of Liefmann's attempt to combine the theory of costs of production, adopted from the classics, with conceptions of the marginal consumer, borrowed from the Austrian school. Liefmann's sweeping promises to build a new theory of prices on the basis of the psychological conception of economy, and to derive an objective law of the equalisation of marginal yields in the exchange turnover (i.e. the average rate of profit) from the subjective law of the equalisation of marginal yields (as psychological sensations) in the consumer economy, cannot be fulfilled. Liefmann himself, apparently, does not deny the possible operation of one of these laws in the absence (or restricted operation) of the other. At least he recognises that in the mediaeval economy the law of the equalisation of marginal yields operated within the consumer economy (insofar as the expenditure of resources in consumer economy occurred at the discretion of a business owner), but it was not the organising principle of the exchange turnover (since the movement of producers from one branch of production into others was restricted by guild rules).[87] And if that is so, then it is obvious that operation of the law of equalisation of marginal money yields (i.e. the rate of profit), as organising principle of the exchange turnover and regulator of the entire process of price formation, finds explanation not in a psychological process of comparing utilities with costs, but rather in a specific social structure of the economy (the dominance of capitalist enterprise and freedom of competition). The law of the equalisation of marginal yields in the exchange turnover cannot be derived from the law of equalisation marginal yields in the consumer economy; to the contrary, the latter, in Liefmann's own portrayal, operates only on the basis of an existing objective system of prices and incomes that develops under the influence of the first law.

In that case, what remains of Liefmann's whole theory of prices? As with other parts of his teaching, what remains of his theory of prices is nothing more than a superficial *analogy*. With indescribable naïveté, Liefmann loudly expresses his delight in stating a verbal analogy between two laws: 'Supply, i.e. the distribution of costs over various goods in the exchange turnover, follows exactly the same *law of the equalisation of marginal yields* that regulates the

---

86   Liefmann 1919, p. 336.
87   Liefmann 1919, p. 36.

allocation of costs within a singular consumer economy'.[88] 'Just as in a singular economy the marginal consumer yield, representing there a psychological magnitude, determines the extent to which each need is satisfied, i.e. the extent to which costs are expended, likewise here (in the exchange turnover, *I.R.*) money yield regulates the allocation of costs'.[89]

Liefmann is forgetting that an analogy, even one that does not provoke particular objections, always remains merely an analogy and does not penetrate the causal connection between phenomena. But additionally, Liefmann's reasoning cannot be recognised as correct even in the modest role of analogies, for their sole basis is use of the same terms in a dual sense – psychological and monetary. In one place yield is understood as a subjective *psychological sensation*, in another as an objective *sum of money*. In the first case what is involved is equalisation of marginal yields within *a single* economy or a single economic plan; in the second case, equalisation of yields for *different* economies that operate independently and are not connected by the unity of an economic plan. In the first case, the marginal yield has a tendency to approach *zero*; in the second case, it represents a *positive* money yield. In the first case, the marginal yield is established, according to Liefmann, for all needs of a given individual at a *single* level; in the second case, the marginal yield is established on *three* different levels (for profit, wages and interest). And this means that in the first case, marginal yields are established *for all the needs* of a given individual; in the second case, equalisation of marginal yields for *all* members of society *never takes place*. From this fact of the *inequality* of marginal yields (incomes) of different members of society follows the central distinction between a singular economy and the exchange turnover: what occurs in the first is the satisfaction of needs in the order of their *decreasing intensity*; in the second what occurs is the satisfaction of demand in the order of the *decreasing effective demand* of purchasers and independently of the needs they experience. This is the fundamental difference between a spontaneous capitalist economy, directed towards acquiring the greatest money yield (rate of profit) and a singular economy that is subordinated to a single economic plan and directed towards receiving the greatest psychological yield (i.e. towards satisfying the needs of the subject). Despite all his efforts, Liefmann does not succeed in obscuring this difference and representing the capitalist economy as one that guarantees maximal satisfaction of the needs of all members of society.

---

88   Liefmann 1919, p. 822.
89   Liefmann 1919, p. 823.

We must remind the reader that Liefmann does not show any particular originality even in the area of constructing analogies. The idea of an analogy between the satisfaction of needs in a singular economy and the satisfaction of demand in the exchange turnover was developed long before Liefmann, although in a somewhat different form, by the Austrian economists. It is enough to read certain arguments by Böhm-Bawerk, who draws an analogy between marginal need and the marginal consumer, and between marginal value and the market price.[90] Unlike Liefmann, Böhm-Bawerk clearly realises that in this case what is involved is merely an analogy, although he too, like Liefmann, vainly tries to demonstrate that 'this analogy is not a game of chance but the result of a recurrence of homogeneous internal causes'. As for the more thorough and thoughtful representatives of the Austrian school, particularly Wieser, he clearly emphasises, along with analogies between a singular economy and the exchange turnover, the elements of difference between them.[91] In this respect Liefmann's work, thanks to the uncritical confusion of methods and the misuse of analogies, is even a step backwards compared to the works of Wieser.

We can now turn to brief summations.

Liefmann promised us that he would derive all the most important phenomena of the exchange turnover, namely, the processes of price and income formation, from 'evaluations of utilities and costs that originate with consumers'. In order to fulfil this promise, Liefmann takes as his starting point an examination of the economic behaviour of an *isolated*, 'natural' individual, who compares his *psychological costs* (i.e. feelings of displeasure, connected with the expenditure of labour) with *psychological utilities* (i.e. the sense of satisfaction provided by items of consumption). We shall not dwell upon the ambiguities and contradictions of Liefmann's psychological conception that we noted in the first chapter. We shall assume that a psychological process of comparing utilities with costs really does occur with an isolated Robinson Crusoe, and that it determines entirely both the scale and the results of his economic activity.

But Liefmann does not stop with Crusoe's economy. He is too much of an expert on the real phenomena of a capitalist economy to follow the example of the Austrian economists and convert the modern economic subject into

---

90   Böhm-Bawerk 1909, p. 157 ff.

91   'Production is regulated not only by needs but also by wealth. In place of the things that could be most useful, things are produced that pay more'. 'While the limit in a singular household economy has a natural character, in a national economy it is also determined by the character of wealth distribution'. Wieser 1889, pp. 57, 59. Cf. the same author's *Theorie der gesellschaftlichen Wirtschaft* (1914, p. 293).

Crusoe. To the contrary, he quickly places Crusoe in the conditions of *money economy* and, after some preliminary psychological exploration, declares that the subject of his investigation will be exclusively the economic phenomena that occur in money form. Paying greater attention to the specific *money form*, or the 'money expression' of economic phenomena, Liefmann favourably distinguishes himself from the Austrian economists. But, instead of explaining money as a *social* phenomenon, Liefmann wants to reveal, beneath the objective money expressions, the *subjective psychological evaluations* of individuals.

There is no need to discuss the fact that Liefmann takes the money form of economic phenomena to be *a ready and given form* that neither requires nor admits of any explanations. Even if questions of the origin and nature of money are left aside, the very existence of money economy overturns Liefmann's psychological conception. The basic concepts upon which Liefmann creates his theoretical structure, namely, the concepts of utility (*Nutzen*), costs (*Kosten*) and yield (*Ertrag*), *split apart* in conditions of money economy and lose all determinacy: they simultaneously denote both a subjective *psychological sensation* and an objective *sum of money*. If we take a simple commodity-money economy (we shall deal with capitalist economy later), all *utilities* in the acquisition economy are essentially sums of money (not psychological sensations), and in the consumer economy all *costs* are essentially sums of money. Consequently, in the acquisition economy costs are essentially *psychological sensations* (labour efforts), and utilities are *sums of money*; and conversely, in the consumer economy costs are essentially *sums of money*, while utilities are *psychological sensations* (feelings of satisfaction). But psychological sensations cannot be compared directly to sums of money. Liefmann's promise to show us how the comparison of utilities with costs occurs separately in the acquisition and consumer economies cannot be fulfilled. It is only possible to speak of a psychological comparison of utilities with costs when referring to the economy of a simple commodity producer (or worker) as a single entity. With this condition, sums of money can be examined as 'transitory items' or 'substitutes' for psychological sensations: through the medium of money the individual compares his psychological utilities with psychological costs. However, this escape also fails to rescue Liefmann's theory. In order to produce a psychological comparison of utilities with costs, the individual (a simple commodity producer or worker) must know in advance the *prices* for which he will be able to sell the products of his labour or his labour power and also the *prices* for which he will be able to purchase items of consumption. A psychological comparison of utilities with costs is produced on the basis of an objectively existing *social system of prices and incomes* and cannot, therefore, serve as an explanation of the latter. Furthermore, Liefmann cannot appeal to a psychological comparison of utilities with costs to explain the *economic behaviour* even of a given individual. Both the scale of the individual's economic activity (e.g. the number of hours of labour being expended by a worker), and the results (i.e. the sum of consumer items being received by the worker) depend upon a series of objective social magnitudes (such as the length of the working day, the price of labour power, and the prices of consumer items). For a money economy, the psychological conception of Liefmann can at best give us a description of an individual's psychological experiences that *accompany* the objective current of economic phenomena. But it is incapable of revealing to us the *regulator* of these phenomena.

Liefmann's position becomes even worse with the transition to *capitalist* economy. In the economy of a simple commodity producer or worker, sums of money can be considered, with reservations, as 'substitutes' for psychological sensations. In the economy of an employer-capitalist, sums of money already play an independent role. 'Costs' are a previously given sum of money or *capital* that is in no way a 'substitute' for psychological costs (i.e. the labour efforts) of its owner. On the other hand, a determinate *sum of money* (profit or interest on capital) takes the place of '*utility*', which is not entirely spent on satisfaction of the capitalist's personal needs and therefore cannot be considered as a 'substitute' for his psychological utilities. In the economy of the capitalist, psychological costs, in the precise sense of the word (feelings of displeasure associated with the need for labour expenditures), are completely missing, and psychological utility plays a subordinate and insignificant role. In place of the 'natural' motivation of an individual, who compares psychological utilities with psychological costs, in capitalist economy there emerges an 'artificial', purely social motivation of the capitalist, who undertakes a *purely quantitative* comparison of one sum of money (profit or net yield) with another (capital or costs) – a method of comparison that is a specific feature of the capitalist economy.

The purely quantitative relation between money yield and money capital (i.e. the rate of profit), plays the role of *objective social regulator* and directs the allocation of capital and labour power in capitalist economy. Liefmann himself is compelled to recognise this fact in his *theory of prices*. His formula of price – 'Price is the marginal costs plus the marginal money yield' – represents nothing more than a new formulation of the classical theory of *costs of production*. The whole process of price formation is regulated not by the psychological evaluations of consumers but by 'social factors', by the 'external objective magnitude' of *marginal money yield* (i.e. by the average rate of profit). Liefmann's attempt to make the magnitude of marginal money yield dependent upon needs of the consumer economy of the marginal *producer* cannot succeed, for what he understands by marginal money yield is profit, not wages. Likewise, Liefmann's attempt to make the formula of price dependent upon the psychological evaluation of the marginal *consumer* also fails – as did the same attempt by the Austrian economists. The formula of price – 'Price is equal to the marginal utility of the commodity for the marginal consumer minus the individual marginal consumer yield for this consumer' – consists, as Liefmann himself recognises, of indeterminate and fluctuating 'individual factors'. The objective price of a commodity cannot be derived from psychological evaluations of the marginal consumer, for the simple reason that which consumer (or group of consumers) turns out to be 'marginal' itself depends upon the level of prices for the given commodity. Liefmann's attempt, in the final formula of prices, to substitute a precisely determined 'universal' factor (namely the marginal *money* yield) for an indeterminate 'individual' factor (i.e. the marginal *consumer* yield), ultimately meets with an even more lamentable end. This construction, which Liefmann himself realises is 'too bold', is a striking illustration of the arbitrary and ridiculous conclusions to which Liefmann is led by the internally contradictory task he has set for himself – the task of explaining the real phenomena of capitalist society with the help of the psychological conception. Whereas the abstract psychological theory of the Austrian economists collapsed due to its lifelessness and scientific sterility, Liefmann's 'empirical-realistic' version has led its author to a series of insurmountable contradictions and arbitrary constructions. The psychological theory, even in the most 'modernised' form provided by Liefmann, has turned out to be unsuitable for explaining the capitalist economy.

The Austrian School[1]

Introduction by the Editor

The central theme of all of Isaak Rubin's writings is that historically formed social production relations between people, as determined by changes in the material conditions of production, are the proper subject matter of political economy. The Austrian theory of marginalism, with its ontological individualism and purely subjective theory of value, is therefore the antithesis of Rubin's own convictions as a Marxist. In this essay, written for the first edition of the *Great Soviet Encyclopaedia*, Rubin provides a scientific critique of marginalism, concentrating upon logical contradictions inherent in the Austrian theory of subjective value as the conceptual basis of price determination.

Whereas Marxism starts with the social whole, analyses it and then reconstructs it concretely in thought, the psychological theory of value looks for the 'final causes' of price changes in judgements of marginal utility by singular individuals. The result, in Rubin's account, is a series of problems involving: a) how to determine the summary value of a series of units, each of diminishing marginal utility; b) how to price means of production when their value is regarded as a derivative of the *differing* values of things they may be used to produce; c) how to impute discrete values to two or more means of production that may be used to produce a particular commodity; and d) how to explain exchange value and profit.

Rubin emphasises the individualistic ontology and methodological subjectivism that distinguished the Austrian school. Reducing the whole of capitalist society to an aggregation of self-determining Robinson Crusoes, the Austrians, in Rubin's judgement, displaced the German Historical School principally because they provided a *theory* that 'corresponds with the ideology of the bourgeoisie in the epoch of capitalism's decline'. Whereas the Historical School limited itself to history, and history objectively pointed to the replacement of capitalism by socialism, the ideological mystification of Austrian theory appeared to be a more 'acute theoretical weapon for the struggle against Marxism'.

---

1 Rubin 1926, pp. 244–54. This translation originally appeared in Day and Gaido 2018, pp. 429–47. For context, readers may refer to Boettke and Coyne 2015; also Alan R. Sweezy 1934, pp. 176–85. A thoughtful comparison of the labour theory and the utility theory of value was written by Alfred Lowe (1981, pp. 786–815).

1   History

The theory that the exchange values[2] and prices of commodities are determined in the final analysis by their use value, or subjective utility, is known as
the Austrian or psychological school of political economy. The rudiments of
such a theory are found in certain eighteenth-century economists, particularly
Condillac. But up to the end of the nineteenth century these views had not
spread. In science the objective theory of value continued to prevail as set out
by the classics (Smith and Ricardo). The mid-nineteenth-century work of Gossen, who was a predecessor of the Austrian school, went unnoticed. It was in
the 70s that works appeared almost simultaneously by Carl Menger, [William
Stanley] Jevons and Léon Walras, the founders of the new school, among whom
Menger developed most thoroughly the psychological foundation of the theory
and Walras the mathematical. During the 80s Wieser and Böhm-Bawerk, students of Menger (all three of them lived in Austria), worked out in detail the
psychological theory that is also frequently called the Austrian theory. By the
end of the nineteenth century, it became widespread in bourgeois university
science in almost all countries of the world. A critical attitude towards this theory has only recently grown up, and even among bourgeois scholars an effort
can now be seen to return to the theory of the classics, although usually in a
half-hearted and compromising manner.

The mathematical theory was also developed at the same time as the psychological, especially in England, America, and Italy (with the result that it
has come to be known as the Anglo-American theory). The focus of research
for both of these theories is the influence of changes in the quantity of goods
upon their price and value. But there are also important methodological differences between them. The psychological theory begins with the motivation
of a separate individual living in conditions of a natural economy; it sees the
ultimate cause of changes in the price and value of a good in the individual's
subjective evaluations, which vary in response to the quantity of goods that he
has at his disposal. The mathematical theory, on the other hand, begins with
the phenomena of developed exchange and studies the correlation between
the quantity of goods and their objective market price. Ignoring the question
of the final cause of changes in prices (i.e. the problem of value), this theory

---

2   Since the Austrian school begins with the concept of subjective utility, for the sake of clarity
in this presentation we use the term ценность [referring to something that is valuable] as
distinct from стоимость [the 'value' of a commodity in terms of its economic cost of production or, more specifically, its labour cost in Marxist terms. Unless indicated otherwise, this
translation will follow Rubin's usage and render ценность in the former sense].

restricts itself to investigating the functional dependence between the level of market prices and the quantity of goods (the laws of supply and demand). The resulting mathematical 'formulae of exchange' are then also applied to the phenomena of production and distribution, thereby restricting the entire purview of economic science to a study of the quantitative changes of market prices.

2 The Subjective Theory and Marginal Utility

In a modern exchange society, commodities have a determinate price in which their objective exchange value is expressed. The Austrian school claims that we can only understand the origin of exchange value and the laws that govern its changes after a preliminary investigation of the subjective value that items possess in the conditions of a natural economy. By *subjective value* is meant the importance that the subject assigns to a particular item as a necessary condition for satisfying his needs. The classical economists observed long ago that items with a very high use value – bread, for instance – are given a much lower evaluation in the market than items that have less use value, e.g. diamonds; and thus they concluded that while only items with use value also have exchange value, the magnitude of the latter does not depend upon the magnitude of the former. In order to surmount this discrepancy between use value and exchange value, the Austrian economists worked out a new concept of need and of use value. In their opinion the economic subject, in his calculations and activities, is led not by need in general, e.g. for bread, but by his concrete need for a specific quantity of bread. For instance, he needs one pound of bread per day in order to sustain life. Once he has this pound of bread, he feels the need for a second pound for the sake of a more bountiful diet. He needs a third pound to feed the household chicken, a fourth pound for making vodka, and a fifth for feeding the parrot. Each of these concrete needs is weaker than the preceding one and stronger than the one that follows. If the first need is felt with an intensity that we can denote by the number 10, the next needs, let us say, are represented by 8, 6, 4 and 1. The intensity of a need diminishes as it is satisfied, and each successive degree of need is less intensive than the previous one, which has already been satisfied ('Gossen's law', or the 'law of the satiation of need'). With the gradual satisfaction of a given need, its intensity diminishes and ultimately declines to nil. If a man has all of his daily five pounds of bread, even including enough to please the parrot, his need for bread will be weaker than his need for items of adornment. Let the scale of need for items of adornment be expressed by the figures 3 and 1. This means that the need for the first item of adornment is equal to 3, while the need for another item of adornment is equal to 1. The scale of need for bread, as we have seen, is 10, 8, 6, 4, and 1. If we divide all of a person's needs into several basic groups (the first being for bread, the second for clothing, the third for housing, the fourth for adornments, etc.), and if we provide for each group a numerical scale for the decline of needs as they are satisfied, then we find that although the generic need for bread is typically greater than the generic need for adornments, the concrete need for adornments (diamonds, for instance) can still be more intensive than the concrete need for the bread that is used, for example, to feed the parrot (Menger's 'scale of needs').

If the intensity of a given need declines as the need is satisfied, the question then is: What determines the degree of satisfaction? Clearly, that depends on the quantity goods at the individual's disposal. If the available supply of a particular good exceeds the quantity needed to satisfy all of the needs for it, then that good – even though it has use value, or the ability to satisfy human need – will not have subjective value since the loss of a unit of this good will have no effect on the individual's well-being. Such goods (air, for example) are said to be 'free', as distinct from 'economic' goods, which are distinguished not only by their usefulness but also by their relative scarcity; that is, they are available in such limited quantity that losing a unit of such a good will compel the individual to forgo satisfaction of some other need. If the supply of bread is only one pound, the subjective value of the latter is equal to 10. If the supply of bread is 3 pounds, then losing one pound of bread will compel the individual to forgo his third need (feeding the household chicken), which is measured by the figure 6. This means that if the supply is 1 pound, the value of one unit of the good is 10; if the supply increases to 3 pounds, the value is 6; and if the supply is 5 pounds, the value of a pound of bread is 1. In the eyes of the person possessing them, all units of the particular good's supply have the identical subjective value, since loss of any one of these units causes him to forgo satisfaction of the least urgent need (e.g. feeding the parrot) among those that can be satisfied with the existing supply of the good. This means that the subjective value of a given good is determined by the utility of the last unit of the existing supply, which enables satisfaction of the least intensive need (the theory of marginal utility). The greater is the supply, the weaker will be the last need it serves to satisfy, the lower will be the marginal utility, and thus the lower will be the subjective value that the individual assigns to a unit of the particular good. Conversely, with a reduction of the supply of a good, the value of a unit rises. The subjective value of the given good depends upon the magnitude of its supply, and it changes in inverse proportion to changes in the magnitude of the latter (the 'law of supply', to use Wieser's expression). The value of a good for different people, or for a single individual at different times, will vary and will have a different individual-psychological or subjective character.

If, with a supply of bread amounting to 5 pounds, the value of each pound is 1, then we may ask: What is the value of the entire supply? The Austrian economists give different answers to this question. Wieser says that once the value of each pound of bread equals 1, the value of all five pounds is $1 \times 5 = 5$; that is, the marginal utility is multiplied by the number of units of the particular good. But Böhm-Bawerk says that even though the value of each pound of bread is 1, loss of the entire supply would mean forgoing satisfaction of the five needs that are expressed by the figures $10 + 8 + 6 + 4 + 1 = 29$. This means that the value of the entire supply is 29. Wieser's view contradicts the foundations of the Austrian theory, while Böhm-Bawerk's contradicts the facts.

3   The Value of Means of Production

Marginal utility determines the value of 'consumer goods' or 'first-order goods', i.e. items of consumption. The value of the latter, in turn, determines the value of the means of production required in order to make them, the so-called 'producer goods' or 'higher-order goods'. If bread is the consumer good, then the flour and labour needed in baking the bread are goods of the second order, while grain, millstones and the labour of grinding the grain are goods of the third order, and so on. The producer goods are regarded as material things, as are labour expenditures. For the sake of simplification, let us suppose that for production of consumer good A it is enough to have only a single producer good of the second order, A_2 (it makes no difference whether this is a thing, labour, or some combination of the two); and for production of the latter we require the third-order good A_3, etc. It is clear that each of these producer goods (A_2, A_3, A_4 and so forth) makes it possible to acquire product A, following one or several stages of production, so that each has a value equal to the value of the latter. Accordingly, the value of the producer good, with the help of which consumer good A can be produced – either directly or through a number of intermediate stages of production – is determined by the marginal utility of the latter. The value of items of consumption and the value of the means of production required in order to make them are equal – not, however, because the former is determined by the latter, as classical theory thought, but rather because the latter is determined by the former.

If, as is generally the case, different units of a given producer good (iron, for example) are used for making various consumer goods with different marginal utilities (such as a stove with a marginal utility of 20, a spade of 17, and a bucket of 15), then it is understandable that the loss of one unit of iron means having to forgo production of the bucket. This means that the value of the means of production depends on the value of the 'marginal product', that is, the product with the least marginal utility among those that are made with the help of the given supply of means of production. In the present case the value of each unit of iron, including that expended in producing the stove, is equal only to 15, in which case the value of the stove itself also falls to 15, since loss of the stove does not entail forgoing the marginal utility of 20 that it provides, but only the expenditure of a unit of iron in making a new stove, and that is valued at 15. It follows that the various consumer goods (the stove, the spade, and the bucket), regardless of their individual marginal utilities, have an identical value if they are produced with the help of an identical quantity of the same means of production (or labour). The value of the products being reproduced is determined by the value of the means of production expended in making them; but the value of the latter is determined, in turn, by the utility of the 'marginal product'. The bucket imparts its value (of 15) to the iron, and the latter imparts the same value to the stove and the spade. In the final analysis, the value of both consumer and producer goods is determined by the marginal utility of the 'marginal product' (the bucket). Thus the Austrian school, although it recognises the action of the 'law of costs of production', regards it merely as a particular instance of applying the 'law of marginal utility' to the goods being reproduced.

4   The Theory of Imputation (or of Distribution)

We have looked at a case in which one producer good (iron) is used in making several consumer goods. But the reverse condition also generally prevails: to make a given consumer good A (the bucket) requires an aggregate or combination of several producer goods, for example, B and C, or labour and the material means of production that the Austrian economists call 'capital' (we are leaving aside land, the third factor of production). The given labour and the given means of production are 'complementary' goods (they complement one another), since it is only possible to make the bucket by taking them together. The aggregate value of the two of them is determined by the marginal utility of the bucket; that is, it is equal to 15. But which part of this value must be assigned or 'imputed' to the labour and which to the iron? In short, how is the value of the final product distributed between the different means of production that are needed to make it (for example, 'labour' and 'capital')? The Austrian school has not managed to provide a satisfactory answer to this problem of 'imputation' or 'distribution'. Wieser suggests comparing the value of the given product (the bucket) with the value of some other product made with the help of the same producer goods B and C, but taken in different proportions. With the help of such method we can find, in his opinion, the comparative value of B and C.

Böhm-Bawerk constructs a very complex theory of 'complementary goods'. He suggests finding first the value of one of the complementary producer goods, B for example. This is possible only in a case where B can be used separately from other means of production and where it thus acquires a separate and 'isolated' value, or alternatively in the case where B can be replaced by some other good having a determinate value of 5 for instance. In that case, B also acquires a value equal to 5. Subtracting the value of the 'replaced member' B, that is, 5, from the value of the product (the bucket), which is equal to 15, we are left with the balance of 10, which represents the value of C. The invalidity of the theory of 'imputation' given by Wieser and Böhm-Bawerk is acknowledged even by certain supporters of the same school.

This teaching, according to which: 1) the value of consumer goods is determined by their marginal utility, 2) the value of producer goods is determined by the marginal utility of the products they are used in making, and specifically by the value of the 'marginal product', while 3) this value is divided in a determinate proportion between all the producer goods involved in making the product – constitutes the theory of 'subjective value'.

5   Objective (Exchange) Value

By this term the Austrian economists understand the possibility of acquiring, in exchange for any given good, a certain quantity of another good, so that the latter represents the price of the first good. The exchange value of any item is expressed in its price. To understand objective exchange value is possible only on the basis of subjective use value, since the market price of a commodity is the result of an encounter between different subjective appraisals on the part of participants in the exchange. First of all, it is obvious that two people can enter into mutual exchange only given the condition that each of them appraises the value of the good to be received in the exchange as higher than the good they will give up in order to acquire it; that is, if the subjective appraisal by each of the two contracting parties is the opposite of the other's appraisal. Let us now take the case of developed exchange, where a multitude of buyers encounter a multitude of sellers, each of whom competes with the others. For this purpose Böhm-Bawerk provides the following scheme (in which the exchange occurs through money):

Buyers	Sellers
A_1 evaluates a horse at the price of 300	B_1 evaluates his horse at the price of 100
A_2 ” ” ” ” ” ” ” 280	B_2 ” ” ” ” ” ” ” 110
A_3 ” ” ” ” ” ” ” 260	B_3 ” ” ” ” ” ” ” 150
A_4 ” ” ” ” ” ” ” 240	B_4 ” ” ” ” ” ” ” 170
A_5 ” ” ” ” ” ” ” 220	B_5 ” ” ” ” ” ” ” 200
A_6 evaluates a horse at the price of 210	B_6 ” ” ” ” ” ” ” 215
A_7 ” ” ” ” ” ” ” 200	B_7 ” ” ” ” ” ” ” 250
A_8 ” ” ” ” ” ” ” 180	B_8 ” ” ” ” ” ” ” 260
A_9 ” ” ” ” ” ” ” 170	
A_{10} ” ” ” ” ” ” ” 150	

The buyers are arranged in a series, beginning with those having the highest evaluations: they are willing to pay a high price and thus enter into exchange sooner and are more 'exchange-ready'. The series of sellers also begins with the more 'exchange-ready', that is, those whose subjective evaluations are lower. It is obvious that only 5 pairs of buyers and sellers will enter into exchange, since the evaluations of the remaining buyers are below those of the remaining sellers, thus excluding the possibility of exchange. This means that all the buyers and sellers below the dotted line are excluded from exchange. The seller A_5 and the buyer B_5 are the final pair participating in exchange, while A_6 and B_6 are the first pair excluded from exchange. Both of these are called 'marginal pairs'. They play the decisive role in exchange since the objective market price that is established for all other exchange participants depends upon their subjective evaluations. That price cannot be higher than the evaluation of buyer A_5, that is, 220 roubles, for otherwise A_5 will withdraw from the exchange and the demand will turn out to be less than the supply, which will cause a decline in price. Yet the price also cannot be higher than 215, or the evaluation of seller B_6, for otherwise B_6 will also want to sell his horse, and the supply will again exceed the demand. Contrariwise, supply will fall below demand if the price is lower than the evaluation of B_5, that is, 200 roubles, or below the evaluation of A_6, namely, 210 roubles. This means that the market price cannot exceed the subjective evaluation of the last actual buyer or of the first excluded seller, and it cannot be lower than the subjective evaluation of the last actual seller or of the first excluded buyer. In the present case the price will be established between 210 and 215 roubles, since only with such a price will the number of those who wish to buy be equal to the number who wish to sell; that is to say, equilibrium will be established between demand and supply. Thus the price of the commodity is determined by the subjective evaluations of the two marginal pairs.

At first sight it may appear that the Austrian school has actually demonstrated that objective exchange value is determined by subjective use value. It must be remembered, however, that as soon as the market price of different items is established, the parties to exchange cease to evaluate them according to their marginal utility or use value. If they wish to determine the subjective value of one or another item for themselves, they start out with its determined price or its objective exchange value.

Consider first a buyer or consumer. Is he really inclined to assign a very high evaluation to his coat, which protects him from the cold? Not at all. The Austrian economists themselves recognise that if the market price of a coat is 100 roubles, then its owner, in the event that he loses it, will buy another coat and will then evaluate it not according to its own marginal utility, which is very high, but according to the 'substitution utility' of those items that he could buy for the 100 roubles if he did not have to use that money to buy a coat. But in order to determine this 'substitution utility' it is first necessary to know the precise quantity of other items that can be purchased for the 100 roubles; that is to say, a determinate price for those other items is presupposed.

Now consider the seller or producer. For him, the marginal utility of his commodities is nil because he personally has no demand for them. He evaluates them not according to their use value but according to the magnitude of their production costs. If the price of the commodity does not cover the costs of production (plus the average profit), the producer will either cease or curtail production. If cotton or textile machinery becomes less expensive, the cloth producer, in order to expand his sales, will lower the price for cloth even when its marginal utility remains unchanged in the eyes of the purchaser. The producer always has to deal with objective exchange value. Even if, for some reason, he wants to determine for himself the subjective value of a given lot of cloth, which can be sold for 1,000 roubles, he will evaluate it not according to its marginal utility but in terms of the utility of those items he could purchase with the 1,000 roubles acquired by selling the cloth. He will evaluate the cloth (as Böhm-Bawerk recognises) according to its 'subjective exchange value', which will be higher, the higher is its objective value or price. Consequently, in a commodity economy it is not prices that are determined by subjective evaluations, but rather the latter emerge on the basis of prices that are determined beforehand. Even if the Austrian theory had correctly explained the laws governing the subjective evaluation of goods in a natural economy, and of the formation of prices in the transition from natural economy to one of exchange – which is also doubtful for a whole number of reasons, particularly since the general possibility of comparing and measuring utilities has not been established – [the theory] would still not apply to the phenomena of an exchange economy. The position of the Austrian school is especially problematic when it attempts to explain the phenomena of a capitalist economy, and this is clearly evident in its theory of profit.

6   The Theory of Profit

If product A, having a value of 110, is produced with the help of producer goods B and C (for example, labour and the material means of production that the Austrian economists call 'capital'), then the value of B and C, taken together, is also equal to 110. The Austrian school considers this to be beyond dispute, even though it cannot resolve the problem of 'imputation' or 'distribution' of the value of 110 between B and C. However, capitalist reality demonstrates that B and C, taken together, in fact have a value not of 110 but of something less, say 100. The capitalist pays 100 roubles altogether for the labour of workers (B) and the means of production C, and after a year he receives product A with a price of 110 roubles. The surplus of ten roubles represents his profit. Does not the fact of the existence of profit contradict the position of the Austrian school, which says that the value of producer goods is equal to the value of the consumer goods made with their help? In order to resolve this contradiction, Böhm-Bawerk constructed his theory of profit.

It is enormously important for an economic subject to know not only the marginal utility of goods but also when the goods are acquired. A pound of bread that is acquired today and a pound of bread subject to a year's wait have different subjective values for the individual. The future good has a lower value than the same good acquired today. The higher evaluation of today's goods is explained by the fact that: 1) the subject calculates that in future he will have a more abundant supply of goods, which therefore have a lower marginal utility for him than today's goods; 2) as a result of insufficient consciousness or lack of will, he cares too little about satisfying his future needs and mistakenly evaluates them as less than current needs; 3) or finally, the third and most important cause of a high appraisal of current needs involves higher technical productivity.

Suppose that a fisherman, having virtually no means of production, acquires with some difficulty the two poods of fish required to sustain himself weekly, or 100 poods in the course of a year. If he had an inventory of 100 poods, he could devote part of the year to making means of production or 'capital' – for example, he could collect wood and iron ore for 3 months, spend 3 months working them up, and 3 months using them to make a boat and instruments – in order to devote the final 3 months of the year directly to fishing. As a result of this 'capitalist' or 'roundabout' production, which is technically more advanced, he would acquire 110 poods of fish by the end of the year, whereas if he occupies himself throughout the year with fishing, but not having the benefit of these means of production, he will have difficulty in acquiring 2 poods weekly or 100 poods in the course of the entire year. Since the current availability of 100 units of the given good makes it possible to acquire, by means of 'roundabout' production, 110 such units in the course of a year, it is clear that the 100 current units have the same value as the 110 future units expected after a year has transpired.

The labour of a worker (B) and means of production (C), purchased by the capitalist, actually represent 'future goods', for only after completion of the production process, which may continue perhaps for an entire year, do they turn into consumer good A, which has a value of 110 roubles. B and C currently have a value that does not exceed 100 roubles, but after a year they 'mature' into consumer good A, whose value is 110 roubles. The capitalist acquires the profit of 10 roubles not from exploiting the labour of workers, but because he has 'waited out' the time required for the 'maturation' process whereby future goods become current goods.

Böhm-Bawerk's theory of profit has been criticised on several grounds. It has been pointed out to him that in capitalist society the work of acquiring the iron, making the boats and nets, catching the fish, etc., is divided up between separate enterprises. Each of them works throughout the year and continuously sends its product to market; the iron, the nets, the fish etc. Since the sequential phases of production are completed simultaneously by different capitalists, not one of them has to 'wait out' the time between first acquiring the raw material and then making the final item for consumption. The bankruptcy of Böhm-Bawerk's theory is recognised even by some Austrian economists: Wieser offers a theory of the 'productivity' of capital; Schumpeter denies the possibility of profit as a continuous income and acknowledges only the possibility of profits being temporarily received by owners of enterprises that surpass the average in terms of their level of technical perfection (differential profit, or super-profit).

7   **Method**

A summary appraisal of the works by the Austrian school comes to this: it has worked out a more or less complete theory of subjective value in terms of logic (although it is psychologically contentious and sociologically barren); in its efforts to deduce the laws of objective exchange value from subjective value it encounters a number of contradictions; and it has been unable to resolve more or less satisfactorily the problems of distribution in general or of the profit of capital in particular. The failure by the Austrian school to explain the basic phenomena of a commodity economy, and especially of a capitalist economy (exchange value and money, capital and profit), is the inevitable consequence of the method it adopts. Political economy does not study the technical side of the economy but rather its determinate social form, namely, commodity-capitalist economy. It begins with the existence of objective-social and histor-ically changing relations between people, which correspond to a given state of the productive forces. The Austrian school begins not with the objective-social relations between people but with the psychology and motives of separate indi-viduals (the subjective-psychological method); it studies 'economic activity' in general, independently of the historical form of the economy; it looks for the economy's motive force not in the sphere of people's productive activity but rather in the sphere of consumption.

The Austrian school takes a single individual, isolated from the entire social environment and confronting nature alone, and asks how this person will sat-isfy his needs with the aid of the material goods on hand and depending upon their greater or lesser scarcity. Insofar as it studies the psychology and 'apprais-als' of such an isolated subject, it cannot possibly construct a bridge from him to a person whose economic activity occurs in a determinate social environment and who occupies a determinate social position in the social production pro-cess. Even in its own special sphere, which deals with the motivation and psy-chology of economic subjects, the Austrian school has been unable to provide fruitful results, since it studies the psychology of 'natural' man, which has noth-ing in common with the psychology of members of a commodity-capitalist society. In the representations of the Austrian school, the latter appear as Robinson Crusoes, and all social-economic phenomena are converted into natural-technical elements of consumption and production that are subject to psychological 'appraisal'; value is the significance of the item for consumption, capital is the means for its production, and so forth. Depriving the production process of its given social – namely, capitalist – form, the Austrian econom-ists thereby dismiss the question of the latter's historically transitory character. They are willing to introduce into capitalist economy modest improvements that alleviate the class struggle, but they respond negatively to any idea of the possibility of eliminating capitalism and the capitalists, in whose initiative and energy they see the sole impetus for powerfully developing the productive forces (Schumpeter).

Certain doctrines of the Austrians have the character not so much of theoretical explanation as of justification for capitalist society (the theory of imputation and especially of profit). These explicit social sympathies on the part of Austrian economists, together with the fundamental peculiarities of their theoretical position – replacement of the capitalist form of economy with 'pure economic activity' in general; transformation of a society consisting of specific classes into an aggregation of individual Robinson Crusoes; the idea that the moving forces of the economy are the psychological experiences and motivations of separate individuals as consumers; transfer of the research focus from the sphere of production to the sphere of consumption; ignoring the dynamic of the economy and its tendencies of development – all of these attributes characterise their doctrine as a theoretical tendency that corresponds with the ideology of the bourgeoisie in the epoch of capitalism's decline, a time when any objective study of the tendencies of social development leads to the conclusion of capitalist economy's inevitable destruction.

In this epoch the objective, social and historical method (the nucleus of which was established by the classics, as the leading ideologists of a young and progressive bourgeoisie) becomes the exclusive property of Marxist economic theory, while bourgeois science appeals to the subjective, psychological and anti-historical method. The allegedly unchanging psychological 'nature' of man comes to serve as the starting point for theoretical research and as an argument for the impossibility of a socialist economy. It is not surprising that the Austrian school has come out with a zealous polemic against Marxism and has enjoyed rapid and clamorous success amongst bourgeois scholars, who have seen in it – following the long period during which the Historical School predominated, with its narrow empiricism and abandonment of theory – an acute theoretical weapon for the struggle against Marxism and socialism.

8   Literature

The most important works by the Austrian economists are: Menger, *Grundsätze der Volkswirtschaftslehre* (Russian translation: *Osnovaniya politicheskoi ekonomii*, 1903); Böhm-Bawerk, *Grundzüge der Theorie des wirtschaftlichen Güterwerts* (Russian translation: *Osnovye teorii tsennosti khozyaistvennykh blag*, 1904); Böhm-Bawerk, *Capital und Capitalzins*, 2 volumes (Russian translation of the first volume: *Kapital i pribyl'*, 1909); Böhm-Bawerk, *Karl Marx and the Close of His System* (Russian translation: *Teoriya Marksa i ee kritika*, 1897); Wieser, *Der natürliche Wert* (1889); Wieser, *Theorie der gesellschaftlichen Wirtschaft* (in Volume I of *Grundrisse der Socialoekonomie*, 1914); *Kritika Avstriiskoi shkoli*; Bukharin, *Politicheskaya ekonimya rant'e*, 1923 (English translation: *The Economic Theory of the Leisure Class*); the collection *Osnovnye problemy politicheskoi ekonomii*, 1924 (edited by Sh. Dvolaitsky and I.I. Rubin); Hilferding, *Bëm-Baverk kak kritika Marksa*, 1923. [Böhm-Bawerk's work and Rudolf Hilferding's response are published jointly in *Karl Marx and the Close of His System* (Böhm-Bawerk) and *Böhm-Bawerk's Criticism of Marx* (Hilfderding), edited with an introduction by Paul M. Sweezy (New York: Augustus M. Kelley, 1949).]

I. Rubin

Isaak Il'ich Rubin on Supply, Demand, and Price Determination

In his *Essays on Marx's Theory of Value*, Isaak Rubin includes a chapter on 'Value and Social Need' that elaborates several of the issues posed in his entry on the Austrian school for the *Great Soviet Encyclopaedia*. Since Marx treats value as the essence of price phenomena, the issue that concerns Rubin is how value relates to social need and demand: 'the value of commodities does not only depend on the *productivity of labour* (which expresses that quantity of labour necessary for the production of commodities under given, average technical conditions), but also on the volume of *social needs* or demand'.[1]

Marx frequently pointed out that demand is determined both by effective demand and by changing commodity prices, with the volume of demand being more or less elastic (i.e. more or less responsive to price changes), depending upon the commodity's position on the scale of subsistence needs.[2] The result, Rubin said, is the familiar demand 'schedule', or curve of social demand. In Volume III of *Capital*, Marx wrote that demand 'moves in the opposite direction to price, expanding when it falls and vice versa'.[3] 'It is evident ... that the expansion or contraction of the market depends on the price of the individual commodity and stands in an inverse relationship to the rise or fall in this price'.[4]

But if we assume constant technology, together with 'a given structure of needs and given purchasing power',[5] then Rubin said the conclusion of marginal utility theorists is refuted: value is what determines the volume of demand, not the reverse.[6] 'The real volume of demand is determined by the

1 Rubin 1990, p. 184.
2 Rubin 1990, p. 186.
3 Rubin 1990, p. 292.
4 Marx 1992, p. 203.
5 Rubin 1990, p. 186; cf. pp. 195–6.
6 Rubin 1990, p. 190. In Volume III of *Capital* Marx writes: 'If the market value changes, the conditions at which the whole mass of commodities can be sold will also change. If the market value falls, the social need is on average expanded (this always means here the need which has money to back it up), and within certain limits the society can absorb larger quantities of commodities. If the market value rises, the social need for the commodities contracts and smaller quantities are absorbed. Thus if supply and demand regulate market price, or rather the departures of market price from market value, the market value in turn regulates the relationship between demand and supply, or the centre around which fluctuations of demand and supply make the market price oscillate' (Marx 1991, p. 282).

© RICHARD B. DAY, 2024 | DOI:10.1163/9789004705661_027

magnitude of the *productivity of labor*';[7] and equilibrium entails all commodities selling at their values (or prices of production), which in turn presupposes equilibrium between the various branches of production (i.e. all commodities selling at a price that yields the social average rate of profit).

Rubin acknowledges that an upward shift in demand 'can take place because of an increase of purchasing power of the population, or because of increased requirements for a given product'.[8] If the production technique is still assumed not to have changed, a higher market price will give producers a 'superprofit', causing an expansion of production and possibly a movement of capital from other industries. Production will then expand until equilibrium between the various branches of production is restored.[9] The value of the commodity, and thus its price of production will remain constant, but a larger volume of the commodity will be produced due to the increased capacity of producers.

The question changes, however, if technology and labour productivity no longer remain constant. Ricardo saw, for example, that an increase of output in agriculture brings diminishing returns and raises the value of agricultural products. If the total output of a manufactured commodity likewise comes from enterprises with differing levels of productivity, then the market value of commodities is 'determined by the value of commodities produced in average or less favorable conditions', which are now the ones that define 'socially necessary' labour.[10] When the price rises, 'production will attract enterprises with average or low productivity'.[11] As a result, value will increase at the same time as supply. This means demand will influence value, but only indirectly, 'namely by changing the volume of production and thus its technical conditions'.[12] Rubin writes that 'the extension of production to worse enterprises changes the average magnitude of socially-necessary labour per unit of output, i.e. changes the value (or price of production). These changes are explained by the technical conditions of a given branch'.[13]

The difference between Rubin's interpretation and that of the 'Anglo-American and mathematical schools in political economy, including Marshall',[14] is that the latter do not ask '*why* prices change'; they only show '*how* simultaneous

---

7   Rubin 1990, p. 188.
8   Rubin 1990, p. 192.
9   Rubin 1990, pp. 192–3.
10   Rubin 1990, pp. 206–7.
11   Rubin 1990, p. 207.
12   Rubin 1990, p. 209.
13   Rubin 1990, p. 211.
14   Rubin 1990, p. 208.

changes in price and demand (or supply) take place'.[15] This relation between demand and supply, which Rubin calls 'functional', is illustrated in the following diagram.

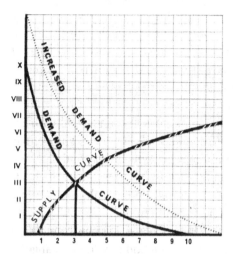

DIAGRAM 1

The diagram appears to show that price is determined 'exclusively by the demand and supply curves'. In the present case, the change of demand causes a rise in price (measured on the horizontal axis) from 3 roubles to 5 roubles and an increase of output from 300,000 units (III) to 450,000 units. Alternatively, a fall in demand might cause production to contract, say, to 150,000 units selling at 1.5 roubles per unit. The diagram implies that *any* level of supply is conceivable, depending upon changes in demand. 'It seems', says Rubin, 'as if the price is not determined by the conditions of production, but exclusively by the demand and supply curves'.[16] However, Rubin objects that 'Such a supply curve is possible [only] if we are dealing with a market situation at a *given moment*'.[17] In extraordinary conditions, and for brief periods, an unusual drop or increase in prices may force some producers to sell at 'catastrophically' low prices or 'to deliver to the market all stocks and inventories and to expand production immediately, if this is possible'.[18]

---

15   Rubin 1990, p. 213. Marshall saw the short-run supply curve as dependent upon rising marginal costs, but he did not develop a long-run average-cost curve as the 'envelope' for short-run average cost curves (see Blaug 1985, pp. 376–80).
16   Rubin 1990, p. 215.
17   Ibid.
18   Rubin 1990, pp. 215–16.

But such a state of affairs cannot long continue. The problem with the diagram is that it 'only gives us a picture of a *momentary state of the market* but does not show us a *long-range, stable equilibrium between demand and supply*, which may be theoretically understood only as the result of *equilibrium between the various branches of production*'.[19] Thus, 'from the accidental price of one day we [must] pass to the permanent, stable, *average price* which determines the *constant, average, normal volume of demand and supply*'.[20] Over a longer period of time, catastrophically low prices would drive capital elsewhere in search of the normal average rate of profit, or extraordinarily high prices would attract new capital to the industry in question.[21]

The result is that, given no significant technological change, and with 'an average, long-range volume of supply and demand', the long-run supply 'curve' would simply be a vertical line, which Rubin represents in a second diagram. Now, 'The magnitude of the value (3 roubles) determines the volume of effective demand for a given commodity and the corresponding volume of supply (300,000 units of output)'.[22] A permanent increase in demand may result in increased supply – for instance, from 300,000 to 600,000 – as new capitals are attracted from other sectors, but the price of production, with no change of labour productivity, would remain constant. 'This price is determined exclusively by the productivity of labour or by the technical conditions of production'.[23]

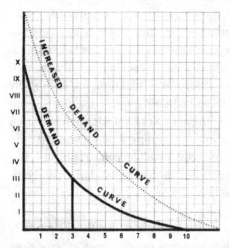

DIAGRAM 2

19   Rubin 1990, p. 216.
20   Ibid.
21   Ibid.
22   Rubin 1990, p. 217.
23   Rubin 1990, p. 218.

Finally, Rubin reintroduces the additional fact that enterprises within a particular sector will normally have differences in their levels of productivity, a condition represented in a third diagram.

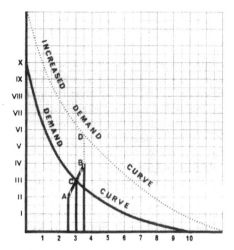

DIAGRAM 3

In this case, the *most efficient* enterprises can produce 200,000 units at a price of 2.5 roubles; if the pressure of demand causes *average enterprises* to add to total output, raising it to 300,000, the price will rise to 3 roubles per unit; and if *least efficient* enterprises then also become involved, supply will rise to 400,000 units at a price of 3.5 roubles. 'Curve ACB is the supply curve. The point of intersection of this supply curve with the demand curve (at point C) determines the actual volume of supply and the corresponding value or center of price fluctuations'.[24] If the new schedule of demand were to become permanent, then, once again, the supply would permanently increase, in this case through a vertical movement upward of the schedule ACB, and the new level of C would be the point of intersection with the new demand curve.

The salient point of Rubin's analysis is that there is, indeed, a demand curve that reflects an inverse relation between quantity and price. Marx understood this, and so, for that matter, did Adam Smith. The demand curve was no unique discovery by marginal utility theory. Secondly, Rubin concluded that there is also a supply curve, albeit objectively limited within a predetermined range by the existing state of labour productivity and the corresponding price of production.[25] Rubin's argument upheld the view that Marx first stated in the

24   Rubin 1990, p. 219.
25   In Rubin's third diagram, a permanent increase in demand, represented by the dotted line,

Grundrisse and ultimately repeated in Volume III of *Capital*: that is, that price is 'nominal' but value is 'real', and the law of the latter 'appears as the law of motions which the former runs through'.[26]

Richard B. Day

---

would have the effect of attracting more capital investment, but price variation would remain confined, other conditions remaining the same, within the range of 2.5 to 3.5 roubles. The difference between Rubin's conclusion and that of conventional liberal theory is that the latter sees the costs of production varying not merely with technology but also with the *scale of output*, in which case the long-run supply curve resembles more closely the one in Rubin's first diagram. An extensive discussion of this and related issues can be found in Blaug 1985, pp. 373–5 et seq.

26   Marx 1993, pp. 137–8. Readers will note that by the time Marx wrote Volume III of *Capital*, the term 'cost of production' was replaced by the 'price of production', which includes the social average rate of profit.

References

Amonn, Alfred 1911, *Objekt und Grundbegriffe der theoretischen Nationaloekonomie*, Leipzig and Wien: F. Deuticke, https://www.gleichsatz.de/b-u-t/can/101/amonnıob jekt.html, accessed 2 August 2019.

Amonn, Alfred 1918–19, 'Liefmanns neue Wirtschaftstheorie ı', *Archiv für Sozialwissenschaft und Sozialpolitik*, 46, 367–421.

Amonn, Alfred 1920–21, 'Liefmann als nationalokonomischer Schriftsteller', *Archiv für Sozialwissenschaft und Sozialpolitik*, 47, 523–41.

Amonn, Alfred 1924, *Ricardo als Begründer der theoretischen Nationaloekonomie*, Jena: G. Fischer.

Amonn, Alfred 1926, *Grundzüge der Volkswohlstandslehre*, Jena: G. Fischer.

Amonn, Alfred 1927, *Objekt und Grundbegriffe der theoretischen Nationaloekonomie*, Leipzig and Wien: F. Deuticke.

Beiser, Frederick C. 2015, 'Rickert and the Philosophy of Value', in *The German Historicist Tradition*, Oxford: Oxford University Press.

Blaug, Mark 1985, *Economic Theory in Retrospect*, Cambridge: Cambridge University Press.

Boettke, Peter J. and Christopher J. Coyne (eds) 2015, *The Oxford Handbook of Austrian Economics*, Oxford: Oxford University Press.

Böhm-Bawerk, Eugen 1909, *Kapital und Kapitalzins*, Vol. ıı, Wagner.

Böhm-Bawerk, Eugen 1949, *Karl Marx and the Close of His System*, New York: Augustus M. Kelley.

Budge, Siegfried 1920, *Der Kapitalprofit. Eine kritische Untersuchung unter besonderer Berücksichtigung der Theorie Franz Oppenheimers*, Jena: G. Fischer.

Bukharin, N.I. 1924, *Ataka: Sbornik teoreticheskikh stat'ei*, Moscow: Gosudarstvennoe Izdatel'stvo.

Cassel, Gustav 1921, *Theoretische Sozialoekonomie*, zweite Auflage, Leipzig: Wintersche Verlagshandlung.

Crimmins, James E. 2020, 'Jeremy Bentham', in *The Stanford Encyclopedia of Philosophy*, (Summer 2020 Edition), ed. Edward N. Zalta, https://plato.stanford.edu/archives/sum2020/entries/bentham/, accessed 26 December 2020.

Curado, Manuel and Steven S. Gouveia (eds) 2017, *Philosophy of Mind: Contemporary Perspectives*, Newcastle upon Tyne: Cambridge Scholars Publishing.

Day, Richard B. and Daniel F. Gaido (eds) 2018, *Responses to Marx's Capital: From Rudolf Hilferding to Isaak Il'ich Rubin*, Leiden and Boston: Brill, pp. 429–47.

Esser, Hans A. 1971, *Power or Economic Law: On the Value and Distribution Theory Controversy between Rudolf Stolzmann and Eugen v. Böhm-Bawerk*, Cologne: Institute of Economic Policy at the University of Cologne.

Esslen, Joseph 1918, 'Nutzen und Kosten als Grundlage der reinen Wirtschaftstheorie', *Schmollers Jahrbuch für Gesetzgebung, Verwaltung und Volkswirtschaft im Deutschen Reiche*, 2.

Fuss, Felicia 1946, 'A Bibliography of Franz Oppenheimer, 1864–1943', *The American Journal of Economics and Sociology*, 6, no. 1 (October), 95–112.

Gottl-Ottlilienfeld, Friedrich von 1923, *Freiheit vom Worte. Über das Verhältnis einer Allwirtschaftslehre zur Soziologie*, München/Leipzig: Duncker & Humblot.

Grossmann, Henryk 1992, *The Law of Accumulation and the Breakdown of the Capitalist System*, London: Pluto Press.

Heinmann, Eduard 1944, 'Franz Oppenheimer's Economic Ideas', *Social Research*, 11, no. 1 (February), 27–39.

Heis, Jeremy 2018, 'Neo-Kantianism', in *The Stanford Encyclopedia of Philosophy* (Summer 2018 Edition), ed. Edward N. Zalta, https://plato.stanford.edu/archives/sum20 18/entries/neo-kantianism/, accessed 18 May 2020.

Hilferding, Rudolf, 1919, 'Review of Franz Petry, *Der soziale Gehalt der Marxschen Werttheorie*, Jena, Gustav Fischer, 1916', *Archiv für die Geschichte des Sozialismus und der Arbeiterbewegung*, 439–48.

Honigsheim, Paul 1948, 'The Sociological Doctrines of Franz Oppenheimer: An Agrarian Philosophy of History and Reform', in Harry Elmer Barnes (ed.), *An Introduction to the History of Sociology*, Chicago: University of Chicago Press, pp. 332–52.

Kant, Immanuel 1923, 'Fundamental Principles of the Metaphysic of Morals', in *Kant's Critique of Practical Reason and Other Works on the Theory of Ethics*, trans. Thomas Kingsmill Abbott, London: Longmans, Green & Co.

Kant, Immanuel 1990, *Kant: Political Writings*, ed. Han Siegbert Reiss, Cambridge: Cambridge University Press.

Kant, Immanuel 1991, *The Metaphysics of Morals*, trans. Mary Gregor, Cambridge: Cambridge University Press.

Keynes, John Maynard 2007, *The General Theory of Employment, Interest and Money*, New York: Palgrave Macmillan.

Kim, Alan 2015, 'Neo-Kantian Ideas of History', in Nicolas de Warren and Andrea Staiti (eds), *New Approaches to Neo-Kantianism*, Cambridge: Cambridge University Press, pp. 39–58.

Kleene, G.A. 1921. 'Liefmann's *Grundsätze der Volkswirtschaftslehre*', *The Quarterly Journal of Economics*, 35, no. 3, 461–8.

Lechner, Gerhard 2017a, 'Rudolf Stolzmann's Philosophy of Economics', *Philosophy Study*, 7, no. 3 (March), 145–52.

Lechner, Gerhard 2017b, 'Der soziale Organismus bei Rudolf Steiner und Rudolf Stolzmann', *Research on Steiner Education*, 8, no. 1, https://www.rosejourn.com/index .php/rose/article/view/386, accessed 28 May 2020.

Liefmann, Robert 1916, *Geld und Gold*, Stuttgart: Deutsche Verlagsanstalt.

Liefmann, Robert 1919, *Grundsätze der Volkswirtschaftslehre*, Vol. II, Stuttgart: Deutsche Verlagsanstalt.

Liefmann, Robert 1920, *Grundsätze der Volkswirtschaftslehre*, Vol. I, Stuttgart: Deutsche Verlagsanstalt.

Liefmann, Robert 1920–21, 'Professor Amonn als Kritiker', *Archiv für Sozialwissenschaft und Sozialpolitik*, 47, 500–22.

Liefmann, Robert 1922, 'The Chief Problem of Economic Theory', *The Quarterly Journal of Economics*, 36, no. 2, 335–42.

Louzek, Marek 2011, 'The Battle of Methods in Economics: The Classical Methodenstreit – Menger vs. Schmoller', *The American Journal of Economics and Sociology*, 70, no. 2, 439–63.

Lowe, Adolph 1965, 'In Memoriam Franz Oppenheimer', *The Leo Baeck Institute Year Book*, 10, 137–49.

Lowe, Alfred 1981, 'Is Economic Value Still a Problem?', *Social Research*, 48, no. 4, 786–815.

Lukács, Georg 1971, *History and Class Consciousness: Studies in Marxist Dialectics*, London: Merlin.

Marx, Karl 1969, *Theories of Surplus Value*, Volume I, London: Lawrence & Wishart.

Marx, Karl 1972, *Theories of Surplus Value*, Volume III, London: Lawrence and Wishart.

Marx, Karl 1976, *Capital*, Volume 1, ed. Ernest Mandel, trans. Ben Fowkes. London: Penguin.

Marx, Karl 1991, *Capital*, Volume 3, trans. David Fernbach, London: Penguin.

Marx, Karl 1993, *Grundrisse*, trans. and ed. Martin Nicolaus, London: Penguin.

Marx, Karl 2010, 'A Contribution to the Critique of Political Economy', in Karl Marx and Frederick Engels, *Collected Works*, Vol. 29, London: Lawrence and Wishart.

Menger, Carl 1985, *Investigations into the Method of the Social Sciences with Special Reference to Economics*, New York: New York University Press.

Menger, Carl 2007, *The Principles of Economics*, Auburn, AL: Ludwig Von Mises Institute.

Odenbreit, Bernhard 1919, *Die vergleichende Wirtschaftstheorie bei Marx*, Essen: G.D. Baedeker.

Olson, Mancur 1993, 'Dictatorship, Democracy, and Development', *American Political Science Review*, 87, no. 3 (September), 567–76.

Oppenheimer, Franz 1903, *Das Grundgesetz der Marxschen Gesellschaftslehre*, Berlin: G. Reimer.

Oppenheimer, Franz 1908, *Der Staat*, Frankfurt am Main: Rüten and Loening.

Oppenheimer, Franz 1919a, *Die soziale Frage und der Sozialismus*, Jena: Fischer.

Oppenheimer, Franz 1919b, *Theorie der reinen und politischen Oekonomie*, Jena: Fischer.

Oppenheimer, Franz 1919c, 'Die Krisis der theoretischen Nationalökonomie', *Zeitschrift für Politik*, 11, 475–506.

Oppenheimer, Franz 1922, *Wert und Kapitalprofit*, Ann Arbor: University of Michigan Library [reprint].

Oppenheimer, Franz 1926, *The State: Its History and Development Viewed Sociologically*, trans. John M. Gitterman, New York: Vanguard Press.

Oppenheimer, Franz 1942–44, 'Critique of Political Economy: A Post Mortem on Cambridge Economics', *The American Journal of Economics and Sociology*, 2, no. 3, 369–76; 2, no. 4, 533–41; 3, no. 1, 115–124, also online at http://www.franz-oppenheimer.de/fo43a.htm, accessed 24 May 2020.

Oppenheimer, Franz 2013, *Moyens économiques contre moyens politiques*, ed. Vincent Valentin, Paris: Société d'édition Les Belles Lettres.

Petry, Franz 1916, *Der soziale Gehalt der Marxschen Werttheorie*, Jena: G. Fischer.

Plekhanov, G.V. 1956, *The Development of the Monist View of History*, Moscow: Foreign Languages Publishing House.

Rickert, Heinrich 1962, *Science and History: A Critique of Positivist Epistemology*, New York: Van Nostrand.

Rickert, Heinrich 1986, *The Limits of Concept Formation in Natural Science*, Cambridge: Cambridge University Press.

Rubin, Isaak I. 1924, *Ocherki po teorii stoimosti Marksa*, 2nd edition.

Rubin, Isaak I. 1926, 'Avstriiskaya Shkola', in *Bol'shaya Sovetskaya* Entsiklopediya, first edition, Volume 1, Moscow, pp. 244–54.

Rubin, Isaak I. 1973, *Essays on Marx's Theory of Value*, 3rd edition, trans. Miloš Samardźija and Fredy Perlman, Montreal and New York: Black Rose Books.

Rubin, Isaak I. 1990, *Essays on Marx's Theory of Value*, ed. Miloš Samardiźija and Fredy Perlman, Montreal: Black Rose Books.

Rubin, Isaak I. 2018a, 'Fundamental Features of Marx's Theory of Value and How It Differs from Ricardo's Theory (1924)', in Richard B. Day and Daniel F. Gaido (eds), *Responses to Marx's Capital*, Leiden: Brill.

Rubin, Isaak I. 2018b, 'The Dialectical Development of Categories in Marx's Economic System', in Richard B. Day and Daniel Gaido (eds), *Responses to Marx's Capital*, Leiden: Brill.

Rubin, Isaak I. 1927, *Sovremennye ekonomisty na Zapade*, Moscow/Leningrad: Gosudarstvennoe Izdatel'stvo.

Sokolov, A. 1923, *Problemy denezhnovo obrashcheniya*.

Solntsev, S. 1922, *Vvedeniye v politicheskuyu ekonomiyu*.

Staiti, Andrea and Luca Oliva 2018, 'Heinrich Rickert', in *The Stanford Encyclopedia of Philosophy* (Fall 2022 Edition), ed. Edward N. Zalta and Uri Nodelman, https://plato.stanford.edu/archives/win2018/entries/heinrich-rickert/, accessed 18 May 2020.

Stammler, Rudolf 1896, *Wirtschaft und Recht Nach der Materialistischen Geschichtsauffassung*, Leipzig: Verlag Von Veit & Comp.

Stammler, Rudolf 1917, 'Review of Franz Petry, *Der soziale Gehalt der Marxschen Wert-*

theorie, Jena, Gustav Fischer, 1916', *Jahrbücher für Nationalökonomie und Statistik*, 108, no. 1, 237–41.

Steinberg, J. 1922, 'Zur Kritik der psychologischen Theorie von Liefmann', *Archiv für Sozialwissenschaft und Sozialpolitik*, 49.

Stolzmann, Rudolf 1896, *Die soziale Kategorie in der Volkswirtschaftslehre*, Berlin.

Stolzmann, Rudolf 1909, *Der Zweck in der Volkswirtschaft. Die Volkswirtschaft als sozialethisches Zweckgebilde*, Berlin: Verlag Puttkammer & Mühlbrecht.

Stolzmann, Rudolf 1914, 'Die Kritik des Subjektivismus an der Hand der sozialorganischen Methode', *Jahrbücher für Nationaloekonomie und Statistik*, 48, 145–92.

Stolzmann, Rudolf 1915, 'Die Kritik des Objektivismus und seine Verschmelzung mit dem Subjektivismus zur sozialorganischen Einheit', *Jahrbücher für Nationaloekonomie und Statistik*, 49, 145–214.

Stolzmann, Rudolf 1918, 'Die soziale Theorie der Verteilung und des Wertes', *Jahrbücher für Nationaloekonomie und Statistik*, 55 (110), 1–27.

Stolzmann, Rudolf 1919, 'Das Reinoekonomische im System der Volkswirtschaft', *Jahrbücher für Nationalökonomie und Statistik*, 57 (112), 385–432.

Stolzmann, Rudolf 1922, 'Liefmanns rein psychisches System der Volkswirtschaft', *Jahrbücher für Nationaloekonomie und Statistik*, 63 (118), 9–45.

Stolzmann, Rudolf 1925a, *Grundzüge einer Philosophie der Volkswirtschaft. Versuch einer Volkswirtschaft auf philosophischem Grunde*, 2nd edition, Jena: G. Fischer.

Stolzmann, Rudolf 1925b, *Die Krisis in der heutigen Nationalökonomie, dargestellt an literarischen Neuerscheinungen, mit Vorschlägen zur Überwindung der Krise*, Jena: G. Fischer.

Struve, P. 1916, *Khozyaistvo i tsena*.

Sweezy, Alan R. 1934, 'The Interpretation of Subjective Value Theory in the Writings of the Austrian Economists', *The Review of Economic Studies*, 1, no. 3, 176–85.

Sweezy, Paul 1946, *The Theory of Capitalist Development*, London: Dobson.

Wagner, Gerhard and Claudius Härpfer, 'Neo-Kantianism and the social sciences: from Rickert to Weber', in Nicolas de Warren and Andrea Staiti (eds), *New Approaches to Neo-Kantianism*, Cambridge: Cambridge University Press, pp. 171–85.

Wagner, Valentin F. and Fritz Marbach (eds), *Wirtschaftstheorie und Wirtschaftspolitik: Festschrift für Alfred Amonn zum 70. Geburtstag*, Bern: Francke Verlag.

Wieser, Friedrich von 1889, *Der natürliche Wert*, Wien: A. Hölder.

Wieser, Friedrich 1914, *Theorie der gesellschaftlichen Wirtschaft. Grundriss der Sozialoekonomik*, Mohr.

Winterberger, Gerhard 1983, 'Alfred Amonn und Joseph Alois Schumpeter', *Schweizer Monatshefte*, 63, no. 5, 387–96.

Index of Names

Amonn, Alfred   xvi, xviii, 147–8n, 149–87, 194, 214n
Austrian School   xii, xv–xvi, 26–7, 85, 91, 97, 108–9, 129, 138n, 151, 154, 176n, 182, 193–4, 196, 197, 198, 216, 221–4, 226, 243n, 271–5, 281, 284, 286, 289, 291–304

Bentham, Jeremy   81
Böhm-Bawerk, Eugen von   xv, 122–3, 135, 137–8, 155, 185, 258, 286, 292, 295, 297–8, 299, 300–1
Bukharin, N.I.   44

Cassel, Gustav   183, 222

Dietzel, Karl August   156
Diehl, Karl   155n, 167n, 191n, 194
Dühring, Eugen   51

Gossen, Herman   218, 221, 292, 293

Hegel, G.W.F   xii–xiii, 196
Hilferding, Rudolf   6, 46n, 138n, 191n, 197, 199, 304n
Honigsheim, Paul   3n, 5n

Jevons, William Stanley   81, 292

Kant, Immanuel   xii–xiii, xviii, 82, 85–6, 97–8, 193, 195, 203, 207
Keynes, John Maynard   xvin, 213
Knies, Karl Gustav Adolf   156

Lenin, V.I.   6
Lukacs Georg   xiv
Luxemburg, Rosa   6
Liefmann, Robert   xiii, xvi, 6, 7n, 87n, 154n, 155n, 194, 211–89

Marshall, Alfred   273, 306, 307n
Menger, Carl   xii, xv, 81, 151–3, 191, 292, 294, 303n
Mill, John Stuart   81

Nakhimson, M.I. (Spektator)   46n

Oppenheimer, Franz   xiii, xvi, 3–78, 115n, 167n, 194, 214n, 215

Petry, Franz   xiii, xvi, xviii, 82n, 147, 168, 186–7, 189–210
Philippovich, Eugen von   147, 155

Ricardo David   3, 9, 30, 81, 108, 113–4, 116–8, 122, 124, 131, 138, 182–3, 196, 198, 204, 205–7, 221, 292
Rickert Heinrich   xiii, xviii, 82, 191–2, 195–6
Rodbertus, Johann Karl   84, 97, 131

Schmoller, Gustav von   3, 156
Schumpeter, Joseph   xvi, xviii, 158, 301, 303
Smith, Adam   xii, 25, 29, 33, 81, 108, 114, 121, 131, 140n, 292
Sombart, Werner   135, 155, 167n, 226
Stammler, Rudolf   85–6, 155, 168, 177n, 191n
Steuart, James   251n
Stolzmann, Rudolf   xiii, xv, xvi–xviii, 79–148, 168, 184n, 186, 194, 196, 203n, 209, 214n, 270
Sweezy, Paul M.   191n, 304n

Wagner, Adolph   3, 84, 151n, 156
Walras, Léon   81, 292
Wieser, Friedrich von   xv, 138n, 147n, 155, 223, 226n, 286, 292, 294–5, 297, 301, 304
Windelband, Wilhelm   xviii, 195